Worship, Tradition, and Engagement

Worship, Tradition, and Engagement

Essays in Honor of Timothy George

Edited by
DAVID S. DOCKERY,
JAMES EARL MASSEY,
and ROBERT SMITH JR.

PICKWICK *Publications* · Eugene, Oregon

WORSHIP, TRADITION, AND ENGAGEMENT
Essays in Honor of Timothy George

Copyright © 2018 Wipf and Stock Publishers. All rights reserved. Except for brief quotations in critical publications or reviews, no part of this book may be reproduced in any manner without prior written permission from the publisher. Write: Permissions, Wipf and Stock Publishers, 199 W. 8th Ave., Suite 3, Eugene, OR 97401.

Pickwick Publications
An Imprint of Wipf and Stock Publishers
199 W. 8th Ave., Suite 3
Eugene, OR 97401

www.wipfandstock.com

PAPERBACK ISBN: 978-1-4982-9849-0
HARDCOVER ISBN: 978-1-4982-4894-5
EBOOK ISBN: 978-1-4982-9850-6

Cataloging-in-Publication data:

Names: Dockery, David S., editor. | Massey, James Earl, editor. | Smith, Robert, Jr., editor.

Title: Worship, tradition, and engagement : essays in honor of Timothy George / edited David S. Dockery, James Earl Massey, and Robert Smith Jr.

Description: Eugene, OR : Pickwick Publications, 2018 | Includes bibliographical references and index.

Identifiers: ISBN 978-1-4982-9849-0 (paperback) | ISBN 978-1-4982-4894-5 (hardcover) | ISBN 978-1-4982-9850-6 (ebook)

Subjects: LCSH: Worship. | Tradition (Theology). | Church. | Evangelicalism—United States. | George, Timothy.

Classification: LCC BR1642.U5 W7 2018 (print) | LCC BR1642.U5 (ebook)

Manufactured in the U.S.A.   04/19/18

Contents

About the Contributors | vii
Preface | ix

Timothy George: An Introductory Tribute | 1
  —By David S. Dockery
Timothy George: A Personal Reflection | 18
  —By Ralph C. Wood

Section One: The Gospel and Worship

The Gospel and the Church | 23
  —Gerald L. Bray
Lose the Church, Lose the Gospel | 35
  —Mark E. Dever
Worship in the Old Testament | 48
  —Kenneth A. Mathews
Worship in the New Testament | 64
  —Frank Thielman
A Pilgrim in Progress: The Doctrine of Baptism | 79
  —Christian T. George
Healing Eucharistic Amnesia | 92
  —Elizabeth Newman

Section Two: The Church and Tradition

Sola Scriptura, Tradition, and Catholicity in the Pattern of Theological Authority | 109
  —Kevin J. Vanhoozer
Kingdom Living at Home and Abroad: The Godly Legacy of Two Church Mothers | 129
  —Sefana Dan Laing

Contemplating a Roman Catholic Reception
of the Heidelberg Confession | 149
    —Karen Petersen Finch

John Calvin and the Construction of a Confessional Church:
A Case Study for Evangelicals | 165
    —Scott M. Manetsch

An Unacknowledged Heritage | 183
    —D. Mark DeVine

Covenant: An Ecclesiology of an Undivided Christ | 200
    —Paul S. Fiddes

The Doctrine of the Church in Evangelical Thought | 217
    —Graham Cole

The Church as a Resurrection Community: The Church's Identity
in Late Modernity | 232
    —Piotr J. Małysz

Vatican II and "Evangelicals and Catholics Together:
A Roman Catholic Perspective" | 247
    —Thomas G. Guarino

Timothy George and Evangelicals and Catholics Together:
An Evangelical Perspective | 262
    —John D. Woodbridge

Section Three: Ministry and Engagement

The Church and Pastor-Theologians | 279
    —R. Albert Mohler Jr.

Preaching and the Church | 292
    —Robert R. Smith

The Church, Preaching, and Christian Music | 307
    —James Earl Massey

Engagement, Constitutional Structures, and Civic Virtues | 318
    —Robert P. George

Recovering the Faith: Timothy George's Theology Embodied
in Beeson Chapel | 333
    —William H. Willimon

Evangelicals and the Global Church | 345
    —Richard J. Mouw

Index of Names | 359
Index of Scripture | 369

About the Contributors

Gerald L. Bray, Research Professor of Divinity, Beeson Divinity School

Graham A. Cole, Dean and Professor of Biblical and Systematic Theology, Trinity Evangelical Divinity School

Mark E. Dever, Pastor, Capitol Hill Baptist Church, Washington, D.C.

D. Mark DeVine, Associate Professor of Divinity, Beeson Divinity School

David S. Dockery, President, Trinity International University/Trinity Evangelical Divinity School

Paul Fiddes, Professor of Systematic Theology and Director of Research, Regent's Park College, University of Oxford

Karen Petersen Finch, Associate Professor Theology, Whitworth University

Christian George, Assistant Professor of Historical Theology and Curator of the Spurgeon Library, Midwestern Baptist Theological Seminary

Robert P. George, McCormick Professor of Jurisprudence, Princeton University

Thomas Guarino, Professor of Systematic Theology, School of Theology, Seton Hall University

Stefana Dan Laing, Assistant Librarian, Southwestern Baptist Theological Seminary at Houston

Piotr J. Malysz, Assistant Professor of Divinity, Beeson Divinity School

James Earl Massey, Dean Emeritus, Anderson School of Theology, Anderson University

Scott M. Manetsch, Professor of Church History and Historical Theology, Trinity Evangelical Divinity School

Kenneth A. Mathews, Professor of Divinity, Beeson Divinity School

About the Contributors

Albert Mohler, President and Joseph Emerson Brown Professor of Christian Theology, The Southern Baptist Theological Seminary

Richard Mouw, Professor of Faith and Culture, Fuller Theological Seminary

Elizabeth Newman, Professor of Theology and Ethics, Baptist Theological Seminary at Richmond

Robert Smith Jr., Charles T. Carter Baptist Professor of Divinity, Beeson Divinity School

Frank Thielman, Presbyterian Professor of Divinity, Beeson Divinity School

Kevin J. Vanhoozer, Research Professor of Systematic Theology, Trinity Evangelical Divinity School

William Willimon, Professor of the Practice of Christian Ministry, Duke Divinity School

Ralph C. Wood, University Professor of Theology and Literature, Baylor University

John D. Woodbridge, Research Professor of Church History and Historical Theology, Trinity Evangelical Divinity School

Preface

Beeson Divinity School celebrates its 30th anniversary in 2018. During this time, this distinctive institution has been blessed with one leader since its inception. In 1988, Timothy George left his faculty post at Southern Seminary at the age of 38 to respond to the invitation from Tom Corts, president of Samford University at the time, to serve as the founding dean. During this anniversary year, friends, colleagues, peers, and former students have worked together to produce this volume of essays to honor the life, leadership, and ministry of Timothy George. The book attempts to capture key aspects of George's multi-faceted interests, built around larger themes of gospel, church, worship, tradition, and engagement. Our prayer is that the work will bring glory to our Lord Jesus Christ while honoring the impact and influence that Timothy George has had on so many.

While the three of us have had the privilege to serve as editors and shapers of the project, many others deserve a word of appreciation. We express our appreciation to Denise George for her encouragement along the way. Le-Ann Little and Evan Musgraves at Beeson Divinity School along with Lisa Weathers at Trinity International University have given much time and attention to this effort, for which we are grateful. We are thankful for the guidance and patience provided by Matt Wimer, Ian Creeger, Chris Spinks, Dave Belcher, and Brian Palmer at Wipf and Stock. For the contributors who joined us in this project and for others who cheered us along the way, we are genuinely grateful.

We trust the book will be used to advance the gospel, strengthen the church, and bring eternal glory to our great and majestic Triune God.

Soli De Gloria
David S. Dockery
James Earl Massey
Robert Smith, Jr.

Timothy George
An Introductory Tribute

By David S. Dockery

How does one briefly provide a tribute to and introduction for Timothy George? An entire chapter attempting to engage his prolific publications would likely be inadequate.[1] An entire chapter on his thirty years of leadership at Beeson Divinity School would be challenging to chronicle. An entire chapter on Timothy George as churchman would require serious understanding of Baptist ecclesiology, of George's thoughtful approach to an ecumenism of the trenches, as well as his commitments to evangelical catholicity.[2] An entire chapter on Timothy George as historian and theologian would require a broad interaction not only with Reformed theology but also with the great Christian thinkers of every period throughout church history. An entire chapter on Timothy George as my good and close friend for more than three decades would more than fill my allotted space in this volume. Still, I must try to bring these things together in one very brief introductory chapter.

---

1. Please see the select listing of publications by Timothy George at the conclusion of this introduction.

2. George served as the co-chair of the steering committee for the statement on Evangelical Catholicity, which was released in the fall of 2017 on the occasion of the 500th anniversary of the beginning of the Reformation.

AN UNEXPECTED FRIENDSHIP

The Southern Baptist Convention struggles were at a peak in the 1980s.[3] At that time Timothy George was teaching church history and historical theology at Southern Baptist Theological Seminary, an institution perceived by most as the heart of moderate or progressive theological perspectives in the SBC. I was teaching theology and New Testament at Criswell College, an institution characterized as conservative and evangelical. Timothy was on the editorial team for the *Baptist Peacemaker*; I was the co-editor of the *Criswell Theological Review*, two publications with very different constituencies. During that time, we developed an initial correspondence long before the days of email. I was invited to serve as visiting professor at Southern Seminary in the summer of 1987, where I met Timothy George face-to-face for the first time. Given the different contexts in which we served, our meeting was expected to have been one of awkward tensions. Instead, we both discovered kindred spirits, which was both unexpected and surprising. A lasting friendship was started, which has continued with God's blessings for three decades. I was invited to join the Southern Seminary faculty in 1988 as the Southern Baptist Convention took serious steps in a more conservative direction. That same year Samford University launched Beeson Divinity School and invited Timothy George to serve as the Founding Dean. We thus have never served together at the same institution, even though we have been privileged to serve together on Boards and denominational committees, to work together on a number of writing projects, and to serve as co-hosts on international, education trips. From these experiences I have been blessed to learn much from Timothy George, beginning with our walks around Cave Hill Cemetery[4] in the summer of 1987, which launched the idea for the *Baptist Theologians* project,[5] and to continue to observe closely his many years of work as scholar, theologian, leader, and churchman. To these things I now turn our attention, but first a brief look at Timothy's background and educational experiences.

---

3. See the various perspectives on this struggle in Dockery and James, eds., *Beyond the Impasse?*; also see George, "Southern Baptist Wars."

4. Cave Hill Cemetery in Louisville, KY is the burial site for numerous shapers of Southern Baptist life including: James P. Boyce, John A. Broadus, Basil Manly Jr., A. T. Robertson, E. Y. Mullins, and others.

5. See George and Dockery, eds., *Theologians of the Baptist Tradition*. George's introductory chapter provided a vision for the revitalization of Baptist theology for this generation, which has at least partly been implemented.

A BRIEF INTRODUCTION

Many people recognize Timothy George as evangelical statesman, founding dean of Beeson Divinity School, and well-published scholar with two Harvard degrees. Few people know Timothy George as the desperately poor kid from Chattanooga, TN.[6]

Timothy George was born on January 9, 1950 at Erlanger Hospital in Chattanooga. His father was an alcoholic who died in prison when George was twelve years old. By his own description, Timothy grew up in a dysfunctional family where his father violently abused him, his mother, and his sister. In God's good providence, George was placed in the care of his two great aunts, who, though uneducated, made sure he went to church and studied hard in school. These two women loved the Lord, loved the church, and loved young Timothy. They lived in the inner city in an area known as "Hell's Half Acre," an interracial neighborhood. People lived in this part of Chattanooga not because they were trying to make a social statement, but because they were too poor to live anywhere else. George often went to bed hungry and went to school ashamed of his clothes and his poverty.

His two aunts provided love, care, protection, and spiritual nurturing, taking him to a fundamentalist Baptist church pastored by Ollie Linkous, who referred to Timothy as his little preacher boy. George came to faith in Christ in August of 1961 and committed his life to the preaching ministry as the pastor's little preacher boy in November of that year. To this day, George interprets his call to ministry not as leader, teacher, scholar, or theologian, but as preacher of the gospel growing out on his reading of Romans 10 while still a young boy.

George became a youth evangelist who was invited to preach in country churches in the region. He was even invited to preach at the Thomas Road Baptist Church, a megachurch in Lynchburg, VA where Jerry Falwell served as pastor. While preaching at the Flintstone Baptist Church as an older teenager, he was introduced to and captivated by the lovely Denise Wyse. At the young ages of twenty and nineteen respectively, Timothy and Denise were married at the Flintstone Church in Chickamauga, GA. While on their honeymoon in Atlanta, George found a discount bookstore where he bought all of Calvin's commentaries, an adumbration of the theological and scholarly interests that would characterize the rest of his life.

In his early years, George was blessed with outstanding teachers in elementary school through junior high school who advanced his love for

---

6. Most of what is contained in this section comes from our personal conversations through the years as well as from one of Dean George's chapel addresses delivered at Beeson Divinity School on September 10, 1996.

learning, reading, books, poetry, and quality music. Following Timothy and Denise's marriage, Timothy continued his education at the University of Tennessee at Chattanooga. After graduation, though neither he nor Denise had ever been outside the South, they packed all of their belongings and moved to the Boston area where Timothy pursued degrees at Harvard Divinity School. During his student days he was able to serve as pastor of a Baptist church in the area.

He was privileged to study with George Hunston Williams, the brilliant church historian, as well as other top-tier scholars, with whom George began to read Luther, Calvin, the Anabaptists, and the Puritans.[7] These historical writings became an anchor for George as his faith was stretched and challenged by other Harvard faculty members. At the end of those years at Harvard, now holding the M.Div. and Th.D. from that prestigious institution, Timothy was invited to join the faculty as a young professor of church history and historical theology at Southern Baptist Theological Seminary. Following ten significant and productive years on the Southern faculty, George was invited to become the founding dean at Beeson Divinity School in 1988, where he has given strategic and statesmanlike leadership for three decades. George's story is an amazing journey made possible by God's amazing grace.

The poverty-stricken kid from Hell's Half Acre, the little preacher boy learning from Ollie Linkous, the youth evangelist who preached at Thomas Road Church became a two-time Harvard graduate, who has shaped the highly regarded Beeson Divinity School, and who has influenced thousands through his marvelous gifts as preacher, teacher, scholar, theologian, author, denominational spokesman, and evangelical statesman. While he thinks of himself first and foremost as a preacher, and while he has invested three decades as an administrator of a highly-respected divinity school, George's reputation has primarily been developed by his work as a top-tier evangelical scholar.[8]

SCHOLAR AND THEOLOGIAN

George entered the publication world with a co-edited festschrift to honor George Hunston Williams (1979).[9] His revised dissertation on *John*

---

7. See George, "George Hunston Williams: A Historian for All Seasons," 15–34.

8. See Garrett Jr., "Timothy Francis George," 696–701.

9. See Church and George, *Continuity and Discontinuity in Church History: Essays Presented to George Hunston Williams* [65th Birthday Celebration].

Robinson and the English Separatist Tradition: (1982) followed shortly thereafter.[10] While most of his work has focused on historical matters, George has also made significant contributions in the areas of theology,[11] biblical studies,[12] as well as cultural-engagement issues.[13] His superb biography of William Carey celebrated the 200th anniversary of the "father of modern missions" and his launch of the global missions movement (1991).[14] He co-edited a major work on Baptist theology and theologians (1990), which was designed to revitalize Baptist theology for a new generation.[15] At the same time he released a helpful volume on James Petigru Boyce (1988), the founder of Southern Baptist Theological Seminary.[16] His stellar contribution to Baptist theology continued with a multi-volume series on Baptist classics (1995–99), co-edited with his wife, Denise.[17]

George established himself as a premier Reformation scholar with the publication of the highly-praised *Theology of the Reformers* (1988), a work that guided readers through the thought of Martin Luther, John Calvin, Huldrych Zwingli, and Menno Simons.[18] The volume was re-released in 2013 to celebrate the 25th anniversary of the book's publication. His edited work on *John Calvin and the Church* (1990) extended his reputation as a serious Reformation historian.[19] Currently, he serves as the general editor of the multi-volume *Reformation Commentary on Scripture,* published by InterVarsity Press.[20] George authored the introductory volume in the series with the title, *Reading Scripture with the Reformers* (2011).[21] His expertise on the thought of Luther and Calvin was reflected in George's outstanding commentary on *Galatians* in the New American Commentary series (1994).[22]

10. See George, *John Robinson and the English Separatist Tradition.*

11. See George, "Evangelical Theology in North American Contexts," 275–92; also see George, "Systematic Theology at Southern Seminary," 31–47.

12. See George, *Galatians,* New American Commentary.

13. See George and Smith Jr., *A Mighty Long Journey*; George, "Southern Baptist Heritage of Life," 79–98; George, "Baptists and Gay Marriage," along with George's important work on "The Manhattan Declaration," (2009).

14. See George, *Faithful Witness: The Life and Mission of William Carey.*

15. See Dockery and George, eds., *Theologians of the Baptist Tradition.*

16. See George, *James Petigru Boyce.*

17. See George, *Library of Baptist Classics,* 1995–99.

18. See George, *Theology of the Reformers.*

19. See George, *John Calvin and the Church: A Prism of Reform.*

20. See George, *Reformation Commentary on Scripture.*

21. See George, *Reading Scripture with the Reformers.*

22. See George, *Galatians.* George's language skills in Greek and Latin surpass that

George's theological contributions have primarily focused on the Trinitarian God, the doctrine of salvation, and the church. An edited volume on *God the Holy Trinity* (2006), followed his excellent exposition of the Trinity in his response to the rise of Islam.[23] Though designed as a popular volume, *Is the Father of Jesus the God of Muhammad* (2002) received serious affirmation from many quarters.[24] A more systematic expression appeared in his chapter on "The Nature of God: Being, Attributes, and Acts," which appeared in the multi-authored volume on Baptist theology edited by Daniel L. Akin (2007).[25]

In 2000, George was invited to write the SBC's annual doctrine study on the doctrine of salvation, which reflected his reformed and Baptist commitments. This work, *Amazing Grace: God's Initiative—Our Response*, rejected any association with hyper-Calvinism, while affirming the doctrine of grace expounded by John Calvin, William Carey, and Charles Spurgeon.[26] His work on the church has included contributions on the Lord's Supper,[27] baptism,[28] the priesthood of all believers,[29] and ecumenism.[30] He joined with a number of other well-known evangelical theologians to honor Millard Erickson with the volume, *New Dimensions in Evangelical Thought* (1999). George's contribution focused on "New Dimensions in Baptist Theology."[31]

A representative listing of George's numerous publications can be found at the end of this chapter. Other noteworthy works from George's pen include books on J.I. Packer (2009),[32] Dwight L. Moody (2004),[33] and volumes to honor Gardner C. Taylor (2010),[34] and Fisher Humphreys (2008).[35] He co-authored a small volume on the Christian intellectual tradition

---

of most New Testament scholars

23. See George, *God The Holy Trinity*.
24. See George, *Is The Father of Jesus the Father of Muhammad?*
25. See George, "The Nature of God," 275–92.
26. See George, *Amazing Grace: God Initiative, Our Response*.
27. See George, "Controversy and Communion," 38–58.
28. See George, "Church Membership and Believers' Baptism," 39–52.
29. See George, "The Priesthood of All Believers."
30. See George, "The Reformation and the New Ecumenism," 319–32.
31. See George, "New Dimensions in Baptist Theology," 136–47.
32. See George, *J. I. Packer and The Evangelical Future*.
33. See George, *Mr. Moody and the Evangelical Tradition*.
34. See George, *Our Sufficiency Is of God: Essays on Preaching in Honor of Gardner C. Taylor*.
35. See George, *Theology in Service of the Church: Essays Presented to Fisher H. Humphreys*.

(2012)[36] and an important volume written with Robert Smith, Jr. on racial reconciliation (2000).[37] Additional volumes on evangelical theology and evangelicalism as a movement included *Evangelicals and the Nicene Faith* (2011),[38] *The Mark of Jesus* (2005),[39] *Pilgrims on the Sawdust Trial* (2004),[40] along with *For All the Saints: Evangelical Theology and Christian Spirituality* (2003).[41] George's prolific publications have left little doubt that he has distinguished himself as one of the most significant evangelical voices over the past thirty years.

CHURCHMAN AND STATESMAN

In this volume, Albert Mohler capably discusses the important role of the pastor-theologian, The concept of pastor-theologian describes well the Beeson Divinity School dean, the one being honored in this book of essays.[42] Having served churches in Alabama, Georgia, Kentucky, and Massachusetts, and preached in every region of the country and around the globe, Timothy George remains in much demand as a gifted preacher of God's Word. Understanding George as preacher, pastor-theologian, and churchman begins with understanding George's commitment to the full truthfulness and authority of the Bible.[43] Having been baptized by Lee Roberson, an influential independent Baptist pastor who reflected well the best of Baptist fundamentalism, George, from his earliest days believed and took seriously the full inspiration of Holy Scripture. Through his study of the Reformers and his studies with premier scholars like George Hunston Williams, Heiko Oberman, and David Steinmetz, George developed a deep appreciation for the role of the Word of God across the ages. The influence of Carl Henry helped George solidify his commitments to *sola scriptura*.[44]

---

36. See Dockery and George, *The Great Tradition of Christian Thinking*.

37. See George and Smith, *A Mighty Long Journey*.

38. See George, *Evangelicals and the Nicene Faith*.

39. See George and Woodbridge, *The Mark of Jesus*.

40. See George, *Pilgrims on the Sawdust Trail*.

41. See George and McGrath, *For All the Saints: Evangelical Theology and Christian Spirituality*.

42. See George, "Foreword," *The Pastor Theologian*, 7–8.

43. See George, "An Evangelical Reflection on Scripture and Tradition," 184–207.

44. Carl Henry was George's choice to deliver the dedicatory address in 1988 at the inaugural service for Beeson Divinity School. Also see George, "Henry, Carl Ferdinand Howard," 316–19.

Over the past three decades, George, in his role as dean, has led Beeson Divinity School as pastor-theologian. His service on the Southern Baptist Convention Reconciliation Committee (1998), the Southern Baptist Convention Theological Study Committee (1992–1994), his involvement with the Baptist World Alliance (2000–2005), his service on the theological committee of the Prison Fellowship Board of Directors (1999–2012), and other similar opportunities all grew out of these foundational commitments. These strategic roles and commitments have strengthened George's identity as churchman and statesman, dedicated to the church as "one, holy, catholic, and apostolic."[45]

George continues to see his work and ministry as one who has been called to bring people together, encouraging them toward reconciliation and renewal, always doing so from the standpoint of genuine biblical conviction.[46] His students, peers, and friends alike view him as a genuine statesman in their midst not because of any kind of convictionless ecumenism, but because he has looked for gospel-centered common ground, doing so as a biblical inerrantist, convinced Baptist, convictional Calvinist, and hope-filled permillenialist. His is an ecumenism of the trenches, making good and wise choices for right reasons.[47] His life reflects the heart of one of his favorite hymns, "For All the Saints," a classic Christian expression, which poetically portrays the theological commitments made known in George's belief in the communion of saints.[48]

The wide-ranging respect that others have for him is seen not only by his leadership at Beeson and his faithful involvements at his home church, Shades Mountain Baptist in Birmingham, but also in his significant leadership, along with that of Chuck Colson and Robby George, in the development of the Manhattan Declaration (2009), in his chairmanship of the Colson Center for Christian Worldview, in his service as trustee at Wheaton College, in his work as senior theological advisor for *Christianity Today*, and in his ongoing service on the editorial boards of *First Things, Books & Culture*, and other periodicals. Some of his most challenging and controversial work in this regard has come from his active role over the past twenty years (1995–) in the Evangelical-Roman Catholic dialogue, often referred to

---

45. See George, "In All Places and in All Ages," 227–41; also, George, "The Unity of Faith: Evangelism and 'Mere Christianity,'" 58–66; George, "The Sacramentality of the Church," 27–39.

46. See George, "Conflict and Identity in the SBC," 195–214.

47. See George, "The Faith, My Faith, and the Church's Faith," 81–93; also George, "Is Christ Divided?," 31–33.

48. See George, "The Pattern of Christian Truth," 21–25; also, George, "Evangelicals and the Present Ecumenical Movement," 44–67.

as Evangelicals and Catholics Together,[49] discussed in this volume by both John Woodbridge and Tom Guarino. It was largely from this highly visible activity that George was invited to provide the Protestant address focused on "Ecumenism After 50 Years" at the Pontifical Gregorian University on the occasion of the 50th anniversary of the Second Vatican Council in 2014.

The chapters in this volume by Robert Smith Jr., Mark Dever, Gerald Bray, and James Earl Massey center on the gospel, church, and preaching, the chapter by Robert George focuses on cultural engagement, and the insightful contribution of Will Willimon creatively describes Timothy George's theology and liturgy embodied in the distinctive Beeson chapel. These essays provide readers with at least some insight into the many sides and multiple interests of Timothy George as an extraordinary Baptist churchman and evangelical statesman.

CONCLUSION

We have merely touched on a few aspects of the life, ministry, and influence of Timothy George. Each contributor to this book could tell his or her story of their own journey with George. Each contributor provides a look at a different piece of George's multi-faceted and wide-ranging interests and areas of expertise. One in particular has had a special seat at the table, the family table. Readers will take note of the contribution by Christian George, a fine young church historian in his own right, and son of Timothy and Denise George. All of the contributors join me in saluting Timothy George and thanking him for lessons learned, and for strengthening and encouraging all of us in the gospel.[50] We offer this volume in deep gratitude for the life, friendship, influence, scholarship, and churchmanship of Timothy George and pray for God's ongoing and abundant blessings on one of the most gifted statesmen and scholars of this generation.

A SELECT LISTING OF PUBLICATIONS BY TIMOTHY GEORGE

Books

Theology of the Reformers. Rev. ed. Nashville: B&H, 2013.

---

49. See George, "Evangelicals and Catholics Together," 34–35; also see Garrison, "Who Knows the Next Pope?"

50. See George, "The Gospel of Jesus Christ," 51–56.

The Great Tradition of Christian Thinking: A Student's Guide. With David S. Dockery. Wheaton: Crossway, 2012.
Amazing Grace. 2nd ed. Wheaton: Crossway, 2011.
Evangelicals and Nicene Faith, editor. Grand Rapids: Baker, 2011.
Reading Scripture with the Reformers. Downers Grove: InterVarsity, 2011.
Our Sufficiency Is of God: Essays on Preaching in Honor of Gardner C. Taylor, edited with James Earl Massey and Robert Smith, Jr. Macon, GA: Mercer University Press, 2010.
J. I. Packer and the Evangelical Future: The Impact of His Life and Thought, editor. Grand Rapids: Baker, 2009.
Theology in the Service of the Church: Essays Presented to Fisher H. Humphreys, editor. Macon: Mercer University Press, 2008.
God the Holy Trinity, editor. Grand Rapids: Baker, 2006.
The Mark of Jesus. With John Woodbridge. Chicago: Moody, 2005.
Mr. Moody and the Evangelical Tradition, editor. London: Continuum, 2004.
Pilgrims on the Sawdust Trail, editor. Grand Rapids: Baker, 2004.
For All the Saints: Evangelical Theology and Christian Spirituality, edited with Alister McGrath. Louisville: Westminster, 2003.
Is the Father of Jesus the God of Muhammad? Grand Rapids: Zondervan, 2002.
Theologians of the Baptist Tradition, edited with David S. Dockery. Nashville: B&H, 2001.
Amazing Grace: God's Initiative, Our Response. Nashville: LifeWay, 2000.
A Mighty Long Journey: Reflections on Racial Reconciliation, edited with Robert Smith, Jr. Nashville: B&H, 2000.
The Axioms of Religion, Library of Baptist Classics, edited with Denise George. Nashville: B&H, 1997.
Baptist Why and Why Not, Library of Baptist Classics, edited with Richard D. Land. Nashville: B&H, 1997.
Galatians. New American Commentary. Nashville: B&H, 1994.
Faithful Witness: The Life and Mission of William Carey. Birmingham, AL: New Hope, 1991.
Baptist Theologians, edited with David S. Dockery. Nashville: B&H, 1990.
John Calvin and the Church: A Prism of Reform. Louisville: Westminster John Knox, 1990.
Theology of the Reformers. Nashville: Broadman and Holman 1988.
James Petigru Boyce: Selected Writings, editor. Nashville: B&H, 1988.
Dear Unborn Child: Personal Letters from a Future Mother and Father, with Denise George. Nashville: B&H, 1984.
John Robinson and the English Separatist Tradition. Macon, GA: Mercer University Press, 1982.
Continuity and Discontinuity in Church History:" Essays Presented to George Huntston Williams [65th Birthday Celebration]. With F. Forrester Church. Leiden: Brill, 1979.

Series

Reformation Commentary on Scripture. General Editor. Downers Grove: InterVarsity, 2011–.
Library of Baptist Classics. Co-edited with Denise George. Nashville: B&H, 1995–1999.

Articles and Chapters

"Foreword." In *Theology, Church, and Ministry: A Handbook for Theological Education,* edited by David S. Dockery, xi–xiii. Nashville: B&H, 2017.
"Foreword." In *Eschatology: Biblical, Historical, and Practical Approaches,* edited by D. Jeffrey Bingham and Glenn R. Kreider, 13–15. Grand Rapids: Kregel, 2016.
"Erasmus Before the Storm." *Midwestern Journal of Theology* 15, no. 1 (2016) 1–4.
"*Unitatis Redintegratio* after Fifty Years: A Protestant Reading." *Pro Ecclesia* 25 (2016) 53–70.
"The Reformation and the New Ecumenism." In *Protestantism after 500 Years,* edited by Thomas Albert Howard and Mark A. Noll, 319–32. New York: Oxford University Press, 2016.
"With David Dockery Among Baptists and Evangelicals." In *Convictional Civility: Engaging the Culture in the 21st Century,* edited by C. Ben Mitchell, Carla D. Sanderson, and Gregory A. Thornbury, 11–18. Nashville: B&H, 2015.
"In All Places and in All Ages: The Holy Spirit and Christian Unity." In *Spirit of God: Christian Renewal in the Community of Faith,* edited by Jeffrey W. Barbeau and Beth Felker Jones, 227–41. Downers Grove: InterVarsity, 2015.
"Foreword," *The Pastor Theologian: Resurrecting an Ancient Vision,* edited by Gerald Hiestand and Todd Wilson, 7–8. Grand Rapids: Zondervan, 2015.
"Let It Go: Lessons from the Life of William Carey." In *Expect Great Things, Attempt Great Things,* edited by Allen Yeh and Chris Chun, 3–14. Eugene, OR: Wipf and Stock, 2013.
"Why I Am an Evangelical and a Baptist." In *Why We Belong: Evangelical Unity and Denominational Diversity,* edited by Anthony L. Chute, Christopher W. Morgan and Robert A. Peterson, 93–109. Wheaton: Crossway, 2013.
"Catholics and Baptists Together." *Christianity Today* 57, no. 1 (2013) 73.
"The Church of the Undivided Christ." *Ecumenical Trends* 42, no. 11 (2013) 1.
"The Man Who Birthed Evangelicalism." *Christianity Today* 57, no. 3 (2013) 61.
"Let God Be God: Martin Luther on Predestination." *Credo Magazine* 2, no. 3 (2012) 20–26.
"Southern Baptists' Long Journey." *First Things* 226 (2012) 16–18.
"Tyndale's One Thing: William Tydale and the Making of the English Bible." In *KJV 400,* edited by Ray Van Neste, 27–39. Memphis: BorderStone, 2012.
"Foreword." In *Whomever He Wills: A Surprising Display of Sovereign Mercy,* edited by Matthew Barrett and Thomas J. Nettles, ix–xi. Cape Coral, FL: Founders, 2012.
"Evangelicals and the Present Ecumenical Moment." In *Critical Issues in Ecclesiology: Essays in Honor of Carl E. Braaten,* edited by Alberto L. García and Susan K. Wood, 44–67. Grand Rapids: Eerdmans, 2011.

"The Faith, My Faith, and the Church's Faith." In *Southern Baptists, Evangelicals, and The Future of Denominationalism,* edited by David S. Dockery, 81–93. Nashville: B&H, 2011.

"William Carey: Faithful Witness." *Carey Pulpit* 31 (2011) 3.

"Tyndale's One Thing." *Southern Baptist Journal of Theology* 15, no. 4 (2011) 8–10.

"Is Jesus a Baptist?" In *Southern Baptist Identity: An Evangelical Denomination Faces The Future,* edited by David S. Dockery, 89–104. Wheaton: Crossway, 2009.

"Do Whatever He Tells You: The Blessed Virgin Mary in Christian Faith and Life." *First Things* 197 (2009) 49–60.

"John Calvin: Comeback Kid." *Christianity Today* 53, no. 9 (2009) 26–32.

"What Baptists Can Learn from Calvin." *Founders Journal* 78 (2009) 19–21.

"Evangelical Revival and the Missionary Awakening." In *The Great Commission,* edited by Martin Klauber and Scott M. Manetsch, 45– 58. Nashville: B&H, 2008.

"John A. Broadus: A Living Legacy." In *John A. Broadus: A Living Legacy,* edited by David S. Dockery and Roger D. Duke, 1–11. Nashville: B&H, 2008.

"Evangelicalism." *Modern Reformation* 17, no. 7 (2008) 23.

"Foreword." In *The Emergence of Evangelicalism: Exploring Historical Continuities,* edited by Michael A.G. Haykin and Keneth J. Stewart, 13–15. Nottingham: Apollos, 2008.

"Foreword." In *The Fugitive: Menno Simons,* edited by Myron S. Augsburger, 9–13. Scottsdale, PA: Herald, 2008.

"Egalitarians and Complementarians Together? A Modest Proposal." In *Women, Ministry, and the Gospel,* edited by Mark Husbands and Timothy Larsen, 267–88. Downers Grove: InterVarsity, 2007.

"Evangelical Theology in North American Contexts." In *The Cambridge Companion to Evangelical Theology,* edited by Timothy Larsen and Daniel J. Treier, 275–92. Cambridge: Cambridge University Press, 2007.

"Love amidst the Brokenness." *Christian History & Biography* 94 (2007) 6–10.

"The Nature of God: Being, Attributes, and Acts." In *A Theology for the Church,* edited by Daniel L. Akin, 275–92. Nashville: B&H, 2007.

"Why Don't Y'all Pass the Bread?" *Preaching* 22 (2007) 40–46.

"Evangelicals and the Great Tradition." *First Things* 175 (2007) 19–21.

"Evangelicals and the Mother of God." *First Things* 170 (2007) 20–26.

"The Jerry I Remember." *Christianity Today* 51, no. 7 (2007) 48–49.

"Foreword." In *Luther as a Spiritual Adviser,* by Dennis Ngien, xiii–xiv. Studies in Christian History and Thought. Milton Keynes, UK: Paternoster, 2007.

"Running Like a Herald to Deliver the Message: Barth on the Church and Sacraments." In *Karl Barth and Evangelical Theology: Convergences and Divergences,* edited by Sung Wook Chung, 191–208. Grand Rapids: Baker, 2006.

"What Faith Isn't." In *The Complete Evangelism Guidebook,* edited by Scott Dawson, 109–27. Grand Rapids: Baker, 2006.

"Theology for an Age of Terror." *Christianity Today* 50, no. 9 (2006) 79–81.

"Southern Baptists after the Revolution." *First Things* 165 (2006) 17–19.

"An Ecclesiastical Mind: An Evangelical Appreciation of Karl Barth." *Touchstone* 19 (2006) 33–39.

"Evangelicals and Others." *First Things* 160 (2006) 15–23.

"The Incarnation: The Word Became Flesh." *Decision Magazine* (2006) 17–19.

"Delighted by Doctrine." *Christian History & Biography* 91 (2006) 43–45.

"Foreword." In *Believer's Baptism,* edited by Thomas R. Schreiner and Shawn D. Wright, xv–xix. Nashville: B&H, 2006.

"Foreword." In *Stewards of the Story,* by James Earl Massey, xi–xiv. Louisville: Westminster John Knox, 2006.

"Martin Luther." In *Reading Romans through the Centuries: From the Early Church to Karl Barth,* edited by Jeffrey P. Greenman and Timothy Larsen, 101–20. Grand Rapids: Brazos, 2005.

"St. Augustine and the Mystery of Time." In *What God Knows,* edited by Harry Lee Poe and J. Stanley Mattson, 27–46. Waco: Baylor University Press, 2005.

"A Distinctive People." *Christianity Today* 49, no. 3 (2005) 62–69.

"Is Christ Divided?" *Christianity Today* 49, no. 7 (2005) 31–33.

"John Paul II: An Appreciation." *Pro Ecclesia* 14, no. 3 (2005) 267–70.

"The Pattern of Christian Truth." *First Things* 154 (2005) 21–25.

"A Peace Plan for the Gender War." *Christianity Today* 49, no. 11 (2005) 51–57.

"The Promise of Benedict XVI." *Christianity Today* 49, no. 6 (2005) 49–52.

"Foreword." In *A History of Apologetics,* by Avery Cardinal Dulles, xi–xiii. San Francisco: Ignatius, 2005.

"The Blessed Virgin Mary: An Evangelical Perspective." In *Mary, Mother of God*, edited by Carl E. Braaten and Robert W. Jenson, 100–122. Grand Rapids: Eerdmans 2004.

"Modernizing Luther, Domesticating Paul: Another Perspective." In *Justification and Variegated Nomism,* edited by D. A. Carson, Peter T. O'Brien, and Mark A. Seifrid, 2:437–63. Grand Rapids: Baker, 2004.

"The Sacramentality of the Church: An Evangelical Baptist Perspective." In *One, Holy, Catholic, and Apostolic: Ecumenical Reflections on the Church,* edited by Tamara Grdzelidze, 27–34. Geneva: W.W.W., 2004.

"A Tribute to Roger Nicole: The Atonement in Martin Luther's Theology." In *The Glory of the Atonement: Biblical, Theological, & Practical Perspective,* edited by Charles E. Hill and Frank A. James III, 9–14. Downers Grove: InterVarsity, 2004.

"Is It OK for Christians to Be Cremated?" *Today's Christian Woman* 26, no. 4 (2004) 25.

"Baptists and the Westminster Confession." In *The Westminster Confession into the 21st Century,* edited by Ligon Duncan, 145–60. Geanies House, UK: Christian Focus, 2003.

"Henry, Carl Ferdinand Howard." In *Biographical Dictionary of Evangelicals,* edited by Timothy T. Larsen, David Bebbington, and Mark A. Noll, 316–19. Downers Grove: InterVarsity, 2003.

"The Sacramentality of the Church: An Evangelical Baptist Perspective." In *Baptist Sacramentalism,* edited by Anthony R. Cross and Philip E. Thompson, 21–35. Waynesboro, GA: Paternoster, 2003.

"The Blessed Evangelical Mary." *Christianity Today* 47, no. 12 (2003) 34–39.

"Doctrinal Preaching." *Proclaim! The Journal of Biblical Preaching* 33, no. 3 (2003) 19–20.

"The Sacramentality of the Church." *Pro Ecclesia* 12, no. 3 (2003) 309–23.

"The Unity of Faith: Evangelism and 'Mere Christianity.'" *Touchstone* 16 (2003) 58–66.

"Foreword." In *Against the Gates of Hell: The Life & Times of Henry Perry, A Christian Missionary in a Moslem World,* by Gordon and Diana Severance, xi–xii. Landham, MD: University of America Press, 2003.

"Controversy and Communion: The Limits of Baptist Fellowship from Bunyan to Spurgeon." In *The Gospel in the World—International Baptist Studies—Studies in*

Baptist History and Thought, edited by David Bebbington, 1:38–58. Edinburgh: Paternoster, 2002.

"The Life and Mission of William Carey—Part 1- Part 2." In *Reclaiming the Gospel and Reforming Churches*, edited by Thomas K. Ascol, 571–612. Cape Coral, FL: Founders, 2002.

"Islam and the Christian Faith." *Christian Life Report* 12, no. 2 (2002) 1.

"Battling for the Past: Reformation Views of History." *Christian History* 20, no. 4 (2001) 37.

"A Call to Freedom." *Decision* 42, no. 4 (2001) 32–36.

"*Dominus Iesus*: An Evangelical Response." *Pro Ecclesia* 10, no. 1 (2001) 15–16.

"Keeping Truth Alive as a Holy Calling." *Harvard Divinity Bulletin* 29, no. 4 (2001) 4–6.

"The Lasting Contribution of a 'Wretched Worm.'" *Christian History* 11, no. 4 (1992) 38–39.

"The Big Picture: Does God Have a Plan for the World?" In *This We Believe*, edited by John N. Akers and John D. Woodbridge, 221–37. Grand Rapids: Zondervan, 2000.

"Toward an Evangelical Ecclesiology." In *Catholics and Evangelicals: Do They Share a Common Future?*, edited by Thomas P. Rausch, 122–48. New York: Paulist, 2000.

"Big Picture Faith." *Christianity Today* 44, no. 12 (2000) 88–93.

"An Evangelical Reflection on Scripture and Tradition." *Pro Ecclesia* 9, no. 2 (2000) 184–207.

"Foreword." In *Reconstructing Theology: A Critical Assessment of the Theology of Clark Pinnock*, edited by Tony Gray and Christopher Sinkinson, 7–11. Edinburgh: Paternoster, 2000.

"The Gospel of Jesus Christ: An Evangelical Celebration." *Christianity Today* 43, no. 7 (1999) 51–56.

"Learning and the Lordship of Jesus Christ." In *The Future of Christian Higher Education*, edited by David S. Dockery and David P. Gushee, 55–58. Nashville: B&H, 1999.

"George Hunston Williams: A Historian for All Seasons." In *The Contentious Triangle: Church, State, and University*, edited by Rodney L. Petersen and Calvin Augustine Pater, 15–34. Kirksville, MO: Thomas Jefferson University Press, 1999.

"Afterword." In *Baptists against Racism*, edited by Denton Lotz, 182. McLean, VA: Baptist World Alliance, 1999.

"The First Easter: God's Great Coming Out Party." *Books and Culture* 5, no. 2 (1999) 4.

"Overlooked Shapers of Evangelicalism." *Southern Baptist Journal of Theology* 3, no. 1 (1999) 76–77.

"Practicing the Two Kingdoms: The Baptist Ideal of a Free Church in a Free State." *Modern Reformation* 9, no. 5 (2000) 29–31, 51.

"The Reformation Connection." *Christian History* 19, no. 4 (2000) 35–38.

"Southern Baptist Ghosts." *First Things* 93 (1999) 18–24.

"Why We Still Need Moody." *Christianity Today* 43, no. 14 (1999) 66.

"You Must Be Born Again—But at What Age?" *Christianity Today* 43, no. 3 (1999) 62.

"New Dimensions in Baptist Theology." In *New Dimensions in Evangelical Thought: Essays in Honor of Millard J. Erickson*, edited by David S. Dockery, 136–47. Downers Grove: InterVarsity, 1998.

"The Gift of Salvation." *First Things* 79 (1998) 2–3.

"Putting Amazing Back into Grace." *Home Life* 51 (1998) 58–59.

"A Theology to Die for." *Christianity Today* 42, no. 2 (1998) 49.

"What I'd Like to Tell the Pope about the Church." *Christianity Today* 42, no. 7 (1998) 41–44.

"Calvin's Use of Natural Law: A Response to Susan E. Schreiner." In *A Preserving Grace: Protestants, Catholics, and Natural Law*, edited by Michael Cromartie, 77–83. Grand Rapids: Eerdmans, 1997.

"The Ecclesiology of John Gill." In *Life & Thought of John Gill—1697-1771,*" edited by Michael G. Haykin, 225–36. Leiden: Brill, 1997.

"Believers' Baptism: More Than American Individualism." *Modern Reformation* 6, no. 3 (1997) 41–47.

"Evangelicals and Catholics Together: An Evangelical Assessment." *Christianity Today* 41, no. 14 (1997) 34–35.

"The Baptist Tradition." In *Theological Education in the Evangelical Tradition*, edited by D. G. Hart and R. Albert Mohler, 27–44. Grand Rapids: Baker, 1996.

"Promoting Renewal, Not Tribalism." *Christianity Today* 40, no. 7 (1996) 14–15.

"Why We Still Need Luther." *Christianity Today* 40, no. 12 (1996) 13.

"Southern Baptist Heritage of Life." In *Life at Risk: The Crises in Medical Ethics*, edited by Richard D. Land and Louis A. Moore, 79–98. Nashville: B&H, 2005.

"Passing the Southern Baptist Torch." *Christianity Today* 39, no. 6 (1995) 32–34.

"What We Mean When We Say It's True." *Christianity Today* 39, no. 12 (1995) 17–21.

"Catholics and Evangelicals in the Trenches." *Christianity Today* 38, no. 6 (1994) 16.

"Five Marks of an Effective Seminary: How to Evaluate Theological Education." *Christianity Today* 38, no. 10 (1994) 78.

"Why We Believe in the Virgin Birth." *Christianity Today* 38, no. 14 (1994) 18–19.

"The Reformed Doctrine of Believers' Baptism." *Interpretation* 47, no. 3 (1993) 242–52.

"Foreword." In *A Marvelous Ministry: How the All-round Ministry of Charles Haddon Spurgeon Speaks to Us Today*, by Tim Curnow et al. Ligonier, PA: Soli Deo Gloria, 1993.

"Conflict and Identity in the SBC: The Quest for a New Consensus." In *Beyond the Impasse? Scripture, Interpretation, and Theology Among Southern Baptists*, edited by David S. Dockery and Robison B. James, 195–214. Nashville: B&H, 1992.

"Doctrinal Preaching." In *Handbook of Contemporary Preaching*, edited by Michael Duduit, 93–102. Nashville: B&H, 1992.

"Baptists and Gay Marriage." *Christianity Today* 36, no. 6 (1992) 15.

"Carey, the Linguist." *Reformation Today* 130 (1992) 9–12.

"Dr. Luther's Theology." *Christian History* 11, no. 2 (1992) 18–22.

"Luther's Legacy to the Laity." *Table Talk* 16, no. 10 (1992) 13–16.

"The Faithful Witness of William Carey." *Evangelical Missions Quarterly* 28, no. 4 (1992) 350–56.

"Christian Faith in History." In *Holman Bible Handbook,* edited by David S. Dockery, 856–77. Nashville: Holman, 1992.

"The Southern Baptist Wars." *Christianity Today* 36, no. 3 (1992) 24–27.

"The Subtle Lure of Liberalism." *Table Talk* 16, no. 4 (1992) 10–14. Reprinted in *Founders Journal* 9 (1992) 17–21.

"Consensus Tigurinus," "Marburg Colloquy," "Wolfgang Capito," and "John Robinson" in *Encyclopedia of the Reformed Faith*, edited by Donald K. McKim, 82, 58. Louisville: Westminster John Knox, 1991.

"Conflict in Baptist Zion." *Perspectives* 6, no. 1 (1991) 21–23.

"Election" and "Providence." In *Holman Bible Dictionary*, edited by Trent C. Butler, 407, 409, 1147–48. Nashville: B&H, 1991.

"Faithful Shepherd, Beloved Minister: The Life and Legacy of Basil Manly, Sr." *Alabama Baptist Historian* 27, no. 1 (1991) 14–33.

"Sovereignty of God." In *The Handbook of Themes for Preaching*, edited by James W. Cox, 222–25. Louisville: Westminster, 1991.

"Bible." In the *Mercer Dictionary of the Bible,* edited by Watson E. Mills, 101–103. Macon, GA: Mercer University Press, 1990.

"Jeter, J. B.," "Leachman, Emma," "Mabie, H. C.," "Marney, Carlyle," "Martin, T. T.," and "Scarborough, L. R." In the *Dictionary of Christianity in America,* edited by Daniel S. Reid. Downers Grove: InterVarsity, 1990.

"Mt. Zion in a Wilderness: A Profile of Pilgrim Spirituality." In *This Sacred History: Anglican Reflections for John Booty*, edited by Donald S. Armentrout, 61–76. Cambridge, MA: Cowley, 1990.

"Southern Baptist Relations with Other Protestants." *Baptist History and Heritage* 25, no. 3 (1990) 24–34.

"Partly Fearing, Partly Hoping: Evangelicals, Southern Baptists, and the Quest for a New Consensus." *Perspectives in Religious Studies* 17 (1990) 167–72.

"The Challenge of Evangelism in the History of the Church." In *Evangelism in the Twenty-First Century*, edited by Thom S. Rainer, 9–20. Wheaton: Harold Shaw, 1989.

"The Priesthood of All Believers and the Quest for Theological Integrity." *Criswell Theological Review* 3, no. 2 (1989) 283–94. Revised and reprinted as "The Priesthood of All Believers," in *The People of God*, edited by Paul A. Basden and David S. Dockery, 283–94 (Nashville: B&H, 1989).

"The Reformation Roots of the Baptist Tradition." *Review and Expositor* 86, no. 1 (1989) 9–22. Reprinted in *SOLA* 2, no. 2 (1989) 13–18.

"John Calvin and Menno Simons: Reformation Perspectives on the Kingdom of God." In *Calviniana: Ideas* and *Influence of John Calvin*, edited by Robert V. Schnucker, 195–214. Kirksville, MO: Sixteenth Century Journal, 1988.

"Holy Scripture," "Last Things," "Proclamation," "Revelation," "Salvation," "Worship." In *The Disciple's Study Bible*, 1677–78, 1689–92, 1696, 1678–80, 1683–85, 1695. Nashville: B&H, 1988.

"Early Anabaptist Spirituality in the Low Countries." *Mennonite Quarterly Review* 61 (1988) 257–75.

"An Open Letter to Honest Doubters." *Student* 67, no. 9 (1988) 40–42.

"Calvin's *Psychopannychia*: Another Look." In *Proceedings of the International Calvin Symposium* 1986, edited by E. J. Furcha, 297–329. Montreal: McGill University Press, 1987.

"A Radically Christian Witness for Peace." In *Education for Peace*, edited by Haim Gordon and Leonard Grob, 62–76. Maryknoll, NY: Orbis, 1987.

"Dogma beyond Anathema: Historical Theology in the Service of the Church." *Review and Expositor* 84, no. 4 (1987) 691–713.

"Interpretation, History, and the Ecumenical Movement: Response to Jeffrey Gros." *Ecumenical Trends* 16, no. 7 (1987) 131–32.

"Spirituality of the Radical Reformation." In *World Spirituality: An Encyclopedic History of the Religious Quest,* edited by Ewert H. Cousins and Jill Raitt, 334–70. New York: Crossroad, 1987.

"Church Membership and Believers' Baptism: A Southern Baptist Perspective." In *Baptism and Church: A Believers' Church Vision,* edited by Merle D. Strege, 39–52. Grand Rapids: Sagamore, 1986.
"A Right Strawy Epistle: Reformation Perspectives on James." *Review and Expositor* 83, no. 3 (1986) 369–82.
"The Southern Baptist Cooperative Program: Heritage and Challenge." *Baptist History and Heritage* 20, no. 2 (1985) 4–13.
"Systematic Theology at Southern Seminary." *Review and Expositor* 82, no. 1 (1985) 31–47.
"The Presuppositions of Zwingli's Baptismal Theology." In *Prophet, Pastor, Protestant: The Work of Huldrych Zwingli after Five Hundred Years,* edited by E. J. Furhca and H. Wayne Pipkin, 71–87. Allison Park, PA: Pickwick, 1984.
"Between Pacifism and Coercion: The Early Baptist Doctrine of Religious Tolerance." *Mennonite Quarterly Review* 58 (1984) 30–49.
"Predestination in a Separatist Context: The Case of John Robinson." *Sixteenth Century Journal* 15, no. 1 (1984) 73–85.
"Three Marks of the Church." *Proclaim* 15, no. 1 (1984) 28–30.
"War and Peace in the Puritan Tradition." *Church History* 53, no. 4 (1984) 492–503.
"The Bones of Joseph." *Pulpit Digest* 62, no. 457 (1982) 301–4.
"Waging Peace in a World of Conflict: A Conference at Harvard." *Baptist Peacemaker* 2, no. 1 (1982) 5.
"The Historical Development of the Doctrine of Baptism." *Church Training* 11, no. 5 (1981) 8–10.
"Though It Tarry." *Pulpit Digest* 59, no. 437 (1979) 47–50.

In addition, George has published numerous book reviews, website articles, participated in forums, and given a variety of interviews and lectureships across the country and around the world.

SECONDARY SOURCES CITED

Dockery, David S., and Timothy George. *The Great Tradition of Christian Thinking: A Student's Guide*. Reclaiming the Christian Intellectual Tradition. Wheaton, IL: Crossway, 2012.
Dockery, David S., and Robison James. *Beyond the Impasse? Scripture, Interpretation, and Theology among Southern Baptists*. Nashville: B&H, 1992.
Garrett, Leo, Jr. "Timothy Francis George (1950–): Evangelical/Calvinist and Baptist Historical Theologian." In *Baptist Theology: A Four-Century Study,* 696–701. Macon, GA: Mercer University Press, 2009.
Garrison, Greg. "Who Knows the Next Pope? Maybe a Baptist Divinity School Dean in Alabama." *Alabama Living* (March 1, 2013). http://www.al.com/living/index.ssf/2013/03/who_knows_the_next_pope_maybe.html.
George, Timothy, and David S. Dockery, eds., *Theologians of the Baptist Tradition*. Nashville: B&H, 2001.

Timothy George
A Personal Reflection

By Ralph C. Wood

Timothy George and I finished our doctoral work—he at Harvard and I at Chicago—at about the same time, just as we also began our teaching careers almost simultaneously, in the early 1970s—he at the Southern Baptist Theological Seminary in Louisville and I at Wake Forest University in Winston-Salem. He was emerging already as a luminary among American evangelicals, while I was still toiling to finish my dissertation. Therein lay a prophecy of the paths we would traverse. His academic future would be meteoric, while mine would be pedestrian. He would remain utterly faithful to the Reformed tradition in general and to Southern Baptists in particular, while I would become increasingly drawn to both Roman Catholicism and Eastern Orthodoxy.

    Yet these differences have never divided us; on the contrary, they have solidified our friendship of four and a half decades. Timothy asked me to teach a course on Karl Barth, for example, during my short but happy stay at Samford. He has also invited me to return to Beeson for lectures after my move to Baylor in 1998. And from the very beginning, I have sought his wisdom. He helped me to discern, early in our exchanges, that John Calvin was no naïve supernaturalist. Not for Calvin does God act as a sort of heavenly factotum in response to our entreaties, no matter how fervently we beseech Him to change his mind. Timothy reminded me that Calvin was loath to probe the wonder of divine operations in the world. With Aquinas and the great preponderance of orthodox theologians, Calvin held that God acts chiefly through secondary causes, i.e., through the natural connections inherent in his good creation. The great Genevan was thus content to confirm one of the deepest Christian mysteries—that God is impassible and unchanging, the One in whom there is no shadow of turning. Yet concerning one matter, Timothy taught me, Calvin was absolutely sure: whatever change authentic prayers may or may not effect in God, they radically realign our wills with his.

On another occasion, I had complained to Timothy about the easy comfort that too many Christians in the Reformed tradition find in their faith. The doctrine of election makes for a dangerous religious complacency, cheap grace as Bonhoeffer called it. Our Lord's anguish in the Garden seems to drop out of sight. Too few evangelicals plead, like the publican, for God to help their unbelief. Where, I asked Timothy, is the fear and trembling that is so central to Scripture, especially to the theologian such as Søren Kierkegaard? I was teaching a course in existentialism and we had been wrestling with Kierkegaard's text with its eponymous title from Philippians 2:12. Not long afterwards, I received a note from Timothy; he had appended the Archangel Michael's speech on human ails and ills from Book XI of *Paradise Lost*. Milton's discourse on death stopped my mouth from any further complaint about the absence of *angst* in the Reformed imagination:

> Death thou hast seen
> In his first shape on Man; but many shapes
> Of Death, and many are the ways that lead
> To his grim cave, all dismal; yet to sense
> More terrible at the entrance, than within.
> Some, as thou saw'st, by violent stroke shall die;
> By fire, flood, famine, by intemperance more
> In meats and drinks, which on the earth shall bring
> Diseases dire, of which a monstrous crew
> Before thee shall appear; that thou may'st know
> What misery th' inabstinence of Eve
> Shall bring on Men. Immediately a place
> Before his eyes appeared, sad, noisome, dark;
> A lazar-house it seemed; wherein were laid
> Numbers of all diseased; all maladies
> Of ghastly spasm, or racking torture, qualms
> Of heart-sick agony, all feverous kinds,
> Convulsions, epilepsies, fierce catarrhs,
> Intestine stone and ulcer, colic-pangs,
> Demoniac frenzy, moping melancholy,
> And moon-struck madness, pining atrophy,
> Marasmus, and wide-wasting pestilence,
> Dropsies, and asthmas, and joint-racking rheums.
> Dire was the tossing, deep the groans; Despair
> Tended the sick busiest from couch to couch;

> And over them triumphant Death his dart
> Shook, but delayed to strike, though oft invoked
> With vows, as their chief good, and final hope.[1]

Timothy George's remarkable witness both to and for evangelicals stems, in no small part, from such breadth and depth of learning. When in 1995 Mark Noll complained, at book length, about *The Scandal of the Evangelical Mind*, he was not thinking of Timothy. On the contrary, George's stellar scholarship—displayed in a clutch of books on the Protestant Reformers as well as biblical interpretation—has brought sustained respect for evangelicals in the ecumenical arena. What other Baptist theologian has written so sympathetically on the Virgin Mary, the source of the deepest divide between Protestants and other Christians? Who else among us has spent several hours conversing with Pope Benedict XVI, and in Latin, no less? If Christian antagonism remains the chief scandal afflicting our Lord's Body, thus crippling its witness in a time of terrible crisis, Timothy George is to be honored and saluted for offering his own faithful answer to Christ's prayer that his disciples "may all be one."

BIBLIOGRAPHY

Milton, John. *Paradise Lost*. In *Selected Works of British Poets: A Chronological Series From Ben Jonson to Beattie with Biographical and Critical Notices*, edited by John Aikin and John Frosts. 10th ed. Philadelphia: Wardle 1843.

---

1. *Paradise Lost* XI.101.

SECTION ONE

The Gospel and Worship

The Gospel and the Church

Gerald L. Bray

No two words are more uniquely characteristic of Christianity than "gospel" and "church." Many religions have priests or other kinds of clergy, and most have sacred books, holy sites, specific rituals, and a body of beliefs. But none has a gospel of salvation that is meant to be proclaimed to all people, and none has a church made up of those who have heard that gospel and received it into their own lives. Furthermore, the gospel and the church are not peripheral to the Christian faith but central to its very being. In a word, the gospel (or "good news") of Jesus Christ is the foundation of the church, the body of believers that is the public face that Christianity presents to the world. Without the gospel the church would not exist, because it would have no reason to. It was because Jesus Christ came into the world to pay the price of human sin, making it possible for those for whom he died to be set free from the condemnation it entails, that there is a gospel, or "good news" of salvation. The church, though manifested in many forms, is essentially the community of those who have received that "good news" and who have been charged with the duty of proclaiming it to the world.

But the gospel is more than just a message that the church proclaims to others and the church is more than just a vehicle for its proclamation. The gospel is above all a spiritual experience that church members are called to live for themselves. The church is meant to be the place where the gospel can be seen at work, transforming lives and through those transformed lives changing the world. That at least is the theory. It is the doctrine that the church officially holds and teaches about itself and its purpose here on earth. In many places and at different times in history, the effects of this combination are and have been quite dramatic. We have seen people on the verge of self-destruction who have been turned around by the power of the gospel message. We have watched as communities of believers have revolutionized villages, tribes, and even entire nations as the message of Christ has come to them. In a very real sense, they have been born again—the old has become new, the effects of evil have become instead a power for good and human beings have been set free to live a new life.

Most importantly, those of us who have met with Jesus Christ and received his gospel have been, and are being, changed by its power at work in our own lives. Some of us have heard the message of salvation in and through the church. Others have heard it elsewhere and been drawn to the community of the church as a result. There is no fixed formula, no one-way that must be followed in every case. But whatever the details may be in individual circumstances, the basic framework is always the same. We hear the gospel, we receive it and we are made members of the church, which is the spiritual body of Christ himself.

It cannot be stressed too strongly that it is the gospel that creates the church and not the other way around. Belonging to a community of believers is no guarantee that we have heard the message of salvation and responded to it. From the beginning, there have always been people who have been attracted to the outward signs of the Christian community and attached themselves to it without having experienced the spiritual transformation that created it in the first place. Spiritual things are by their nature invisible, but the church manifests itself in time and space. It acquires a visible presence that is meant to reveal its spiritual heart, but that all too often conceals it from view. The church should, and often is, a means to further the proclamation of the gospel, but in some of its manifestations it can, and sometimes has been, a hindrance to it instead.

The reason for this is that there is a sense in which the visible body of the church extends further than the spiritual power that it proclaims. The gospel is at work in the hearts and minds of individual believers, but we are not always as obedient to its demands as we should be. As long as we remain in this world, the residue of our former lives remains with us—we are not perfect, and shall not be as long as we live on this earth. Those who observe us from without may see our good works and glorify God for them, but they may also see the imperfections that we still carry with us. Once a spiritual movement becomes a social institution it is subject to the pressures of the world in which it is placed. The church as we know it is scarred by the wounds of battles with the powers of evil that are out to destroy it. Forces that want to render the gospel message it proclaims harmless and ineffective often imprison it. In its vulnerability, it bears witness to its own infallibility and impermanence in a universe that will one day come to an end. As the apostle Paul told the Corinthians, we hold the treasure of the gospel in "jars of clay" (2 Cor 4:7), so we should not be surprised that what we see on the outside does not adequately reflect the reality that lies within. But that did not dishearten Paul. He explained this apparent paradox as having been designed "to show that the surpassing power belongs to God and not to us." His words are the charter of the church and explain its relationship to the gospel it professes perhaps better than any learned treatise could do:

> We are afflicted in every way, but not crushed; perplexed, but not driven to despair; persecuted, but not forsaken; struck down, but not destroyed; always carrying in the body the death of Jesus, so that the life of Jesus may also be manifested in our bodies. (2 Cor 4:8–10)

In some mysterious way, the sufferings of the church, which are the sufferings of its members both individually and collectively, are themselves part of the gospel message, the reminder that we must die to self and be born again in the life of Jesus, who rose from the dead and who gathers us to himself in his resurrection body.

When we examine the relationship of the gospel to the church in the light of this, we discover that there are three essential aspects to the process by which Jesus Christ transforms the lives of those who hear and receive the salvation which he has brought and which provide the links that tie the gospel proclamation to the means by which it is proclaimed and the purpose for which it has been given. The first of these aspects is the message that he came to proclaim. The second is the ministry through which he proclaims it, and the third is the mission through which the message is preached to the world in time and space. The message must be preached, understood, and accepted in its fullness, without being added to or subtracted from. The ministry, which is the work of those who have been chosen to preach the message, must be formed and guided by what that message says and those who exercise it must bear witness to its transforming power in their own lives. Finally, the mission encapsulates the purpose for which the message and the ministry have been given, which is to spread the "good news" and win others to the faith that the church exists both to manifest and to proclaim.

THE MESSAGE OF THE GOSPEL

Paul lays out the essential ingredients of the gospel message with exceptional clarity in Titus 3:5–7:

> [H]e saved us, not because of works done by us in righteousness, but according to his own mercy, by the washing of regeneration and renewal of the Holy Spirit, whom he poured out on us richly through Jesus Christ our Savior, so that being justified by his grace we might become heirs according to the hope of eternal life.

He begins with the straightforward statement that Christ has saved us. This may seem obvious to us, but it was not necessarily self-evident to people in New Testament times, nor are its implications fully understood even now. Salvation is not a process that is evolving as time passes and human knowledge increases. The gospel is not a message that we modern people understand better than our forbears, nor will it become even more comprehensible in the future. Salvation has been given, once and for all, in and through the work of Jesus Christ. That work cannot be supplemented, nor can it be set aside by something greater that is still to come. In this respect, the New Testament message is quite different from that of the Old, as the letter to the Hebrews reminds us. The Law of Moses and the priestly sacrifices for sin that it supported were intended only for a time—they were not definitive and something better was expected at some point in the future. Christ, on the other hand, has fulfilled the law. There is no more sacrifice for sin, no higher knowledge to which we must aspire, no additional contribution that we must make in order to benefit from what he has done. He has saved us—fully, uniquely, and forever!

Furthermore, Christ has achieved this quite apart from any "works of righteousness" done by us. In theory, it might be possible for someone to keep the commandments of God and earn salvation by doing so, but in practice this is impossible. The reason is that although the works required are beyond human ability, nobody can actually do them because we are in a state of alienation from God to begin with. Jesus accomplished our salvation as a human being, but he was able to do that because he was *not* cut off from God by sin. It is paradoxical to say that the man who knew no sin became sin for us, but a moment's reflection will tell us that that was the only way our salvation could have been achieved. If Christ had been a sinner, he would not have been able taken our sins upon him. He could have died for his own sins, as anyone can, but he could not have brought new life to overcome them, because his death would have been no more than the full and just reward for his wrongdoing.

To put this another way, to rely on human efforts for salvation is to build a house on sand. Such a foundation is not capable of bearing the weight of the edifice that would be erected on it and the whole project would collapse. A "work of righteousness" displayed by an unrighteous person has no merit in the sight of God. However good it may be, it lacks the foundation in which it needs to be anchored, because someone who is righteous has not done it. In God's eyes, an action is only valid if it is performed by the right kind of person in the right way, and sinful human beings are not capable of producing "works of righteousness" that have any saving power of their own.

The only sure basis for Jesus' saving work is the divine mercy, which he has shown us by taking our burden of sin on himself. This mercy is not a thing or an act but an attitude of heart and mind, a movement of the spirit that proceeds from the will of God. It is, in short, a manifestation of his love. It is a response to our sinfulness that is designed to correspond to the problem it intends to resolve. Christ meets the need that we have because of his love for us, which would be there even if we had not sinned, but would have taken a different form. God did not show kindness to Adam and Eve only after they had disobeyed him, but the gospel of salvation would hardly have been necessary if there was nothing that human beings need to be saved from. In other words, the gospel is the form that God's love takes when he reaches out to sinners, and those sinners are people like you and me, whom he is calling to become members of the church, which is his "body."

The process by which our salvation has been accomplished is described as a "washing of regeneration," a phrase that immediately makes us think of baptism. The church's rite of baptism is a visible witness to this washing, but it is not the washing itself, which can only be spiritual and therefore invisible. If salvation could be achieved merely by being baptized in water, there would be good reason to baptize everyone, regardless of his or her faith or lack of it, since by doing that we could save the entire world. It is not the physical washing that produces regeneration but the regeneration that effects what can be described as a spiritual "washing." Regeneration means new birth—a fresh start. The old life has been put to death by the power of Christ's shed blood. It is the blood that cleanses us from sin—a spiritual paradox, because physical blood would leave a stain on anything it touched, not remove it. Sin is not a stain on the soul, but is a barrier that prevents our reconciliation to the Father. It is this barrier that has been broken down by the sacrifice of Christ on the cross and our relationship with him has been restored. By his forgiveness we can begin again.

The new life we have received in Christ is only possible by the renewal of the Holy Spirit, a point that emphasizes the spiritual nature of our salvation. The Holy Spirit reaches into human beings to a depth of which none of us is fully conscious. He goes beyond our mind and our will to something more profound, to that spiritual character that determines who we are as creatures made in the image and likeness of God. It is at that level that our relationship with him has been renewed and at that level that we can now function as his children and as heirs of the salvation that he has won for us.

The practical consequences of this are that God the Father has poured out his Holy Spirit on us through Jesus Christ, so that we are fully equipped to live the new life that he wants us to enjoy and to share. We are justified, not by our own achievements but by his grace, which makes it possible for us to live in a way that would otherwise not be humanly possible and to become heirs of eternal life. For Christians, the life that we live now is a foretaste of the kingdom of heaven. It is not perfect, because as long as we remain in our created, material body we must live with the sinfulness that we have inherited from our first parents, but the grace of God allows us to confront this handicap and to deal with it in a way that is honoring to God.

Proclaiming this is the command that God has given to the church, but as we all know, the reality does not always live up to the promise. In its earthly form, the church is a mixed body in which the wheat and the tares grow together until the harvest. Too many people assume that belonging to the social institution known, as the "church" is a guarantee of salvation, as if we can be made holy by association. It is the glory of the Baptist tradition that it reminds us that this is not so. Every church member is called to make a personal commitment to Christ, to be born again of his Holy Spirit and to participate actively in building up the community of the faithful. But as Baptists will be the first to admit, that in itself is no guarantee that this desired outcome will always be achieved in practice.

Nevertheless, although spiritual perfection will always elude us in this world, the promise of the first fruits of eternal life remains to focus our attention and set our goal. In New Testament times, Christians were perceived by their pagan neighbors to be different in the way they lived, and the same challenge faces us today. Individuals filled with the grace of the Holy Spirit must relate to others who enjoy the same blessing in a way that bears witness to the reality of what we claim. This does not mean that we must tolerate anything and everything! The early church exercised discipline over its members, and we are called to do the same. We cannot tolerate false teaching or loose morals now any more than the apostles and their congregations could. Yet sadly, we are forced to admit that standards have slipped over the years and that the reputation of the gospel in wider society has suffered as a result of our collective unfaithfulness. Christians should be in the forefront of social reform, advocating universal health care for example, and strict gun control laws, yet all too often they are associated with the exact opposite. Christians should regard divorce with horror and do everything possible to avoid it, yet according to some statistics, the divorce rate is higher among churchgoers than it is in the general population. Excuses are made, people look the other way, and before anyone notices, the purity of God's people has been compromised. Here, perhaps more than anywhere, we need to repent of our spiritual laziness and recover a sense of the true meaning of the gospel. Lives can be turned around by the power of Christ's atoning sacrifice, but if the church is not the place where the fruits of that can be seen, how will anyone come to believe it?

THE MINISTRY OF THE GOSPEL

The second aspect of the relationship between the gospel and the church is what we call its "ordained" ministry. Ordination takes different forms, but the essence of it is that there are some individuals who have been set aside to teach the gospel message and apply it in the life of the church. Paul did not tell his helpers like Timothy and Titus to treat everyone in their congregations with absolute equality, as if there were no valid distinctions among them. On the contrary, he urged them to find and appoint individuals who had the qualities need to instruct and discipline the congregations they belonged to. They did not constitute a breed apart, a higher class of being to which everyone else ought to be subservient, but they *were* given a specific task as members of the body of Christ, and were expected to fulfill it for the good of everyone, including themselves.

The church cannot be shaped according to the demands of the gospel if its ministers do not set an example of what that reform ought to look like. What kind of people should these individuals be? Paul sets out what we would now call their "job description" in Titus 1:6–9:

> [I]f anyone is above reproach, the husband of one wife, and his children are believers and not open to the charge of debauchery or insubordination. For an overseer, as God's steward, must be above reproach. He must not be arrogant or quick-tempered or a drunkard or violent or greedy for gain, but hospitable, a lover of good, self-controlled, upright, holy and disciplined. He must hold firm to the trustworthy word as taught, so that he may be able to give instruction in sound doctrine and also to rebuke those who contradict it.

The general principle is that a minister of the gospel must be above reproach, and few people would disagree with that. Someone in a public position will inevitably come under scrutiny, not only from those whom he is serving but also from those who observe proceedings from outside. The devil is ready to attack church leaders, and the *Schadenfreude* of the popular press when one of them falls into open sin must be a warning to us all. Unfortunately there is a strong tendency within the church to protect ministers in that situation, often for the best of reasons. It is not right for Christians to turn their backs on those who find themselves in trouble, and it is important for us to help them in any way that we can. But at the same time, a minister has responsibilities and if he fails to live up to them he cannot be allowed to continue in his ministry. The history of Catholic pedophile priests who have been moved to other parishes, or of Protestant philanderers who have been dismissed in one place only to be hired again elsewhere, is a reminder to us of the dangers that lurk when this tendency gets out of control. All too often, a pattern of behavior emerges in which the individual concerned carries on the activities for which he has been suspended or dismissed, and when this is finally discovered (as it often is) the reputation of the church suffers great damage.

The preaching of the gospel must be entrusted only to those who have shown themselves worthy of that trust. Paul tells Titus to make sure that the individuals he selects as elders have a proven track record in the management of their own affairs, a reputation for sober and responsible behavior and what we would now call a healthy work ethic. In ancient times, managing one's affairs meant controlling the activities of the household, where most business and social intercourse took place. That is less true today, and the modern minister cannot be held accountable for the activities of his grown-up children if they should abandon the faith, but the principle that he should manage what is under his control in a way that is consistent with his profession remains valid. In particular, a minister's wife should be fully committed to the work to which he is called. This does not necessarily mean that she should be equally involved in it, but she must be supportive of its aims. A disengaged or hostile spouse can do great harm to a man's ministry, and the gospel message will not be honored in a church where that is tolerated. It is not a requirement that a minister should be married, but those who are must remember that their marriage and family life is part of their witness to the wider world, and treat them accordingly.

For the same reason, there is no place in the ministry for convicted felons or for those who have been divorced for reasons other than adultery committed by a spouse (Matt 19:9). Even if there has been repentance and forgiveness, the nature of the ministerial task is such that those who bear such scars should not exercise it. These unfortunate people lack the authority, which the ministry requires and are likely to be weak or feel compromised if they are called to apply discipline in an area where they themselves have conspicuously failed. Of course, they should not be condemned or cast aside-there is a place for them in the Lord's service and it is the duty of the church to help them find it. But the public ministry of preaching and teaching must be protected for the good of all concerned, and for the reputation of the gospel itself.

As long as the church fails in this respect it will lack credibility, and if it is weakened in that way, the message that it is called to proclaim is bound to suffer. Unfortunately, we are seeing this unfold before our eyes. The increasing willingness to excuse divorce and remarriage among church teachers and pastors has compromised our witness to the sanctity of marriage and is being used as a stick to beat Christians when they oppose same-sex unions, for example. How can we attack something that Jesus said nothing about when we so obviously disregard what he commanded? There is a heavy price to be paid for laxity of this kind, and the muted reaction of so many churches to the sexual disorders of our time is a sad and silent witness to our failure in this area.

A minister must not only lead an upright life in private, but he must also teach only sound doctrine in public. The apostle Paul is very insistent on this. A person who betrays the gospel message, either by twisting it in some way or by failing to deliver it in its fullness, is a liability that the church cannot afford. Discipline of this kind is essential, though we must admit that it is extremely difficult to implement, especially in our democratic society with its exposure to the pressures of the mass media. Heresy trials play into the hands of secularists who accuse the church of bigotry and injustice whenever it seeks to enforce its standards, and we must face up to the consequences of that for our freedom to proclaim the gospel. Yet at the same time, false teaching cannot be allowed to spread unchecked, because when it is, the entire church suffers.

This has been the sad fate of much "mainline" Protestantism. There have been too many cases of individuals who have had to leave positions in conservative denominations being then taken up by more liberal ones, sometimes with a vague hint that the conservatives' attempt at discipline was "unloving" or "unchristian." This is wrong of course, but in the fragmented state of modern Christianity it is almost impossible to prevent. Yet difficult as it is, the church must do all it can to maintain the quality of its ministry, not out of pride or a misplaced sense of spiritual superiority, but out of concern for the health of the gospel. The Bible warns us time and again that if the minister fails in his duty the people of God will suffer, and when the issue at stake is nothing less than the gospel of salvation, that warning must be heeded all the more.

THE MISSION OF THE GOSPEL

Finally we come to the place where the gospel and the church merge into one—its calling to mission. Read Titus 2:11–15, where this is set out as clearly and as forcefully as anywhere in the New Testament:

> For the grace of God has appeared, bringing salvation for all people, training us to renounce ungodliness and worldly passions, and to live self-controlled, upright and godly lives in the present age, waiting for our blessed hope, the appearing of our great God and Savior Jesus Christ, who gave himself for us to redeem us from all lawlessness and to purify for himself a people for his own possession who are zealous for good works. Declare these things; exhort and rebuke with all authority. Let no one disregard you.

The grace of God has appeared and it has come with a gift—a message of salvation "for all people." This does not mean, as some have assumed, that everyone will be saved. Paul was writing against a background of Judaism, which thought of divine blessing exclusively in relation to the people of Israel. If a non-Israelite wished to enjoy it, he (or she) had to join the Jewish people first, which was not an easy thing to do. The message of Jesus Christ however was that salvation could be preached to non-Jews, who could obtain it on the same basis as God's covenant people of old. What mattered was not physical descent from Abraham, but a faith that was the same as his, and in principle that faith is available to anybody.

In practice, of course, not everybody accepts it, for reasons that are hidden from our eyes. We have to be prepared for rejection, but that should not deter us from proclaiming the "good news" of the gospel. Those who hear and receive it will be saved, and there can be no greater blessing than that. Furthermore, those who receive it will form the next generation of the church, because as Paul says to Titus, it was the purpose of Christ "to redeem us from all lawlessness and to purify for himself a people for his own possession who are zealous for good works."

It has become common, especially in Evangelical Protestant circles, to portray the gospel as a message of liberation—from sin, from anxiety, from psychological traumas of all kinds. In some ways, and for certain people, it can be all of these things and more. But that is not the central emphasis of the New Testament. When Paul talks about the gospel, he does not usually say much about what we have been set free *from*, although he occasionally reminds forgetful believers of what they were once like. Rather, he places his emphasis on what we have been set free *for*, which is a godly life in this world and the hope of better things to come in the next. The godly life is essential for pastors and teachers, but it is also intended for every member of the church. It is not something that comes naturally, which is why Paul tells Titus that the grace of God is training us "to renounce ungodliness and worldly passions, and to live self-controlled, upright, and godly lives in the present age."

It is the duty of our preachers to emphasize this and to recall us to our duty when we are tempted to fall away. How many Christians have a reputation for being God-fearing on Sunday and then behaving like pagans for the rest of the week? Often they have an excuse—a pastor can live in his own pious bubble, they think, but ordinary people have to mix with the world, and that is not always easy. Compromises may have to be made and sinful behavior may have to be tolerated in an environment where standards are different from those that the church would expect. Being honest in a corrupt world is very difficult, and there are cases where those who have stood up for their beliefs have suffered as a result. The church cannot hide the fact that to follow Christ is to take up his cross, to be crucified with him. Persecution of one kind or another is the lot of every faithful witness and we must not hide this unpleasant fact under a bubble bath of blissful joy that is supposed to be the mark of the saved. Christians are not called to be popular—they are called to make a difference, and living the godly life is sure to do that.

The other problem with a lot of public evangelism nowadays is that it puts so great an emphasis on salvation by faith alone that the place of good works is completely forgotten. It is quite true that we can do nothing to earn our salvation and that our so-called "good works" are worthless when set next to the sacrifice of Christ on our behalf. On that point we can all agree. But as Paul tells Titus, in Christ we have been set free *for* good works. They are not the cause of our salvation but its effect. Those who know Christ will be determined to order their lives in a way that will please him, and doing good to others comes at the top of the list. Too many Christians today never hear this part of the message; if they absorb anything at all about how to live as believers it will be only that they should go out and tell others and spend as much time as possible in pious activities like prayer and Bible study.

Those things are necessary and important, but they are not the whole story. We are called to be a transforming element in society—the salt of the earth, the light of the world. The assertion that faith is a purely private matter that has no place in public life is a myth that is doing great harm to the world in which we live. If Christians abdicate their responsibilities in this area, they do not create a neutral space in which all beliefs and none can flourish equally. On the contrary, they leave the field wide open to anti-Christian forces that will do their best to suppress the message of the gospel. We are seeing this at the present time in the great push for homosexual rights. This has gone far beyond the initial quest for tolerance and has become an unholy crusade that is determined to change social values in a way that can only do great harm. Marriage has been dissociated from procreation to such an extent that surrogacy, with all its attendant dangers and uncertainties, has become an accepted norm in many places. Sexual identity has been divorced from natural biology and become a plaything of the mind, allowing people to choose what "gender" they want to be—and to force others to accept them at their own self-evaluation. Even children, some as young as eight, are being encouraged to adopt a gender of their choice when they are barely old enough to understand what the difference between boys and girls is.

We are witnessing a form of collective madness that can only destroy the foundations of our society, but where is the voice of the church? Where is the message of the gospel that can set people free from such delusions and give them the "blessed hope" of the appearing in glory of our God and Savior Jesus Christ? Accused (sometimes rightly) of having supported widespread injustice in the past, apparently incapable of self-discipline in the present, the compromised church flounders in a morass of "ungodliness and worldly passions" and has lost its authority to exhort and rebuke the world as we are called to do. Instead of distancing ourselves from sin and from false solutions to the world's needs, we pander to them, claiming that we too understand the plight of the poor and the oppressed, and ape the world's cries for justice. It is not that we are against such things in principle, but that we propose a radically different solution to the problems we face—the gospel of Jesus Christ.

That is what the church exists for and that is what we are called to proclaim, both to those who will listen and to those who will not. We shall suffer for it, yes, but in suffering we will also be glorified and our sacrifice will be vindicated. We are not put here on earth in order to build vast megachurches with parking lots that stretch to infinity, but the one, true church of God that is seated around the throne of glory in the heavenly places, singing for all eternity the praises of the Lamb who was slain for the sins of the world. The gospel is at the center of that church. The gospel gives it its unity and sense of purpose. The gospel is the means whereby it grows and flourishes, both in this life and in the next. May God have mercy on us his pilgrim people as we head towards that heavenly glory, and may our light so shine before others that they may see our good works and glorify their Father in heaven even as we seek to glorify him here on earth. Amen.

Lose the Church, Lose the Gospel

Mark E. Dever

I AM CONCERNED THAT too often in our day, holiness and grace are presented as mutually exclusive emphases. After all, do not Paul Washer and Tim Keller preach the same gospel?

But how is Keller's Luther-like liberation from legalism to be joined with Washer's MacArthur-like insistence on repentance? I actually do not think it is too difficult. In fact, I contend that the grace and holiness and truth and love that underpin these approaches to gospel communication should be reconciled and even mutually reinforced in a single place on this side of heaven—and that place is the local church.

The nineteenth-century Anglican pastor Charles Bridges began his classic *The Christian Ministry* with the observation that "The Church is the mirror, that reflects the whole effulgence of the Divine character. It is the grand scene, in which the perfections of Jehovah are displayed to the universe. The revelations made to the Church, the successive grand events in her history, and above all, the manifestation of "the glory of God in the Person of Jesus Christ"—furnish even to the heavenly intelligences fresh subjects of adoring contemplation."

I am convinced the gospel cannot be well and practically addressed without addressing the topic of the church. The church is so beautiful as to be described in the Bible as "coming down out of heaven from God prepared as a bride adorned for her husband" (Rev 21:2). "The church of God," which Paul could describe under the inspiration of the Holy Spirit as "the church of God which he obtained with his own blood" (Acts 20:28). It is common in current evangelical circles for the universal church to be extolled while the local church is ignored or even belittled. But I would like to argue that the integrity of our claim to love God is intended to be confirmed by our membership in a local church. That is my simple, underlying assumption to my title's claim that if we lose the church, we inevitably and eventually lose the gospel. We all accept the notion that ideas have consequences. And in our contemporary world, we are increasingly aware of how our community influences our ideas. I would expect this idea to be as uncontroversial as it is largely unconsidered; I would also expect its implications to be significant, both corporately and personally. Because I am an evangelical Protestant, I want to locate everything I am about to say in the Bible, and then attempt to glean some pastoral and practical insights on the basis of the Bible's teaching. So first, let us consider the Old Testament background of Israel as a community whose life was not only founded on its special doctrine, but whose special doctrine was cultivated by and even expressed, protected, and preserved by their special life together. Then, we will turn to the New Testament and consider how the church was made not only *by* the gospel, but also to both propagate and protect the gospel. Third, I want us to consider how it is that the local church is normally meant to define the gospel in a given place and time. And, finally, I want us to reflect historically and practically on the dangerously partial and unbalanced nature of the typical American conservative evangelical decline narrative.

OLD TESTAMENT ISRAEL

First and foremost, in the Old Testament, we find that disobedience led to misrepresenting God. The special life of Israel was intended to protect and preserve God's truth. But sometimes, even those entrusted with protecting that special life failed in their important job. Disobedience to God seemed to lie about him. I will give two examples—one individual, the other national. First, as an example of the individual, consider Saul:

> And Samuel said, "Has the Lord as great delight in burnt offerings and sacrifices, as in obeying the voice of the Lord? Behold, to obey is better than sacrifice, and to listen than the fat of rams. For rebellion is as the sin of divination, and presumption is as iniquity and idolatry.
>
> Because you have rejected the word of the Lord, he has also rejected you from being king."
>
> Saul said to Samuel, "I have sinned, for I have transgressed the commandment of the Lord and your words, because I feared the people and obeyed their voice. (1 Sam 15:22–24)

Have you ever noticed how clear Saul's confession is? He displays stunningly clear self-knowledge:

> "because I feared the people and obeyed their voice." Saul disobeyed God's rule and so he came to misrepresent it. Saul's apparent mercy—which he had shown earlier—is really a misplaced fear of the people, rather than the LORD. But Saul's use of authority was meant to be an expression of God's; therefore, for Saul to remove himself from obedience to God was to unplug himself from God's authority that he was to exercise in his role. In fact, the only authority he legitimately had was from God. Saul disqualified himself by following in the way of the original sin, listening to human voices, rather than the voice of God. Do you remember what God charged Adam with doing wrong in Gen 3:17? "Because you have listened to the voice of your wife" ... instead of *my* voice!" Here in 1 Samuel, Saul misprioritize the will of the people over the will of the Lord, which in turn causes him to confuse the relative merits of obedience and ritual sacrifice. His ethical error led to a theological error. If nothing else, we must say that thought and life, theology and ethics, are deeply intertwined in the life of the people of God in the Old Testament. And sin distorts it all. But is it any surprise to a Christian heart that sin has this refracting power? Take disordered love as an example. Not too long ago, I was sitting with a man married for over 40 years, claiming to be a Christian, yet who was having a hard time seeing that the adultery he was committing was "sin." How can it be so wrong if it feels so right! But is love always so straightforward a matter for fallen human beings? Can we be surprised that God's people needed to be instructed even on love?

In the founding of Israel, the LORD made it clear in Lev 19:2 that "You (Israel) shall be holy, for I the LORD your God am holy." (This—with all its ramifications—is *not* a self-evident truth to fallen people.) God meant for the holiness of his people to express itself ethically in many ways, especially in the command, "you shall love your neighbor as yourself" (Lev 19:18). But they were to show themselves holy most supremely in their love for him: "You shall love the LORD your God with all your heart and with all your soul and with all your might" (Deut 6:5). The repeated "all" stressed that God was one and not many, and that there was no other divine being to rival the LORD, no one to whom Israel could ever legitimately divide their affection. We are aware that not loving God can lead to us not loving others, but I wonder if we are aware that not loving others can expose the fraying nature of the love we claim to have for God, and eventually cause it to unravel altogether. Again, it is not essential for our purposes to prove which one caused the other, but simply to note how intertwined they are.

But let us get back to Saul in 1 Samuel 15. By fearing people, he did not love them, as he should—and by disobeying God, he did not love God as he should. Saul was proving that, while he may have been a part of God's people nominally and naturally, we have reason to question whether he was spiritually and supernaturally. To further illustrate sin's tendency to generate distortion and lies, we turn to the corporate example of the northern kingdom, Israel, and its idolatry. In the eighth century, the only writing prophet from the northern kingdom, Hosea, condemned Israel for its idolatry. Hosea wrote,

> Hear the word of the Lord, O children of Israel, for the Lord has a controversy with the inhabitants of the land. There is no faithfulness or steadfast love, and no knowledge of God in the land; there is swearing, lying, murder, stealing, and committing adultery; they break all bounds, and bloodshed follows bloodshed. Therefore the land mourns, and all who dwell in it languish, and also the beasts of the field and the birds of the heavens, and even the fish of the sea are taken away. Yet let no one contend, and let none accuse, for with you is my contention, O priest. You shall stumble by day; the prophet also shall stumble with you by night; and I will destroy your mother. My people are destroyed for lack of knowledge; because you have rejected knowledge, I reject you from being a priest to me. And since you have forgotten the law of your God, I also will forget your children. The more they increased, the more they sinned against me; I will change their glory into shame. They feed on the sin of my people; they are greedy for their iniquity. And it shall be like people, like priest; I will punish them for their ways and repay them for their deeds. They shall eat, but not be satisfied; they shall play the whore, but not multiply, because they have forsaken the Lord to cherish whoredom, wine, and new wine, which take away the understanding. My people inquire of a piece of wood, and their walking staff gives them oracles. For a spirit of whoredom has led them astray, and they have left their God to play the whore. They sacrifice on the tops of the mountains and burn offerings on the hills, under oak, poplar, and terebinth, because their shade is good. Therefore your daughters play the whore, and your brides commit adultery. (Hos 4:1–13)

Idolatry is so perfectly expressed by adultery because idolatry is spiritual unfaithfulness to our sworn love. God's plan was to bring the nations to himself through Israel: "It is too light a thing that you should be my servant to raise up the tribes of Jacob and to bring back the preserved of Israel; I will make you as a light for the nations, that my salvation may reach to the end of the earth" (Isa 49:6). David prophesied similarly in Psalm 86: "All the nations you have made shall come and worship before you, O Lord, and shall glorify your name!" (Ps 9).

The nation of Israel was to be a message from Creator to creation—but Israel was exchanging the truth for a lie! After all, what could be *less* in line with the world-wide redemptive purposes of God than to have the very people he had specially set apart become indistinct in their lives, indistinguishable from the nations around them, even to the point of actually losing their copies of God's written Word?

Moses' destruction of the tablets in light of Israel's sins symbolizes how the people's idolatry and adultery caused them to break God's laws, even making those laws effectively vanish. In fact, this is *exactly* what the LORD foretold would happen if the people were unfaithful to the LORD: "And the LORD will scatter you among all peoples, from one end of the earth to the other, and there you shall serve other gods of wood and stone, which neither you nor your fathers have known" (Deut 28:64).

And so it came to pass that the people were unfaithful, and the Assyrians destroyed the northern kingdom and the southern kingdom went into exile, scattered among the nations. Ezekiel describes it this way: "But when they came to the nations, wherever they came, they profaned my holy name, in that people said of them, 'These are the people of the LORD, and yet they had to go out of his land.' But I had concern for my holy name, which the house of Israel had profaned among the nations to which they came" (Ezek 36:20–21).

Forfeiting their special practices, God's people distorted the truth about their God. And with the truth obscured and seemingly denied by their lives, the nation's purpose—like Saul's centuries before—had been compromised. So they would be scattered into the nations they had chosen to emulate. The nation whose very existence was intended to be an argument *for* serving God actually led in rebellion against him, which led to God's judgment on them in the Exile.

To summarize this first point: in the Old Testament, disobedience led to misrepresenting God. Marrying the idol-worshippers would lead to idolatry. Moral error often preceded and gave rise to theological error. Israel was to be a light to the Gentiles, a beacon to the world of God's holiness and truth. Their mission, though, required them to be distinct from the world, and when that distinction was lost, they ceased to hold up and display the truth about God to his watching world.

NEW TESTAMENT CHURCH

When we arrive at the New Testament, we see that the church is presented as the pillar and foundation of the truth (1 Tim 3:15) As the LORD called Israel in the Old Testament, so, too, would the Messiah call his own assembly, one that would be created and shaped by the same gospel they are called to hold on to and share. Just like the Old Testament people of God were called to steward God's great truths by lives which reinforced their distinction from the people around them, so the church has been called to live like those who are God's special possession, as Paul says a little earlier in 1 Tim 2:14. In other words, the church's identity is shaped by the truth of God; in turn, the church keeps that truth and proclaims it to the world.

This means every church should be marked by holiness and love and unity. And why is this the case? Because God is holy and loving and one. For instance, when Paul is presented with reports of division in the Corinthian church, he asks a profoundly theological question: "Is Christ divided?" (1 Cor 1:13) Paul's powerful assumption here is twofold: not only must the Corinthians' doctrine reflect God's truth—as we see in Galatians 1–but their life together must also reflect God's being. Therefore, any satisfaction or contentment with sinful divisiveness in the body imperils the congregation's hold on truth itself. As surely as personal idolatry followed marriage to idolaters in the Old Testament, so false teaching about God and the gospel will follow in the wake of sin ignored and accommodated in the church. That reinforcing relationship between life and doctrine is rooted in Matt 28:20, where Christ commissions the church to "teach them to obey all that I have commanded." It is also how we might expect verses like Eph 3:10 to be fulfilled, in which Paul says that *"through the church* the manifold wisdom of God might now be made known to the rulers and authorities in the heavenly places" (Eph 3:10, emphasis added). As I heard pastor Mark Ross say years ago: "Paul's great concern (Eph 4:1–16) for the church is that the church manifest and display the glory of God, thus vindicating God's character against all the slander of demonic realms, the slander that God is not worth living for. God has entrusted to his church the glory of his own name."

In 1 Tim 3:15–16, Paul returns to the building metaphor of the church as the house of God. Paul calls Timothy to lead the Ephesian church to hold up God's truth; by their lips and by their lives they were to support and protect the truth. He is clearly concerned with right teaching. But he is also adamant that right conduct testifies to the truth. The church *should* be the pillar and foundation of the truth—and they uphold this truth by living it and teaching it and preaching it. I say this not as someone of Eastern Orthodox or Roman Catholic persuasion, but as a biblical, Baptist Congregationalist: *normally, we can no more understand the truth of the Christian gospel without the church than we can learn a language we never speak, never read, and never use.* Signs and symbols without being joined by faith to that which they symbolize are, as Richard Sibbes said, but "seals to a blank" and worth nothing. The life of faith expresses and encourages the gospel that first gives rise to it. The love of God we claim to come to know in Christ is shaped by Scripture's requirements and prohibitions in our relationships with others. The church is the pillar and foundation of the truth. It is the setting—the God-ordained, Christ-purchased, and Spirit-created prongs that hold the diamond of the gospel and keep it from being lost.

HOW THE LOCAL CHURCH DEFINES THE GOSPEL FOR YOU AND ME

This all brings me to a third point: the local church is the community which defines what the gospel means in a given time and place. Of course, some evangelicals will understand rule-establishing bodies *above* the local church to have responsibility for theological definition. For example, Presbyterians recognize a unique authority in the Presbyterian Church of America's General Assembly. But who would want to deny the local church's front-line responsibility to define and therefore de-limit gospel boundaries? So, the man in 1 Corinthians 5 can claim he will inherit the kingdom of God, and the local church can even affirm him in it, but the truth is not created by him or by the local church. The truth has been revealed that he, as an unrepentantly immoral person, will not. To preach anything else would be false. So then, under the inspiration of the Holy Spirit, does Paul revise God's condemnations of such immorality? No. Does he correct some official outside of Corinth who has responsibility for the church's discipline? No. Does he correct the sinner himself? Not directly. Does he take to task the pastor or elders of the church? Not distinctly. To whom does Paul express, in the strongest language, God's warning? To the same group Jesus in Matt 18 entrusted with the final say in the composition of the local church—the *ecclesia*, the local congregation.

Jesus initiated the church and pledged his very self as the guarantee of its success in Matt 16 and 28. This does not, of course, mean that no local church can err. But it *does* entail a historical claim that—despite deception from within and persecution or indifference from without—Christ has given his church the unerring, life-creating promise that she will not only survive, but prevail over Hell's strongest defenses—its gates!

Christ's church will fail in its purposes only to the degree Christ failed in his. As he told his heavenly Father in John 17:4: "I glorified you on earth, having accomplished the work that you gave me to do." He goes on to pray for his followers, that God would keep them—that he would keep us. This prayer is being and will continually be answered, and all that, in no small part, through the local church as it embodies the character of God.

But how does this work practically? The local church acts as a kind of assurance of salvation cooperative, where we are cared for, even as we care for each other's life and doctrine. Paul envisions the local church in Rom 15:14 as a place where Christians instruct one another. We see in 1 Corinthians that our holiness and love and unity reflect God's own. We testify to our commitment to the Christian life and our reliance on Christ alone as we partake in the public signs of our initial baptism and our regular taking of the Lord's Supper together. These two signs stand strong and together, testifying against ever-threatening evils.

Baptism in particular stands against the evil of hypocrisy as we *personally* testify to our own sincere, comprehensive all-in-ness, as we confess our hope is in our new life with Christ. The Lord's Supper, then, stands against the evil of any individualism that allows us to claim to love God privately, with no love shown to our brothers and sisters; through the Supper, we proclaim Christ's death until he comes, picturing his sacrifice at the Table, reflected in our self-sacrificing love both for God and for each other. Normally, how will people know what we mean by the gospel we speak without a community filled by God's own Spirit, living out what holiness and love, repentance and faith, forgiveness and hope actually look like? Do we make the mistake that because the church no longer has the ethnic distinction of the Old Testament people of God, that we have no distinction at all from the world around us, or that our distinction serves no purpose? The local church is the community which defines what the gospel means in a given time and place.

WHAT CHURCHES WILL HOLD ON TO THE GOSPEL?

If the points above are true, then our evangelical decline narrative should not only emphasize that liberal doctrine kills churches, but it should also include the observation that churches increasingly indistinct from the world will lose their hold on the gospel, both in its soundness in the pulpit, and in its appearance in its members' lives. A confession: when I read someone's biographical blurb, I want to know what church he or she are a member of and what they do there. I wonder if I am the only one. When was the last time you considered the spiritual significance of your own church membership?

We are well familiar with the defensive importance of the pulpit. That is, we are aware that the proclamation of the truth and the denunciation of error are hallmarks of true and faithful gospel ministry. Our own self-understanding as evangelicals is that we are the rightful heirs of the New Testament, that our orthodoxy is older and truer than both Eastern and Roman Catholic churches. We understand ourselves to be children of the sixteenth-century Reformation—all of whom would together say that it is faith alone in Christ that saves, even as we acknowledge that saving faith never stays alone. We exult in the freeness of the grace and mercy of the gospel of Jesus Christ, and we mean to protect it and its doctrinal entailments. But how is our diligence in defining doctrine accompanied by defining obedience as well?

In our local churches, we define the gospel not only by what we say and what we deny, but also by whom we accept into membership, by whom we allow to remain in membership, and by whom we put out of membership. Our membership roles are intended to reflect our confessions. And it all comes together very practically in the local church and its membership. If we give up any ability to say what a Christian is *not*, can we meaningfully say what a Christian *is*?

Take the most wonderful descriptions of the Christian life—as a life of love, for example, in 1 Corinthians 13. Love is described by what it is *not*, as well as by what it is: "If I have prophetic powers, and understand all mysteries and all knowledge, and if I have all faith, so as to remove mountains, but have not love, I am nothing" (1 Cor 13:2).

In 1 Corinthians 6, Paul is at pains to warn the Corinthians not to be deceived. And then he lays out a list of some of those who will not inherit the kingdom of God—as damning a prediction as the Bible knows. Interestingly, though, Paul populates that list not with those holding various heresies, but with those indulging unrepentantly in sin.

I wonder if Reformation studies these days underplay the outrage at the widespread moral hypocrisy of the clergy? There was a great deal of immorality that was widely known and decried. If you read Shakespeare, you'll see a phrase that gets thrown around: "Hie thee to a nunnery!"—which means, "Go to a whorehouse." So widespread was the knowledge of the common immorality of the clergy at the time. This is why church discipline was so naturally a part of the recovery of the gospel in the sixteenth century. For so long, people had not expected holiness from people who called themselves Christians—leaders, ministers, priests. So the Belgic Confession of 1561 states in Article 29: "The marks by which the true Church is known are these: If the pure doctrine of the gospel is preached therein; if she maintains the pure administration of the sacraments as instituted by Christ; if church discipline is exercised in punishing of sin; in short, if all things are managed according to the pure Word of God, all things contrary thereto rejected, and Jesus Christ acknowledged as the only Head of the Church."

If the church is to reveal God's character, the nature of God's own holy love must be displayed in our care for each other in our local churches. And this love has many functions, among the most important of which are to display the Creator's character to his creation, to validate our own claims to love and to be loved by God.

By nature, we think we are the world's experts on us, but the truth is we are not. We can deceive ourselves. We do not know ourselves completely or unerringly—and, in some ways, others may know us better than we know ourselves. And so, we are thankful for the community that can reveal false positives in our claims and teach us the truth about ourselves, while there is still time. Perhaps this is what John the Apostle is getting at in 1 John 4:20–21: "If anyone says 'I love God,' and hates his brother, he is a liar; for he who does not love his brother, whom he has seen cannot love God whom he has not seen. And this commandment we have from him: whoever loves God must also love his brother."

The way we often tolerate an unholiness that is typified by a lack of love is *not* by denying the truth of 1 John. More likely, it happens when we isolate ourselves from communities that would be able to call us out on our loveless-ness, and call us more into Christ-like, inconvenient love. When *we have* made the Scripture and its demands convenient for *us* and for *our* lives, can we be surprised that others do the same?

In short, unholiness leads to heterodoxy. What strange fruit was borne in the twentieth century by the abandonment of discipline even by congregations that defended the Bible's authority? Does the Bible's authority transfer from the words in the pulpit to the lives in the pew? Can such a conversation only be heard as a forerunner to an ingrown, cultish legalism? Could we find a way to have this conversation about church health and membership again? Do you see how we need to, in part, because of the importance of the health of the local church to our own spiritual soundness and well being?

Robert Murray M'Cheyne reflected on the importance of a regular practice of church discipline in addition to the right preaching of the Word. He said, "When I first entered upon the work of the ministry among you,

I was exceeding ignorant of the vast importance of church discipline. I thought that my great and almost only work was to pray and preach. I saw your souls to be so precious, and the time so short, that I devoted all my time, and care, and strength, to labor in word and doctrine. When cases of discipline were brought before the elders, and me I regarded them with something like abhorrence. It was a duty I shrank from and I may truly say it nearly drove me from the work of the ministry among you altogether. But it pleased God, who teaches his servants in another way than man teaches, to bless some of the cases of discipline to the manifest and undeniable conversion of the souls under our care; and from that hour a new light broke in upon my mind, and I saw that if preaching be an ordinance of Christ, so is church discipline. I now feel very deeply persuaded that both are of God—that two keys are committed to us by Christ, the one the key of doctrine, by means of which we unlock the treasures of the Bible, the other the key of discipline, by which we open or shut the way to the sealing ordinances of the faith. Both are Christ's gift, and neither is to be resigned without sin."[1]

Brothers-pastors, being careful about inerrancy and careless with your membership rolls is a recipe for disaster. We can as little afford to dispense with vigilance in our membership as we can dispense with diligence in our teaching.

Could your own local church be helped as much by putting out unrepentant members as by refuting false doctrines? Could you yourself ever stand in need of such help? Does our lack of concern about the lives of our fellow church members belie our stated love for the church? What does it truly matter if your young people love reading theology books but will not get up an hour early to take an older person to church? It is tragic when a commitment to sound doctrine is used to justify such inconsistent lives.

To repeat this final point: Liberal, unbelieving doctrine kills churches, but it should also be said that churches indistinct from the world lose their hold on the gospel. Are you seeing something of God's character in *your* local church, something of God's love and purity and self-giving nature?

CONCLUSION

To recap what I have been trying to argue: God's unchanging purpose over time has been to have a people special to himself, a people whose life-commitments to him helps them both understand and preserve the truth about him. We can preach better than we live—we have to! We also must realize

---

1. Bonar, *Robert Murray M'Cheyne*, 87–88.

that how we live does affect how we preach. It is dangerously naïve to ignore the fact that life affects doctrine.

Therefore, in the New Testament the church is concerned not merely with truth, but also with holiness—not only with the Scriptures, but also with the fruit of the Spirit in the believer's life. In other words, God intends the local church to be a living picture of what the gospel looks like when truly believed. Mere professions of faith or arguments for good actions fail to convey the power of God's salvation. Professions and arguments should be made; preaching and evangelizing should be done; and all of it should exist in connection with a community of people whose lives are being reshaped by the gospel.

It is in part because of Timothy George's friendship and kind encouragement that I declined an opportunity to teach in a seminary and have, instead, given the past twenty years to pastoring the Capitol Hill Baptist Church in Washington, DC. Timothy had been the supervisor of my ThM thesis in the mid-1980's and had become a close friend. Unlike many professors however, Timothy has never understood his own profession as the apex of Christian callings. He has a humble and profound joy in the pastoral office, and a respect and esteem for it often lacking in academics. And so, when others counseled against my accepting the pastorate of a largely—elderly congregation in typical, inner-city decline, Timothy alone spoke to me of what wonderful things God might do there. He seemed to understand intuitively what I have been arguing in this chapter. For Timothy, Bible truth and Christian life come together in the local church.

I have argued that contesting for the truth of the Bible and the truths in the Bible, while simultaneously neglecting the life of the local congregation, is disintegrating what Jesus created together. It is like trying furiously to scoop out water with a bucket and doing nothing to plug the leak in the boat. For a church to denounce abortion without really knowing who its members are—are there abortion doctors as members who are allowed to take the Lord's supper, Is self-contradictory and self-defeating. Paul warned about this kind of church, like the one in Corinth who welcomed the unrepentant, adulterous man (1 Cor 5).

I will say it again: the integrity of our claim to love God is intended to be confirmed by our membership in a local church. And so it is that we pastors must contend for the inerrancy of the Bible, *and* the gracious nature of the gospel of salvation only by faith in Christ *and* the importance of a loving commitment to our own local congregations. To ignore the local church while pursuing studies in the name of Christ falls somewhere on the scale between ignorance and hypocrisy. And if ignorance is no excuse, how much less hypocrisy? To ignore the fundamental nature of the local church to your own discipleship can be damaging to the church—as it is robbed of you and your assiduous care. But it can be disastrous for you, especially if you are a preacher. I appreciate Spurgeon's plainness on this point: "God never saved any man for being a preacher."[2] Thus, I say again, "Loose the church, Loose the gospel."

BIBLIOGRAPHY

Bonar, Andrew. *Robert Murray M'Cheyne*. 1844. Repr., Edinburgh: Banner of Truth, 1960.
Spurgeon, C. H. *Lectures to My Students*. Peabody, MA: Hendrickson, 2010.

---

2. Spurgeon, *Lectures to My Students*, 1:7.

Worship in the Old Testament

Kenneth A. Mathews

Christian readers have a spiritual intuition about worship in the OT. On the one hand, we immediately recognize that Israel's tabernacle/temple worship is not for the church to practice, but on the other we see that traditional Christian worship reflects in many ways the practice and perspective of worship in Israel. Those who consider the OT no more than preface to the Christian gospel and discipleship the teaching that OT revelation and Israel's worship are indispensable to our Christian experience. In other words, we would not be "Christian" in its fullest sense if there were no OT revelation and people (Gal 4:4–6; 1 Tim 2:6; Titus 1:3). What confounds us is the *form* of worship that Israel practiced. It is strange to us but was common in the Ancient Near East . Formal worship at the tabernacle/temple required choreography of a complex drama, with moving and interconnecting parts. Daniel Block observes that worship services today may include drama *in* worship, but in Israel's worship drama was an act *of* worship.[1] The primary features of the performance were the worshiper, the worship offering, the worship functionary/mediator, and the response of the divine Recipient. Compulsory times and space/place—again foreign to Christian conception of worship—were also vital aspects that contributed to the painstaking demands of conducting acceptable worship. The choreography by both mystery and imagery, when rightly understood and performed, expressed profound theological thought and elicited deep spiritual devotion.

The idea of worship was of critical importance to Israel as the number of diverse Hebrew expressions for worship suggest. Of these the most telling are *abad*, meaning "to serve," and *chawah*, meaning "to bow, prostrate." "Serve/servant" describes the activity of a slave and worship functionary

---

1. Block, *For the Glory of God: Recovering a Biblical Theology of Worship*, 271.

(Exod 13:5; 21:2; Num 8:15). "Bow/prostrate" particularly describes a person's subservient position to a superior (Ps 99:9; cf. Ruth 2:10). In both cases the terms refer to someone in service to God or a human. Worship then involves acknowledgment of one's subordinate standing before the person/object worshiped. The structural principle that underlay worship in its cultic sense was the concept of the holy (sacred). Although a diachronic approach to describing Israel's worship practices has its merit, I am taking a topical approach, focusing on the vital concept of "holy." Since our study coalesces around the theme of "holy," we begin with defining the concept and then move on to selected features of Israel's worship that expressed intellectual and experiential (emotional/spiritual) knowledge of the Holy One of Israel.

THEOLOGY OF THE HOLY

Leviticus 10:10 says, "You [priests] must distinguish between the holy and the common, and between the clean and the unclean" (ESV). This is the task of the priests when teaching and applying the Levitical laws to individuals and to the community. Many readers today confuse the concepts of "holy" (*qodesh*) and "clean/unclean" (*tahor/tame*). It is best to think of them as two parts of the same system, just as is intimated in Lev 10:10. Perhaps it is useful to illustrate what the Bible means by "holy" and "clean/unclean" in terms of their coordination. At fleeing King Saul, David and his men sought food from Ahimelech the priest at the sanctuary in Nob. Ahimelech replied to David's request, "There is no ordinary (*chol*) bread on hand. However, there is consecrated (*qodesh*) bread, but the young men may eat it only if they have kept themselves from women" (1 Sam 21:4[Hb. 5]). The consecrated bread, restricted for food to the priests, was the twelve loaves of the "bread of the Presence" on the table in the tabernacle's holy place (1 Sam 21:6[Hb. 7]; Exod 25:30; Lev 24:5–9). Ahimelech agreed to give the consecrated bread to David but only if the men had not engaged in sexual relations. The purity laws declared a person who had engaged in sexual relations was *ritually* unclean (*tame*) until evening (Lev 15:18; cf. Exod 19:15). The reasoning for Ahimelech's answer was the consecrated bread was ritually holy (versus ordinary bread) because of its special affiliation with God, and only those in a ritually clean state was permitted to eat it.

But what was the standard for measuring the holy? The definition of what *is* holy is the Holy One himself who is *inherently* holy. Whatever is exclusively devoted to God was declared holy because it was uniquely connected to him. Since no other is by nature holy, God chose to share his holiness with others through "consecration" (declared holy). Two examples help show this. (1) When God from the midst of the burning bush commanded Moses to remove his sandals, the Lord explained, "for the place where you are standing is holy ground" (Exod 3:5). What marked the ground as holy was the presence of God himself. (2) The prescription for making the special anointing oil and incense solely for tabernacle worship was deemed holy. Exodus 30:37 explains, "As for the incense you are making, you must not make any for yourselves using its formula. It is to be regarded by you as sacred to the Lord." Consecration typically involved the ritual act of applying anointing oil to declare that the common is now holy, such as consecrating the tabernacle and the priestly functionaries (Exod 28:41; 40:10; Lev 8:10–11): "I (the Lord) will consecrate the tent of meeting and the altar; I will also consecrate Aaron and his sons to serve Me as priests" (Exod 29:44). Consecration then depicted the idea of moving a person/thing from its ordinary state to the sacred sphere of life.

Next, how was the relationship between the holy and the clean/unclean? The classifications "clean" and "unclean" were not necessarily equivalent to the conception of holy/common. Clean/unclean described what was *symbolically* appropriate/inappropriate for God's presence. Clean/unclean categories were based on physical material appearance (visual images), such as skin disorders (Lev 13–14) whose deviations from the norm would be unsuitable symbolically in the divine *Presence*. "Command the Israelites to send away anyone from the camp who is afflicted with a skin disease, anyone who has a bodily discharge, or anyone who is defiled because of a corpse. You must send away both male and female; send them outside the camp, so that they will not defile their camps where I dwell among them" (Num 5:2–3). Thus, "unclean" did not necessarily indicate a person's sinfulness, but unclean may be only because of the mismatch in visual aid between imperfection in the community and the perfection of God. Nevertheless there may be a person who was *morally/spiritually* "unclean" because of violations, such as sexual incest. Thus people could "defile" (make unclean) themselves by following the "detestable customs" of the nations (Lev 18:24–30). That God demanded holiness in character and purity in worship secured a fellowship with God that was exceptional among the religions of the ANE. "For what great nation is there that has a god near to it as the Lord our God is to us whenever we call to Him? And what great nation has righteous statutes and ordinances like this entire law I set before you today?" (Deut 4:7–8). This declaration indicated God was "near" by virtue of his revealed Word. Although Yahweh was a national deity, he was also the personal deity of every one under his lordship, regardless of social class. Moreover, the meticulous regulations for proper worship and life (e.g., Exod 20:24–25) were theologically vital to Israel's identity by distinguishing Israel from its neighbors (Lev 20:26; Num 23:9; Deut 26:18–19) and by achieving God's witness to the nations (Exod 19:5–6; Deut 4:6; Ps 33:10–12). This leads us to consider the community life of worship.

SACRED COMMUNITY

Related to the ethos of holy was the national life of "covenant" (*berith*, a solemn mutual agreement) under God. Covenant relationship was essential to Israel's self-understanding as a unique community among the nations. Promissory blessings given to Abraham and his descendants by divine declaration expressed the personal, patron relationship of the Lord and the Hebrew fathers (Gen 12:1–3; 15:19–21; 17:1–14; Deut 1:8; Isa 41:8; 51:2). When God and Israel at Sinai entered into a mutual pact of obligation, Israel submitted to live under the stipulations of a *national* covenant (Ten Commandments; Exod 20:1–19; 24:1–11; 34:27–28; Deut 4:13; 5:1–21). "Now if you (Israel) will listen to Me (God) and carefully keep my covenant, you will be My own possession out of all the peoples, although all the earth is Mine and you will be My kingdom of priests and My holy nation" (Exod 19:5–6; Deut 7:6).

The covenant stipulations required them to observe God's commandants that entailed an individual and community life of holy conformity to him. "You are to be holy to Me because I, Yahweh, am holy, and I have set you apart from the nations to be Mine" (Lev 20:26). The nation enjoyed protective care by the Lord, but with that advantage was the highest standard of spiritual and purity life. Failure to heed the covenant jeopardized their benevolent standing with God. God's holy character both compelled and repelled the worshiper. The mystery of the *Presence* attracted but the threat of death for the worshiper who came inappropriately before God produced fearful awe (e.g., Exod 28:35,43; Lev 10:1–5; Deut 5:22–30). Since the common person did not have access to inside the tent, the curtain between the courtyard and the tent preserved the mystery of the Presence and reminded the worshiper of the danger that loomed behind it.

The threat of divine manifestation however was not limited to the location of the cult. The Presence extended to the whole of the Israelite camp. "For the Lord your God walks throughout your camp to protect you and deliver your enemies to you; so your encampments must be holy. He must not see anything improper among you or He will turn away from you (Deut 23:14). Completing the general covenant stipulations were sets of various laws that applied the general stipulations to various concrete circumstances that were designed to guard against violations of the holy. What is important for our purpose is to recognize that sacred worship was not restricted to cultic activities but involved every aspect of human life. This was true of any transgression of law pertaining to human relations, humanitarian values, economic activities, societal justice, and many other facets. Worship then was a *lifestyle*, a perpetual awareness that God was present by virtue of his revealed Word and thus every feature of life was subject to God. There was no demarcation between secular and religious authority, such as we acknowledge in the West. All was under covenant and therefore all was under its sanctions.

From this perspective, it is obvious that the community was commanded to have an authentic spiritual response to the Lord; in other words, performance of ritual observance would not be an acceptable substitute for spiritual relationship with God—in truth, taken as evil offense against the Lord. The Psalmists expressed this inner spiritual passion for communion with the Lord best: "As a deer longs for streams of water, so I long for You, God" (Ps 42:1; cf. 16:9; 73:25).

SACRED PLACE

An Appropriate place for worship was essential to worship gatherings in Israel. "Calling on the Name of the Lord" as acts of worship and proclamation of the one true God was evidenced in the earliest times (Gen 4:26; 12:8). "Name" reminds us of the "Name theology" so important to Deuteronomy's perspective on prayer and worship (Deut 12:5,13–14). Authentic community worship could only occur at those places that his Name alone was honored, meaning that his *real* presence was recognized at the exclusion of any other deity. For Solomon's temple, the Lord declares, ". . . I have consecrated this temple you have built, to put My *name* (italics mine) there forever; My eyes and My heart will be there at all times (1 Kings 9:3). In the ANE the temple mount was considered the residence of the gods and provided the "portal" between earth and heaven whereby the worshiper accessed the divine world.[2] Authentic Yahwism, however, declared that he was not restricted to an earthly manifestation at a particular location or series of locations. Solomon's prayer at the dedication of the Jerusalem temple made this clear. "But will God indeed live on earth? Even heaven, the highest heaven, cannot contain You, much less this temple I have built" (1 Kings 8:27). Yet, the tabernacle/temple was identified as the "house of the Lord" (Jer 7:2; and its variations, Exod 23:19; Ps 122:1; Zech 8:9). Yahwism acknowledged that the Presence was a voluntary act of God that

---

2. Walton, *Ancient Near Eastern Thought and the Old Testament*, 113–18.

could *not* be manipulated by incantation and ritual. The prophets especially condemned Israel for its assumption that the tabernacle/temple was inviolate because God had irrevocably attached his Presence to the tabernacle/temple structures. The political and religious leaders believed no foreign power or any moral collapse could ultimately corrupt the place of worship and precipitate God's abandonment. He was in effect locked into the covenant arrangement as long as the Israelites carried out ritual offerings in the Jerusalem sanctuary. Evidence of this in their minds was the demise of the Northern Kingdom (722 BC) whose sanctuaries were illegitimate, whereas the Jerusalem temple was established and sanctified by the Lord's anointed servant, King Solomon. The response by the religious authorities to Jeremiah's famous "Temple of the Lord" sermon demonstrated their misdirected trust in the divine *place* instead of the divine *Presence* (Jer 7:2–15; 26:6–9). Ezekiel's vision saw the "glory" of the Lord (Presence) depart the temple, leaving the temple defenseless before the Babylonians (586 BC) (Ezek 10:3–19; 11:22–23).

Although the tabernacle/temple was the chief physical component in Israel's worship, the plan and its constituent parts symbolized *spiritual* realities, "a shadow of heavenly things" (Heb 8:5; cf. 9:1–10:1). Both the tabernacle and temple plans were revealed respectively to Moses (Exod 25:8) and to David (1 Chron 28:9). The architecture of ancient church buildings achieved the same kind of theological presentation. "The church is not a work of engineering. It is a symbol. . . . To see the church as only a building, a material structure, is like deconsecrating it, emptying it of its fundamental significance as a symbol."[3] Just as the church basilicas reflected the common Roman public basilica, the basic tabernacle/temple plan also reflected the common plan of sanctuaries in the ANE, in particular the Phoenicians. Tyrian specialists were hired to build David's palace (1 Chron 7:14; 14:1) and after David's death the Jerusalem temple was erected with Solomon's craftsmen (1 Kings 5:17–18; 7:13–14; 2 Chron 2:7,13–14).

Beginning with the tabernacle floor plan, the rectangular-shaped structure faced the east and was enclosed by linen hangings. It encompassed (1) a courtyard and (2) a two-room tent. The courtyard comprised the bronze altar of burnt offering and the bronze water basin for washings. Next, the sacred tent, also facing east, consisted of two enclosed rooms, the posterior room was the holy place and the anterior room was the most holy place containing the ark of the covenant/testimony. A veil separated the courtyard and the entrance into the holy room, which contained the table of the Presence (north), the lamp stand (south), and the golden altar of incense

---

3. Demetrescu, "Symbols in Sacred Architecture and Iconography," 28.

(west) at the back of the room fronting the second veil that separated the two rooms within the tent. Solomon's temple was permanent, made of stone and cedar timbers. It was far more ornate but had the essential two-room arrangement and furniture. The temple platform consisted of three sections, however: a portico, holy place, and most holy place. The rooms were shored up by a three-story structure that supported the temple walls on its three sides, used for housing and storage. There were two bronze pillars located in the portico at the entrance (1 Kings 7:15–22). Much more could be said here but the point is that the temple structure was reminiscent of the simpler tabernacle construction.

What is important for our purposes is the relationship of the tabernacle/temple within the camp of the Israelites and beyond. Imagine a series of five concentric circles that depict the sectors ranging from the inner-most circle to the outer-most circle. (1) For this "sacred compass"[4] the center was the most holy place where the high priest only on the Day of Atonement (*Yom Kippur*) entered before the ark of the covenant to present the atoning blood of the sacrificed animals (Lev 16). This was the most sequestered locale of the whole and it was symbolically the pulsating heart of the community. The high priest's vestments included a linen ephod joined together at the shoulders by two stones each engraved with six names of the twelve tribes. Also, he wore an embroidered, yarn and linen breast piece, displaying twelve stones each inscribed with a tribal name. The symbolic meaning of the engraved stones that high priest represented the whole nation and brought the tribes "over his heart before the Lord" (Exod 28:29–30). (2) The next sector was the holy place in which only Aaronic priests served. (3) Outside the two-room tent was the tabernacle's courtyard where the Levitical priests assisted the priestly functions at the bronze altar. (4) The next sector was the camp of Israel's twelve tribes. (5) And the last sector was "outside of camp," that is, it had no boundary and was the realm of the nations. Increasingly, from the courtyard to the most holy place, there were stages of segregation based on functional holiness.

By the progression in the sectors, we see that all holiness was rooted in the Presence, centered spatially in the most holy place, and flowing out from God. Also, the Presence required increasingly holy conditions to maintain the Lord's communion with his people, including guarded space, consecrated persons, and sacred convocations. The structure showed that God's presence on earth was an earthly reflection of the heavenly reality. The cosmos (Gen 1:1–2:4), Eden (Gen 2–3; cf. Deut 8:7–10; 26:15), Sinai (Exod 24:1–11), tabernacle (Exod 25–31; 35–40), the land (Ps 78:54; Zech 2:12),

---

4. Walton, "Equilibrium and the Sacred Compass: the Structure of Leviticus."

and the temple (1 Kings 6–8) each depicted the holy by the staging of holy gradations, deriving from God as the source of the holy.[5] For example, there was progression in the account of Eden's sacred space. The movement is from the land, to Eden, to Eden's garden, and finally exile outside Eden (Gen 2–3). Also, Eden faced the east (and other connections to temple worship) all implying retrospectively that the tabernacle/temple was Eden *redivivus.* Similarly with hindsight, Sinai was holy space (tabernacle/temple) because of the presence of the Lord. God established limits for those he permitted to climb the mountain to meet with him: first the people could not "touch" the mountain, then the next boundary was selected priests and elders, then Moses and Joshua came to the top, and finally Moses alone encompassed by the cloud of glory (Exod 19:12; 24:1–2,9,13–14,18).

At entering the tabernacle/temple from the east, the worshiper first saw the bronze altar where sacrifice took place. The range of heightened senses to the sounds, smells, and sights alerted the worshiper that the approach to God involved life and death (Num 3:10). The "smell" of death was pervasive. Moreover, approaching the sacred required a costly offering by the worshiper. Yet, the temple's ringing of praise and thanksgiving were a comforting message of hope and acceptance (see Sacred Music below). Additionally, the altar "belonged" to the priest alone, so to speak, in the sense that the layperson did not carry out the ritual practices of handling the blood or animal parts. The basin's water indicated sacramental purity since it was used in the washings of the offering by the priestly functionaries. The procedures for proper discharge of sacrifice requirements were in the hands of the priests (see Sacred Sacrifice below).

At the entrance to the tent, the veil prohibited the worshiper from viewing the inside of the tent, leaving it to the priest who was qualified to enter. This feature preserved the awe and mystery that surrounded the worship of God. Inside, of course, only the priests witnessed firsthand the three furnishings that conveyed (1) the message of divine provision (table of bread), (2) divine illumination/guidance (lamp stand), and (3) the intercessory prayers offered to God (incense altar). The incense altar was "especially holy" to the Lord, meaning it was used for the purposes the Lord instructed (Exod 30:10). The smoke of the incense altar and the second veil protecting the ark of the covenant from wandering eyes functioned as a "buffer" between the priests and the most holy place.

---

5. See Block, *For the Glory of the Lord,* 297–332.

SACRED TIME

As in the Christian liturgical year (e.g., Advent, Holy Week), the feast days and liturgical seasons in the Hebrew calendar memorialized the works of God in creation and for his people. Two factors underlay the stories and rituals that were essential to acceptable worship. (1) The first was the rhythm of Sabbath's (seventh's) that marked weekly, monthly, and annual times of worship. For example, the seventh month in the year included the most celebrated convocations—Weeks, Trumpets, Day of Atonement, and Booths/Tabernacles (see below). Why Sabbath's? Exodus 20:8–11 (fourth commandment) explains that the Sabbath pattern of six + one corresponds to the creation pattern (Gen 2:2–3, "seventh day"). Sabbath then was an acknowledgement that the Lord was Creator. The Sabbath also served as the chief sign of the Sinai covenant (Exod 31:12–17). What is striking about Hebrew observance is there was no parallel in the ANE for sacred Sabbath's (seven's). Religious calendars in the ancient world were tied to astral movements, the sun and moon, which were believed to be deities. Deuteronomy, on the other hand, ties Sabbath practices to the deliverance of Israel from Egyptian slavery (5:12–17). Sabbath was a reminder that God is Redeemer. These two pillars of theology, Creator and Redeemer, undergird all biblical revelation and worship.

(2) The second factor is the connection between the sacred calendar and the times of harvest in Canaan. The ritual of presenting firstfruits, for example, was the setting for the classic historic confession of the worshiper.[6]

> 5You are to respond by saying in the presence of the Lord your God: My father was a wandering Aramean. He went down to Egypt with a few people and lived there. There he became a great, powerful, and populous nation. . . . . 10I have now brought the first of the land's produce that You, Lord, have given me. You will then place the container before the Lord your God and bow down to Him. (Deut 26:5,10).

The link between harvest and salvation history was based on the promissory gift of land and its harvests for the nation. Unlike the nature deities of the nations, Israel's religion placed an emphasis on God actions in history as he carried out his promises. Accordingly, all male leaders of households undertook three annual pilgrimages to the tabernacle/temple to acknowledge God's deliverance in Israel's national memory (Exod 23:14–17; 34:23–24; Deut 16:16–17). These pilgrimage events were *week-long* celebrations. (1)

---

6. The Feast of First Fruits described below was annual whereas the one described here was probably the one time event when the nation successfully possessed the land and enjoyed its first harvest.

The Feast of Unleavened Bread with Passover and Firstfruits (March–April) recalled the deliverance of Israel from Egyptian bondage and celebrated the beginning of barley harvest (Exod 12–14; Lev 23:5–14; Deut 26:1–11). (2) The Feast of Weeks (Pentecost) fifty days later (May–June) joyfully recognized the harvest of wheat and first summer fruits (Lev 23:15–21); in Jewish tradition it was the time of the giving of the law at Sinai. (3) The Festival of Booths/Tabernacles (September–October) recalled God's provision during the wilderness sojourn and celebrated the ingathering of the last summer fruits (Lev 23:33–43; Deut 16:13–17). The purpose for the mandatory appearance of the male leaders was to renew the covenant vows of the households. The worshiper declared that the Lord was the Landowner and they were tenants, owing strict obedience to the terms of the tenure (e.g., Lev 26:3–13). Of the sacred *day* celebrations the two most important were the Feast of Trumpets (later reckoned New Year's Day) (Lev 23:23–25; Num 29:1–6) and the Day of Atonement (Lev 16; 23:26–32), both occurring in the seventh month. Trumpets summoned the people to a full day of sacrifice and worship, preparing them spiritually for the holy convocations of the seventh month. The Day of Atonement was especially important since it was the only sacred day of national fasting and repentance. Its unique events dramatized the reconciliation of the whole covenant nation to God, ensuring that the Lord and the people continued in spiritual union. The day included sacrifice for sins, ritual purging of the sanctuary and people, and a scapegoat (for *azazel*) that carried away the corruption/sins out of the camp into the wilderness (Lev 16:8,10,21–22). Repeated connection with their historic faith and community reinforced their fidelity and unique role and mission (e.g., Exod 12:25–27). The need for community cohesion was the development of their distinctive tribal traits over time, such as linguistic differences (e.g., *sibboth/shibboth*, Judg 12:1–7).

SACRED SACRIFICE

The instructions for acceptable worship were demanding: the proper place, time, kind of offering, officiant, and ritual state of the worshiper. But the commands also indicated the Lord's grace by providing a means for continuing his presence with Israel. Moreover, everyone, whether poor or rich, had the opportunity to worship, because the regulations for the kind of offering (animal or flour) were calibrated on the basis of a person's financial ability (e.g., Lev 5:7; 27:8; Deut 16:17). The very poor, for example, offered a small quantity of flour.

Worship always involved an offering (*qorban*, "gift") when a person appeared before the Lord (Deut 16:16; 2 Sam 24:24). Both animal and vegetable offerings were presented at the altar and were supervised by the authorized priest on duty. The most imposing physical feature of sacrificial worship was the bronze altar located in the courtyard. An altar for the purpose of worship was ubiquitous in the ANE. The patriarchs, for example, typically constructed altars for worship in their various journeys (e.g., Gen 12:7–8; cf. Exod 17:15). The tabernacle's altar always burned, and there was a burnt grain offering made every morning and evening (*tamid* "perpetual," Exod 29:38–42; Num 28:1–8), indicating a perpetual act of atonement and worship. Yet, it was the blood of the slain animal that was the most important ritual symbol since it was representative of a life given, that is, the blood indicated death (Gen 9:2–5; Lev 17:11). Special directives therefore dictated the taking and handling of blood. For instance, blood could never be eaten, since the life-blood of the animal belonged to God (Lev 17:12–14; Deut 12:23–24; Ezek 33:25). As we will see below, the blood functioned symbolically as a purgative that eliminated sin's corruption of the sanctuary.

An important aspect theologically is the question whether Yahwism believed the offerings were food for the deity, as was the case in pagan thought. The expression for food for the Lord (Lev 3:11; 22:25; Num 28:2; Ezek 44:7) must be a figure of speech since a priest never presented a food item from the altar *inside* the tent before the Lord (Ps 50:12–13; Isa 1:11). Only blood was presented, while the priest and/or laity consumed the food portions of the offerings.

The listing of the five common sacrifices as they are arranged in Leviticus 1–7 is topical, emphasizing the full commitment of the worshiper. The three listed first were *voluntary*.

(1) The (whole) burnt offering was completely consumed by fire, expressing total devotion by the worshiper and resulting in atonement. (2) The grain offering expressed thanksgiving for the Lord's provision; it typically accompanied burnt and fellowship offerings, thereby providing meat and bread. (3) The fellowship offerings (peace, vow, and freewill) involved a shared meal showing that there was peace with God and also peace with fellow community members. Covenant ritual between parties included a common meal to seal the agreement. The fellowship's meat offering was the main source of meat for the priests' and laypeople's diets. The final two, sin and guilt offerings, were *required* for atonement of unintended sins (Lev 4:2; 5:15,18; Num 15:24–29). Intentionally committed sins (lit., "high-handed," Num 15:30–31; "brazenly violate," NLT) had no corresponding offering for atonement. The only possible resolution to these was the Day of Atonement that remedied all the accumulated sin community wide. (4) The sin offering

(purification offering) atoned for specific sins and purged ritual defilement (symbolic impurities). When verbal confession was made by the offender, sins were "forgiven" (Lev 4:20; 5:5–6). By applying the blood of the animal to the sanctuary altar or/and to the incense altar *inside* the tent, the sanctuary was purged of corruption created by sins and impurities. The priest applied the blood to the bronze altar or inside the tent according to the extent of penetration of the corruption based on the degree of the sin's impact on the common person. The higher the social position of the offender (priest, community, civic leader, and layperson) the closer the priest brought the blood to the most holy place. For example, for priest and community, the priest brought the blood inside the tent and sprinkled the veil that fronted the most holy place as well as applied it to the horns of the altar of incense. Purging the sanctuary ensured that it was an appropriate dwelling place for the holy Presence. (5) Last, the guilt offering (restitution offering) differed from the sin offering in two major ways. One, it made atonement specifically for sacrilege against God's holy things or for defrauding a fellow covenant member. The remedy involved animal sacrifice preceded by full restitution plus a 20% surcharge of the evaluation. Two, while the sin offering focused on *ritual* pollution which could be transmittable, the guilt offering addressed depriving someone (God or human) of his rightful due, and this sin was not transmittable.

The proper sequential order of the offerings, however, followed this pattern (Lev 9:1–4; Num 6:16–17): (1) sin or guilt offering to purge sin's corruption or make restitution; (2) the burnt offering to indicate renewed full commitment to God; and (3) fellowship and grain/drink offerings to indicate restored covenant reconciliation with God and neighbor. The significance theologically was that the supplicant could not worship acceptably unless he was first purged of sin and forgiven (Ps 24:3–4; 26:6). The fellowship offering expressed the joy of feasting with God as a sign of reconciliation.

SACRED PRAYER

That the OT contains a diverse vocabulary of the idea of "prayer" shows that it was a rich theological concept and was an important feature of worship and spiritual life. Prayers in the ANE and in Israel were typically offered in a cultic setting, both at personal and national levels. The nations and the Israelites practiced praise, invocation, supplication, confession, and lament. The polytheistic versus the monotheistic worldview undergirded the differences in the perspectives of their prayers. Two substantive differences—apart from the deity addressed—were the purpose of prayer and the perplexity over the reason for the deity's anger.[7] (1) A person's plea in the ANE was primarily to redress public shame and to reestablish reputations in the eyes of the community since it was assumed that the penitent had outraged the god(s). The supplications of the Israelites, however, focused on covenant guilt, not public standing although shame was not irrelevant (Ezra 9:7). (2) The pagan's prayers were offered in ignorance of why the god(s) was offended. What ritual performance or behavior drew the wrath of the deity? And which deity? (Jonah 1:6–16). The Israelites, on the other hand, focused on their personal identity with God spiritually, especially the Psalmists evidenced this. The difference that Israelites had received God's covenant revelation, giving them knowledge of God's ritual and spiritual standards. They therefore could couple their proper sacrifice with a true inner acknowledgement of their specific transgression. The efficacy of ritual was accepted by God only when it was a genuine expression of a person's heart, never as a substitute for obedience to covenant.

Allen Ross notes that worship often followed a "prayer-praise" sequence. The prayers of supplication were followed by praises of thanksgiving for deliverance.[8] A person's prayer was composed, set to music, became a part of the congregational experience through liturgy and singing. Psalm 22 exemplifies this "prayer-praise" sequence. David lamented his suffering and sought God's rescue from his enemies (vv. 1–21); the following declarative praise of deliverance showed that his prayer was answered (vv. 22–31).

We limit our comments to five primary kinds of prayer in the OT. (1) Strikingly, lament is the most common genre in Psalms (e.g., Ps 3:13, 51), but certainly occurs elsewhere, as the book of Lamentations illustrates. There was lament over Saul's death (2 Sam 1:17–27), lament over fallen Israel (Amos 5:1–2), lament over sickness (Isa 38), and even over one's birth (Job 3:3,7). Communal lament over enemies, plague or famine was also practiced (e.g., Ps 44; 74). (2) Confession of sin was essential to right relationship spiritually with God and neighbor, as the classic penitential prayers demonstrate (Ps 6; 32; 38; 51; 102; 130; 143). Sin and guilt offerings required confession before the congregation, and the high priest's confession of Israel's sins on the Day of Atonement was compulsory (Lev 16:21). (3) Supplications were petitions calling on God to meet various individual and national needs (1 Sam 1:10; 2 Kings 19:15–34; Ps 118:25; 122:6). (4) Invocations for blessing upon the nation, such as the priestly benediction, were

---

7. Walton, *Ancient Near Eastern Thought*, 146–47.

8. Ross, *Recalling the Hope of Glory: Biblical Worship from the Garden to the New Creation*,

rehearsed for generations (Num 6:24–26). (5) Intercessory prayers, such as by Moses in behalf Israel's rebellious actions (Exod 32; Deut 9:26–29), concerned national deliverance.

The flip side were three major categories of praises and thanksgiving. (1) Declarative praises (testimonials) especially declared that God rescued the worshiper from his oppression or met his need (Ps 18; 32; 138). (2) Descriptive praises proclaimed the truthful, powerful character of God's revelation in creation and Word and his salvation in history by his sovereign grace (Pss 33; 135). (3) Thanksgiving hymns were common, coupled with thanksgiving sacrifices, acknowledging the blessings of God (e.g., Ps 34; 100; 107; 118).

SACRED MUSIC

Temple worship involved music performed by singers and musicians, accompanying the prayers and praises of compositions (Ps 30:1; 68:1,5,26; cf. 1 Sam 18:6). Antiphonal singing (Pss 120; 121), liturgy (Ps 136), and dance (Ps 150:4) were features that created the atmosphere of loud, enthusiastic, creative, and skillful praises (Ps 33:1–3). The connection between God's holy presence and sacred music in temple worship was captured in Psalm 22: "But You are holy, enthroned on the praises of Israel" (v. 3 [Hb 4]). Songs of thanksgiving and praise were a daily, even hourly, feature of temple services. There was a range of compositional tenor, from confessional lament to praise and thanksgiving. Also, orchestration included percussion (cymbals and timbres), wind (trumpets, horns, flutes, and pipes), and strings (lyres harps, strings, and lutes) (1 Chron 16:37–42; 23:30; Neh 11:23). An occurrence of the complementary nature of rite and music was the "Songs of Ascents" that pilgrims sung on way to Jerusalem's temple at festival assemblies (Ps 120–34; Isa 30:29). By this summary we see that it was unimaginable to participate in temple services without a prominent musical feature.

Therefore, we are not surprised that sacred music and spiritual renewal in the history of Israel occurred in tandem. The entrance of the Ark of the Covenant into Jerusalem under David's supervision is such an example (1 Chron 15:16–22; 16:4–6). Others included the dedication of the temple by Solomon (2 Chron 7), the rebuilding of the post-exilic foundation of the temple (Ezra 3:10–11), and Nehemiah's dedication of Jerusalem's walls (Neh 13:27–47). Reformation movements, too, included the return of music in temple service, as in the reforms of Hezekiah (2 Chron 29:25–30) and Josiah (2 Chron 35:15).

Who were these gifted and spiritual leaders? David, "the sweet psalmist of Israel" (2 Sam 23:1), was the famous patron of Israel's temple music (Amos 6:5) and the prominent composer of temple songs in Psalms. He established the three Levitical families of temple musicians, Asaph, Heman, and Ethan (1 Chron 6:33–46; 15:1–16:6) and named Jeduthun, Korah, and their families as gatekeepers who also played roles as singers and instrumentalists (1 Chron 16:38–42; 25:1–6; 2 Chron 5:12; 29:14; 35:15; Neh 11:17; for Korah, see 2 Chron 20:19). Additionally, the Psalter names Levites who were noted composers and performers: Asaph (Ps 73–83; 88); Jeduthun (Ps 39:1; 62:1; 77:1); and the "sons of Korah" (Ps 45–49; 84–85; 87–88). Music also inspired prophecy (1 Sam 10:5–13; 2 Kings 3:15–19). But music played a significant role in the worship of Israel long before the golden era of Jerusalem's temple. "The Song of the Sea" was Moses' memorial to deliverance from Pharaoh's armies (Exod 15:1–19; cf. Exod 15:20–21; Deut 31:30–44; Judg 5). This emancipation of Israel became a common theme by poets and lyricists (Pss 78:12–16; 106:6–12; 114; Hab 3).

CHRISTIAN UNDERSTANDING

Yet, OT worship was not complete unless it had its fullest meaning and realization in the Christian revelation. This is because the nature of OT practices were intrinsically lacking—yes, a compass indicator pointing toward the magnetic north but not the *true* north itself. Cult anchored in covenant and holy living portended the person and work of Jesus Christ and the spiritual benefits we Christians have received. The *essentials* to acceptable worship in Israel's covenant relationship with God have not changed, however. We discovered that authentic worship occurred only when it was a person's heart-felt submission to the Lord, recognizing him as sole Creator and Covenant-Lord. Deuteronomy's *Shemaʿ* expressed it best: "Listen, Israel: The Lord our God, the Lord is One. Love the Lord your God with all your heart, with all your soul, and with all your strength" (Deut 6:4–5). The objective was to experience spiritual relationship at both an *individual* and *communal* level that only God could achieve in behalf of Israel's loyal subjects by his sacred Presence. This we enjoy now through Jesus and through him exclusively. Adam Johnson comments on the significance of the OT temple and the atonement by Jesus: "This standpoint also offers far more resources to the church for integrating the doctrine of the Holy Spirit within that of the atonement, for it is the Spirit's indwelling in Christ by which he is the new temple, and it is through the repetition of this fact by the indwelling of the Spirit in believers that they are made to be part of this temple."[9]

This divine-human relationship was founded at the initiative of the Lord and worship was the response of his people. The initiative was the grace-filled promissory blessings that the Lord extended toward Israel's ancestors and the nations. The classic expression of such grace was the redemptive act at Passover that points ahead to the cross event of Christ who secured the salvation and ultimate final sanctification of his people (John 17:17–19; 1 Cor 11:30; 5:7). By Jesus Christ's incarnational initiative the relationship between the holy Father (John 17:11) and the sanctified church (1 Pet 2:9) enjoy a communal experience that is deeper than what the OT images pointed to and could not fully enable. The writer to the Hebrews identifies Christ and church in terms of the OT cult's imagery ("high priest," 2:17; chaps. 5–10). Israel's requirements for daily perpetual fires (*tamid*) upon the altar, the recurring annual Day of Atonement, the exacting measures mandatory for ritual performance, and the demanding purity laws—all revealed a tentative relationship between the Lord and Israel. These show inherent spiritual deficiency in the people, a gap that God must transcend to regulate and maintain the sacredness of his people. The outcome was only temporary, however, for God's gracious "restraint" of justified wrath provided the foil for the final remedy in the atonement provided by Jesus Christ (Rom 3:25–26; Heb 9:11–14; 10:1–18). A life of holiness is no longer measured in the people of God extrinsically by places, rites, and holy things, but by the believer's "new way of the Spirit" (Rom 7:6; 8:9–11). Yet, as was the case with Israel, Christians today manifest holy living as an act of worship through love and blameless conduct (Eph 4:1; Col 1:10; 1 John 4:7–21).

BIBLIOGRAPHY

Block, Daniel I. *For the Glory of God: Recovering a Biblical Theology of Worship* Grand Rapids: Baker, 2014.
Demetrescu, Camilian. "Symbols in Sacred Architecture and Iconography," *Journal of Sacred Architecture* 3 (2000) 28.
Johnson, Adam. "A Temple Framework of the Atonement." *JETS* 54 (2011) 225–37.
———. "The Temple Framework of the Atonement." *JETS* 54 (2011) 236.
Ross, Allen P. *Recalling the Hope of Glory: Biblical Worship from the Garden to the New Creation*. Grand Rapids: Kregel, 2006.
Walton, John. *Ancient Near Eastern Thought and the Old Testament*. Grand Rapids: Baker, 2006.
———."Equilibrium and the Sacred Compass: The Structure of Leviticus." *BBR* 11 (2001) 293–304.

9. Johnson, "The Temple Framework of the Atonement," 236.

Worship in the New Testament

FRANK THIELMAN

THOSE OF US WHO work with Dean George at Beeson Divinity School have benefited in practical ways from his careful thinking about worship in our Tuesday chapel services, which he oversees. I offer this essay with gratitude to God for what he has enabled Timothy to accomplish over the last thirty years at Beeson, and with the prayer that God may give him many more fruitful years to come.

The New Testament tells the story of God's merciful transformation of his people from idolaters to worshipers of the one true God. God's people, like the rest of humanity, were once mired in the foolish, self-destructive worship of the creature rather than the creator, but through the gospel of his Son and the power of the Holy Spirit, God has renewed their minds, restored them to the true worship of himself, and started to heal their societally destructive behavior. The New Testament teaches that worship lies at the center of the human plight and God's gracious solution to that plight in the gospel.

HUMANITY'S FALL FROM THE WORSHIP OF THE CREATOR

Right at the beginning of the most detailed and systematic explanation of the gospel in the New Testament, Rom 1:16–15:13, Paul describes the importance of worship. It is a negative description, but it demonstrates clearly how critical worship is to purposeful human existence. Human beings,

Paul argues, expressed their rebellion against God, and the reason why they needed God's salvation, by refusing to acknowledge him as the gracious creator of the universe and the one object within the universe worthy of worship (1:18–32).

God justly pours out his wrath on human beings, Paul explains, because, although he had clearly revealed to them his eternity, power, and divinity in creation, they foolishly and rebelliously refused to give him the praise and thanks that rightfully belonged to him. The two expressions "they did not honor him" and "they did not. . .give thanks to him" show where the problem lay. As the echo of the term "grace" (*charis*) in the expression "give thanks" (*eucharisteō*) implies, God had given humanity a wonderful gift in creation (Rom 1:21).[1] He had given them existence and provided them with all that they needed. According to the expectations of gift giving that existed throughout antiquity, those who received and benefited from freely given gifts were obligated to honor and thank the giver.[2]

For Paul, the human refusal to thank God for his gracious gifts in creation was so egregious that it constituted an act of war. That is why, when he explains justification and redemption in 5:1–11, he uses terms commonly reserved for ending warfare. Believers now have "peace" with God and "access" to him, as if to a king (5:1–2).[3] God "reconciled" us to himself while we were still his "enemies," and we boast in this "reconciliation" (5:10–11).

The human declaration of war against God through refusing to acknowledge him appropriately for his gifts was a foolish move (1:21–22, 28, 31). Since he is just, God could not leave such massive ingratitude unpunished, and so he poured out his wrath on humanity (1:18), but, as a just God, he did so in a measured and proportional way, not in a frenzy of bad temper. This is the burden of Paul's threefold "God gave them up. . .God gave them up. . .God gave them up" (1:24, 26, 28). The dishonor they showed to God led them to dishonor one another (1:26). Their refusal to acknowledge God led them to debased minds (1:28), and their debased minds led them into all kinds of religious and societal mayhem (1:29–32). The foolish refusal to acknowledge God (1:21–22) led people foolishly to mistreat each other (1:26–27), and so society fell apart in the violent and irrational ways Paul describes in Rom 1:29–31.

The rest of Paul's letters confirms Paul's perspective here. According to Paul's prayer of praise to God in Eph 1:3–14, God "chose," "predestined," and "adopted" his people "for the praise of his glorious grace" (1:6); he

---

1. Barclay, *Paul and the Gift*, 577–78.
2. Ibid., 11–78.
3. Cranfield, *The Epistle to the Romans*, 1:259.

"predestined" them to exist "to the praise of his glory" (1:12); and, when God's people finally receive their eschatological inheritance of eternal existence with this gracious God (cf. 2:7), it will be "to the praise of his glory" (1:14). Just as in Romans, then, the primary purpose for which God created his people was that they might worship him in response to the grace he had shown them.

On the flip side, before they have heard and believed the gospel and entered the family of God, they are like zombies, walking in a benumbed daze (2:1; cf. 4:19) through a world dominated by the devil's schemes (2:2), their own rebellion against God (2:3), and the death that all this deals out (2:1). People were created to praise God's glorious grace, and when they live instead in rebellion against God, they end up "darkened in their understanding, alienated from the life of God because of the ignorance that is in them," "callous. . .given. . .up to sensuality," and "greedy to practice every kind of impurity" (4:18–19).

Similarly, in First Corinthians and First Timothy Paul says briefly but clearly that human beings were created to worship God. In 1 Cor 8–10 Paul describes how the Corinthian church should negotiate the worship of God in the complexities of an environment awash with the worship of pagan deities. He begins by affirming the basic principle that "although there may be so-called gods in heaven or on earth—as indeed there are many 'gods' and many 'lords'–yet for us there is one God, the Father, from whom are all things and for whom we exist, and one Lord, Jesus Christ, through whom are all things and through whom we exist" (1 Cor 8:5–6). The reason, then, that the Corinthians should "flee from idolatry" (1 Cor 10:14) is that everything, including the Corinthians themselves, has come from God through Jesus Christ, and the Corinthians exist "for" God. Participating in seemingly harmless pagan worship rituals is a large step in the wrong direction, because "what pagans sacrifice they offer to demons and not to God" and, Paul says, "I do not want you to be participants with demons" (1 Cor 10:20).

In First Timothy, the central problem with the heresy that has plagued the Ephesian church is its ascetic refusal to acknowledge the goodness of marriage and food as creations of God "to be received with thanksgiving by those who believe and know the truth" (1 Tim 4:3). "Everything created by God is good," Paul responds, "and nothing is to be rejected if it is received with thanksgiving, for it is made holy by the word of God and prayer" (1 Tim 4:4). The heretical teachers in Ephesus have misrepresented the good and pleasurable experience that God intended his human creatures to have with his creation. A critical element in putting this church back on the right footing, then, is the restoration of a form of worship in the Ephesian church that acknowledges God as the gracious creator of everything.

This is not simply a Pauline perspective on worship, but is characteristic of the New Testament generally. In Revelation 4, for example, John's striking vision of the throne room of God is designed to convey the same perspective: worship is something that human beings were created to do. God himself, in that vision, has the appearance of beautiful, colorful elements of his own creation ("jasper and carnelian"), and surrounding God's throne is a rainbow that looks like an emerald (Rev 4:3). The twenty-four elders who sit on thrones that encircle God's throne are clearly the people of God, stretching from the period of Israel (with its twelve tribes) into apostolic times (with its twelve apostles), and their thrones and crowns show that they share the kingly rule of God over his creation (Rev 4:4). The four living creatures that also surround the throne seem to represent all creation (Rev 4:6b–8a).[4] Together, all God's creation and all God's people praise God with the hymn, "Worthy are you, our Lord and God, to receive glory and honor and power, for you created all things, and by your will they existed and were created" (Rev 4:11). When an angel announces "the eternal gospel" to all the earth prior to the outpouring of God's judgment, he calls on the earth's inhabitants to "give" God "glory. . .and worship him who made heaven and earth, the sea and the springs of water" (Rev 14:6–7).[5]

Similarly, the primary reason why God was about to punish the inhabitants of the earth was their failure to acknowledge him in worship as the one God and the creator of everything. Instead, they worship Satan because he gave his authority to Rome (Rev 13:2, 4), and they worship Rome because of its military might (Rev 13:4). They view the emergence of Rome from the ashes of governmental chaos that followed Nero's suicide as if it were the miraculous recovery of a beast from a mortal wound.[6] This blasphemous parody of the resurrection of Jesus, and a series of weird mimicries of the miracles of the prophets, lead them to worship the image of the beast (Rev 13:3, 11–15).[7]

---

4. Swete, *The Apocalypse of St*, 71.
5. Bauckham, *Revelation*, 48.
6. Caird, *A Commentary on the Revelation of St. John the Divine*, 164.
7. Ibid., *Revelation*, 172.

Just as in Romans, this perversion of true worship creates perversions in the way people relate to one another and to the creation. As Rome comes tumbling down toward the end of the book, the client kings of the Roman empire, who enriched themselves by doing business with Rome, "weep and wail over her" (Rev 18:9), but watch her burn from a safe distance, since it is only their self-interest that fuels their pity (Rev 18:10).[8] The merchants of the earth weep tears of even greater self-interest at her destruction since, with Rome's destruction, their lucrative market for exotic, luxury imports has now disappeared. The injustice and oppression that made such a market possible become clear in the last item on John's grocery list of imports: "slaves, that is, human souls" (18:13). The early twentieth century commentator Henry Barclay Swete eloquently described the significance of this final item:

> The world of St John's day ministered in a thousand ways to the follies and vices of its Babylon, but the climax was reached in the sacrifice of human life which recruited the huge *familiae* of the rich, filled the *lupanaria*, and ministered to the brutal pleasures of the amphitheatre.[9] The Satan-inspired worship of the goddess Roma led to disaster both for those she oppressed and, eventually, for Rome's ruling classes and their allies.

THE RESTORATION OF TRUE WORSHIP IN THE GOSPEL

In the narrative of Satan's desert temptation of Jesus in both Matthew and Luke, it becomes clear that Satan understood how essential human worship of the one true God was to the accomplishment of God's saving purposes for humanity. Just before Jesus begins his public ministry, Satan attempts to thwart his mission with a bribe: if Jesus will only fall down and worship him, he will give Jesus the world's kingdoms (Matt 4:9; cf. Luke 4:6–7). Jesus answers Satan with the biblical instruction to worship God and offer religious service to him alone (Matt 4:10; Luke 4:8; cf. Deut 6:13).

As commentators often recognize, in resisting this temptation, Jesus was re-enacting, only successfully, the desert temptation of Israel after the Exodus.[10] Israel had failed the test and succumbed to the temptation to worship the golden calf (Exod 32:1–10), but Jesus refused to worship anyone

---

8. Swete, *Apocalypse*, 231–32, 236.
9. Ibid., 235.
10. Davies and Allison, *The Gospel according to Matthew*, 1:373.

other than the one true God. With the coming of Jesus, the restoration of the true worship of God not only within Israel but among all the peoples of the earth had begun.

THE WORSHIP OF JESUS AS THE WORSHIP OF GOD

In a move that must have been surprising within the theism of their Jewish context, the gospel writers all affirm that, since the coming of the gospel, the true worship of the one God, creator of the universe, must include the worship of Jesus of Nazareth.[11] The word that Jesus uses in the temptation narrative to emphasize the critical importance of "worshiping" the one true God (*proskyneō*) shows up frequently in Matthew's subsequent narrative to refer to the "worship" that people give to Jesus.

Matthew prepared the way for this theme at the beginning of his narrative by pointing out to his readers that Isaiah gave Jesus the name "Immanuel," meaning "God with us" (Matt 1:23). So when, in the following paragraph, magi from the east appear in Jerusalem hoping "to worship" the child Jesus (Matt 2:2, 11), Matthew probably meant for his readers to know immediately that this was not some well-intentioned pagan error but a case of Gentiles doing what everyone else, including the leaders of Israel, should do. Matthew could certainly use the term translated "worship" in its less significant sense of "kneel in respect" (Matt 18:26; 20:20), but he makes unmistakably clear that it could also refer to the worship of Jesus, just as Jesus used it in the temptation narrative of the worship of God. Jesus' disciples worship him as the master of the wind and waves (Matt 14:33; cf. Ps 107:23–32) and as one who has been victorious over death (Matt 28:9, 17).

Worshiping God as he has revealed himself through Jesus is also an emphasis of John's gospel. The word that was with God and was God according to the opening paragraphs of the gospel "became flesh and dwelt among us. . .full of grace and truth" (Matt 1:14). In John's narrative, the Baptist testifies that he has seen the Spirit come upon Jesus from heaven (Matt 1:32). Nathanael identifies Jesus as a rabbi who is much more than a rabbi—he is the great Messiah-King of Israel, and Jesus, in response, tells him that he is actually much more than even this. He is the very means by which God descends to live among human beings (Matt 1:51). Jesus manifests his glory by changing water to wine (Matt 2:11), and the reader knows that he has this glory because of his eternal pre-existence with the one God (Matt 1:14; cf. 17:5). By the time John's readers arrive at Jesus' dialogue with the woman at the well and hear him say to her that "true worshipers will

---

11. Bauckham, *Jesus and the God of Israel*, 127–51.

worship the Father in spirit and truth" (Matt 4:23–24), it is natural for them to think of worshiping Jesus (cf. Matt 1:14, 32).

This impression becomes clearer as the narrative proceeds. The blind man knows that it is important to be "a worshiper (*theosebēs*) of God" (Matt 9:31), and then, a little later, he worships (*proskyneō*) Jesus, uttering the confession, "Lord, I believe" (Matt 9:38). At Jesus' arrest, John records the odd detail that when Jesus identified himself to the soldiers who had come to arrest him saying, "I am he," they "drew back and fell to the ground" (Matt 18:6). Not only is this the sort of detail an eyewitness might remember, but it is the sort of detail that John especially might think significant: Jesus' statement of self-existence (*egō eimi*) seems to echo God's statement of self-existence in Exod 3:14, and when some clumsiness at Jesus' arrest ended with people falling to the ground, John took this as a sort of accidental obeisance before God himself. Like the high priest Caiaphas who prophesied the significance of Jesus' death better than he knew (11:51), the very soldiers sent to arrest Jesus had paid him homage as God. It is not unexpected, then, when Thomas finally, and climactically, sees the risen Lord and confesses, "My Lord and my God!" (20:28).

To summarize, true worship of God in the New Testament begins with the "good news" that God himself has come in Jesus to reveal the truth about himself in even clearer terms than are found in Israel's Scriptures. This worship of the one God lines up with the truth about God and the world he created and has a positive, transforming effect on those who engage in it.

CHRISTIAN WORSHIP AS THE RENEWAL OF MINDS AND THE TRANSFORMATION OF LIVES

Paul shows how this transformation works in his letter to the Romans. At the beginning of Romans, when Paul was describing the quintessential human sin as the failure to worship the one true God (Rom 1:18–32), he focused on the irrationality of this failure. Human ingratitude to God was foolish and led to equally foolish treatment of one's self and other human beings. This correspondence between an irrational idolatry and an irrationally shameful and harmful society was God's measured, just punishment of humanity for its "ungodliness and unrighteousness" (Rom 1:18).

At the other end of Romans, after he has thoroughly explained God's compassionate response to the human plight in the gospel, Paul describes how the gospel transforms Christian worship. The "mercies of God," he explains, now lead Christians to the "rational worship" (*logikēn latreian*) that logically follows from appreciating who God is and the gracious gifts of justification, reconciliation, and peace that he has given them (Rom 12:1).[12] Believers have started a process through which they are being "transformed by the renewal of" their "mind" (Rom 12:2). Paul's use of the expressions "transform" (*metamorphoō*) and "renewal of" the "mind" (*noos*) recall his earlier statements about how believers now "set their minds (*phronousin*) on the things of the Spirit" (Rom 8:5) and are predestined "to be conformed (*symmorphous*) to the image" of God's Son (Rom 8:29). Rather than the futile thoughts and foolish, darkened minds (Rom 1:21) that led them ever deeper into an exchange of God's glory for the images of God's creatures (Rom 1:23), the image of God, instilled in them at creation, is being restored through their union with God's Son (cf. 2 Cor 5:17; Eph 4:22–24; 5:1; Col 3:9–10). The worship of images is being replaced with the worship of God, and God is polishing the divine image that they bear as a result.[13]

Despite his cultic language, the "rational worship" Paul has in mind here is not the observance of a particular liturgy in corporate gatherings but the presentation of Christian "bodies as a living sacrifice, holy and acceptable to God" (Rom 12:1). "Bodies" that God had once given up to dishonorable conduct because they belonged to people that "worshiped and served (*elatreusan*) the creature rather than the creator" (Rom 1:25) are now the means of the appropriate "worship" (*latreian*) of God.[14] Paul spends much of the rest of the letter describing what this kind of worship looks like. It involves humble service to other believers (Rom 12:3–8), genuine love (Rom 12:9–10), responding to persecution and evil with blessing and good (Rom 12:14, 20–21), helping to maintain an orderly society (Rom 13:1–7), loving one's neighbor (Rom 13:8–10), avoiding self-indulgence at the expense of others (Rom 13:11–13), and welcoming into Christian gatherings those who are weak and who differ from the majority (Rom 14:1; 15:7).

We should probably add to this list Paul's own service to God as an apostle who takes the gospel to others in obedience to the call of God (Rom 1:9; cf. 1:1). He calls this "serving" (*latreuō*) God in his "spirit" (Rom 1:9), using the verbal form of the noun that he uses in Rom 12:1 for rational "worship" (*latreian*). He sees his traveling around proclaiming the gospel in places where Christ has not been named (Rom 15:19) as worshiping God with sincerity. Not surprisingly, then, he can call himself "a minister (*leitourgon*) of Christ Jesus to the Gentiles in the priestly service (*hierourgounta*) of the

---

12. Longenecker, *The Epistle to the Romans*, 921.
13. Beale, *We Become What We Worship: A Biblical Theology of Idolatry*, 202–22.
14. Dunn, *Romans 9–16*, 707–14.

gospel of God, so that the offering of the Gentiles may be acceptable, sanctified by the Holy Spirit" (15:19). Paul's obedience to his apostolic vocation is one way in which he gives to God the "rational worship" God deserves.

Paul calls this service "with my spirit" (1:9), not referring primarily to the empowering, mind transforming work of God's Spirit, but to his inner life, his sincerity. This is clear from the pronoun "my." At the same time, however, Paul's later talk of living as "a Jew. . .inwardly" through circumcision "of the heart, by the Spirit, not by the letter" (2:29) makes it hard to avoid the notion that his own sincere worship of God through his apostolic service is also worship empowered by the Spirit of God.[15] This is confirmed by Phil 3:3 where Paul describes Christians as those "who worship (*latreuontes*) by the Spirit of God and glory in Christ Jesus and put no confidence in the flesh." Worshiping by or with the spirit, therefore, is for Paul more than just sincere worship. It is worship that involves Spirit-empowered obedience to God.

This is how God is transforming his people from those who foolishly failed to worship their Creator, and reaped the disastrous consequences, to people who worship God and work to establish the peaceful, loving society he intended humanity to be. All this is a work of God's Spirit and begins with the Spirit's transformation of Christian minds so that believers respond appropriately and sincerely to the gracious character of God.

CORPORATE WORSHIP AS AN EXPRESSION OF RENEWED MINDS AND TRANSFORMED LIVES

The logical way to worship God was to live a divinely transformed life, but this does not mean that the language of religious ritual was merely metaphorical in the New Testament. It is clear from the New Testament's many references to Christian gatherings that this was not the case, although there is not much evidence for a set order of corporate worship among the early Christians. The Corinthians assembled in the same place for the Lord's Supper (11:18, 20), and they also met together to exercise various spiritual gifts (12:4–11, 28–30), especially speaking in tongues and prophecy (11:4–5, 13; 14:4–5, 12, 19, 23). It would not be surprising if the Lord's Supper, tongues, prophecy, hymns, and teaching all occurred whenever "the whole church" came "together" (14:23, 26), although it is not clear that any of these elements was always present at every time and place the church assembled. Probably gatherings took place, at least in many locations, "on the first day

---

15. Fee, *God's Empowering Presence: The Holy Spirit in the Letters of Paul,* 484–86.

of every week" (16:1–2; Acts 20:7; cf. Rev 1:10) to commemorate the Lord's resurrection from the dead (Mark 16:2; cf. Justin, *1 Apol.* 67.8).

When Luke outlines the devotional habits of the "three thousand souls" who received the "word and were baptized" after Peter's Pentecost sermon (Acts 2:41) he may, at the same time, be describing the standard components of religious ritual for the earliest Christians.[16] These believers, he says, "devoted themselves to the apostle's teaching and the fellowship, to the breaking of bread and the prayers." The expression "devoted themselves" translates a term (*proskartereō*) often used in the context of religious observance, especially prayer (Acts 1:14; 2:46; 6:4; Rom 12:2; Col 4:2). The term describes habitual religious conduct, and would make sense as an introduction to the basic elements of regular Christian worship.

"The apostles' teaching" referred to what the authoritative eye and ear witnesses of Jesus' ministry and resurrection (Acts 1:21–22) communicated to the believing community about what they had seen and heard (e.g., Acts 4:2, 18; 5:42). "Fellowship" probably referred especially to taking care of the needs of the poor in their midst (Acts 2:44–45; 4:32, 34), but perhaps also simply to the close relationship that these early Christians had with one another and that was especially expressed in their common meetings (2:46–47).[17] "The breaking of bread" echoes the language Luke uses to describe the Lord's Supper, but since no wine is mentioned, it may refer to the celebration of the Lord's Supper at a common meal (cf. 1 Cor 11:17–34).[18] The expression "the prayers" (*tais proseuchais*), in the plural and with the article, seems to refer to set prayers.[19] Could Luke have had in mind prayers such as those recorded in his first volume: the *Magnificat* (Luke 1:46–55), the *Nunc Dimittis* (2:29–32), and the Lord's Prayer (Luke 11:2–4)?

Justin Martyr, writing from Rome in the mid-second century, describes early Christian worship assemblies in much the same terms (*1 Apol.* 67).[20] On Sunday people came from various locations and gathered "in one place."[21] Someone read from the apostles' memoirs or the prophets, everyone stood to pray, bread and wine were brought in for the Lord's Supper, and a collection was taken for the needy. Justin's description is more detailed than Luke's brief summary, but the basic outline of what happened in his time in Rome is remarkably similar to what Luke says happened over a

---

16. Keener, *Acts*, 1:1000–1001.
17. Barrett, *The Acts of the Apostles*, 1:163–64.
18. Ibid., 1:165.
19. Ibid., 1:166.
20. Keener, *Acts*, 1:1000–1001; A. W. F. Blunt, ed., *The Apologies of Justin Martyr*, lii.
21. Richardson, ed. and trans., *Early Christian Fathers*, 287.

century earlier in Jerusalem. All four elements, moreover, seem to have been present in the Corinthian assemblies of Paul's time (1 Cor 10:16; 11:17–34; 12:28–29; 14:29; 16:2).

It is curious that neither Luke nor Justin mentions hymn singing. At least some of the Christian assemblies connected with Paul sang "psalms and hymns and spiritual songs" in their assemblies (1 Cor 14:26; Eph 5:19; Col 3:16). The "psalms" were probably the canonical Psalms of the Jewish Scriptures. "Hymns and spiritual songs" may have included newer compositions based on Scripture, such as "the song of Moses, the servant of God, and the song of the Lamb" recorded in Rev 15:3–4. They may have also included brand new songs celebrating various elements of Christian teaching, like the "hymn. . .to Christ as to a god" sung by Christians in Bithynia in the early second century (Pliny, *Ep.* 10.96).[22] Eph 5:14 may record part of one such song: "Awake, O sleeper, and arise from the dead, and Christ will shine on you."

There was, then, some variety in the way early Christians worshiped together, but one constant seems to lie beneath the various references to these gatherings in the New Testament. At least when they were functioning properly, those who participated in them did so sincerely, out of hearts and minds that had been transformed by the Holy Spirit. The rituals followed in early Christian worship were outward expressions of the renewed minds Paul describes in Romans 12:2. So, Paul describes worship in Corinth as empowered by God's Spirit (1 Cor 14:12–16, 32, 37). In Ephesians, too, Paul connects the singing and thanksgiving that take place in Christian worship with life in the Spirit (Eph 5:18–20). Similarly, in Colossians, Paul prefaces instructions on the teaching and singing that happen in Christian worship with the command to "let the peace of Christ rule in your hearts" (Col 3:15–17). All this correlates with Luke's description of worship among the earliest Christians in Jerusalem. Their ritual of teaching, fellowship, eating together, and prayer, was a matter of devotion accompanied by an "awe" that "came upon every soul" and by "glad and generous hearts" (Acts 2:42, 46).

In a way that is consistent with the pattern of inner transformation leading to loving conduct (Rom 12:1–2, 3–10, 14, 20–21; 13:1–10; 14:1; 15:7), early Christian worship gatherings were also supposed to be opportunities for demonstrating love toward one another. In 1 Corinthians, for example, Paul spends a lengthy portion of the letter discussing how the Corinthians should order their Christian assemblies in Corinth (11:1–14:40). He pleads with wives to honor their husbands by following the custom of covering their heads in the assembly rather than dispensing with the sign of

---

22. Melmoth, 2:403; Fee, *God's Empowering Presence*, 722.

their marriage and communicating that they are sexually available to others (11:2–16).²³ Similarly, he rebukes the Corinthians for humiliating the poor at the Lord's Supper (11:22), reminding them that the Supper itself is a memorial of the Lord's sacrificial attitude toward others, an attitude that Christians must imitate (11:23–26). He prefers prophecy in the assembly to speaking in tongues because it affords a greater opportunity to edify others (14:3–5, 12, 17, 26).

In the midst of the discussion, in 13:1–13, he plants an essay on love that has the effect of urging the Corinthians to make their assemblies for Christian worship into an expression toward one another of this, the "greatest" Christian virtue (13:13). The way they dress, observe the Lord's Supper, and use their spiritual gifts when they assemble together should reflect love for each other.

Similarly, in Ephesians, a few paragraphs after urging his audience to "be renewed in the spirit of" their "minds" (4:23), Paul urges them to walk "wisely, making the best use of the time, because the days are evil" (5:15) and to "understand what the will of the Lord is" (5:17). This introduces a section in which Paul seems to describe what should happen in the Christian assembly (5:18–21). Christians met for worship in private homes, and a house or apartment large enough for a sizeable meeting would have probably been owned by a wealthy member of the privileged class (Acts 20:8–9; Rom 16:5; Col 4:15). In the Greco-Roman world, such homes were frequently the setting of dinner parties that featured drunkenness and debauchery, and, if that is what Paul had in mind in Eph 5:18–21, then he is contrasting what corporate Christian worship should look like with one of these dinner parties.²⁴

There should be no drunkenness (cf. 1 Cor 11:21–22), no drunken singing, sexual immorality, and mistreatment of slaves, but instead, the whole meeting should take place within the boundaries laid down by God's Spirit (5:18; cf. 2 Peter 2:13; Jude 18). There should be Spirit-inspired singing of Scripture and of the gospel story (5:19). There should be thanksgiving to God, and Christ-like submission to one another (5:21). Ideally, all this should take place in a home where wives and husbands display respect and love for one another (5:21–31), where children and parents work together to honor the Lord in their relationship (6:1–2), where slaves and masters have a relationship with each other so transformed by their common "Master. . .in heaven" that the Master stops even the threat of violence against the

---

23. Winter, *After Paul Left Corinth*, 123–31.
24. Gosnell, "Ephesians 5:19–20 and Mealtime Propriety," 363–71.

slave and treats the slave exactly the same way that the slave, "with a sincere heart," treats the master (6:5–9).

Much the same pattern appears in Colossians. Paul sums up an admonition to the Colossian Christians to treat each other with compassion, kindness, humility, meekness, patience, a forgiving spirit, and love with the command to "let the peace of Christ rule in your hearts" (3:12–15). This then leads into a description of the teaching, admonition, and singing that was characteristic of corporate Christian worship. In Colossians, once again, corporate worship arises out of hearts that Christ has transformed so that peace rules over them.

Paul's letter to the Roman Christians shows the same emphases. The kindness that the "strong" and the "weak" among the Roman Christians are to show one another (Rom 15:1), despite their differences over whether to observe certain Jewish customs (14:2–3, 5, 13–23), arises from the renewed minds of 12:2 and leads to living "in such harmony with one another in accord with Christ Jesus, that together you may with one voice glorify the God and Father of our Lord Jesus Christ" (15:6). This seems to be a description of corporate Christian worship in Rome as Paul hopes these Christians will experience it.

That all this was not merely an abstraction for Paul becomes clear in an unexpected place in the letter: the closing greetings. Rom 16:3–16 is by far the longest section of greetings in any of his extant letters and the only place in them that urges the audience in the imperative mood to greet more than a few people by name (cf. Col 4:15; 2 Tim 4:19). Paul urges his audience to greet twenty-four individuals that he names, two others that he does not name, and six groups, including the entire assembly itself ("Greet one another. . .").

Scholars have speculated at length about why Paul did this, and, in the end, it is probably impossible to know. It is hard to imagine that Paul himself would have derived any great personal advantage from the list of greetings. Contrary to what interpreters sometimes say, he does not even seem to have personally known many of the people that he greets since he gives no descriptive phrase for some names and only identifies others by the group to which they belong (16:10b, 11b, 14–15).

The effect of these instructions, however, seems fairly certain: they would have brought this diverse and divided group of believers together by urging them to show affection for each other, and by honoring people of low social standing.[25] Many people in the list were Jews (Aquila, Andronicus,

---

25. Jewett, *Romans: A Commentary* 952.

Junia, Herodion, and probably Prisca and Miriam).[26] Nine were women, seven of whom receive special commendation from Paul for the risks they had taken, the hard work they had done, or the special concern they had shown for Paul (16:3, 6, 7, 12, 13). Some of the names, such as Ampliatus, Tryphaena, Tryphosa, Philologus, and Nereus, were common among slaves, and some were typical "wish names" (Urbanus, Asyncritus), functional names (Phlegon, Hermes, Hermas), or origin names (Persis).[27] Such names seem to be contrived from the viewpoint of someone who thought of the person they named as no more than the demeanor or function that a master hoped they would have ("Refined," "Matchless," "Blazer," "Messenger"), or as little more than their place of origin ("the Persian"). In other words, these were probably slaves or freedmen whose existence had been defined, at least for many years, by the de-humanizing institution of slavery and the horrific idea that those caught up in it were merely living tools (Aristotle, *Nicomachean Ethics* 8.11, 1161b, 4–6).

The assembled Roman Christians, therefore, should embrace one another as equals, greeting each other "with a holy kiss," whether Jew or Greek, slave or free, male or female. The God whom they praised with one voice because of the gracious good news that had transformed them all expected their corporate worship to lead to practical, loving acceptance of each other as equals.

CONCLUSION

In summary, the New Testament views worship as a central element of the gospel. When people hear and believe the gospel, God's Spirit begins to transform their minds and their way of life. Rather than worshiping false gods with all the alienation and social chaos that inevitably follows this act of immense ingratitude, they take their rightful place as grateful creatures, made in the image of God and designed to praise him for his grace. This new way of life leads them to live in loving ways toward one another. The New Testament reveals that this form of living sacrifice often expressed itself in corporate worship where Christians, meeting together, received and handed on the teaching of the apostles, tended to each other's physical needs, celebrated the Lord's Supper, and praised God and his Son Jesus Christ. In the New Testament, then, worship is about praising God in word and deed for his abundant grace, and about living in loving community with other

---

26. Thielman, *Romans*.
27. Lampe, *From Paul to Valentinus*, 181 (on "Urbanus").

human beings, beginning with the other human beings next to us when we gather for worship.

BIBLIOGRAPHY

Barclay, John M. G. *Paul and the Gift*. Grand Rapids: Eerdmans, 2015.
Barrett, C. K. *The Acts of the Apostles*. 2 vols. ICC. Edinburgh: T. & T. Clark, 1994–1998.
Bauckham, Richard. *The Theology of the Book of Revelation*. New Testament Theology. Cambridge: Cambridge University Press, 1993.
———. *The Climax of Prophecy: Studies on the Book of Revelation* Edinburgh: T. & T. Clark, 1993.
———. *Jesus and the God of Israel*. Grand Rapids: Eerdmans, 2008.
Beale, G. K. *We Become What We Worship: A Biblical Theology of Idolatry*. Downers Grove, IL: InterVarsity, 2008.
Blunt, A. W. F., ed. *The Apologies of Justin Martyr*, Cambridge: Cambridge University Press, 1911 Caird, G. B. *A Commentary on the Revelation of St. John the Divine*. HNTC. New York: Harper & Row, 1966.
Caird, G. B. *A Commentary on the Revelation of St. John the Divine*. San Francisco: Harper, 1966.
Cranfield, C. E. B. *The Epistle to the Romans*. 2 vols. ICC. Edinburgh: T. & T. Clark, 1975–1979.
Davies, W. D., and Dale C. Allison. *The Gospel according to Matthew*. 3 vols. ICC. London: T. & T. Clark, 1988–1997.
Dunn, James D. G. *Romans 9–16*. WBC 38b. Dallas: Word, 1988.
Fee, Gordon D. *God's Empowering Presence: The Holy Spirit in the Letters of Paul* Peabody, MA: Hendrickson, 1994.
Gosnell, Peter W. "Ephesians 5:19–20 and Mealtime Propriety." *TynBul* 44 (1993) 363–71.
Jewett, Robert. *Romans: A Commentary*. Hermeneia. Minneapolis: Fortress, 2007.
Keener, Craig S. *Acts: An Exegetical Commentary*. 4 vols. Grand Rapids: Baker, 2012–2015, 1:1000–1001.
Lampe, Peter. *From Paul to Valentinus: Christians at Rome in the First Two Centuries*. Edited by Marshall D. Johnson. Translated by Michael Steinhauser. Minneapolis: Fortress, 2003.
Longenecker, Richard N. *The Epistle to the Romans*. NIGTC. Grand Rapids: Eerdmans, 2016.
Melmoth, William, trans. *Pliny: Letters*. 2 vols. Rev. W. M. L. Hutchinson. LCL. London: Heinemann, 1915.
Osborne, Grant. *Matthew*. ZECNT. Grand Rapids: Zondervan, 2010.
Richardson, Cyril C., ed. and trans. *Early Christian Fathers*. New York: Macmillan, 1970.
Swete, Henry Barclay. *The Apocalypse of St John*. London: Macmillan, 1909.
Thielman, Frank. *Romans*. ZECNT. Grand Rapids: Zondervan, 2018.
Winter, Bruce W. *After Paul Left Corinth: The Influence of Secular Ethics and Social Change*. Grand Rapids: Eerdmans, 2001.

A Pilgrim in Progress
The Doctrine of Baptism

Christian T. George

In John Bunyan's seventeenth-century allegory *The Pilgrim's Progress*, the main character, Christian, encounters a colorful cast of characters—Evangelist, Pliable, Talkative, Flatterer, Faithful. Along the path, he sinks into a Slough of Despond, climbs Delectable Mountains, resists Vanity Fair, and is seduced by Enchanted Ground.

The turning point comes when Christian discovers a cross. Suddenly, the burden falls from his back and rolls down the hill into a tomb. Christian's posture straightens, he leaps for joy, and he shouts, "He hath given me rest by his sorrow, and life by his death."[1]

Bunyan's prison-damp publication became the most popular seller in the English language, second only to the King James Bible. It represents the journey every Christian undertakes—that sacred trek from destruction to deliverance, from bondage to breakthrough, from fire to glory.

Surprisingly though, Bunyan's famous allegory lacks one essential ingredient. Christian passes through the Wicket Gate, enjoys refreshment at Palace Beautiful, defeats Apollyon with the sword of the Spirit, escapes Doubting Castle, and almost drowns in the River Jordan (symbolizing death). Yet entirely absent from the narrative is any mention or metaphor of baptism.

Six years and ten editions later, Bunyan did include a reference to the aqua-ordinance in his 1684 sequel, when Christiana (Christian's wife) and her four children were washed in the garden bath at Interpreter's House. Six years. For so central command (Matthew 28:19), six years is a long time to wait.

---

1. Bunyan, *The Pilgrim's Progress*, 35.

Thankfully, I only had to wait *three* years between the moment of my conversion and the splash of my baptism. I was eight years old when the Lord began pulling at the strings of my soul. It was as if Jesus Christ swept me to himself when I surrendered my life to him. Alone and in my room, the burden fell from my second-grade shoulders and rolled off the bed into the closet.

Baptism seemed to me like a natural next step so I prepared myself for the plunge. But then the trajectory of my life bent in a different direction. Instead of diving headfirst into the baptistery, my father encouraged me to wait until I gained a deeper grasp of its significance. With the Ethiopian Eunuch I wondered, "Can anyone withhold the water to baptize? (Acts 10:47)

Third grade became fourth. Fourth became fifth. By the sixth grade, three long years had come and gone. Three years is a long time for an adolescent to wait. You can earn a ninety-six-hour Master of Divinity degree in three years! Jesus Christ himself considered three years long enough before exiting the earth after the launch of his public ministry. For me, three years felt like three hundred.

But there was wisdom in the waiting. Shortly after my conversion, my father gave me a 9.5-inch by 6-inch Nu-bound notebook complete with one hundred and fifty narrow-lined pages. A golden flap concealed its metallic spinal coil. In large red letters—not quite cursive—I penned my name on its mustard yellow cover: "Christian Timothy George." Then I dignified the notebook with a proper title: Baptism Workbook.

This workbook became my window into the biblical, theological, and historical significance of my faith. With my dad as my docent, we embarked on a pilgrimage into the past—a journey that strengthened my confidence in Christianity. Almost every night he and I discussed the progress—or regress—of my elementary scholarship.

He quizzed me on the creeds, confessions, and catechisms that shaped the identity of the church. "What is man's chief end?" That one was easy. "What is my only comfort in life and death?" Well, that one took much longer to learn: "That I am not my own, but belong—body and soul, in life and in death –to my faithful Savior, Jesus Christ . . . "

My father also tasked me with researching some of the heroes of the Baptist tradition: John Bunyan, Roger Williams, William Carey, and Ann and Adoniram Judson. How fascinating I found their stories. From an imprisoned Bedford preacher to a courageous missionary to India, I gleaned wisdom from their daring witnesses and came to appreciate their unified differences.

When I outgrew the workbook, my father graduated me to *field*work. Quite literally. Through grassy shires of Essex we hiked. Beneath rotating windmills in Belgium we biked. Sometimes, we had to confess with David, "there is but a step between me and death" (1 Samuel 20:3). Like the time our boat endured twenty-foot swells in the North Atlantic before we scaled a one-thousand-year-old staircase up the slippery slopes of Skellig Michael.

Reading *The Pilgrim's Progress* prepared me to follow Bunyan to Bedford. We visited the very jail ("gaol") where the Puritan penned his publication. We visited Westminster Abbey where, in 1646, the Westminster Confession was written. We traveled to Heidelberg, Basel, Geneva, and Wittenberg. Slowly, I came to connect what I knew to what I experienced. Pilgrimages helped me *own* history and see myself as part of it. Memorization led to internalization and, eventually, application.

Other times, our souls were in far more danger than our soles. At the French monastery of Taizé, for instance, I encountered a way of worship that brought me so close to the throne of God that it nearly ruined me for all other forms. My father and I also traveled east, as Paul attempted but failed to do (Acts 16:6). We ventured to Nagasaki, Japan, where nineteen youthful Jesuit missionaries chose crucifixion over compromise. We woke up long before dawn to join fellow Christians in prayer meetings in the South Korean mountains.

Like the pages of my baptism workbook, each pilgrimage was tailored to trespass me beyond the boundaries of my comfort zones. Sure, every once in a while we caught a ball game, rode a roller coaster, or visited a museum. But we were *pilgrims*, not tourists. We were hunting for the holy—magnetized to the places and faces turned inside out and upside down by the power and presence of God.

Our travels also led us to places pertaining to the practice of baptism. We ventured to Milan where Ambrose immersed Augustine. We fought the overgrown banks of the River Lark to see where Charles Spurgeon's timidity "floated down the river into the sea, and must have been devoured by the fishes."[2]

This chapter is primarily fed by the tributaries of those travels. My goal here is not to offer a comprehensive survey of the doctrine of baptism, or even engage deeply with competing perspectives. Rather, I hope to offer a general reflection by one whose father not only introduced me to the practice, but *practiced the practice* on me.

As I read the baptism workbook now at the age of thirty-five, the content solicits more than a few smiles. My early syntax and grammar are in desperate need of a thorough editing; yet, I have chosen to retain the childish spelling, capitalization, and punctuation. After all, as Christian discovered in Bunyan's allegory, every pilgrimage is punctuated with potholes and problems.

A definition of baptism is found in the opening pages of the workbook:

---

2. *Spurgeon's Autobiography*, 1:152.

Baptism is the way People are marked as followers of Jesus. When you get Baptized, you either get sprinkled with water or you get *dumped* under the water."[3]

At the end of this chapter, I will share my experience of being "dumped" by my father in the baptistery of Shades Mountain Baptist Church in Birmingham, Alabama. Until then, join me—join us—on a journey into the theology, history, and practice of baptism.

A SYMBOL OF SALVATION

"Water is a symbol of baptism. The water is a symbol because we could not live without it. . . . Water also gets us clean. Jesus wants to make us clean."[4]—Baptism Workbook

In his work *Baptist Theology*, Stephen Holmes identifies two primary perspectives of the practice from which Baptists borrow their name. Baptism is first a *symbol* representing the death, burial, and new life of the regenerated believer (Romans 6:4). As such, baptism becomes an "enacted sermon" bearing witness to "the narration and display of the gospel story."[5] Holmes explains:

> Baptism is important because it is commanded by Jesus, but nothing special happens when a person is baptized. Baptism is an act of witness and obedience, and the personal testimony of the baptismal candidate to the workings of grace in their lives, and their enacted obedience to the instruction of Jesus, form the core of the rite.[6]

The *Philadelphia Confession of Faith,* adopted by American Baptists in 1742, echoes this perspective:

> Baptism is an ordinance of the New Testament, ordained by Jesus Christ, to be unto the party baptized a sign of his fellowship with Him in His death and resurrection; of his being engrafted into Him; of remission of sins; and of his giving up unto God, through Jesus Christ, to live and walk in newness of life.[7]

---

3. C. George, "Baptism Workbook," 31; italics added.
4. Ibid., 31–32.
5. Holmes, *Baptist Theology*, 93.
6. Ibid., 93–94.
7. *Philadelphia Confession of Faith*, 97.

In its precursor, *The London Confession* of 1644, baptism was described as a "sign" of "the washing the whole soul in the blood of Christ" and "that interest the saints have in the death, burial, and resurrection."[8] That "interest the saints have" is animated in the drama of this doctrine where "actors" are buried (or drowned, as Ian Bradley noted)[9] before being resurrected.[10]

While the strain to locate a direct line of unbroken succession of those practicing immersive baptism (Baptist Successionism) will not be chased in this chapter,[11] there may be value in pulling a different thread through history—a trail, not of blood, but of *flood*.

In the Jewish practice of ritual washings, or *tevilah*, the concern for purity and fear of pollution was central. *Mikvehs* were constructed to allow running water to flood into the pool from springs or reservoirs. In the Mishnah Mikvaot, "Rabbi Tzadok testified regarding flowing sources that [their waters] were greater than [those of] dripping sources."[12]

First-century Christian baptisms adopted the Jewish tradition of using flowing, water. A symbol of new life, vitality, washing away, and regeneration, *living* (or flooding) waters were preferred in both traditions to stagnant ones. In the first century, the *Didache* instructed: "And concerning baptism, baptize this way: Having first said all these things, baptize into the name of the Father, and of the Son, and of the Holy Spirit, in living water."[13]

Post-Constantine baptisteries followed suit. In the fourth century, Ambrose immersed Augustine beneath the flowing waters of a "gushing fountain," as Peter Brown described."[14] My father and I recently visited the excavated site beneath the Milan Cathedral where Augustine was baptized on Easter Sunday, AD 387. Originally in a separate building, the octagonal pool still retains the original marble tiles upon which Augustine stood. Central to the design was a large canal entering and exiting the building and allowing for the flow of fresh water.

---

8. George and George, eds. *Baptist Confessions, Covenants, and Catechisms*, 46; italics added.

9. Bradley, *Water: A Spiritual History*, 31.

10. Hammett, *Biblical Foundations for Baptist Churches*, 262.

11. For discussion of Baptist origins, see Bebbington, *Baptist through the Centuries: A History of a Global People*, 25–41; and Chute, Finn, and Haykin, *The Baptist Story: From English Sect to Global Movement*, 11–37.

12. *Mishnah*, Mikvaot 5:5. http://www.sefaria.org/ Mishnah_Mikvaot.5?lang=en (accessed November 19, 2016).

13. Roberts-Donaldson, trans., *Didache*, "Concerning Baptism," www.earlychristianwritings.com/text/didache-roberts.html, accessed November 22, 2016.

14. Brown, *Augustine of Hippo: A Biography*, 124.

In the post-Reformation era, rivers were often chosen for baptismal locations, not for symbolic reasons but for pragmatic and geographical ones. The continuity, however, should not be missed. Following the pattern of Jesus's own baptism in the River Jordan (Matthew 3:13–17), English Separatists and later Baptists flocked to rivers: William Bradford to the Don River, John Bunyan to the Ouse River, Krishna Pal (William Carey's first convert in India) to the Hooghly River, Gerhard Oncken to the Elbe River, etc.

In his commentary on Matthew 3:6, John Gill captured the sweeping symbolism of baptism by emphasizing the etymology of the Hebrew name of the River Jordan "because it descended."[15] In North America, many Baptist churches reflected this movement: Riverside Baptist, Zion Spring Baptist, Catfish Creek Baptist, Living Water Baptist, and countless others.

Long before the use of indoor baptisteries in the nineteenth century, Baptists went "down to the river."[16] For slaves in America, to "wade in the water" was not only an allegory of exodus across the Red Sea (Atlantic Ocean) to the Promised Land (Africa); it was also a call for baptism.

> One version of the spiritual reads:
> Wade in the water, Chillen
> Oh wade in the water, chillen,
> Wade in the water, chillen,
> Wade in the water to be baptize'.[17]

The symbolism and dynamism of baptism is reflected in the experience of those like my father. It was not through a careful study of ecclesiology that he came originally to embrace his Baptist roots. Rather it was, as he reflected, "as a person who finds himself standing, wading, and eventually swimming in a flowing mountain stream."[18] It is fitting, then, to identify Baptists as my father does, as a renewal movement within Protestant Christianity. Regardless of geography or chronology, Baptists are those who have been immersed, renewed, and rejuvenated in living water.

A "MEANS OF GRACE"

Historically, Baptists have understood baptism as a symbol. But Holmes also identified a second perspective of the practice: baptism as a sacrament.

---

15. Gill, *An Exposition of the New Testament*, 1:19.
16. "Down to the River to Pray" [http://www.hymnary.org/text/as_i_went_down_to_the_river_to_pray]. See also Stuckey, *Slave Culture*, 36.
17. Stuckey, *Slave Culture*, 37.
18. T. George, "Recovering the Baptismal Theology of the Early Church."

Some recent writers, drawn from across the Baptist world, have suggested an alternative understanding, which they claim is both more adequate theologically and exegetically, and has deep roots within the Baptist tradition. Core to this view would be a belief that the fact of being baptized changes something about a person. Baptism on this sacramental understanding is a "means of grace," an act which is accompanied by a promise that the Holy Spirit will be at work in and through this act.[19]

Baptisma Semper Reformandum[20]—a refining and defining impulse for Baptists—is continuing in the discovery, or recovery rather, of its *sacredness*. In his chapter, "Sacramentality of the Church," my father writes, "The church always exists in a state of becoming, buffeted by struggles, under the sign of the cross."[21] J. I. Packer, who self identifies as a "Reformed evangelical of Puritan-pietists type within Anglicanism," was "surprised" but encouraged by this burgeoning modification within Baptist circles.[22]

For many Baptists, however, the word "sacramental" solicits somatic reactions. This is biblically warranted if one understands baptism as the transferring of actual grace through the act (*ex opera operato*). Spurgeon was right to challenge such thinking in his controversial 1864 sermon, "Baptismal Regeneration."[23] However, if one understands sacramentality as a "means of grace," as John Hammett argues, and "not the grace that saves, but that which strengthens and upholds a believer,"[24] then a recovery of the sacredness of this practice does not threaten our identity. In fact, it may inform it, reform it, and conform it to a more faithful reading of Scripture.

Spurgeon's baptism may shed light on the subject. Paedo-baptized by his grandfather, Spurgeon began having "serious thoughts about baptism" in April 1850.[25] His thoughts soon grew legs, and on May 3, he walked eight miles from Newmarket to Isleham to be immersed by Rev. W. H. Cantlow in the River Lark.

As Charles stood on the banks of the narrow river, his "thoughts were in the water, sometimes with [his] Lord in joy, and sometimes with [himself] in trembling awe at making so public a confession." Spurgeon reflected:

---

19. Holmes, *Baptist Theology*, 94.

20. See Cross, *Recovering the Evangelical Sacrament: Baptisma Semper Reformandum*.

21. Cross and Thompson, eds., *Baptist Sacramentalism*, 35.

22. Ibid., xiii–xiv.

23. See *The Metropolitan Tabernacle Pulpit*, Vol. 10, Sermon 573.

24. Hammett, *Biblical Foundations for Baptist Churches*, 262.

25. Spurgeon, *Autobiography*, 1:129.

> It was a new experience to me, never having seen a baptism before, and I was afraid of making some mistake. The wind blew down the river with a cutting blast, as my turn came to wade into the flood; but after I had walked a few steps, and noted the people on the ferry-boat, and in boats, and on either shore, I felt as if Heaven, and earth, and hell, might all gaze upon me; for I was not ashamed, there and then, to own myself a follower of the Lamb.[26]

Born and bred in anti-Catholic country, Spurgeon went on to become the most popular preacher in the world (his first biography was written when he was twenty years old). From the meandering stream in Isleham to the mighty River Thomas, Spurgeon docked on South London in 1854 to pastor the famed New Park Street Chapel. By the end of his ministry in 1892, Spurgeon's Metropolitan Tabernacle had baptized thousands in its much larger location at Elephant and Castle.

Yet for the Essex-bred teenager whose first great literary work was a 295-page treatise against Roman Catholicism, "Antichrist and Her Brood; or, Popery Unmasked," his baptism was more than merely symbolic. God *did something* to Spurgeon in that chilly stream. The same Spirit once likened to the wind, which "blows where it wishes (John 3:8), and who "moved upon the face of the waters" (Genesis 1:2), took something of Spurgeon's down the river:

> My timidity was washed away; it floated down the river into the sea, and must have been devoured by the fishes, for *I have never felt anything of the kind since*. Baptism also loosed my tongue, and from that day it has never been quiet. I lost a thousand fears in that River Lark.[27]

The theology of baptism is not the only practice being revisited along sacramental lines. Particularly among younger evangelicals in flavored Southern Baptist churches, there is a recovered sense of the sacredness of the Lord's Supper. Though outside the scope of this chapter, perhaps here is the more fitting place to trace through the centuries a "trail of blood."

Regardless, Baptists of sacramental and symbolic stripes stand united in their unflinching repudiation of infant baptism. For many Baptists, their convictions cost them everything for, as David Bebbington notes, "Baptists were taken to be social subversives."[28] In *The Dippers Dipt*, a seventeenth-

---

26. Ibid., 1:152; italics added.
27. Spurgeon, *Autobiography*, 1:152.
28. Bebbington, *Baptists through the Centuries*, 48.

century refutation of the Anabaptists, Anglican apologist Daniel Featley summarized their immersive practice: "Therefore the adminiſtration of baptiſme upon infants is a meer device of mans brain, and no baptiſme of Chriſt." Then Featley noted, "This argument ſtands as it were upon two legs, and both of them are lame."[29]

Many Christians throughout the centuries have stood upon those lame legs. In his interpretation of Colossians 2:12, Thomas Schreiner makes the point that infant baptism stands only on one of the two legs, so to speak, of the biblical command:

> It is difficult to see, then, how infants can fit with what Paul says since they cannot exercise faith. Those who support infant baptism rightly see the objective work of God's grace in Christ's death and resurrection that is applied in baptism, but they delay the subjective appropriation of God's gift by faith. Such a view truncates, as we have now seen in several texts, the fullness of the biblical witness.[30]

Central to believers' baptism is not only what God does and says, but also what *we* do and say. Baptism is a reflection of the mysterious synergy of salvation—the obedient response to God's active initiative.

Yet in Baptist circles, where the trend is to baptize children younger and younger, my father's advice should give pause: "While seeking to stem the decline in the number of baptisms, Baptists today would do well to recover the rich theological meaning of baptism itself as set forth by those who were first called Baptists."[31] He makes the argument in his article "The Reformed Doctrine of Believers' Baptism" that a faithful demonstration of baptism is not only about the *age* of life but also the *stage* of life:

> In many of our churches, both paedo- and credobaptist, baptism is as American as the Statue of Liberty or Sunday afternoon football. By becoming safely routinized as part of the ecclesiastical landscape, baptism is apt to lose its basic New Testament meaning as the decisive transition from an old way of human life to a new way, as an act of radical obedience in which a specific renunciation is made and a specific promise is given.[32]

---

29. Featley, *The Dippers Dipt*, 76.

30. Schreiner and Wright, eds., *Believer's Baptism: Sign of the New Covenant in Christ*, 77–78.

31. T. George, "Troubled Waters."

32. T. George, "The Reformed Doctrine of Believers' Baptism," 243.

Looking back on my own baptism, I am grateful my father encouraged me to postpone the practice. Baptism is not a private discipline but a public testimony—one that I was privileged to give in 1992 at Shades Mountain Baptist Church in Birmingham, Alabama.

After three years of studying Puritans and Patriarchs, pouring over confessions and creeds, I was finally ready to offer my own before God, the church, and the devil. One week prior, my pastor, Charles Carter, prayed with me in his office and offered words of counsel (he still prays for me, even today). With every page of the workbook fresh in my mind, I entered the baptistery where my father awaited, hand extended. He pitched a simple but serious question: "Is Jesus Christ the Lord and Savior of your life?" He was. In the name of the Father, and of the Son, and the Holy Spirit, he then "dumped" me into the waves.

I have seen many baptisms over the years in which the pastor barely dips the candidate's head beneath the surface of the water (a sanctified form of waterboarding). In their defense, the word "baptize" does come from βαπτίζω, which means "to dip." James Dale explains, "*To dip* expresses a gentle, downward motion, entering slightly into some diverse element, with immediate return."[33]

Not so with my father. That morning, I was neither gently dipped nor immediately returned. I was plunged into the depths! I was "*dyed*"—a word also associated with βαπτίζω in the ancient world, which means "*to stain, to smear, to gild, to temper, to imbue*."[34] So *dyed* was I, my back scrapped the bottom of the baptistery. My father later confessed he wanted to make sure I was *really* buried with Christ in baptism. For about three seconds, liquid silence suspended me before a swirling surge raised me to walk in newness of life.

Long after my baptism, my father continued taking me on pilgrimages around the world. Each travel, each lesson, serves as an extension of that baptism workbook, pressing me to push beyond the periphery of my comfort zones and see what God has in store. Each journey corrects the trajectory of my life and replaces a monochrome mindset with a multi-ethnic, multi-cultural, kaleidoscopic Christianity.

My father once said, "I came to see that being a Baptist was the most faithful way I could be an evangelical, a Protestant, and a Christian. But this has not stifled my desire to learn from Christians of many different ilks."[35] His desire for Christian unity as expressed by Jesus in John 17:21, "that they

---

33. Dale, *Classic Baptism: Baptizo*, xiii; italics in the original.
34. Ibid.; italics in the original.
35. T. George, "Recovering the Baptismal Theology of the Early Church."

may be one," is a helpful contribution and corrective to twenty-first century evangelicalism. His is an ecumenism of conviction, not of compromise. And by modeling this mindset, my father has encouraged not only me, but evangelicals throughout the world, to retain our denominational distinctives while also recognizing God is up to something in other places, faces, and spaces.

Twenty-four years have passed since I completed the final page of my baptism workbook. Yet its words still glow in my mind, reminding me of my name, my calling, my pilgrimage, and my father's gentle guidance. On page eighteen, after listing several symbols of resurrection (tomb, fish, peacock, butterfly, and phoenix), I recorded the following words:

> Finally comes the egg. It's a very strong resurrection symbol because it means it has a knew life. It's in the egg living and then it comes out and it lives again. That's like us. We live here on earth than we hatch out of our old life and come into our knew life.[36]

Experientially and theologically, baptism ushers us onward and upward. It divides but unites. It points us backward and forward, reminding us of the past while giving us courage to travel into the future. Baptism is both memory and prophecy:

> So will it be with the resurrection of the dead. The body that is sown is perishable, it is raised imperishable; it is sown in dishonor, it is raised in glory; it is sown in weakness, it is raised in power; it is sown a natural body, it is raised a spiritual body (1 Corinthians 15:42).

BIBLIOGRAPHY

Bebbington, David W. *Baptist through the Centuries: A History of a Global People* Waco, TX: Baylor University Press, 2010.

Bradley, Ian. *Water: A Spiritual History.* London: Bloomsbury, 2012.

Brown, Peter. *Augustine of Hippo: A Biography*. Berkeley: University of California Press, 1967.

Bunyan, John. *The Pilgrim's Progress As Originally Published, Being a Fac-simile Reproduction of the First Ed.* London: Stock, 1877.

Chute, Anthony L., Nathan A. Finn, and Michael A. G. Haykin. *The Baptist Story: From English Sect to Global Movement*. Nashville: B&H Academic, 2015.

Cross, Anthony R. *Recovering the Evangelical Sacrament: Baptisma Semper Reformandum*. Eugene, OR: Pickwick, 2013.

Cross, Anthony R., and Philip E. Thompson, eds. *Baptist Sacramentalism*. Studies in Baptist History and Thought 5. Carlisle, UK: Paternoster, 2003.

---

36. C. George, *Baptism Workbook*, 18.

Dale, James W. *Classic Baptism: Baptizo, An Inquiry into the Meaning of the Word as Determined by the Usage of Classical Greek Writers*. 1867. Repr., Wauconda, IL: Bolchazy-Carducci, 1989.

Featley, Daniel. *The Dippers Dipt, or The Anabaptists Duck'd and Plung'd over Head and Ears, at a Disputation in Southwark*. 5th ed. London: printed for N. E. and Richard Royston at the Angel in Ivy-lane, 1647.

George, Christian. *Baptism Workbook*. Unpublished booklet, 1989–1992.

George, Timothy. "Recovering the Baptismal Theology of the Early Church." Nevin Lectures, Trinity House Institute, 2014.

———. "The Reformed Doctrine of Believers' Baptism." *Interpretation: A Journal of Bible & Theology* 47, no. 3 (1993) 242–54.

———. "Troubled Waters." *First Things*. June 2, 2014. Accessed November 19, 2016. https://www.firstthings.com/web-exclusives/2014/06/troubled-waters.

George, Timothy, and Denise George, eds. *Baptist Confessions, Covenants, and Catechisms*. Nashville: Broadman & Holman, 1996.

Gill, John. *An Exposition of the New Testament, in Three Volumes: In Which the Sense of the Sacred Text Is Given; Doctrinal and Practical Truths Are Set in a Plain and Easy Light, Difficult Places Explained, Seeming Contradictions Reconciled; And Whatever Is Material in the Various Readings, and the Several Oriental Versions, Is Observed. The Whole Illustrated with Notes Taken from the Most Ancient Jewish Writings*. Vol. 1. London: printed for the author, 1746.

Hammett, John S. *Biblical Foundations for Baptist Churches: A Contemporary Ecclesiology*. Grand Rapids: Kregel Academic, 2005.

Holmes, Stephen R. *Baptist Theology*. London: T. & T. Clark, 2012.

Mishnah. Mikvaot 5:5. Sefaria. Accessed November 19, 2016. http://www.sefaria.org/Mishnah_Mikvaot.5?lang=en.

Philadelphia Confession of Faith being The London Confession of Faith Adopted in 1742 by The Baptist Association with Scripture References and Keach's Catechism. Sterling, VA: G. A. M., 1981.

Schreiner, Thomas R., and Shawn D. Wright, eds. *Believer's Baptism: Sign of the New Covenant in Christ*. Nashville: B&H Academic, 2006.

Spurgeon, C. H. *Autobiography. Compiled from His Diary, Letters, and Records, by His Wife, and His Private Secretary*. 4 vols. London: Passmore & Alabaster, 1899–1900.

———. *The Metropolitan Tabernacle Pulpit: Sermons Preached and Revised by C. H. Spurgeon*. Vols. 7–63. Pasadena, TX: Pilgrim, 1970–2006.

Stuckey, Sterling. *Slave Culture: Nationalist Theory and the Foundations of Black America*. 1987. Repr., Oxford: Oxford University Press, 2013.

Healing Eucharistic Amnesia

Elizabeth Newman

For Baptists and some other Protestants, the Lord's Supper has come to hold a minor place in worship. As children of the Reformation, we have rightly celebrated the weekly and even daily preaching of the Word of God. The Lord's Supper, however, practiced much less frequently, has often been seen as an "occasional intruder[ ] on a normal pattern of worship."[1] A common view is that the Lord's Supper is a symbol, meaning in this case a sign pointing to a reality that lies elsewhere. In this essay, I look at how this disconnect between real and symbol prevents Baptists and others from seeing the Lord's Supper as an abundant feast, a sacrament[2] that brings all creation into communion with God.

---

1. White, *Protestant Worship, Traditions in Transition* 37.

2. My use of "sacrament" is not opposed to "ordinance." Both "sacrament" and "ordinance" may be "understood as the 'making visible' of the Word of God who rules the church" ("The Word of God in the Life of the Church," 61). It is also important to note, as do Cross and Thompson, that [some] "Baptists from the seventeenth century to the present have held to sacramental views of baptism and the Lord's Supper." They also note, however, that, "as children of the Enlightenment, Baptists have too often unconsciously imbibed Enlightenment presuppositions" (*Baptist Sacramentalism*, ed. Cross and Thompson, 36–54). See also Philip Thompson's essay in this volume, "Sacraments and Religious Liberty," where he states, "There is ample evidence that early Baptists regarded the sacraments as means of grace appointed by God to strengthen and increase faith unto salvation. 'And as [Israel] had the manna to nourish them in the wilderness to Canaan,' confessed the Midlands General Baptists, 'so have we the sacraments, to nourish us in the church, and in our wilderness conditions.'" 40.

REAL VERSUS SYMBOL: A MODERN DICHOTOMY

Our dominant culture has grown accustomed to accepting the real as that which appears within the limits of what William H. Poteat calls the "religion of modernity."[3] For this modern religion, the real is that which can be measured, tested or seen. The white styrofoam cup sitting before me is real; the dream I had last night is not. Wendell Berry describes this religion of modernity as essentially an empirical orthodoxy.[4] The official faith of this religion of modernity is scientism and technology.[5] Berry acknowledges a legitimate confidence in the "workability and soundness" of the scientific method, but, he argues, this legitimacy veers off "into a kind of religious faith in the power of science to know all things and solve all problems, whereupon the scientist may became an evangelist and go forth and save the world."[6] At the heart of this religion of modernity lies a dualism between knowledge and faith, and between fact and value.[7] While this dualism has been criticized many times over, Poteat emphasizes that it continues to pervade the air "like chronic depression."[8]

One sees the pervasive hangover in the tangled debate about whether the Lord's Supper is real or symbolic. Consider the following thought experiment. What is the difference between the Lord's Supper and the supper you eat at your family table? A key difference that will likely come to mind is that while the Lord's Supper is only a sip of juice and a piece of bread, the family meal is *really* a meal. If we were to create a *real* Lord's Supper, perhaps something like DaVinci's "Last Supper" would come to mind. DaVinci portrays the disciples as animated and quizzical, their gestures and faces alive with wonder and curiosity. Jesus sits serenely in their midst. The table before them is filled with plates of food and loaves of bread. Of course, we cannot create the DaVinci scene entirely; that would require much more, not the least of which would be bringing the disciples into our time. We are

---

3. Poteat, *Recovering the Ground, Critical Exercises in Recollection* 124.
4. Berry, *Life Is a Miracle*, 99.
5. Poteat, *Recovering the Ground, Critical Exercises in Recollection*, 125–26.
6. Berry, *Life Is a Miracle*, 19.
7. Kant stated, "I cannot even make the assumption—as the practical interests of morality require—of God, freedom, and immortality, if I do not deprive speculative reason of its pretensions to transcendent insight . . . I must, therefore, abolish knowledge, to make room for belief," in Kant, *Critique of Pure Reason*, 10.
8. Poteat, *A Philosophical Daybook, Post-Critical Investigations* 5. The fuller quotation is that "Cartesianism as an explicit philosophical doctrine is virtually without effect in this culture. It functions however at a tacit level like a repetition compulsion; it is ubiquitous and pervades the atmosphere of our life like chronic depression."

therefore left, so it seems, with a symbolic re-enactment of the real meal Jesus had with his disciples.

THE REAL IS THE ESSENCE

If the real is not identified with an historical event or time, then the real, modernity imagines, has to do with the essential. What is water, for example? A scientist would likely say, "H20" or perhaps "a liquid substance." Water might be many other things, but a basic definition focuses on the essential components. Is not real bread what you buy at the store (or possibly make)? Are not its ingredients flour, yeast, milk, butter and so forth?

Years ago, I was sitting with my children on the banks of Lake Naylor when, we suddenly realized, a large group was headed our way. It turned out to be a lovely baptismal service. Congregants stood on the shore and some entered the water. The pastor lifted up his hand showing his wedding ring. The wedding ring could be lost, he said, pretending to throw it in the water, but, he continued, this would not change the love he had for his wife. The ring is just a symbol. He compared this to baptism by saying that baptism, too, was just symbolic; what was real was the conversion and commitment to Jesus.

On this view, the surrounding ritual is important only in the sense that it points to the real essence. If we apply this familiar logic to the Lord's Supper, then we would say that the small piece of bread and the sip of grape juice are only symbols; what is real is that Jesus gave his body and blood for our sins. Like the ring, the bread and juice are secondary. From this perspective, the alternative seems to be that if the grape juice were *really* scientifically Christ's blood, it would taste and feel like blood. This is like the child who "after making her first communion, refused an ice-cream because she 'did not want to make Jesus' head cold.'"[9]

"Everything is what it is"?

Whether one is thinking about the real historically (the historical event) or scientifically (the empirical essence), the words of the eighteen century philosopher Joseph Butler pertain, "Everything is what it is, and is not another

---

9. Lash, *His Presence in the World,* 150. Lash is arguing that this way of thinking of Christ's presence is a distortion of the teaching of the Catholic Church.

thing."[10] A circle is a circle and not a square. You attended this school and not that one. Grape juice is juice and not blood. This all seems obvious.

In *The Screwtape Letters*, C. S. Lewis has Screwtape, the senior devil, instruct his young protégé, Wormwood, in exactly this kind of thinking:

> "The whole philosophy of Hell rests on recognition of the axiom that one thing is not another thing,. . .Even an inanimate object is what it is by excluding all other objects from the space it occupies. . ."[11]

It seems, at first reading, that if one were to drop the word "Hell" from the quotation, Lewis is simply describing the real world: the physical universe of objects in space and time. He emphasizes that objects do not share space with other objects. If you occupy a space, then no one else can be in that same space. If a loaf of bread sits on a table, then nothing else can take up that space. Bread is bread. The way of thinking, also known as the "principle of simple identity" assumes that x, whatever its content, "has its identity in itself, apart from or outside of relation to non-x."[12]

Why does Lewis put this apparently innocuous and obvious philosophy into the mouth of Screwtape? To respond, we can turn to the David L. Schindler who states that the principle of simple identity sees any relation between x and non-x as *external*. I can relate to you through my choice to do so but there is nothing inherent in my being as such that connects me with others. This is significant because the principle of simple identity says that who I really am or who you really are, or what anything really is, lies essentially within itself. Schindler identifies the primary features of the logic of simple identity as externality and closure That is, x and non-x are "turned in on themselves, closed to each other."[13] The principle of simple identity thus leads, according to Schindler, to patterns of thinking marked by fragmentation (identity is only in x), and domination (since there is an original closure to relation, then relations will seem domineering, external and not-x).

We see this logic of closure and domination in the words of Screwtape when he applies it to persons: "Even an inanimate object is what it is by excluding all other objects from the space it occupies. . .A self does the

10. Wedgewood, "Butler on Virtue, Self-Interest and Human Nature."

11. Lewis, *The Screwtape Letters*, 81.

12. Schindler, "Faith and the Logic of Intelligence: Secularization in the Academy," 173.

13. Ibid. Schindler states that these features come to expression when primacy is accorded to doubt, and when meaning is "first and essentially discrete (*bounded*), and is gotten at most properly by analysis ('breaking up' into ever smaller discrete bits)."

same...'To be' *means* 'to be in competition.'" Thus, "the whole philosophy of Hell rests on recognition of the axiom that...one self is not another self."[14] Lewis is describing a world in which nothing can exist but individual things. The "vertical" or "interior" dimension of reality is effectively eliminated.[15] That is, there is no sense of being as created or of being as participation in the Divine Logos. There is no notion of created beings as signs of a reality that exceeds them infinitely. The demonic world is rather closed in on itself and thus inherently competitive. The harmony of creation can only be heard as discordant noise.[16]

At stake here, as Screwtape well understands, is an argument about being, about ontology. Screwtape is showing his young charge, Wormwood, how he can lead his "patient" (the human) to forget who he really *is*. Analogously, the Lord's Supper as only symbolic, by reinforcing the conviction that a "thing is what it is," leads to forget who we are and who Christ is at the Table.

Eucharistic Amnesia

In "The Pleasure of Eating," Wendell Berry diagnoses our culture as suffering from a culinary amnesia. Food, he says, has become an abstraction, leading to a loss of memory about the food we eat, where it comes from and, most fully, who we are as creatures of God. Those familiar with Berry and his writings will recognize his emphasis: "When food, in the minds of eaters, is no longer associated with farming and with the land, then the eaters are suffering a kind of cultural amnesia that is misleading and dangerous."[17] It is dangerous because "how we eat determines, to a considerable extent, how the world is used."[18] The cure for such amnesia, says Berry, is to practice eating with "the fullest pleasure," which means "we experience and celebrate our dependence and our gratitude, for we are living from mystery, from creatures we did not make and powers we cannot comprehend."[19] His analysis is not just about eating; it is about the way we live in relation and dependence upon each other, the natural world and God.

---

14. Lewis, *The Screwtape Letters*, 81.
15. Caldecott, *The Radiance of Being, Dimensions of Cosmic Christianity*, 29.
16. Lewis, *The Screwtape Letters*, 102.
17. Berry, *What Are People for?* 146.
18. Ibid., 149.
19. Ibid., 152. Berry closes this essay with this eucharistic poem by William Carlos Williams: "There is nothing to eat/seek it where you will, but the body of the Lord. The blessed plants and the sea, yield it/to the imagination/intact."

Analogously, the Lord's Supper is not just a symbolic meal occasionally celebrated. Rather it has to do with the mystery of God in the one Body of Christ and with the kind of life this mystery produces, one that is eucharistic (meaning "thanksgiving" or "praise"). It thus has to do with a whole way of ecclesial life together for the sake of the world. To believe otherwise is to suffer eucharistic amnesia.

What, then, is the cure? Understanding the Lord's Supper has, of course, been the subject of heated argument in the life of the church. My purpose here is not to engage the nuances of these debates as much as it is to try and discern the "'crucial difference. . .between telling a story differently and telling a different story.'"[20] We can acknowledge that churches will practice the Lord's Supper differently, but at what point does the practice and reflection on the Lord's Table come to tell a different story? Thus far, I have argued that the Lord's Supper as only a symbol, celebrated infrequently, reflects a loss of memory. The result is that the practice becomes more determined by modern rationalism than by the life, death and resurrection of Christ and the church as Christ's body. How can we tell the story of the Lord's Supper in a way that avoids the modern dualism between symbol and real, a dualism which rests on a distorted ontology?

THE LORD'S SUPPER: AN ONTOLOGY OF GIFT

Key to a faithful understanding of the Lord's Supper is a Chalcedonian Christology that affirms Jesus as one person, fully human and fully divine. Of particular significance for the Lord's Supper is the further affirmation that Jesus not only became a human, but assumed humanity as such and, in a sense, all of creation. In and through Christ, all of creation is united with God. Pope John Paul II states this point succinctly:

> The Incarnation of God the Son signifies the taking up into unity with God not only of human nature, but in this human nature, in a sense, of everything that is "flesh": the whole of humanity, the entire visible and material world. The Incarnation, then, also has a cosmic significance, a cosmic dimension. The "first-born of all creation," becoming incarnate in the individual humanity of Christ, unites himself in some way with the entire reality of man, which is also "flesh" and in this reality with all "flesh," with the whole of creation.[21]

---

20. Harvey, *Another City, An Ecclesiological Primer for a Post-Christian World*, 19.
21. Paul II, *Dominum et Vivificantem*, no. 50.

To say that Christ's incarnation pertains to all being is to emphasize that Christ, through forgiving sin and defeating death, brings all of creation to its final purpose: union with God. That is, "in Christ God was reconciling the world to himself..." (1 Cor 5:19) This seems like a straightforward point, but it stands in stark contrast with modernity's definition of the "real" as neutral, flat, and what simply "is." In other words, embedded in the logic of Christ's life, death and resurrection is the reality that all being, as created and recreated, is inherently oriented toward God. If it were otherwise, salvation would not have a cosmic reach. There would be "things" or "objects" or "beings" outside of the sphere of God's creating and recreating love in Christ. To be in not "to be in competition," as Screwtape maintained, but to be in communion. Even when persons reject this communion, it remains a reality; apart from the Divine gift of being, they would cease to be.

The Lord's Supper itself depends upon an ontology of gift. At its most basic level, the Lord's Supper is about life. "Just as the living Father sent me, and I live because of the Father, so whoever eats me will live because of me" (Jn 6:57). This is not a magic potion, but rather a participation through the Spirit in the true life that the Son shares with the Father. St. Augustine notes with approval that "in several Punic dialects the word used for Eucharist is simply the word for 'life.'"[22] That the eucharist is a synonym for life is an ontological claim; it is saying that true life itself is thanksgiving and gift. This is why, in contrast to the religion of modernity, the Lord's Supper is not a kind of add-on to an otherwise real world. It is not a liturgy in contrast to the non-liturgical being of daily life. It rather has to do with that fact that intrinsic to *all* being everywhere is communion. Augustine captures this understanding in his familiar prayer, "My heart is restless, O God, until it rests in you." An ontology of gift says that this restlessness is true of everyone. I am calling this "gift" because the desire for God as well as communion with God are both gifts. The Lord's Supper, relying upon exactly this ontology, is the offering of the gift of Christ's body and blood. Through the body and blood of Christ, the gifts of bread and wine and the gathered bodies around the table, Christ through the Spirit enables the body to be what it is intended to be: communion with Christ.

---

22. Cavanaugh, "The Eucharist in the Streets: Eucharist and Politics," 384; See also Zizioulas, *Being As Communion,* 82. Zizioulas argues that Christians in the early church developed an understanding of life in contrast to an Aristotelian view that life was a quality *added* to being. In part through reflecting on the Eucharist, early Christians came to the conviction that one could say being and life in the same breath. As Zizioulas puts it: "[T]he eucharistic experience implies that life is imparted and actualized only in an event of communion, and thus creation and existence in general can be founded only upon the living God of communion."

One could object that is it not necessary to partake of the Lord's Supper in order to have this life. This is true, of course, if one is talking about life in a strictly biological sense. But, as we've seen, true life is life in communion with Christ and his body. Some Christians, particularly Protestants, might object that the Lord's Supper is not necessary for such communion. It can be received in other ways: through preaching, prayer, bible study and so forth. Certainly these are means of communion with God and so also means of building up the body of Christ. But full life speaks to the full reception of God's gifts to the church. The present tense of these familiar verses is significant: "This is my body broken for you" (1 Cor 11:24) and "for this is my blood of the covenant, which is poured out for many for the forgiveness of sins" (Matt 26:28). "Divine love made food"[23] brings the church into communion with Christ, enabling its being as gift to be fully realized.

The Lord's Supper: Koinonia

Paul writes, "Because there is one bread, we who are many are one body, for we all partake of the one bread" (1 Cor 10:17) A key implication of this passage is that one does not have to *think* or *feel* certain thoughts or emotions when sharing in the sacrificial meal. In chapter ten, Paul is arguing that those who eat bread sacrificed to idols in a pagan religious rite are becoming "partners [κοινωνοὺς] with demons" (v. 20) though idols have no real existence, Paul emphasizes that such eating constitutes idolatry. One's inner thoughts or feelings are beside the point in this regard; it is rather the action itself that makes this demonic partnership a reality. By contrast, Paul emphasizes that partaking of the cup of blessing and the bread is a sharing (κοινωνία) in the body and blood of Christ (v. 16). And because it is a sharing in Christ's gift of life, it is inherently unitive. When you eat the food of idols in the context of worship, you are uniting yourselves with demons. When you eat the cup and bread, you are uniting yourself with Christ.

For any number of reasons, one might not feel or experience anything during the Lord's Supper. One might be tempted to wonder, "Am I (or we) just going through meaningless motions?" Paul's description, however, emphasizes that it is the liturgical action that drives the significance of the celebration. In other words, when the pagans sacrificed at the altar they were in fact practicing idolatry and becoming partners with the demons. So also, when Christians gather at the Lord's Table to receive the body and blood of Christ, they are in fact becoming partners with Christ. The power of this understanding is that it serves as a reminder that the Lord's Supper is not

---

23. Schmemann, *For the Life of the World*, 4.

first of all about us, i.e., our feelings, experiences, thoughts and so forth.[24] Nor is it a mere ritual, the external shell of which can be discarded (like the wedding ring) while the inner essence or meaning remains. It is rather a real sharing of Christ's body, as real as sharing a meal with a friend. And, as Paul indicates, if one were at a pagan sacrifice, that would be a real sharing as well.

Such action depends, of course, on God's prior action of gathering a people and feeding them; the manna in the desert, the multiplication of fish and loaves and other such Divine feedings prefigure the Lord's Supper in this sense. The Latin word "*sacramentum*" translates the Greek word "*mysterion*"; both words refer to the faithful action or pledge of God and to the mystery of God's saving work.[25] The Lord's Supper, then, is ultimately about the mystery of God's action in the world, not about one's subjective thoughts or feelings. The language of "sacrament" designates how this Divine mystery/action makes "*koinonia*" at the Lord's Table possible. The human response is to participate, to collect the manna, to receive what God is giving.

The Lord's Supper: Re-membering One Body

If the Lord's Table is really a unitive meal, however, then why is it that Christians are unable to celebrate it together? It often seems, rather, to highlight the brokenness of Christ's body. There is, of course, a long history of how theological differences around the Lord's Supper (or mass) have increased division in the church. In light of such division, James Buckley rightly emphasizes the need to preserve painful memories in a way that heals. One of the painful memories that we live with is the inability fully to worship together at the Lord's Table. When the Lord's Table becomes a minor liturgical event in the life of the church, however, even the memory of eucharistic unity easily fades. By contrast, attending to the Lord's Table—as truly *koinonia*—is a way of *remembering* the unity that Christ desires for the

---

24. What Ellis notes about baptism can be applied to the Lord's Supper as well: "Too often interpretations of . . . baptism have been reduced to an *illustration* of the gospel, an expression of subjective faith or an opportunity to encourage commitment," Ellis, *Gathering, A Spirituality and Theology of Worship in Free Church Tradition* 178. If the Lord's Supper is primarily expressive, then the meaning of the Supper depends on one's subjective experience or emotions.

25. "The Word of God in the Life of the Church," 63. A Report of International Conversations Between the Catholic Church and the Baptist World Alliance, 2006–2010," 61. It is also important to note, as do Cross and Thompson, that [some] "Baptists from the seventeenth century to the present have held to sacramental views of baptism and the Lord's Supper."

whole church. Rightly understood, such memory is not just about the past; memory in the sense of *anamnesis* refers to "a participation *in the present* in the mighty acts of God that are being remembered from the past."[26]

To participate in God's mighty acts is to allow ourselves, as Barry Harvey states, to be "re-membered" or reconfigured so that false stories of division no longer form our lives.[27]

Harvey states that "the dismembering of Christian identity by means of 'religion' during the modern era further eviscerated the public and bodily character of biblical and patristic Christianity." That is, "sequestering religion in the private sphere reserves the public realm exclusively for the coercive rule of both state and market. . ."[28] Alexander Schmemann similarly describes how the body has been malformed by means of a sequestering of religion. He describes particularly how Ludwig Feuerbach, the German materialist thinker, is the heir of a Christianity turned into a religion. Feuerbach famously argued that "man is what he eats." He meant by this that "man" is fundamentally a material reality; the "spiritual" is essentially a projection of our material conditions. Schmemann argues that Feuerbach's materialism, far from simply arising in opposition to Christianity, is "in fact the natural heir to Christian 'idealism' and 'spiritualism.'"[29] Once Christianity becomes a religion that belongs in a sphere, then a material or secular sphere separate from the "spiritual" is inevitably imagined.

This modern dis-memberment of Christ's body relegates the Lord's Supper to a symbolic or spiritual realm, having little to do with so-called secular sphere. One thus assumes that the Lord's Supper has nothing to do with politics or economics or education. In trying to bridge this gap, some have viewed the Lord's Supper as primarily a moral exercise: the sharing of bread means we ought to share bread with our neighbor. While sharing bread is of course a good thing, moralizing the supper in this way is similar to interpreting Jesus as a persuasive moral figure, but not the fully human

---

26. Ibid., 77; my emphasis. As Lohfink describes it, "What once happened is happening for us . . . For all faithful Jews, and not only for them, it is a matter of course that at the Passover meal the foundational history of the people of God is made present," *Does God Need the Church?*, 239.

27. Harvey, "Re-membering the Body: Baptism, Eucharist and the Politics of Disestablishment," 96–116; See Bullard, *Re-membering the Body: The Lord's Supper and Ecclesial Unity in the Free Church Traditions*.

28. Harvey, "Re-membering the Body: Baptism, Eucharist and the Politics of Disestablishment," 106

29. Schmemann, *For the Life of the World* 3.

and fully divine person who is the Son of God. In this sense, such a moral interpretation repeats the Kantian reduction of religion to morality.[30]

When William Cavanaugh, then, states that the eucharist reconfigures bodies in space and time, he rightly describes this as an alternative to all other political and economic configurations.[31] The Lord's Supper is not simply about helping the old creation to function better; it is rather about a new creation. In contrast to the "religion of modernity" that equates religion with spiritual values, the reconfiguration of the Lord's Supper is not about value as opposed to fact, nor about the spiritual or symbolic separated from the real. In seeking alternative language to this kind of modern assumption, Stanley Hauerwas states that "learning to pray is the way Christians discover *how to speak*."[32] Rightly understood, the language of prayer pertains to all speech: to all "spheres" of life. Thus, we can say that "prayers are the making *of us*."[33] This is surely true as well of the Lord's Supper, which is an embodied prayer. The Lord's Supper enables us to speak of all creation as communion, meaning that any autonomous self, sphere or subject is a fiction. So understood, the Lord's Supper reconfigures our bodies to be the one Body of Christ over against all other configurations, such as nationalism, denominationalism, etc. Though this unity is often "clouded by our sinfulness and 'slowness of heart' (Luke 24:25)," it nonetheless "already exists among us as God's gift."[34]

The Lord's Supper: Sacrifice

The Lord's Supper moves beyond strictly "historical" time. As we saw, the "religion of modernity" equates real time with that which can be measured and assessed by the modern historical method. But the time of Christ is not strictly linear. The particularity of the incarnation, life and death of Jesus in

---

30. As White notes, in the Enlightenment, "religion was basically seen as an instrument for the improvement of human society . . . The message of the eucharist became 'be good' rather than 'God is good,'" White, *Protestant Worship*, 53. As Cavanaugh states, "the Eucharist spills well beyond the confines of the altar and out into the world. To do this, however, is for me more than an attempt to reduce the Eucharist to a *meaning* that can be translated in a secular idiom, or a model of society that can be replicated in other contexts," "The Eucharist in the Streets: Eucharist and Politics," 391.

31. Cavanaugh, "The Eucharist in the Streets: Eucharist and Politics," 389.

32. Hauerwas, *Where Resident Aliens Live,* 42; my emphasis.

33. Hemming, and Parsons, "Editor's Preface," xvii.

34. Daley, "Rebuilding the Structure of Love: The Quest for Visible Unity among the Churches," 74. Daley states that to live ecumenically is to allow this unity "to become more fully evident in the way Christians look upon each other, articulate their faith, carry out their worship, and act in the world."

human time is of course crucial. God became human at a particular time, in a particular place. But the resurrection points to the reality that Christ is not limited by linear or historical time. At the Lord's Table, one does not need to be locked into only remembering a past event. Rather, Christ is now present at *this* table in *this* particular congregation. The Divine abundance of the Lord's Supper is that Christ unites participants with one another across time and place, thus bringing a particular congregation more fully into God's time. This is not liturgical time *versus* real time, or religious time *versus* time in the world of work. It is rather the lens through which one sees all time as communion with God.

If Christ is present in all time, this means that the Lord's Supper is not a gesture only pointing to an event that happened long ago. A familiar debate between Catholics and Protestants has had to do with the word "sacrifice," and whether or in what sense to see the Lord's Supper itself as a sacrifice. Catholics have argued that it is the sacrifice of Christ (the real body and blood, and thus their teaching "transubstantiation"). A common Protestant worry has been that Christ's unique sacrifice cannot be repeated: he made only one sacrifice, "once for all when he offered himself" (Heb 7:27). Protestants do not have to accept transubstantiation, however, to acknowledge that the one sacrifice of Christ is efficacious across time. It is not limited to a particular time or place. Early Baptists as well as some Baptists today see themselves as participating, in the Lord's Supper, in the "very events of the death and resurrection of Jesus," and "sharing in 'all the benefits' of Christ's saving sacrifice."[35] The sacrifice that Christ gives is always available; indeed to worship God is to receive this gift again and again. This ongoing reception of the Lord's Supper is not because Christ's sacrifice is somehow inadequate. It is rather because our own blindness and sin prevent us for living fully out of this divine gift. We receive Christ's sacrifice when we gather at the Lord's Table, and partake of the bread and wine.

Understandings of the Lord's Supper as sacrifice are found not only in Scripture but also in the Baptist hymnody. Philip Thompson, for example, notes that the following hymn appears in many Baptist hymnals: "Here at thy table Lord, we meet/To feed on food divine; Thy body is the bread we eat,/Thy precious blood the wine. He that prepares the rich repast,/Himself comes down and dies; /And then invites us thus to feast/Upon the sacrifice."[36] To feast on food divine is to feast upon Christ's sacrifice. Is this

---

35. "The Word of God in the Life of the Church" 124; and The London Confession of Faith, 1677.

36. Samuel Stennett, "Here at Thy Table, Lord, We Meet," #302, in Burdette, *Baptist Harmony*, cited by Thompson, "Re-Envisioning Baptist Identity," 299.

just symbolic? It rests, rather, on an ontology of gift: we live through the food divine, the sacrifice of Christ.

CONCLUSION

The religion of modernity thinks of the Lord's Supper in strictly historical or scientific terms. Either the eucharist is a magical intrusion into the natural scientific order or it is only symbolic in an otherwise real, historical world. I have argued that this dualism results in eucharistic amnesia, a sign of which is the Lord Supper's relegation to a sphere, divorced from both regular worship and more broadly from the rest of life. My analysis points to how the Lord's Supper as a true sharing in the body of Christ unites us as one body. Through the body and blood of Christ, we discover how all creation, all being, is created for communion with God the Father, Son and Holy Spirit. There is therefore no area of life outside of which this communion does not pertain, no real thing or substance that exists only in itself. The Lord's Supper as a genuine, albeit mysterious, reception of Christ frees the church to be more fully Christ's one eucharistic body for the world.

BIBLIOGRAPHY

Bullard, Scott W. *Re-membering the Body: The Lord's Supper and Ecclesial Unity in the Free Church Traditions* Eugene, OR: Cascade, 2013.
Berry, Wendell. *Life is a Miracle*. Washington, DC: Counterpoint, 2000.
———. *What Are People for?* San Francisco: North Point, 1990.
Burdette, Staunton S. *Baptist Harmony*. Philadelphia: Ustick, 1834.
Caldecott, Stratford. *The Radiance of Being, Dimensions of Cosmic Christianity*. Tacoma, WA: Angelico, 2013.
Cavanaugh, William. "The Eucharist in the Streets: Eucharist and Politics." *Modern Theology* 30, no. 2 (2014) 384.
Cross, Anthony R., and Philip E. Thompson. "Baptists' Sacraments and Religious Liberty: From Critical Ally to Rejected Encroachment." In *Baptist Sacramentalism*, edited by Anthony R. Cross and Philip E. Thompson, 36–54. Studies in Baptist History and Thought 5. Carlisle, UK: Paternoster, 2003.
Daley, Brian. "Rebuilding the Structure of Love: The Quest for Visible Unity among the Churches." In *The Ecumenical Future*, edited by Carl E. Braaten and Robert W. Jenson, 73–105. Grand Rapids: Eerdmans, 2004.
Ellis, Christopher. *Gathering: A Spirituality and Theology of Worship in Free Church Tradition*. Norwich, UK: Hymns Ancient & Modern, 2004.
Harvey, Barry. *Another City: An Ecclesiological Primer for a Post-Christian World* Harrisburg, PA: Trinity, 1999.

———. "Re-membering, the Body: Baptism, Eucharist and the Politics of Disestablishment." In *Baptist Sacramentalism*, edited by Anthony R. Cross and Philip E. Thompson, 96–116. Carlisle, UK: Paternoster, 2003.

Hauerwas, Stanley. *Where Resident Aliens Live*. Nashville: Abingdon, 1996.

Hemming, Laurence Paul, and Susan Frank Parsons. "Editor's Preface." In *Corpus Mysticum, The Eucharist and the Church in the Middle Ages*, by Henri de Lubac, edited by Laurence Paul Hemming and Susan Frank Parsons, translated by GEmma Simmonds, ix–xviii. Notre Dame, IN: University of Notre Dame, 2006.

Kant, Immanuel. *Critique of Pure Reason*. In *The Critique of Pure Reason; The Critique of Practical Reason, and Other Ethical Treatises; The Critique of Judgment*. Translated by J. M. D. Meiklejohn et al. 2nd ed. Chicago: Encyclopedia Britannica, 1990.

Lash, Nicholas. *His Presence in the World, A Study of Eucharistic Worship and Theology*. Dayton, OH: Pflaum, 1968.

Lohfink, Gerhard. *Does God Need the Church?* Collegeville, MN: Liturgical, 1999.

Lewis, C. S. *The Screwtape Letters*. New York: Macmillan, 1961.

Paul II, John. *Dominum et Vivificantem*. No. 50. Accessed January 19, 2018. http://w2.vatican.va/content/john-paul-ii/en/encyclicals/documents/hf_jp-ii_enc_18051986_dominum-et-vivificantem.html#-1E.

Poteat, William H. *Recovering the Ground: Critical Exercises in Recollection*. Albany: SUNY, 1994.

———. *A Philosophical Daybook: Post-Critical Investigations*. Columbia, MO: University of Missouri Press, 1990.

Schindler, David L. "Faith and the Logic of Intelligence: Secularization in the Academy." In *Catholicism and Secularization in America: Essays on Nature, Grace and Culture*, edited by David L. Schindler., 170–93 Notre Dame, IN: Communion, 1990.

Schmemann, Alexander. *For the Life of the World: Sacraments and Orthodoxy*. Rev. and exp. ed. New York: National Student Christian Federation, 1965.

Thompson, Philip E. "Re-Envisioning Baptist Identity: Historical, Theological, and Liturgical Analysis." *Perspective in Religious Studies* 27, no. 3 (2000) 299.

Wedgewood, Ralph. "Butler on Virtue, Self-Interest and Human Nature." http://wwwbcf.usc.edu/~wedgwood/Butler.htm.

White, James F. *Protestant Worship, Traditions in Transition*. Louisville: Westminster John Knox, 1989.

"The Word of God in the Life of the Church: A Report of International Conversations between the Catholic Church and the Baptist World Alliance, 2006–2010." *American Baptist Quarterly* 31, no. 1 (2012) 61.

Zizioulas, John. *Being as Communion: Studies in Personhood and the Church*. Contemporary Greek Theologians 4. Crestwood, NY: St. Vladimir's Seminary Press, 1985.

SECTION TWO

The Church and Tradition

Sola Scriptura, Tradition, and Catholicity in the Pattern of Theological Authority

Kevin J. Vanhoozer

> O Captain! my Captain! our fearful trip is done,
> The ship has weather'd every rack, the prize we sought is won
>
> —Walt Whitman

The above lines from Whitman's poem always come to mind each time I head to New York City for another round of Evangelical and Catholic Togetherness. Timothy George has for some years been the captain of the Good Ship Evangelical, and I have learned implicitly to trust his good judgment each time we set sail on a new dialogical doctrinal adventure. Each voyage—whether it be towards a common statement on justification by faith, or Mary, or the saints, etc.—has its share of challenges, navigation being chief among them. As a church historian, Captain George is well-acquainted with previous expeditions, especially those of the Reformers. He has studied the charts and is familiar with the rocks and shoals that have sunk others. Like his namesake Timothy, whom the apostle Paul commended for "holding faith," Captain George has not made shipwreck (1 Tim 1:19).

Some outside observers may nevertheless wonder whether George has gone off the theological rails, at least to some extent, given what they perceive to be his conflicted, even contradictory identity. He is a Baptist, and some in his own denomination wonder why he is also an Evangelical. He is an evangelical, and some of that tribe wonders why he has set his compass, *Touchstone*-style, towards Christian unity. A few may even wonder why, if he is an evangelical, he is interested in church history rather than the Bible!

In an essay for *Pro Ecclesia*, George identifies himself with three adjectives: "I find my theological bearings within the Reformed tradition . . . I am affiliated with the world evangelical movement . . . I am an ordained minister in the Southern Baptist Convention."[1] In other words, he is a Protestant, an evangelical, and a Baptist.

It gets worse. Despite Southern Baptists' tendency to be "notoriously suspicious of 'entangling alliances' with other denominational groups,"[2] George has at least on one occasion been named a "Bapto-Catholic."[3] That's what you get when you require an essay on the Apostles' Creed as part of the admissions process, to the Beeson Divinity School. Although George does not self-identify as "Bapto-Catholic," perhaps because the term has not caught on, he would no doubt embrace the epithet "evangelical Baptist catholicity," particularly when it describes those who hold to the supreme authority of Scripture and understand catholicity as a function of canonicity.[4] Writing in a confessional mode, George once said: "I learned how to 'think with the church,' with the body of Christ extending throughout time as well as space."[5] This is the hallmark of catholic Christianity.

I am no psychoanalyst, nor do I think that Timothy George suffers from inner conflicts that require theological therapy.[6] However, if Ludwig Wittgenstein was right in suggesting that philosophy—in particular, ordinary language analysis—is a kind of therapy that resolves the linguistic confusions speakers sometimes get themselves into, then those who perceive George's identity statements to be contradictory may themselves need therapy: conceptual therapy. My aim will therefore be to achieve clarity on the three descriptors (four, if we include "catholicity") George uses to articulate his theological identity. I shall argue that, far from being at war with one another, they actually belong together. Each of these terms—Protestant, evangelical, Baptist, and catholic comes into its own only when they qualify and are qualified by one another. I shall demonstrate this indirectly, namely, by arguing that church, tradition, and catholicity are perfectly compatible with one of the signature themes of the Reformation and defining marks of evangelical Baptists like Timothy George—*sola scriptura*— and therefore are essential ingredients in the Protestant pattern of theological authority.

1. George, "The Sacramentality of the Church," 310.
2. Ibid.
3. Jorgensen, "Bapto-Catholicism," 126n172.
4. As do Emerson and Stamps, "Baptists and the Catholicity of the Church." Catholicity here is a function of the church's reception of biblical authority and history of biblical interpretation.
5. George, "Why I Am an Evangelical and a Baptist," 101.
6. Ibid., 93

"PROTESTANT": PREMISES, PROBLEMS, AND PROSPECTS

The Bible, says Luther, is the manger where we find the baby Jesus—and the living Christ. We do well to remember that the high view of scripture that characterizes the Reformation, and the best of the evangelical tradition, is at the service of the subject matter of scripture. *Sola scriptura* is in the service of *solus Christus*. But it is not enough to have a high *view* of scripture; Christians must also know how to read and use the Bible rightly if they want to teach doctrine and make disciples: "Do your best to present yourself to God as one approved, a worker who has no need to be ashamed, rightly handling [*orthotomounta*] the word of truth" (2 Tim 2:15). Right opinion (orthodoxy) matters, to be sure, but so does "orthotemnology" (the study of right handling of scripture [from *ortho* + *tomeo* "to make a straight cut"]). *Sola scriptura* names both a theory *and* a practice. And, inasmuch as it is a practice, *sola scriptura* is inextricably linked to the community that handles it. A thick description of *sola scriptura* therefore obliges us to discuss the church, the priesthood of all believers that exists as the domain of God's Word. The church is a creature of God's triune Word, *sola scriptura* its confession of the Bible's constitutional authority.

Protestant Premises of Sola Scriptura: Five Theses on What the Bible is

The Bible's authority derives from its nature as holy: set apart by God for a divine purpose. First, the Bible is the word of God written in human words inspired by the Holy Spirit "who spoke through the prophets" (and apostles). God elected and set apart certain human authors to be the instruments through whom God communicated his word. God has commissioned just these human words to be the means by which he shares with us the knowledge he has of himself (cf. 1 Thess 2:13).

Second, in *authoring* the Bible God also *authorizes* it. The special office of scripture—to be the creaturely agent of God's special self communication—derives from its divine authorship. God has spoken. Would-be disciples (followers) cannot believe or behave (i.e., follow) any way they like, for there is a prior word that holds them accountable.

Third, the Bible is divine discourse fixed in writing: something God says about something to someone in some way for some purpose. Scripture is not simply a handbook of information, but a medium of divine action:

God can do many things with human words, including tell the truth, make promises, issue commands, and reveal the end of history.

Fourth, different types of discourse exercise authority in different ways over different domains. For example, the authority of "exalted prose" may work differently than that of law or history. What we read in Isaiah 55:11 is true "[my word] shall not return to me empty, but it shall accomplish that which I purpose, and shall succeed in the thing for which I sent it" yet we have to discern the intent and domain of particular biblical passages.

Fifth, the different forms of biblical discourse are all divinely authored and serve the same ultimate divine end (in particular, to communicate Christ to God's chosen people). In many and various ways, the Father commissions the human authors of scripture, prophets and apostles, to communicate his light and life, his Son and Spirit. In the eloquent words of J. I. Packer: the Bible is "God the Father preaching God the Son in the power of God the Holy Spirit."[7] This is the Word whose promise and demand constitute the Church as a creature of triune discourse.[8]

Protestant Problems with Sola Scriptura: Five Salvos

Despite its Reformation pedigree, or maybe because of it, *sola scriptura* has acquired a host of negative connotations. It's no exaggeration to say that, of all the *solas*, none has been more despised and rejected by men than *sola scriptura*. *Sola Scriptura* has been blamed for everything from secularism and pluralism to skepticism and individualism.

What follows is a list of five problems—five *salvos* against one *sola*—that any Protestant account of biblical authority must eventually address. I share some of the concerns, but I view them as flesh wounds only, not mortal weaknesses unless left untreated.

1. It is to blame for modern secularization, skepticism, and schism

   Probably the biggest critical blast, a 21-gun reproof, comes from Brad Gregory, author of *The Unintended Reformation*, a magisterial deconstruction of the magisterial Reformation.[9] Gregory's core complaint is that Luther, by rejecting the authority of church tradition, accidentally opened a Pandora's box, out of which flew the evil spirits of modernity: secularization, skepticism, and schism. These all derive, says Gregory, from the Reformers' insistence, directed against Rome, "not thine

---

7. Packer, *God Has Spoken*, 97.
8. See Vanhoozer, "Holy Scripture," 30–56.
9. Gregory, *The Unintended Reformation*.

interpretation but mine." In a word, the unintended consequence of the Reformation was that every individual now claimed independent authority to interpret scripture for him or herself, a sure recipe for turning the Bible into a Babel of competing claims.

2. It is modern

William Abraham worries that *sola scriptura* encourages using the Bible as an epistemic criterion, a canonical slide-rule as it were for distinguishing true from false beliefs, instead of using it to make us wise unto salvation or cultivate godliness.[10] On his view, *sola scriptura* makes what should be a house of prayer into a den of epistemologists—typical of modernity's concern for method and certain knowledge.

3. It is dangerous

Alister McGrath calls *sola scriptura* "Christianity's dangerous idea" because of its tendency to produce chaos rather than consensus. Once you locate authority in scripture rather than the church, and once you say that every church member has as much right to interpret the Bible for herself as another, how then can you regulate, much less stop, the proliferation of interpretations, he wonders, and what else should we call the uncontrolled division of opinions that spread through the body of Christ but *cancer*?

We do well to bear in mind Spinoza's sobering observation: "the chief concern of theologians on the whole has been to extort from Holy scripture their own arbitrarily invented ideas, for which they claim divine authority." This is indeed dangerous, even idolatrous to the extent that it exchanges the truth of God for a lie (Rom 1:25). Theologians especially have to remain vigilant not to conflate what "the Bible says" with what they want the Bible to say. The danger is real—and not for fundamentalists only.

4. It is self-defeating

The sociologist Christian Smith's book, *The Bible Made Impossible*, is an attack not on the Bible but on biblicism, a theory about biblical authority, about how the Bible is used to support moral and theological opinions.[11] His fundamental claim is that biblicism is self-defeating, collapsing in upon itself. The interaction of Luther's twin principles, *sola scriptura* and the priesthood of all believers, produce what we might call the second law of "hermodynamics": the hermeneutical en-

---

10. Abraham, *Canon and Criterion*.
11. Smith, *The Bible Made Impossible*.

tropy (interpretive disorder) of a theological system increases through interaction with other systems. As one Roman Catholic thinker puts it: "No honest religious historian can deny that the result of *sola scriptura* has been doctrinal chaos."[12] This, then, is the fundamental problem: that in protesting the authority of Rome and relocating authority to the scripture, the Reformers left themselves without a referee to settle interpretive disputes about what scripture means. Stated differently: biblicism gives rise to what Smith calls pervasive interpretive pluralism, namely, the situation of Bible-believing Christians disagreeing about what they believe the Bible to be saying.

5. It detracts from Christ

Finally, several critics raise the specter of *sola scriptura* functioning as an epistemic criterion in abstraction from—or worse, as a rival to—*solus Christus*. No one can serve two *solas* (cf. Matt 6:24). As I hope we shall see, however, "scripture alone" does not mean that the Bible functions as an authority *independently of Christ*. That would be an extreme version of going it alone indeed: *sola-ism* as solipsism!

These five salvos are formidable objections—at the very least, a public relations disaster. Wittenberg, we have a problem!

Prospects of Sola Scriptura

In spite of these formidable problems, I remain positive about the prospects of *sola scriptura* for the next 500 years, and this for three chief reasons: First, most if not all of the criticisms miss their target. They hit a straw *sola*, not what the Reformers were talking about. Everything depends on getting the definition right. *Sola scriptura* is shorthand for a principle of biblical authority, but the principle is *not* alone, for it is part of a pattern of authority, and is accompanied by a practice. Put it this way: *sola scriptura* is shorthand for a practice of theological authority by a particular kind of theological community (the church) in the context of a broader *pattern* of theological authority (the economy).

To mention the economy is to invoke the whole plan of revelation and redemption that unfolds in the history of Israel and culminates in the event of Jesus Christ. This is vital because, and this is my second reason for being positive, *sola scriptura* comes into its own when we remember its role in the economy of God's self-communication. *Sola scriptura* is not simply a formal

---

12. Rose, *The Protestant's Dilemma*, 87.

principle that the Reformers invented to resolve interpretive disputes; rather, scripture is part and parcel of the gospel message, one of the mighty acts of God, a set-apart means that the triune God employs to communicate his light and life.

Third, the gospel Paul delivered to the Corinthians was of "first importance." What matters is not only that Jesus died for our sins and was raised by God on the third day, but also that Jesus died for our sins and was raised on the third day *in accordance with the Scriptures* (1 Cor 15:3–4). What is of first importance is what accords with scripture. *Sola scriptura* means that scripture is "first and foremost" when it comes to authorizing statements about the God of the gospel and the gospel of God.

Sola Scriptura and Church Tradition: Exclusion or Exclamation?

What did the Reformers really mean by insisting on "scripture alone"?

THE DEFINITION

A picture of an individual interpreting the Bible for himself, without consulting any other authority holds modern critics captive. But wait: isn't that what the phrase means: Scripture *alone*? What is striking about this caricature of *sola scriptura* is its literalism. The words *sola scriptura*, literalistically interpreted, may indeed give rise to the thought that the Bible is the *only* authority for theology, but this is not the *literal* meaning of the phrase. The literal meaning is a function of what its authors meant by the phrase, and this in turn is a function of how they used it. To interpret *sola scriptura* as meaning "Scripture is the only authority a theologian may consult" is to rip the phrase out of its original context.

The Reformers never intended *sola scriptura* to exclude the use of secondary sources. If there is an exclusionary dimension, it pertains only to what is first and foremost as concerns authority (there can be only one "first"). Yet to say that scripture alone is the supreme or primary authority leaves open the possibility that there are other, secondary authorities. I therefore propose the following definition: "*Sola Scriptura* means that *only scripture, because it is God's inspired Word, is our inerrant, sufficient, and final authority for the church.*"[13]

---

13. Barrett, *God's Word Alone*, 10; emphasis his.

The Context

In Luther's late medieval context, the *solas* were indeed exclusionary. For example, *sola gratia* and *sola fide* deny the meritorious nature of good works, but they do not exclude the importance of human obedience. Similarly, *sola scriptura* denies the equal authority of church traditions as well as the claim that Rome has the authority to decide the rightness of biblical interpretations. *Sola scriptura* does not exclude church tradition as a theological resource altogether, however; rather, it seeks to put tradition in its rightful place.

It's true that Luther lost his temper when, in the heat of doctrinal disputation, Eck could not give him biblical reasons for his position, only quotations from church fathers. Appeal to tradition is no good unless it ultimately derives from scripture. Yet, though Luther believed that scripture is the final authority, and the only infallible authority, he did not believe in *nuda Scriptura*, namely, the idea that scripture is the one and only authority. This is why we have to speak not only of a principle but also of a *pattern* of authority.

The Purpose

Tradition has a legitimate place in the Protestant pattern of theological authority. It is therefore incumbent upon evangelicals to combat the misleading picture of *sola scriptura* as necessarily excluding tradition and, by extension, the church and the Holy Spirit.

1. *"Scripture alone to rule"*

   Luther's appeal to *sola scriptura* occurs in the context of arbitrating the conflict of theological interpretations: "by whose judgment is the question settled if the statements of the fathers are in conflict with one another? Scripture ought to deliver this judgment." This is the context in which to understand Luther's affirmation *solam scripturam regnare*: "Scripture alone to rule." Scripture is alone in its *magisterial* authority.

2. *"Scripture is its own interpreter"*

   Luther also describes scripture as its own interpreter. When accused of interpreting scripture according to his own ideological agenda, or "private spirit," he insisted that his only agenda was to interpret scripture by its *own* spirit. Luther believed that scripture's spirit was best discerned by the Spirit leading the whole church. The priesthood of all believers was not a license for epistemic egoism as much as a mandate for epistemic conscientiousness, that is, for acknowledging that other Christian believers have "the same natural desire for truth and the same general powers and capacities that I have."[14] The Reformation was not a charter for individuals to do what is hermeneutically right in their own eyes only.

3. *The importance (but not final authority) of interpretive communities*

The Reformers realized that not all interpreters or interpretive communities are created equal. In particular, they distinguished between communities that nurture a primary trust in their own authorized interpreters—whether this be the Roman Catholic magisterium or groups of Anabaptist Enthusiasts, on the one hand—and those who nurture a primary trust in scripture as its own best interpreter (and the Spirit's ability to mortify one's interpretive will to power). *Sola scriptura* is a warning to the former (interpretive communities can err) and an encouragement to the latter (interpretive communities can pass on the truth when illumined by the Holy Spirit to understand scripture). The Reformers, then, were far from despising church tradition. Indeed, they regularly appealed to the church fathers as secondary authorities *because they acknowledge the fathers as (often) faithful expositors of scripture*. *Sola scriptura* is best understood not as an exclusionary but exclamatory word: Scripture first! Scripture *above all other earthly powers and authorities!*

SOLA SCRIPTURA AND THE PROTESTANT PATTERN OF AUTHORITY

We have now briefly surveyed the contemporary objections to *sola scriptura* as well the reasons the Reformers had for emphasizing it in their own historical context. What began as a necessary corrective—an exclusionary gesture—is at root a positive exclamation: "the word of the Lord!" *Scripture alone constitutes God's authorized self-presentation in human words.*

The proper dogmatic location of the doctrine of scripture is in the triune God's economy of self-communication and communicative action oriented to communion: a fellowship of the reconciled. It follows that we must not separate scripture's formal authority from its material covenantal purpose, or the ecclesial context in which this purpose comes to fruition.

I sometimes wonder to what extent the criticisms of *sola scriptura* are protests against the concept of authority itself. People resent authority when

---

14. Zagzebski, *Epistemic Authority*, 55.

they think of it as an oppressive power that impinges on their freedom. Before we can truly appreciate the supreme authority of scripture, then, we have to clarify what authority is.

A Unique (and user-friendly) Authority

1. *Authority is rightful say-so, the power to commend belief and command obedience.*

   Who has more right to say-so, over a certain domain, than the author of that domain? As creator, God is author of all domains and thus has authority over all, as Paul says in Romans 13:1: "For there is no authority except from God, and those that exist have been instituted by God."

2. *The authority principle in Christianity is the say-so of the triune God.*

   The question is whether God has *expressed* his authority and, if so, where. *Sola scriptura* is the answer to the question concerning the locus of divine authority. That God speaks human words to human creatures, and that there is an authoritative word of the Lord to which God's people is accountable, is a central and conspicuous theme in scripture from Genesis onwards: "Speaking is not incidental to God, as if it were simply one more thing he happens to do. It is central to who he is, what he does, and how he relates to his creation."[15] Authority must be verbally expressed—*said*—because, apart from meaningful content, there is nothing else that holds persons accountable. God uses human words to say and do things with determinate content and force. God's promise to Israel via Moses is neither vague nor idle, but specific and sure: "I will bring you up out of the affliction of Egypt to the land of the Canaanites" (Exod 3:8). To the extent that scripture's meaning is unclear, its authority is short-circuited: the bugle that gives an indistinct sound cannot summon soldiers to battle (1 Cor 14:8).

3. *The speaking God is a writing God.*

   There are also intriguing indications in scripture that God cares about preserving his word in writing. I'm thinking, for example, of the injunction against adding to or taking away from the words God gave Israel, an injunction that occurs in both testaments (Deut 4:2; Rev 22:18–29). It's also interesting to note that one of the very few things that *happen* in Deuteronomy is that YHWH writes (Deut 4:13; 5:22;

---

15. Nafzger, "These Are Written," 67.

9:10; 10:4) and "Moses writes" (see Deut 31:9, 19). And what God does in writing is *covenant*.

A covenant is "a relationship established by an oath-bound commitment."[16] There can be no covenanting without communicative action: speech. Yes, God uses other things, like rainbows, to signify his covenant, but these signs must be accompanied by divine words for the covenant to have meaningful content and hence binding authority. Deuteronomy depicts God fixing his discourse, first, by writing words on stone (the tables of the Law to be deposited in the ark of the covenant) and second, by making provision for Moses' Torah to be preserved and read on a regular basis so that Israel will learn to fear YHWH (Deut 31:10–13). What we learn from Deuteronomy bears on *sola scriptura* in two ways: first, we learn that there is a set apart (i.e., holy) set of writings authorized by God; second, we learn that the purpose of these set-apart writings is to establish and administer covenant relations between God and his people.

4. *A user-friendly authority.*

We now see why the Bible's authority is unique, but why am I calling it user-friendly? It's user-friendly because its purpose is not to oppress but release us. The Old and New Testaments orient human freedom to the created order and the risen Christ, and hence to wise living and human flourishing in Christ. God's word has supreme authority because God is the sole author of all that is, visible and invisible, and this authoritative word *authorizes* us to live with others before God in ways that are *good* for us.

5. *A Unique Authority*

Here's my best attempt at saying what is unique about the Bible's authority: scripture alone is holy, set apart as supreme the church's authority, because God, its ultimate author, commissions just these texts to serve as permanent witnesses to his covenant of grace. Scripture is a divinely authorized creaturely medium through which the Lord, out of love and freedom, communicates his light (i.e., revelation, knowledge, truth) and life (i.e., redemption, fellowship, salvation) to us. Scripture is the means by which the risen Christ announces the gospel, administers his new creational kingdom, and imparts his light and life to readers made right-minded and right-hearted—fit for communion with God—through the illumination of the Holy Spirit.

---

16. Cf. Hugenberger, *Marriage as a Covenant*, 11.

A Truthful (infallible) Authority

How does this view of scripture as covenantal discourse bear on the earlier concern that *sola scriptura* reduces the Bible into an epistemic criterion with which to distinguish true from false doctrine? Must we, like Israel before crossing into the Promised Land, choose this day whom—or rather, what—we will serve: epistemology or soteriology?

The concern, as you may recall, is that *sola scriptura* encourages people to treat the Bible as a handbook of propositional truth with which to "prove" things by citing chapter and verse rather than appreciating, and participating in, the broader economy of redemption that those chapters and verses serve. The worry is that *sola scriptura* encourages interpretive pride, and prideful certainty.

I see *sola scriptura* rather differently, namely as a standing challenge to interpretive pride and prideful certainty. Scripture has meaning: what God said/did with human words (discourse) has been fixed by writing. Accordingly, as a past communicative act, its meaning is there, independent of the interpreter's language and thought. Scripture *alone* is authoritative, not our interpretation of it.

I'm not forgetting, much less contradicting, what Luther says about the clarity of Scripture. Laypeople don't need professional interpreters in the church or the academy to follow the basic plot of scripture: God makes world; God loses world; God wins world back. The basic story is clear, clear enough to evoke faith in its hero. That we don't follow the story, or the Master whose story it is, owes more to our ignorance, darkened minds, and hard hearts than any deficiency in the text. No, scripture is clear because it is the word of God, and God is the great communicator, whose law and testimonies are perfect (Ps 19:7).

As perfect, scripture has veridical authority: the authority of truth. In Revelation 21:5, Christ declares: "Write this down, for these words are trustworthy and true." Christ here associates truth with what can be relied on. Scripture *alone* can be relied upon ultimately, for Scripture *alone* is the utterly reliable personal word of the triune God. What God says goes. We can count on everything God says—promises, warnings, commands, and yes, statements—to accomplish the particular purpose for which they were written. The truth and trustworthiness of God's word are intimately connected with God's covenant faithfulness. Throughout the biblical narrative, God proves himself true, by time and time again keeping his word. Think of truth as covenantal correspondence: a faithful fit between God's words and God's deeds, between what scripture says and the way things are, between who God says he is and who he really is. True words communicate reality—what is, was, and will be—and they do so reliably.

As God is true, utterly reliable, so Jesus is the truth in person: the utterly reliable promise of God made good, and the exact representation of God being made flesh (Heb. 1:3). We can go further into what we might call the triune economy of truth: as the Son faithfully communicates who and what the Father is, so the Spirit speaking in the Scriptures inspires true and faithful testimony to who the Son is and what is "in Christ." Scripture is thus a vital ingredient in the economy of truth, the pattern by which the Father reliably represents himself through the Son and the Son reliably represents himself through the testimony of the Spirit. *Sola scriptura* is shorthand for Scripture's role in the economy of God's truth. This is the ultimate reason why scripture is the supreme authority in all matters concerning God and the gospel, the identity of Christ's person and the significance of his work. Scripture is the "canon" of Christ, the rule that tells us *what is in Christ*, thus enabling us to distinguish true or false testimony, sound or unsound doctrine. *Sola scriptura* means that Scripture alone is sufficient to teach us about Christ, and to do so authoritatively, especially when the Spirit of truth leads the church into all truth.

A SUPREME (BUT NOT SOLITARY) AUTHORITY

To describe scripture as the final court of appeal leaves open the possibility that there are lower courts. For example, here in the United States in addition to the Supreme Court there are also thirteen appellate courts, ninety-four district courts, and many more municipal courts. We might describe this as an economy of judicial authority. Something similar pertains to Scripture's role in what we could call the *economy of theological authority*.

1. The Economy of Authority

    The risen Christ makes a stunning claim: "All authority in heaven and on earth has been given to me" (Matt 28:18). There is *no limit* to the domain of dominical authority. At first glance, Christ's claim to exclusive and inclusive authority seems to contradict what we have said about the supreme authority of Scripture. Bernard Ramm states the problem: "The difficulties of a single principle of authority (rather than a pattern of authority) appear clearly in discussions of the authority of Jesus Christ. Frequently the authority of Christ and the authority of the Scriptures are opposed."[17] The way forward, as should by now

---

17. Ramm, *The Pattern of Religious Authority*, 46.

be clear, is to view biblical authority not as an isolated principle, but as an element in the larger economy of authority. Remember: the *sola* in *sola scriptura* means "only *final* or *supreme* authority," not "one and only source of authority."

All authority has been given to Jesus Christ, yet Christ did not count divine authority "a thing to be grasped" (Phil 2:6), but delegated it to others. Jesus commissions the apostles to preach (Mark 3:14) and "proclaim the kingdom of God" (Luke 9:2). He both appoints and *anoints* the apostles with the Holy Spirit, empowering them for their authoritative office, to be his witnesses (Acts 1:8). *The apostles are delegated authorities, commissioned witnesses of Jesus's person and work, inscribers of the meaning of the Christ event, whose written discourse is part and parcel of the word of God.*

There is therefore an economy—a divinely instituted plan or pattern—of authoritative testimony: God the Father makes himself known in and through Christ; Christ makes himself known to the apostles; the apostles make Christ known to the church. The Holy Spirit is involved at every stage as well, witnessing to Christ and empowering his witnesses. What about the church and church tradition: do these have a place in the economy of theological authority too, or does *sola scriptura* exclude them? May it never be! "Scripture alone" does not mean "Scripture apart from the community of faith" or "Scripture independent of church tradition." *Sola scriptura* excludes rivals, such as the teaching office of the church or man-made tradition, only when it's a question of *supreme* authority. *Sola* does not mean "so long": it does not eliminate other sources and resources of theology altogether. Once again, the challenge is to locate scripture in the broader pattern as the first-born, but not the only, child of theological authority. Once we understand this we can set forth a more positive account of the Scripture /Tradition relationship.

2. Magisterial and ministerial authority: the role of Tradition

    Scripture is the sole magisterial authority—it is both the canonical cradle of Christ and the scepter by which the ascended Christ now rules the church (Luther)–*but it does not play this role independently of the Holy Spirit or of the church's tradition and teaching ministry.* These have *ministerial* authority, like Abraham's servant "who had charge of all he had. . ." (Gen 24:2).

    Neither Luther nor Calvin advocated traditionless interpretation. It is vitally important not to confuse *sola* with "solo" scriptura. The problem with thinking that individuals interpret the Bible alone—that is, by and for themselves, in isolation from the church and tradition—is not only the lack of checks and balances on their readings, but the inevitable ensuing neglect of the gifts the Spirit has provided. In particular, "solo" scriptura—call it Tradition 0—denies the importance of catholic Christianity, that is, the importance of reading in communion with the saints. As Keith Mathison says: "Scripture itself indicates that the Scriptures are the possession of the Church and that the interpretation of the scripture belongs to the Church as a whole, as a community."[18] *Sola scriptura* comes into its own only when God's people read Scripture in God's way for God's purpose. That purpose, I suggest, is to serve as the instrument by which God rules his people, administers his covenant, and shapes the people into a holy nation. The church—including her tradition and her teachers—is the context in which the biblical text makes sense (thanks to the illumination of the Spirit) and exercises its authority. This is the Reformers' understanding of sola scriptura, in contrast to reduced versions of "scripture alone" that announce "No creed but the Bible," and then abstract Scripture the broader pattern of authority.

What God has therefore joined together—canonicity and catholicity—let no one (especially evangelical Baptists!) put asunder. This is an important point, so let me be perfectly clear: the Reformers objected to the church magisterium of their day not because it used Tradition as a resource, but because it narrowed catholicity to the institution centered at Rome. Luther and Calvin had no problem appealing to the church fathers as ministerial authorities. Think of Tradition as "the church's stance of abiding in and with apostolic teaching through time."[19] *Sola scriptura* is perfectly compatible with this notion, and with what we could call reformed catholicity, by which I mean catholicity governed first and foremost by canonicity. One important expression of Reformed catholicity was conciliarism: the use of fully representative church councils to make theological judgments about issues that threatened the integrity of the gospel and the unity of the church. John McNeill argues that conciliarism is the "constitutional principle" of "unitive Protestantism," or what I like to call "mere Protestant Christianity."[20]

3. Creeds, confessions, and the role of the Holy Spirit

---

18. Mathison, *The Shape of Sola Scriptura*, 245.
19. Allen and Swain, *Reformed Catholicity*, 34.
20. See McNeill, *Unitive Protestantism*, 89.

I mentioned previously that Luther and Calvin were very interested in patristic tradition because, as persons of epistemic conscientiousness, they realized that the fathers too were motivated by their desire to get Scripture right. Those who wish to be biblical do well to attend to those who have wrestled with the text before us, especially when they reached consensus on fundamental truths, such as they did at Nicaea with regard to the Trinity. I like Herman Bavinck's construal of tradition as "the method by which the Holy Spirit causes the truth of scripture to pass into the consciousness and life of the church."[21] *Sola scriptura* is the practice of attending to the Spirit speaking in the Scriptures and to those, equally attentive, who do the same.

It is a grievous mistake to think that *sola scriptura* entails either *nuda scriptura* or *nulla traditio* (Tradition 0). The biblical authors and Reformers rightly show disregard for merely human traditions because they lack divine authorization. When I speak of Tradition, though, I mean the postapostolic conversation about the meaning and implications of apostolic discourse, a conversation that the Spirit uses to guide the whole ("catholic") church into all truth. Tradition too is an element in the economy of grace that, like the church, exists to nurture the society of Jesus.

I see the products of Tradition—the Rule of Faith, creeds, and confessions—as sanctified instruments the Holy Spirit uses to lead the church into all truth, "effects of pedagogical grace."[22] Please don't misunderstand: everything we need to know about Jesus Christ for our salvation is in Scripture. Scripture is materially sufficient: its content needs no supplement. Tradition does not add new content to Scripture, not does Tradition have any independent capacity to communicate light.

Light is the operative term. God is light (1 John 1:5), Christ is the light of the world (John 8:12; 9:5), light from light, and Scripture is the appointed instrument through which the light of Christ shines—more light from light. God is light, yet interestingly enough he appointed lights in the expanse of heaven to give light upon the earth (Gen 1:15). The parallel between these lights and our subject is closer than you might first think. Genesis 1:16 says, "And God made *two* great lights—the greater light to rule the day and the lesser light to rule the night." Tradition is the lesser light: the moon to Scripture 's sun. What light the moon gives off is always and only a reflection of the sun, yet it is real light. Indeed, a full moon casts enough light for a pilgrim to find her way. . . So too with Tradition. Tradition has a derivative,

---

21. Bavinck, *Reformed Dogmatics* vol. 1, 494.
22. Allen and Swain, *Reformed Catholicity*, 45.

secondary, ministerial authority insofar as its creeds and confessions reflect the light that shines forth from the biblical text.

How do Scripture and Tradition relate in the Reformation pattern of authority where Scripture holds pride of place? Scripture is the *norma normans* (norming norm), the "unnormed norm." Tradition is a *norma normata*, a "normed norm." I've already said that Tradition has ministerial (as opposed to magisterial) authority. Let me now be more precise: tradition has *testimonial* authority. Tradition is corporate testimony to the meaning, significance, and implication of Scripture's teaching. Attending to this testimony—the doctrine of the Trinity, for example—means that individual interpreters do not have to start from scratch in order to reinvent the wheel of orthodoxy. It would be silly to neglect this testimony to the deeper implications of biblical teaching. The testimonial authority of Tradition nevertheless stands under the *judicial* authority of Scripture. Tradition resembles the Supreme Court, to the extent that the Justices' interpretations serve or minister the meaning of the Constitution (and as we know, we can't always count on their doing so!).

Interpreters often need help, like the Ethiopian eunuch who answered Philip's question, "Do you understand what you are reading," by saying, "How can I, unless someone guides me?" (Acts 8:30–31). Tradition at its best is our Philip. Scripture *alone* is the supreme authority, yet God in his grace decided that it is not good for scripture to be alone. He thus authorized tradition so that, when Scripture saw it, Scripture said, "This at last is norm of my norm and light of my light; she shall be called postapostolic testimony, because she was taken out of apostolic testimony."

Scripture alone authorizes, yet the Scripture that authorizes is not alone. Philip Schaff, in his book *The Principle of Protestantism*, saw the connection too: "Faith alone justifies, but produces at the same time good works as its necessary fruit; the word of God is the only fountain and norm of knowledge, but it flows forward in the church, and comes there continually to clearer and deeper consciousness."[23] Tradition on this view is nothing less than "the necessary, ever-deepening onward flow of the sense of scripture itself."[24]

---

23. Schaff, *The Principle of Protestantism*, 98.
24. Ibid., 225.

CONCLUSION: *SOLA SCRIPTURA*, CATHOLIC TRADITION, AND THE CHURCH TODAY

I trust that by now it is clear that, when we properly understand it as a vital ingredient in a broader economy of theological authority, *sola scriptura* does not fall prey to the problems I listed at the outset. Let me make three summary points in conclusion.

Scripture First in Authority (but not entirely alone in the pattern)

Sola scriptura is the declaration that scripture alone is of "first importance" for making wise unto salvation, developing doctrine, making disciples, and in general for knowing God and cultivating godliness. Scripture *alone* is the divinely authorized standard for measuring all attempts to present Christ, and to form Christ in us. And yet, "The Spirit who enables and sustains our reading of Holy Scripture *also provides a community to aid us* in our reading."[25]

Why Evangelical Baptists should Affirm Catholicity as well as Canonicity

There is therefore now no condemnation for those who whole-heartedly affirm both canonicity (the supreme authority of Scripture as a rule for Christian faith and life) and catholicity (the divinely appointed nurturing role of the church and church Tradition). The problem with the Roman Catholic Church is not that it is catholic but that it is Roman. It circles the wagons too narrowly or, to change the image, builds a fence around the term catholic, which means "universal." The Reformers cared about catholicity too, but they wanted it centered on the gospel, not Rome. For Reformation Christians, like evangelical Baptists, it is the Spirit speaking Christ in the Scriptures, in the context of the household of faith, that is the final authority in questions of interpretation. *Sola scriptura* is not a blank check individuals can cash in to fund their own idiosyncratic interpretations of the Bible. Interpretive egoists should not think they can bypass the pattern of theological authority. *Sola scriptura* includes the call to listen for the Spirit speaking in the history of the church's interpretation of Scripture.

Sola scriptura is both a confession of faith that God's word is infallible, and a confession of sin that our human interpretations are, by contrast,

---

25. Swain, *Trinity, Revelation, and Reading*, 100.

fallible. *Sola scriptura* is the admission that the church, and her tradition, is ultimately accountable to an authoritative word that is not her own. It is an acknowledgment that our primary responsibility as pastors and theologians is not to our denominational home team but to the whole scriptural witness to Jesus Christ. And yet, this confession, admission, and acknowledgment is not strictly speaking *alone*, for it is part of a broader pattern of theological authority, one that includes the church, her tradition, and her teachers as means the Holy Spirit uses to minister right understanding.

A *Singular* (not solitary) Authority

In sum: *sola scriptura* reminds us of the set-apart nature and function of the Bible and its role in the pattern of divine communication and authority. It is no contradiction to say both that Scripture is not alone in this economy and that it plays a singular role. *Sola* indicates not solitariness but *singularity*. *Only* Scripture provides the final say-so as to doctrine and discipleship, for only Scripture provides the final say-so concerning the person and work, the *who* and the *what,* the alpha and omega of Jesus Christ. If we confess Jesus as Lord, we must confess the canon as his scepter.

Far from needing therapy, Timothy George's complex self-description as a Protestant Baptist evangelical catholic captures the heart of what the Reformation was all about: preserving the supreme authority of scripture and the consensus or the Great Tradition of its interpretation in a Spirit-led church. George's "evangelical and Baptist" not a contradiction in terms. On the contrary, inasmuch as it signals both the supremacy of the gospel (apostolic canonicity) and its reception in a particular church tradition (apostolic catholicity), it is one of the many ways we can and must think of the future of Protestantism.

BIBLIOGRAPHY

Abraham, William J. *Canon and Criterion in Christian Theology: From the Fathers to Feminism.* Oxford: Oxford University Press, 1998.

Allen, Michael, and Scott Swain. *Reformed Catholicity: The Promise of Retrieval for Theology and Biblical Interpretation.* Grand Rapids: Baker Academic, 2015.

Barrett, Matthew. *God's Word Alone: The Authority of Scripture. What the Reformers Taught . . . and Why It Still Matters.* 5 Solas. Grand Rapids: Zondervan, 2016.

Bavinck, Herman. *Reformed Dogmatics.* Vol. 1, *Prolegomena.* Edited by John Bolt. Translated by John Vriend. Grand Rapids: Baker Academic, 2003.

Emerson, Matthew Y., and R. Lucas Stamps. "Baptists and the Catholicity of the Church: Toward an Evangelical Baptist Catholicity." *Journal of Baptist Studies* 7 (2015) 42–66.

George, Timothy. "The Sacramentality of the Church: An Evangelical Baptist Perspective." *Pro Ecclesia* 12, no. 3 (2003) 309–23.

———. "Why I Am an Evangelical and a Baptist." In *Why We Belong: Evangelical Unity and Denominational Diversity*, edited by Anthony L. Chute, Christopher W. Morgan, and Robert A. Peterson, 93–110. Wheaton, IL: Crossway, 2013.

Gregory, Brad S. *The Unintended Reformation: How a Religious Revolution Secularized Society.* Cambridge, MA: Belknap, 2012.

Harmon, Steven R. *Baptist Identity and the Ecumenical Future: Story, Tradition, and the Recovery of Community.* Waco, TX: Baylor University Press, 2016.

Hugenberger, George. *Marriage as a Covenant: A Study of Biblical Law and Ethics Governing Marriage Developed from the Perspective of Malachi.* Leiden: Brill, 1994.

Jorgensen, Cameron H. "Bapto-Catholicism: Recovering Tradition and Reconsidering the Baptist Identity." PhD diss., Baylor University, 2008.

Mathison, Keith A. *The Shape of Sola Scriptura.* Moscow, ID: Canon, 2001.

McNeill, John T. *Unitive Protestantism: The Ecumenical Spirit and its Persistent Expression.* Richmond, VA: Knox, 1964.

Nafzger, Peter H. *"These Are Written": Toward a Cruciform Theology of Scripture.* Eugene, OR: Pickwick, 2013.

Packer, J. I. *God Has Spoken: Revelation and the Bible.* Grand Rapids: Baker, 1979.

Ramm, Bernard. *The Pattern of Religious Authority.* Grand Rapids: Eerdmans, 1957.

Rose, Devin. *The Protestant's Dilemma: How the Reformation's Shocking Consequences Point to the Truth of Catholicism.* San Diego: Catholic Answers, 2014.

Schaff, Philip. *The Principle of Protestantism.* Translated by John W. Nevin. 1845. Repr., edited by Bard Thompson and George H. Bricker. Lancaster Series on the Mercersburg Theology 1. Eugene, OR: Wipf and Stock, 2004.

Smith, Christian. *The Bible Made Impossible: Why Biblicism Is Not a Truly Evangelical Reading of Scripture.* Grand Rapids: Brazos, 2011.

Swain, Scott R. *Trinity, Revelation, and Reading: A Theological Introduction to the Bible and Its Interpretation.* London: T. & T. Clark, 2011.

Vanhoozer, Kevin J. *Biblical Authority after Babel: Retrieving the Solas in the Spirit of Mere Protestant Christianity.* Grand Rapids: Brazos, 2016.

———. "Holy Scripture." In *Christian Dogmatics: Reformed Theology for the Church Catholic*, edited by Michael Allen and Scott R. Swain, 30–56. Grand Rapids: Baker Academic, 2016.

Zagzebski, Linda Trinkhaus. *Epistemic Authority: A Theory of Trust, Authority, and Autonomy in Belief.* Oxford: Oxford University Press, 2012.

Kingdom Living at Home and Abroad
The Godly Legacy of Two Church Mothers

Sefana Dan Laing

In a fairly recent *Christianity Today* article, Timothy George gave a testimony to the work of God in his life as he deliberated whether to begin a new stage in his academic career: should he go to Samford University and start a new seminary, or should he continue in his productive and satisfying career at Southern Seminary in Louisville, Kentucky?[1] In making this decision, he sought the Lord in the company of many other Christians with a legacy of influential ministry. These Christians could not advise him directly, though: while George was still part of the church on earth, the Christians about him that day formed part of "the church at rest." In true historian fashion, he sought an answer by considering from where, and through what, and by whom, God had brought him to the crossroads at which he found himself that day in Cave Hill Cemetery.

As he reflected on those who had been most influential in his life and spiritual development, several significant women came to mind. First, two great-aunts, Hattie Ann Nash and Mary Elizabeth George.[2] These women cared for him, took him to school, and equally importantly, to a church where he heard the gospel message and was saved. In addition to these two faithful women, George reflected on his mother's influence: Nancy Norman George was a devout Baptist and participated in the ladies prayer ministry at her church.[3] George appreciated his mother's love and guidance, despite the physical challenges (presented by her struggle with polio) of raising two children alone, as her husband was an alcoholic who eventually died in

1. George, "Pilgrim's Progress."
2. Ibid.
3. "An RRJ Interview," 135.

prison. George believes he received his call to evangelistic ministry through reading an article printed in a magazine his mother brought home from prayer meeting, *Royal Service*.[4] George also mentions as a godly influence his grandmother, Bessie Jane Hamil, with whom he spent summers, and who he accompanied to church.[5] This intergenerational group of the family's women had mothered him and tended to his well-being. Although they were not expertly equipped to educate him in the secular and the sacred (his two great-aunts were actually illiterate), they nevertheless lovingly and faithfully created the conditions for his academic and spiritual formation, by taking him to school and to church, encouraging him in his educational and spiritual pursuits, and offering a loving Christian home. They served as channels of God's blessing and revelation in George's life, gifts of God for which he is deeply grateful, remembering them each time he relates his testimony.

It wouldn't be the first time that faithful women guided a boy named Timothy toward the Lord. The apostle Paul mentored a protégé, Timothy, for whom he was a spiritual father, calling him, "my true child in the faith" (1 Tim 1:2; also 2 Tim 1:2). As an apprentice to Paul, Timothy regarded the apostle as a father figure, and Paul, for his part, wrote of Timothy that he had served in the missionary endeavor "as a son with his father" (Phil 2:22). But Timothy had godly influences in his life far in advance of meeting Paul. In 2 Tim 1: 5, Paul remembers Timothy's mother Eunice, a Jewish-Christian believer, and his grandmother Lois, whose godly faith had such a strong impact on the young man. Where was Timothy's father? The book of Acts explains that he was a gentile ("a Greek") and thus absent from Timothy's faith walk, though other scholars conjecture that he had already passed away and was no longer a part of Timothy's life by the time Paul came preaching to the city of Lystra (Acts 16).[6] Even so, Timothy seems to have been a man of high character, for he was highly esteemed in the congregation at Lystra and Iconium (Acts 16:2). His sterling reputation was a tribute to the women who had taught and nurtured Timothy in the faith.

These stories lead us to think about other women who invested themselves into the spiritual lives of brothers and sons and other family members, leaving the church a rich legacy of faith and a robust gospel harvest. Some of these family members memorialized their mothers and sisters, paying them tribute for their critically important influence on the family's spiritual vitality and character formation. The two writers examined here are

4. Ibid.
5. Ibid.
6. Longenecker, *The Acts of the Apostles*, 455.

the great Eastern theologian and mystic, Gregory of Nyssa (ca. 335–394), and the equally great Western churchman and theologian of sin and grace, Augustine of Hippo (354–430). By commemorating a sister, Macrina, and a mother, Monica, each man respectively paid homage to formative influences in his life. In their narrative descriptions of Christian character, conduct and life in community, each also portrays for us his theological vision of the Kingdom of God, consistent with each man's theological vision. These visions remain relevant for us, despite a remove of sixteen centuries.

Within these cosmological and eschatological visions, two overriding and interrelated themes emerge: goodness and harmony. These themes express the connection of the beloved family member to God, who is Goodness itself. Although God's goodness cannot be contained in matter, it can be "*reflected* in material things."[7] This quality may be called "*derived* goodness," and both Gregory and Augustine reference it very intentionally. Each man refers to the goodness of God in giving gifts, recognizes and describes those gifts mediated through his subject, and intentionally attributes these gifts to their true Source, with praise and thanksgiving. God's goodness, moreover, is manifested in harmonious order, a subset of goodness. Therefore, as Slater explains, "harmonizing goodness" is an "expression of the divine will."[8] Harmony and order within the individual soul as well as outwardly in a community characterize the Kingdom of God, which Gregory calls the "life of the angels," and Augustine describes as the only perfect state, namely life in the City of God. Whoever lives in spiritual and communal harmony, driven ever more fervently by love to move toward the Source of Goodness Himself is already in some sense living a Kingdom life even here below. For that person, the yearning for the Lord's will "on earth as it is in heaven" is fulfilled. In this essay, we will examine how each woman reflected God's "harmonizing goodness" within her own context, whether at home, in a domestic setting, or abroad, in the constant flux of pilgrimage, restlessly seeking the stability of a city.

MACRINA: LIVING A KINGDOM LIFE IN A DOMESTIC SETTING

Devoted Daughter and Big Sister

After the peace of the church in AD 312, martyrdom was no longer a viable means of discipleship and spiritual refinement, so many devout men,

---

7. Slater, "Goodness as Order and Harmony in Augustine," 152.
8. Ibid.

women, and even teenagers began to practice an ascetic lifestyle. Sometimes they undertook this *askesis* (training) in seclusion, withdrawing to an isolated desert place, or in any case, away from urban areas so they could practice their faith in solitude (eremitism) or like-minded community (coenobitism) undisturbed. This was not the only brand of asceticism around, however. It was not at all unusual (especially for females who had less social and geographical mobility) to remain in one's own city or household, and to incorporate ascetic practices such as prayer, fasting, worship, scripture reading, and acts of service into one's daily routine. These ascetic activities were seen as an enthusiastic pursuit of mature discipleship, and an attempt to live out the legacy of the martyrs, for by the 4th century (even earlier, for example in Clement of Alexandria), the ascetic life was termed a "bloodless martyrdom."[9]

Macrina was born around AD 327, the eldest daughter of Basil (Sr.) and Emmelia, into an aristocratic Cappadocian family at Annisa. Theirs was a Christian household, one which was renowned not only for its staunch Christian convictions but also for its wealth; in fact, their family had suffered loss of life and property in the Diocletianic persecution (or earlier).[10] Macrina was the eldest of 9 (possibly 10) children. At the age of 12, Macrina's parents arranged a marriage for her, but her fiancé died before their marriage. Upon his death, Macrina vowed not to marry anyone at all, insisting that the young man was not fully dead, but rather "was 'living in God' through hope of the resurrection."[11] When their father passed away, Macrina served as a second mother to Gregory and his siblings (perhaps with the exception of the arrogant second-born Basil), since Emmelia was burdened with administration of the family's properties—extending over several provinces—as well as ensuring good marriages for her children. Gregory writes that Macrina "shared with her mother full responsibility in running the household," and was "partner of her mother's labors."[12] Little Peter, the youngest child, was born the year his father died. Macrina took him from his nurse/nanny, and cared for him herself, becoming "everything for the little boy: father, teacher, tutor, mother, counselor in all that was good."[13] Macrina further became a "mother" to several young girls whom she rescued from destitution during a famine, taking them into her

---

9. Bowersock, *Martyrdom and Rome*, 67.
10. Gregory of Nyssa, *Life of Macrina* 20 (trans. Peterson, 67).
11. Ibid., 5 (trans. Peterson, 55).
12. Ibid. (trans. Peterson, 55–56).
13. Ibid., 12 (trans. Peterson, 61).

domestic monastery. Upon Macrina's death, these girls wept bitterly, "calling her nurse and mother."[14]

The brief, rich hagiographical account by Gregory relates his experience of Macrina's final days in about the year 379. The narrative of his letter describes Gregory's grief at the recent loss of their brother, Basil, as the reason for his desire to visit his sister, whom he had not seen for about 8 years. Upon reaching her monastery, he quickly realized that she herself was gravely ill, and a few days later, Macrina took to her (death) bed. Despite her weakened condition, Macrina was positively philosophical about death, and for her strength of character and theological acumen, she is sometimes known as "the fourth Cappadocian." Instead of bemoaning her plight, she expounded to Gregory on the soul and the resurrection, most likely the basis of a later dialogue composed by Gregory on the *Soul and the Resurrection*.[15] She began, at some point, to speak in penitent prayer to God and to no one else, until she "ended her life and her prayers at the same moment."[16]

Macrina's Community: A Little Lower Than the Angels

Harmony

A striking image used by Gregory—and indeed by many ascetic writers—to describe life in monastic communities was the "angelic life." This image relates to the theme of harmony because this life is one lived in concord on multiple levels: spiritual/ theological, personal, communal, and global. What is the "life of the angels?" References to "the angelic life" abound in ascetic literature, but it is not described at length. From comments in various sources, we can gather several ideas about its nature. Patristic writers often began with reflection upon the nature of angels in order to elucidate the nature of life in God's kingdom. Angels are rational but incorporeal creatures, therefore they are devoid of passions, and are in complete harmony with God, perfectly submitted to His will and attuned to God's kingdom and priorities. They are unconcerned with corporeal matters, as Jesus indicated in Matthew 22:30 when he taught that in the resurrection there will no longer be marriage; rather people "are like angels in heaven." As Evagrius of Pontus taught, "By true prayer, a monk becomes (the equal of) an angel, for he

---

14. Ibid., 26 (trans. Peterson, 73).
15. Ibid., 18 (trans. Peterson, 65–66).
16. Ibid., 25 (trans. Peterson, 72).

ardently longs to see the face of the Father in heaven."[17] He also admonished his disciples who are learning to pray, ". . .banish the things of this world. Have heaven as your homeland and live there constantly—not in mere word but in actions that imitate the angels and in a more god-like knowledge."[18] Monks and other ascetics desired God Himself and the beatific vision as the goal of their spiritual practice.

Humans, like angels, are rational but corporeal. They have a rational soul, capable of freely making good decisions. At the beginning of the creation, humans were at one with the angels, or as Gregory of Nyssa writes, humans had sung in harmony with the heavenly chorus, and had "danced along with the angelic powers."[19] However, because of sin, humans are now subject to disordering passions which act on the body and spoil that spiritual harmony; their souls then struggle to bring the passions into order. Through ascetic practice (*askesis*), humans may, to some degree, participate in God's goodness, the goodness for which they long, for God Himself is the ultimate Good. Humans will never perfectly conform to God's will until the final restoration of all things (*apokatastasis*) when God will bring all things into alignment with Himself, as He will be "all in all" (1 Cor 15:28). Nonetheless even in this life, through the virtue produced in the soul by ascetic practice, humans may grow by progressive degrees into harmony with the life of the angels. By worship, prayer, fasting and contemplation, and especially by the chanting of the Psalms, they bring the passions into order and are at peace and in harmony within themselves, a harmony which is outwardly evident and extends further out towards the community in acts of loving service.[20] This "angelic life" attuned to God is characterized not only by rational contemplation, but also by sacrificial love and service to others.[21] In fact, as many ascetic masters of the Egyptian and Syrian deserts indicate, ardent love for God was the goal of all ascetic practice, for *agape* is the ultimate unifying and harmonizing force.[22]

17. Evagrius of Pontus, *Chapters on Prayer* 113 (trans. Bamberger, 74).

18. Ibid. (trans. Bamberger, 78).

19. Gregory of Nyssa, *Commentary on the Inscriptions of the Psalms*, 75.

20. On this idea, Athanasius is also in agreement, in lilting and instructive passages from his *Letter to Marcellinus*. The musical harmony in the singing of the Psalms brings into spiritual harmony the disordered movements in a person's soul, bringing the person into harmony with himself, so that he truly knows himself rather than being self-alienated. This kind of spiritual harmony produced by chanting the Psalms produces "calmness and tranquility" of the soul, conforming the bodily members to the dictates of the reasoning faculty. (Athanasius, *Letter to Marcellinus*, in Charles Kannengiesser ed., *Early Christian Spirituality*, 73).

21. Evagrius, *Chapters on Prayer* 39 (trans. Bamberger, 61n26).

22. Chryssavgis, *In the Heart of the Desert,* 103–8; Theodoret, "Epilogue on Love" in

Macrina's life is characterized by harmony in multiple ways. From the beginning of the account, Gregory describes Macrina as cosmically beautiful at the marriageable age of 12: while artists boldly paint grand objects like the "sun and planets themselves," they were "unable to represent accurately the harmonious beauty of her form."[23] Before the formation of her extended community, while Macrina was growing up with her mother, there was a harmonious relationship between them, in which the "mother cared for her daughter's soul, and the daughter, her mother's body," resulting in a "fruitful exchange."[24] In a movingly symmetrical account, Gregory describes his sister as luminously beautiful, equally in death as in life. The "beauty and the holiness of her character" shone radiantly even as she lay prone, and "her beautiful form seemed to throw out rays of light."[25] Her beauty is proportionate (harmonious, *harmostheisa*) to the beauty of the divinely-created cosmos, and reflects the beauty of God.[26] When she is reposed in death, her entire body is in good order and proper proportion, eyes closed, hands folded, so that "no hand was needed to lay it out" (*kosmounton*).[27] She has finally attained to a state of perfection—short of the resurrection—for as Ramelli explains, "harmony implies unity, and unity perfection."[28]

Macrina's religious community is described in sublime terms as "in harmony with the angels."[29] There was a harmony of care and reciprocity, equality of status and of relating to one another as sisters through the obliteration of rank based on wealth and social class, and there was regularity and balance of manual labor and worship. Gregory describes the community in terms of the angelic life, indicating that although they lived corporeally, it was as though they had completely subdued the bodily passions and no longer bore the burden of material concern. "Just as souls, when released from bodies by death, are at the same time freed from the cares of this life, so was their life similarly liberated. It was lived apart from all worldly trivialities and was brought into harmony with the life of the angels."[30] All passions in them had been quelled, and they desired only self-control, pov-

---

A History of the Monks of Syria, 190–207. Also see Ramelli, "Harmony between *Arkhe* and *Telos*," 9–10.

23. Gregory of Nyssa, *Life of Macrina* 4 (trans. Peterson, 54).
24. Ibid., 5 (trans. Peterson, 55).
25. Ibid., 32 (trans. Peterson, 77).
26. Nicomachus the Pythagorean, *The Manual of Harmonics*.
27. Gregory, *Life of Macrina*, 25 (trans. Peterson, 72).
28. Ramelli, "Harmony between *Arkhe* and *Telos*," 13.
29. Gregory, *Life of Macrina* 11 (trans. Peterson, 60).
30. Ibid. (trans. Peterson, 59–60).

erty, and obscurity (the exact opposite of worldly desires), "having shaken offall material superfluity from their bodies as though it were dust."[31] Their work was Kingdom work, not about the things of "this life" but about "the things of God, prayer without ceasing, and the uninterrupted chanting of the Psalms," day and night.[32] This community of sisters and worshippers hovered between heaven and earth in their way of life, "bounded by both human and incorporeal nature. . .On the one hand, the liberation of their nature from human passions was something which made them superhuman; on the other, their appearance in a body. . .made them into beings lower than those whose nature is angelic and incorporeal. . .their life was elevated above the earth, and they walked on high with the heavenly beings."[33] Gregory thus describes communal life at Annisa as a long-term progress in virtue by successive degrees, adding that they "advanced ceaselessly towards greater purity with the help of the good gifts which they had discovered."[34] These "gifts," i.e., spiritual and moral virtues, derive from God, and are not innate, but rather develop over "a long time," allowing life transformation and gradual growth in virtue until death allows entry into the beatific vision and eternal life in God.[35] In fact, by the time Macrina's life was ebbing seriously, Gregory says it was as if she had actually ceased being a human and was more like an angel than a human being; she had transcended her human nature;[36] her room was a "holy place," her words and her teaching lifted him into "the inner sanctuary of heaven," as she spoke of "the future life," guiding his ascent and speaking with the power of the Holy Spirit.[37] These descriptions manifest the full fruits of asceticism, as well as the force which drives Macrina's ascetic practice, namely, a fervent love for her "unseen Bridegroom" toward whom she hastened.[38]

Finally, at the end of Macrina's holy life, Gregory relates a further—quite literal—harmoniousness, her funereal bier was accompanied by the harmonies of the church through the singing of the men and women of her community. This harmony "proper and fitting" was only broken by the passion of grief, requiring Gregory once again to bring the singers back into

---

31. Ibid.
32. Ibid.
33. Ibid.
34. Ibid.
35. Ibid. (trans. Peterson, 63).
36. Ibid., 22 (trans. Peterson, 69).
37. Ibid., 17 (trans. Peterson, 65).
38. Ibid., 22 (trans. Peterson, 70).

harmony with one another.[39] "Indiscipline and confusion broke out" at the grave, he relates, "which destroyed the good order and sacred character of the chanting."[40] As the presiding cleric, Gregory divided the monastic community into two choirs, organizing them by gender so that the women and men sang antiphonally, and thereby some balanced order was restored.[41]

God's Good Gifts: Tois Theiois Agathois

Divine harmony experienced even in this life is both a gift of God and a conduit of God's gifts in the world. Macrina had an acute and deep-seated sense of this fact, and always saw the goodness of God in her circumstances, even His gifts in the vicissitudes of life, which sometimes overtake us or the tragedies, which overwhelm us. Goodness is God Himself, through whose grace that goodness is shared as gift. God had gifted their family two generations prior with wealth and abundance, and the family had a reputation for generosity and philanthropic activity. Although they experienced privations of property, God restored their wealth and they continued to serve as a conduit of blessing to the surrounding community in times of hardship. For example, during a food-shortage in 368/9, Gregory reports, under his brother Peter's administration, the family fed so many people that the crowds "made the desert look like a city."[42]

God's gifts of natural manual ability were imparted to Macrina, who used them to serve their mother;[43] to her brother Naucratius, who used them to serve a community of elderly men who were "living together in poverty and ill-health"[44]; and to their brother Peter, who used his gifts to serve and oversee the monastic men's community.[45] Macrina herself (not surprisingly) turns out to be a great gift of God to her family and community: she was a gift to her mother whose physical and spiritual needs she tended, comforting her in the debilitating loss of her son, Naucratius, and teaching her to rejoice "in the goodness she could see";[46] and to her brothers, Gregory, who called her his "Teacher," and to Basil whose pride in his own natural ability (in rhetoric) she had deflated, turning him rather toward

---

39. Ibid., 33 (trans. Peterson, 78).
40. Ibid. (trans. Peterson, 79).
41. Ibid. (trans. Peterson, 78).
42. Ibid. (trans. Peterson, 61).
43. Ibid., 20 (trans. Peterson, 55, 68).
44. Ibid. (trans. Peterson, 57).
45. Ibid. (trans. Peterson, 61).
46. Ibid. (trans. Peterson, 59).

"the true philosophy." She was a gift to the community of women whom she saved from destitution and homelessness at the time of the famine;[47] and to her youngest brother, Peter, who she nursed from birth, becoming his mother, nurse, teacher, spiritual trainer, and role model in goodness.[48] Macrina drew all of these people into a community striving toward "the goal of the angelic life."

She also recognized that God's goodness extended out globally in ministry to the church. In response to the dejected Gregory who had complained to his big sister about his harassment by Arian bishops, his persecution and exile by Valens the Arian emperor, and his unpleasant assignments to resolve various church disputes, Macrina upbraided him: "Will you not give up your hardheartedness towards God's good gifts?"[49] She reminded him that he was a "celebrated man," a bishop whom the churches entrusted to "bring help and achieve reform."[50] She considered his reputation a great grace and blessing, and scolding Gregory, she reminded him that he had these privileges ("goods," *agathon*) due to "the prayers of your parents. . .when you yourself have little or no predisposition for such things."[51] Basil became the bishop of Caesarea, a celebrated man himself, "the glory common to all our family" and "a man of importance among the saints,"[52] and through Macrina's training, Peter later became bishop of Sebaste, ordained by Basil himself. Gregory remarks that Peter became no less respected and renowned a bishop than Basil.[53]

For all the goodness she poured into others' lives, God poured out His goodness on her in another way: miracles. Some of these were for her own healing, such as when a cancerous lump in her breast was healed upon prayer and signing the spot with the cross; while other miracles were intended by God's grace through Macrina to treat others. Gregory states that there were many more miracles which helped visitors seeking out his sister, for cures, exorcisms, or prophecies (common characteristics of desert ascetics), but he refrained from recording them all because of doubters, and "those who have little faith in the gifts of God," and who may be punished for their unbelief.[54]

---

47. Ibid., 26 (trans. Peterson, 73).
48. Ibid., 12 (trans. Peterson, 61).
49. Ibid., 21 (trans. Peterson, 68).
50. Ibid.
51. Ibid., 21 (trans. Peterson, 68–69).
52. Ibid., 14 (trans. Peterson, 62).
53. Ibid., 12 (trans. Peterson, 61).
54. Ibid. 39 (trans. Peterson, 82).

As Macrina proved to be a gift to her family, we find that Monica is presented/ remembered in much the same way by her son Augustine. In contrast to Gregory's descriptions, though, Augustine is much more emphatic that his mother was not a saint in and of herself. Whereas Gregory associates his sister with saints and martyrs, and even goes so far as to say that at one point it was as if Macrina had been completely replaced by an angel, Augustine associates his mother with Eve, a mortal prone to sin.[55] Monica is no less a gift though, because Augustine paints himself a very great sinner with respect to his mother. Both of them are imperfect pilgrims, journeying to the New Jerusalem, but they only gradually leave "Babylon" (i.e., this life with its worldly priorities). While Monica was growing in faith and had "escaped from the centre of Babylon" before him, she still "loitered in its outskirts," a reference to her motherly ambitions for her gifted child's career advancement.[56] Still, she is ahead of him and has some distinct advantages of character and spirituality, while Augustine is mired in his pride and ambition and lust, and bogged down in his surfeit of knowledge, through which he justified his vices. Nevertheless, Monica will not go without him, pleading and weeping to God for Augustine's salvation, as Augustine describes graphically and somewhat melodramatically, "Night and day my mother poured out her tears to you and offered her heart-blood in sacrifice for me"; and so they journey together, spiritually and literally.[57]

MONICA: LIVING A KINGDOM LIFE ABROAD

Prayer Warrior or Helicopter Parent?

Monica was born around 331 and grew up in a Christian household in Thagaste, North Africa. She was taught and disciplined by an elderly family servant, who trained her in modesty, obedience, and temperance. About the age of 12, her parents married her to an unbeliever, Patricius (Patrick), who was about a decade her senior. There is no mention of her education, so it may be assumed that she was taught the skills of a proper matron who managed a household, rather than given any formal education. It is not even certain if she was literate. She proved to be a good, submissive wife, who knew how to deal with her hot-tempered and sometimes unfaithful husband. These personal qualities, along with patience and a peaceable nature, kept

---

55. Augustine, *Confessions* 5.8, 5.9 (trans. Pine-Coffin, 101, 102).

56. Ibid., 2.3 (trans. Pine-Coffin, 36).

57 Ibid., 5.7 (trans. Pine-Coffin, 99).

her safe from any husbandly abuse—which seems to have been disturbingly common at the time—and also garnered favor with her mother-in-law.

Monica proved to be a strong personality and an ambitious mother, investing herself in Augustine's education and career. She also took the lead over her husband in advising Augustine on moral and spiritual matters, so that it appeared she wanted God, not Patricius, to be his father.[58] Her husband eventually converted in 370, when Monica was 39 or 40, but he died the following year, when Augustine was about 16 or 17.[59] After Patricius's death, Monica continued to fund her son's education in law and rhetoric, and lived the life of a virtuous widow, as described in 1 Timothy 5. She apparently broke table fellowship with Augustine and may have even banned her son from the house because of his involvement in the heretical cult of the Manichees.[60] He may have also embarrassed her in the eyes of the church, gaining himself a reputation as a troublemaker. Monica had asked a bishop to speak with Augustine about his heretical beliefs, but the bishop refused because Augustine had been very vocal about his new ideas, and in his ardor as a Manichaean devotee, he had spread his doctrines, confusing and misleading simpler Christians.[61] This attempt at spiritual intervention was just the beginning of her life-long pursuit of her son's spiritual well-being.

Around 383, Augustine left Carthage to take a position in Rome as a professor of rhetoric and logic. Monica tried to dissuade him, wishing to keep him closer to home, and she followed him to the harbor, pleading with him to remain or take her with him.[62] He deceived her, though, and left secretly by night without her. Augustine later remembered this incident with great emotional agony, since he had lied to his own mother—"and to such a mother, too!—yet he saw with hindsight that God had orchestrated matters so that he moved from Monica's tears on the Carthaginian shore, safely through the waters of the Mediterranean to Rome, and eventually to be reborn in the waters of holy baptism in Milan under the godly influence of his spiritual father, Ambrose.[63] Two years later (AD 385), Monica joined her son in Milan, having heard about Ambrose's influence on him, and impressed that the bishop had shaken her son's Manichaean certainties.[64] Monica followed him there with the sure knowledge that God would bring

58. Ibid., 1.11 (trans. Pine-Coffin, 32).
59. Ibid., 3.4 (trans. Pine-Coffin, 59).
60. Ibid., 3.11 (trans. Pine-Coffin, 68).
61. Ibid., 3.12 (trans. Pine-Coffin, 69).
62. Ibid., 5.8 (trans. Pine-Coffin, 100–101).
63. Ibid.
64. Ibid., 6.1 (trans. Pine-Coffin, 111–12).

about his conversion. This sense of certainty upheld Monica on the sea voyage to Italy, and Augustine relates a delightful story, which highlighted this woman's stalwart faith and strength of character, strongly reminiscent of Paul in Acts 27 and 28 relating the shipwreck and marooning on the island of Malta. He asserts, "her piety had given her strength to follow me over land and sea, facing all perils in the sure faith she had in you. When the ship was in danger, it was she who put heart into the crew, the very men to whom passengers unused to the sea turn for reassurance when they are alarmed. She promised them that they would make the land in safety, because you had given her this promise in a vision."[65]

Monica's confidence in God's plans for her son also led her to begin arrangements for a suitable wife. Even though her immediate plans had not materialized as she had hoped, God used that situation to fulfil her highest hopes for Augustine. She sent away Augustine's African concubine and contracted a respectable match for her son; but his fiancé was underage, and Augustine was impatient for marriage (or rather for consummation), so he took another concubine. While Monica continued making plans for a wedding and entertained hopes for more grandchildren, Augustine was reaching a crisis point on his spiritual journey. The next year (386), he converted fully to a celibate Christianity, and all talk of marriage and grandchildren melted away in the happiness of his mother's fondest and deepest hope fulfilled. Monica spent several happy months with two of her sons at Cassiciacum, a small town in the Milanese countryside. Augustine, his son, and several other catechumens, lived there in community as they awaited baptism the following year under the hand of Ambrose, at Easter in Milan. After their baptism, Monica prepared to journey back to Africa with the entire group, presumably to re-settle at Thagaste while Augustine determined the best course of service to the church. While in Rome at the port of Ostia, waiting for their ship homeward, Monica fell ill, developed a high fever, and within a few days she went to her eternal home with God in the autumn of 387 at the age of 56. In her final moment of death, Augustine writes "her pious and devoted soul was set free from the body."[66] She died peacefully, gracefully, and courageously.

---

65. Ibid. (trans. Pine-Coffin, 111).
66. Ibid., 9.11 (trans. Pine-Coffin, 200).

Mother on the Move: Pilgrimage toward the Celestial City

God's Good Gifts: Loving God in Others

As Augustine remembers his mother, he considers all that she meant to him and to his community of friends, offering what could be termed an extended eulogy in the form of a *vita* in Book 9 of his *Confessions*. Yet he does not praise Monica for all her attributes directly, as if they were innate and stemmed from her; rather the gifts she possessed (her virtues and good qualities) were *derived* goods, manifestations of God, and the great gift-giver. God is the ultimate source of Goodness, as He is Goodness itself. In fact, Augustine asks, ". . .if any man makes a list of his deserts, what would it be but a list of Your gifts?"[67] As Monica was attuned to God and loved God, she became to Augustine both a channel of blessing and an example of Christian virtue. He recognized that he—on the contrary—fell woefully short of her many virtues, since he had turned away from the source of Goodness and toward himself, finding "only pain, confusion, and error."[68] Upon Monica's death, he writes, "I will omit not a word that my mind can bring to birth, concerning your servant, my mother. In the flesh she brought me to birth in this world: in her heart she brought me to birth in your eternal light. It is not of *her gifts* that I shall speak, but of *the gifts you gave to her*. For she was neither her own maker, nor her own teacher"; rather, he continues, Christ was her teacher.[69] It was therefore proper for Augustine to thank God and love God as the source of goodness in which Monica participated.

Augustine praises her characteristic obedience: to her parents, God, and her husband.[70] She respected Ambrose and regarded him "as God's angel," drinking in his teaching and obeying his admonitions concerning the proper, church-sanctioned celebration of martyrs' feast days.[71] For her "pious submission" and "regular churchgoing," Ambrose warmed to her equally. He commended her "zealous good works," praised her to Augustine, and congratulated him on "having such a mother."[72] Her other virtues included modesty, temperance, patience, consistent efforts to evangelize her husband, and a concomitant faith in God for his conversion. As Augustine

---

67. Ibid., 9.13 (trans. Pine-Coffin, 203).
68. Ibid., 1.20 (trans. Pine-Coffin, 40–41).
69. Ibid., 9.8 (trans. Pine-Coffin, 192).
70. Ibid., 9.9 (trans. Pine-Coffin, 194).
71. Ibid., 6.1, 6.2 (trans. Pine-Coffin, 112).
72. Ibid., 6.2 (trans. Pine-Coffin, 113).

notes, God in fact spoke both to him and to his father, through Monica's admonitions against fornication and adultery to the teen-aged Augustine, and through her forgiveness and encouragements to a life in God to Patricius. Her virtues served as "so many voices constantly speaking to him of you," channeling God's grace and compassion in His search for the lost.[73]

She gave the gift of spiritual motherhood to both Augustine and his newly converted friends. Augustine writes of her during the months at Cassiciacum, "She had the weak body of a woman, but the strong faith of a man, the composure of her years, and the devotion of a Christian."[74] Nevertheless, Monica is only indirectly praised, as praise is properly due only to the Supreme Good: "Those who knew her praised You, honored You, and *loved You in her*, for they could feel your presence in her heart and her holy conversation gave rich proof of it."[75] In reflecting God's nature, Monica displayed other gifts like a conciliatory nature, earthly detachment, and experienced divine visions, helping create harmonious conditions in her family, as we shall see below.

Harmony: The Fruit of Goodness

Augustine enjoyed thinking about beauty and harmony, and in fact in his younger pre-conversion years, he had composed a book (which he lost) entitled "On the Beautiful and the Harmonious," or "On Beauty and Proportion."[76] Later, during his post-conversion retreat to Cassiciacum in 387, Augustine wrote a treatise on music (*De Musica*) which dealt in more detail with the value of music as an integral part of the liberal arts, its effect on the passions via rhythm, and its value for understanding the nature of spiritual realities.[77] Much later, in his sweeping opus, *City of God*, Augustine describes progressive aspects of the harmony and
concord which obtain in the Celestial City, evoking an eschatological state much like Gregory's descriptions of a state of harmony and unity of creaturely willing directed exclusively toward God, the Supreme Good.

In Augustine's understanding, all material things are metaphysically ordered in a hierarchy of being, and derive their existence from God as their source.[78] Further, all beautiful things must be admired, desired, and

---

73. Ibid., 9.9 (trans. Pine-Coffin, 194).
74. Ibid., 9.4 (trans. Pine-Coffin, 186).
75. Ibid., 9.9 (trans. Pine-Coffin, 196).
76. Ibid., 4.13 (trans. Pine-Coffin, 83).
77. Deusen, "De Musica," 574–76.
78. Slater, "Goodness as Order and Harmony in Augustine," 155.

loved *in* God. They must not replace God in our hearts as objects of our love; rather, our love must be continually oriented toward God/ The Good.[79] Perfect harmony is driven by willing rightly on a personal level. When the soul is properly oriented toward God, the passions are at rest (ordered) and the person is in harmony with himself. Peace of body and soul results in a harmonious, well-ordered and healthy life. This state leads to harmony with God, and extends to the domestic sphere, bringing peace between rulers and their subjects as well as concord among citizens. The ultimate harmony, however, may only be perfectly enjoyed in the Kingdom, as citizens enjoy dwelling peacefully with God and enjoy one another *in* God.[80] Thus, harmony begins with the individual soul and extends by degrees to the entire Kingdom, making it, as Augustine calls it in the *Confessions* (composed long before the *City of God*), a "Land of Peace." This is a perfect state in which, as Slater explains, "the reason, will, and physical act of the individual would be fully harmonious. Body would obey spirit."[81] This explanation accords well with Gregory's description of the harmonious workings of Macrina's community, thereby constituting Augustine's version of "the life of the angels."

Although he enjoyed dwelling on philosophical aspects of harmony and proper proportion, before his conversion Augustine struggled to experience that harmony within himself. His soul failed to control the disordered impulses of his flesh, and his "rational mind" was corrupt, leading to false ideas about God and His nature. These heretical thoughts kept him outside the Kingdom, spiritually speaking: "though I did not know it, I was in exile from my place in God's city among His faithful children, my fellow citizens."[82] He was prevented from attaining to true beauty and harmony, by his errors, errors which drowned out "the voice of the Bridegroom of my soul."[83]

As Augustine describes Monica's virtues and gifts, he essentially describes her as a citizen of the Heavenly City by enumerating ways in which Monica lived a harmonious life and created harmony around her. At Cassiciacum, her piety extended to serving Augustine and his friends, as he describes it, "She took good care of us, as though she had been the mother of us all, and served each one as though she had been his daughter."[84] In her own household, Monica exercised obedience to her husband, not con-

79. Augustine, *Confessions*, 4.12 (trans. Pine-Coffin, 82).
80. Augustine, *The City of God*, 19.13.
81. Slater, "Goodness as Order and Harmony in Augustine," 157.
82. Augustine, *Confessions*, 4.15 (trans. Pine-Coffin, 87).
83. Ibid.
84. Ibid. (trans. Pine-Coffin, 196).

demning him for his shortcomings and infidelities, not antagonizing him and thereby keeping the peace in her marriage. Augustine admires his mother for her peace-making inclinations, a great gift from God. By her conciliatory attitude, she created concord with her mother-in-law, sought reconciliation among her friends, and refused to be a slanderer or gossiper that divulges secrets and promotes strife.[85] She exercised kindness, a sense of duty, self-restraint, and gentleness. "This was my mother's way," Augustine wrote, "learned in the school of her heart, where You were her secret teacher (*magistro intimo*)."[86] Monica's spiritual life gave evidence of harmonious progress as well. Toward the end of her life, Monica achieved detachment from certain earthly desires which (in Augustine's mind) were useless and vain, like being buried next to her husband back in Africa. Her detachment from earthly things (also a "gift") signaled to Augustine her full harmony and attunement to Kingdom priorities, confirmed by the fact of her participation with him in the awesome and mysterious vision at Ostia.

As God gave miraculous gifts of healing to Macrina, He granted several prophetic visions to Monica, whom Augustine calls "a holy woman."[87] However, none equaled the famous vision at Ostia. Five days prior to her fatal illness, Monica and Augustine together experienced a mystical vision of Heaven.[88] This vision constituted the zenith and consummation of her spiritual life. She and Augustine were conversing about life in the Kingdom, "the eternal life of the saints," and as they spoke, they rose toward God in mystical and mental ascent, obtaining a glimpse of "the eternal Wisdom," a reference to Christ.[89] By the uplifting power of the "flame of love" (the Holy Spirit) they passed beyond bodily senses and material things, and "reached out in thought and touched the eternal Wisdom which abides over all things."[90] Their ultimate goal was that of the Christian mystic: the beatific vision of God. "This single vision entranced and absorbed the one who beheld it and enveloped him in inward joys. . ." so that life for that person is eternally like that instant of spiritual bliss. That, they conclude, is Heaven.[91] And Augustine further understood (as he had stated earlier in the *Confessions*) that this heavenly land, this "land of peace" for which they longed and

---

85. Ibid., 9.9 (trans. Pine-Coffin, 195).
86. Ibid., 9.9, 196.
87. Ibid., 9.12, 202.
88. O'Donnell, *Augustine, Confessions: Commentary on Books 8–13*, 133.
89. Augustine, *Confessions*, 9.10, 197.
90. Ibid., 197–98.
91. Ibid., 9.10, 198.

strained, was "that blessed country which is meant to be no mere vision but our home."[92]

SPIRITUAL MOTHERS AS CONDUITS OF GOD'S HARMONIZING GOODNESS

The legacies of Monica and Macrina, the two church mothers we have been commemorating are rich and varied, and to them and others like them in sacred history, the church owes a great debt of gratitude. They offered the love and nurture of a mother, intensified in the absence of a husband or father. They spoke truth into the lives of their family members, disciplining them in love, and setting an example of godly devotion. Their devotion to God was driven forward by fervent longing and deep desire for God's beauty and presence. As Monica was borne higher on her ascent by the flame of love to glimpse the Beloved, so Macrina strove in mighty ascetic contests out of "pure love for the unseen Bridegroom."[93]

These women—just as Lois and Eunice, and many mothers before and after them—demonstrated the ideals of the Kingdom on a microcosmic scale in daily opportunities within the family that yielded global results for the church. We need only consider the Ephesian pastor Timothy, a faithful disciple of high repute, and an example for other pastors for nearly two millennia; the bishops which emerged from Macrina's family, –Basil, Gregory, and Peter,–responsible for battling Arianism in the Eastern Church into the late fourth century, explicating the doctrine of the Trinity, consolidating Athanasius's theological legacy, and defending the deity of the Holy Spirit; and the great Augustine, the most dominant of ancient theological voices in the Western Church, whose prodigious literary output left us theological, ethical, and philosophical treatises aplenty, in addition to exegetical commentaries and homilies for the spiritual nurture of the church. Living a "life of the angels" is of such great value, creating harmony in the home

---

92. Ibid., 7.20, 154.

93. Gregory, *Life of Macrina* 22 (trans. Peterson, 69–70). Ancient writers who treat the theme of asceticism at any length emphasize the deep love that gives impetus to the holy man or holy woman to pursue Christ as a lover. In the next century, Theodoret of Cyrus provides a wonderful and extensive epilogue entitled "On Divine Love" at the conclusion of his *Religious History*, brief biographies of fourth- and fifth-century Syrian ascetics. "It is this desire [for God] that...makes them transcend the heavens, reveals the Beloved in so far as it is possible, and through imagination, inflames yearning for contemplation, stirs up longing for it, and kindles the flame more fiercely . . ." for they have "received the goads of divine love." Theodoret of Cyrus, *A History of the Monks of Syria*, 192–93. For the entire Epilogue, see 190–205.

by obedience to scripture and the discipleship of household members: serving, loving, and worshiping God, and keeping a Kingdom perspective at the center of the family. Monica and Macrina understood this prioritization of Kingdom values, and the church reaped rich rewards due in large measure to these women, who could not have foreseen the vast theological and ecclesiological legacy from which we benefit today, but who nonetheless served faithfully in their time and place as conduits of God's grace and of His harmonizing goodness.

BIBLIOGRAPHY

Primary Sources:

Athanasius, Saint, Patriarch of Alexandria. *Athanasius: The Life of Anthony and The Letter to Marcellinus*. Translated by Robert C. Gregg with William A. Clebsch. Mahwah, NJ: Paulist, 1980.

Augustine. *The Confessions*. Translated by R. S. Pine-Coffin. London: Penguin, 1961.

———. *The City of God*. Translated by Henry Bettenson. Introduction by G. R. Evans. London: Penguin, 2003.

Evagrius of Pontus. *Chapters on Prayer*. Translated by John Eudes Bamberger. Cistercian Studies 4. Kalamazoo: Cistercian, 1981.

Gregory of Nyssa. *Commentary on the Inscriptions of the Psalms*. Translated by Casimir McCambley. Brookline, MA: Hellenic College Press, 1994.

———. *The Life of Macrina*. In *Handmaids of the Lord: Contemporary Descriptions of Feminine Asceticism in the First Six Christian Centuries*, edited and translated by Joan Petersen, 51–86. Cistercian Studies 143. Kalamazoo: Cistercian, 1996.

Nicomachus the Pythagorean. *The Manual of Harmonics*. Translated and with commentary by Flora R. Levin. Grand Rapids: Phanes, 1994.

Theodoret of Cyrus. *A History of the Monks of Syria*. Translated by R. M. Price. Cistercian Studies 88. Kalamazoo: Cistercian, 1985.

Secondary Sources:

Bowersock, G. W. *Martyrdom and Rome*. Cambridge: Cambridge University Press, 2002.

Brown, Peter. *Augustine of Hippo: A Biography*. Berkeley and Los Angeles: University of California Press, 1967.

Burton-Christie, Douglas. *The Word in the Desert: Scripture and the Quest for Holiness in Early Christian Monasticism*. New York: Oxford University Press, 1993.

Chryssavgis, John. *In the Heart of the Desert: The Spirituality of the Desert Fathers and Mothers*. Bloomington, IN: World Wisdom, 2003.

Clark, Elizabeth, ed. *St. Augustine on Marriage and Sexuality*. Washington, DC: Catholic University of America Press, 1996.

Cloke, Gillian. *This Female Man of God: Women and Spiritual Power in the Patristic Age, AD 350–450*. London: Routledge, 1995.

Davis, Stephen J. *The Cult of Thecla: A Tradition of Women's Piety in Late Antiquity*. Oxford: Oxford University Press, 2001.

Deusen, Nancy Van. "De Musica." In *Augustine through the Ages: An Encyclopedia*, edited by Allan D. Fitzgerald, 575. Grand Rapids: Cambridge: Eerdmans, 1999.

Fitzgerald, Allan, ed. *Augustine through the Ages: An Encyclopedia*. Grand Rapids; Cambridge: Eerdmans, 1999.

George, Timothy. "My Own Pilgrim's Progress." *Christianity Today*, August 19, 2015. http://www.christianitytoday.com/ct/2015/july-august/my-own-pilgrims-progress.html.

Godwin, Joscelyn, ed. *The Harmony of the Spheres: A Sourcebook of the Pythagorean Tradition in Music*. Rochester, VT: Inner Traditions, 1993.

Joost-Gaugier, Christiane. *Measuring Heaven: Pythagoras and His Influence on Thought and Art in Antiquity and the Middle Ages*. Ithaca: Cornell University Press, 2006.

Kannengiesser, Charles. *Early Christian Spirituality*. Translated by Pamela Bright. Sources of Early Christian Thought 6. Philadelphia: Fortress, 1986.

Longenecker, Richard N. *The Acts of the Apostles*. Expositor's Bible Commentary 9. Grand Rapids: Zondervan, 1981.

McWilliam, Joanne, ed. *Augustine: From Rhetor to Theologian*. Waterloo, ON: Wilfrid Laurier University Press, 1992.

O'Donnell, James J. *Augustine, Confessions*. Vol. 3, *Commentary on Books 8–13 and Indexes*. Oxford: Clarendon, 1992.

Osiek, Carolyn, and Margaret Y. Macdonald. *A Woman's Place: House Churches in Earliest Christianity*. Minneapolis: Fortress, 2006.

Petersen, Joan, ed. and trans. *Handmaids of the Lord: Contemporary Descriptions of Feminine Asceticism in the First Six Christian Centuries*. Cistercian Studies 143. Kalamazoo: Cistercian, 1996.

Ramelli, Ilaria. "Harmony between *Arkhe* and *Telos* in Patristic Platonism and the Imagery of Astronomical Harmony Applied to Apokatastasis." *International Journal of the Platonic Tradition* 7 (2013) 1–49.

"An RRJ Interview with Dr. Timothy George." *Reformation and Revival Journal: A Quarterly for Church Renewal* 13, no. 3 (2004) 133–66.

Slater, Peter. "Goodness as Order and Harmony in Augustine." In *Augustine: From Rhetor to Theologian*, edited by Joanne McWilliam, 151–60. Waterloo, ON: Wilfrid Laurier University Press, 1992.

Contemplating a Roman Catholic Reception of the Heidelberg Confession

Karen Petersen Finch

CHRISTIANS ARE CONTINUALLY IN the process of receiving their own tradition. Whenever we recite the Apostles' Creed, study a confessional document of the past or present, or retrieve the theology of the early church, we are engaging in reception. Yet reception is even more basic to daily Christian life than these particular activities suggest. Elsewhere, I have defined reception as a participation in acts of common meaning.[1] When we read Scripture we are reaching out (with the help of the Holy Spirit) to the earliest Christians and sharing in their knowledge and experience of the Gospel and its transformative power. We are seeking to participate in what Paul calls the *paradosis,* the tradition: literally "that which is handed on" (II Thess 2:15). In this way, even the reading of Scripture is an act of reception.

All Christians for whom the Bible is authoritative are thus engaged in a reception of the *paradosis*, of common Christian meaning. This insight suggests a new perspective on the phrase "ecumenical reception." Normally the word "reception" in ecumenical settings refers to the final stages of dialogue process in which the immediate object of reception is a dialogue report. Rarely do we think about Christians from the divided household of God (the *oikomene*) receiving Scripture together. In fact, our colleague Timothy George is currently engaged in just such an effort through the Paradosis Center, in which Catholic, Orthodox, and Evangelical scholars engage together "in an effort to hear, teach, live, and pass on intact that *doctrina* which is at the heart of the Christian Gospel."[2]

---

1. Finch, "A Deeper Reception" 2016.
2. George, "Engaging John Together," 2016.

> The vision of Paradosis Center builds on the insight of St. Augustine that the erroneous reading of Scripture is not a mere failure of technical exegetical expertise. It results rather from a failure to engage the Bible in a way that builds up the two-fold love of God and our neighbors commended by Jesus. Pope John Paul II reminded us that genuine ecumenism involves the exchange of gifts as well as a sharing of ideas (Ut Unum Sint, 28). Paradosis Center aims to foster this kind of work in the midst of the ecclesial divisions that mar the face of the church in our world today.

In this article I am recommending a particular form in which this "exchange of gifts" and "sharing of ideas" might take place. If ecumenical reception includes listening to Scripture together, could it not also mean listening to the documents that are important to one another's divided lives? On this logic, the more accurately a confession or catechism reflects the paradosis of 2 Thess 2:15, the more likely a candidate it would be for ecumenical reception. The prima facie objection to this project is that so many of these documents are both catholic and polemical by turns. For example, a Catholic believer reading Scripture is not going to encounter an explicit condemnation of the veneration of the saints, while a Catholic reader of the Heidelberg Catechism is going to face just that. And yet, as I hope to demonstrate below, the great majority of the Heidelberg's content is truly catholic and could serve as a winsome example to Catholic believers of the distinctive riches of Reformed and Lutheran piety.

An "exchange of gifts" through confessional documents is even more possible if we have a sufficiently complex view of their reception. It is true that all confessions and catechisms are the work of a particular time and place.[3] Those who author them give priority to the insights and judgments that are urgently needed for faithfulness in that time and place. But they do so with a mind to the history of their community, to the patterns of action and reflection that have given that community a distinctive voice. If this is true, then no confession or catechism is received in isolation, but as one chapter in a longer story, which creates tremendous opportunities for ecumenical sharing. It means, for example, that Catholic believers today can receive the Heidelberg Catechism concomitantly with recent ecumenical agreements in which their community has participated, such as *The Joint Declaration on the Doctrine of Justification* (Roman Catholic-Lutheran) and

---

3. World Alliance of Reformed Churches & Pontifical Council for Promoting Christian Unity, "The Church as a Community of Common Witness to the Kingdom of God," 98.

the three reports of the International Reformed-Catholic Dialogue (IRCD).[4] In these agreements, Catholic and Lutheran, and Catholic and Reformed (respectively), have testified that the condemnations of the past may be left in the past, and need not bind us today.[5] Therefore a more thorough reception of contemporary ecumenical documents—a fuller participation in their meaning—could help separated Christians to put aside the polemical content of older documents and appreciate *both* what is catholic *and* what is distinctive in the writings of another tradition.

This article purports to imagine what it would be like for a Roman Catholic Christian to receive the Heidelberg Catechism. First, we will identify the main doctrinal "pressure points" in the Heidelberg that would be troubling for Catholic readers. (Although I have been studying Catholic theology for some time, I am Protestant and Reformed; therefore my identifications are exercises in theological empathy and are open to correction or confirmation by Catholic readers.) Secondly, I will briefly explain why—in spite of its polemical moments—I find the Heidelberg to be particularly suited for ecumenical reception. Then we will take a closer look at two troubling conflicts and demonstrate how they might be ameliorated through careful study of the Heidelberg itself, and through engagement with other documents that the churches are currently in the process of receiving. Our examination of each "pressure point" cannot be exhaustive in such a constrained space, but we can make a beginning.

The risk of this approach is that it may obfuscate the much larger number of emphases in the Heidelberg that a Catholic reader could enjoy and celebrate; along the way, therefore, we will identify elements of the Heidelberg that would be comfortably received as "catholic" to a "Catholic." The entire procedure will reflect my conviction that, even if reception should be only partially successful, all Christians would benefit from experiencing one another's most authentically Christian texts.

THE POLEMICAL PASSAGES, AND BEYOND

The following chart represents a map of doctrinal "pressure points" in the Heidelberg Catechism. They are of two types. Some of the passages listed are directly antagonistic to sixteenth-century Roman Catholic faith and practice. Question 30 on the veneration of saints is a good example of this kind

---

4. The IRCD reports are WARC/PCPCU, "The Presence of Christ in Church and World," 1977;

5. Lutheran World Federation & Pontifical Council for Promoting Christian Unity, "Joint Declaration on the Doctrine of Justification," paragraphs 3–5 and 13.

of text: "Do those who seek their salvation or well-being in saints, in themselves, or anywhere else, also believe in the only Savior Jesus?" "No. Though they boast of him in words, they in fact deny the only Savior Jesus. . ."[6] The chart also lists passages that, while not overtly hostile, would be likely to strike contemporary Catholics as uncomfortably foreign. An example of this second type is Question 8 on the inevitability of sin: "But are we so corrupt that we are totally unable to do any good and inclined to all evil?" "Yes, unless we are regenerated by the Spirit of God."

Topic	Question (s)
The nature of sin	7, 10, 56, 60, 61,
The inevitability of sin	5, 8, 114
The origins of faith	21, 65
The communion of saints	29, 30, 55, 94–98, 102
Grace and good works	62–64
Nature and number of sacraments	66–68, 75
Baptism	69, 73, 78
The Lord's Supper	78–81
The Keys of the Kingdom	83–85

Why include the second type of passages when they are not as overtly divisive? The intention is to avoid an unrealistically sanguine approach to the text. For example, one could argue that Question 8 represents a distillation of Augustine's doctrine of the bondage of the will as formulated in response to Pelagius, to which Catholic, Lutheran and Reformed all assent. Technically, this is true. Perhaps this is why Barth does not include Question 8 in his list of those sections of the Heidelberg that express "*exclusively* Reformed doctrine."[7] Yet the answer to Question 8 does not clarify what degree of moral impotence remains after regeneration by the Holy Spirit. It leaves the impression that a fierce struggle with sin is the Christian's daily reality, which accords with Reformed and Lutheran sensibilities but not at all with Catholic ones. In Catholic theology it is *concupiscentia*—not sin proper, but the inclination to sin—which remains after the sacrament of baptism. As the authors of the *Joint Declaration on the Doctrine of Justification* explained it, "Since, according to Catholic conviction, human sin always involves a personal element and since this element is lacking in this inclination, Catholics do not see this inclination as sin in an authentic

---

6. Presbyterian Church (U.S.A.), "The Heidelberg Catechism," question 30.
7. Barth, *The Heidelberg Catechism for Today*, 25.

sense."[8] Even a Catholic believer who is unaware of the technical difference between sin and *concupiscentia* would experience the Heidelberg's language on the constant battle with a "sinful nature" as jarring.[9] In other words, not only overt differences but also subtle implications must be acknowledged in the reception of one another's confessional texts, in order to avoid a false irenicism which "obscures" the "genuine and certain meaning" of doctrinal positions that are unique to each community.[10]

While avoiding false irenicism, it is equally important not to let the polemical sections dominate one's acquaintance with the Heidelberg. The situation is rather like getting to know a person who occasionally has a bad temper, but whose passion and faith are immensely edifying. A glimpse of that person's history can sometimes explain the origin of the temper; and this is certainly true of the Heidelberg. Polemical material in the Catechism reflects the interlocking religious and political conditions of 16th-century Germany, in which Lutheran and Reformed competed bitterly with one another, as well as with the Roman Catholic establishment, for power and influence.[11] However, it is wisest to view the Heidelberg as an exception to this contentious atmosphere rather than as a representation of it. As Barth wrote, the Catechism expresses the "positive content" of Reformation thinking.[12] We know that Frederick III was inspired by Philip Melanchthon to commission the Heidelberg as an instrument of theological unity among evangelicals and as a standard for teaching and preaching in the Palatinate and beyond. Zacharias Ursinus (its primary author) had studied with both Melanchthon and Calvin and was influenced by a spectrum of Reformation thinkers in trying to forge an irenic approach to divisive questions of the moment, such as the relationship between the human and divine natures of Christ.[13] Sadly, the Heidelberg Catechism did not "bring peace and unity to the Palatinate"; but the irenic impulse is still powerfully present in the text. According to Dreyer, "[We] cannot say that the Heidelberg Catechism derived its structure from any specific theologian or document. . . Even the articles on the sacraments do not reflect a distinctive doctrinal viewpoint."[14] The Heidelberg was aiming at a catholic perspective, which renders it more immediately accessible to ecumenical reception than other documents, which are more sectarian in origin.

8. LWF/PCPCU, "Joint Declaration on the Doctrine of Justification," Paragraph 30.
9. Presbyterian Church (U.S.A.), "The Heidelberg Catechism," question 114.
10. Vatican II, *Unitatis redintegratio*, 511.
11. Dreyer, "The Heidelberg Catechism," 3.
12. Barth, *The Heidelberg Catechism for Today*, 25.
13. Dreyer, The Heidelberg Catechism," 4.
14. Ibid.

Some Reformers, such as Martin Bucer, did dream of articulating an evangelical theology that was inclusive to Catholic believers.[15] It does not appear that Ursinus and his colleagues considered such an approach. Had they done so, their credibility for trying to bring unity among evangelicals would have been weakened; nor is it likely that the response of the Roman church would have been positive. The authors of *Towards a Common Understanding of the Church* (IRCD) have noted that imperial and papal politics, little direct access to evangelical writings, and a juridical mindset caused the Roman Catholic establishment to miss what was truly catholic in the request for widespread reform.[16] But Roman Catholics today are not in the same situation. They are, for example, heritors and receptors of the "pervasive reorientation in. . .liturgy and life, theology and thought" that characterized Vatican II. From this newer perspective, what is catholic in the Catechism is easier to perceive; for "Roman Catholic theologians today generally acknowledge that many of the issues raised by the Reformers urgently needed to be faced and resolved."[17] It is hoped that Catholic lay people can see the Heidelberg as an imperfect attempt to raise these urgent issues, within an overall exposition that reflects the *paradosis* and invites the participation of all who experience Jesus as Lord.

This brings us to what is most universal about the Heidelberg: its appeal to Christian experience. We naturally expect catechisms to be in some degree personal as well as theological, since they are tools of spiritual formation and discipleship. Yet the Heidelberg is unusual in that it continuously invites believers to identify the "benefit" to themselves in the doctrine they are professing, at the very same moment that they are professing it.[18] This recurring invitation certainly reflects the theological influence of Calvin; yet as an epistemological approach it is profoundly catholic, even profoundly human.

We can picture the epistemology of the Heidelberg as involving three levels:

EXPERIENCE ("Comfort")

FAITH (gift of the Holy Spirit)

DOCTRINAL TRUTH

---

15. Denlinger, "Men of Gallio's Naughty Faith?," 68.

16. WARC/PCPCU, "Towards a Common Understanding of the Church," paragraphs 37–38.

17. Ibid., paragraph 61.

18. Presbyterian Church (U.S.A.), "The Heidelberg Catechism," questions 28, 36, 43, and others.

At the bottom level, the certain foundation of Christian knowledge is the *pura doctrina* found in Scripture. But faith is not simply intellectual assent; it is meant to be experienced in the affective and practical dimensions of life. The Heidelberg's word for this experience is "comfort," which is very close to Calvin's concept of "assurance."[19] Like the saving work of Christ, the truth of Scripture will remain *extra nos* without the work of the Holy Spirit who forges the living connection between the Word of Scripture and our daily experience. That living conduit is faith. What is important for our purposes is that Christian experience is *also* a kind of knowledge, especially when it is founded on the Word of God and enlivened by the Holy Spirit. A Christian cannot be said to really *know* a doctrinal truth unless they can articulate the "comfort" or "benefit" that comes from the Spirit's introduction of that truth into their everyday life.

This honoring of experience gives the Catechism a passionate quality, something akin to Catherine's declaration of "I am Heathcliff" or Luther's "Here I stand; I can do no other." It may also smooth the way for ecumenical reception as participation in common meaning. When I attend Mass, for example, I choose not pray for those who have died in the Lord, since 2 Macc. 12:46 is not an authoritative text in my community. Instead, I think with gratitude of my parents who are with Christ. On the level of doctrinal judgment, it would be false irenicism to claim a unity between my thinking and that of my neighbors with respect to prayers for the dead at such a moment. But on the level of experience, I can fully participate in the confidence in God's faithfulness that inspires my neighbors at Mass to pray in this way, and the joy that attends their confidence. Eschatological hope does not belong only to Catholics, or only to Protestants, whatever the doctrinal language in which it may be packaged. It could be that the authors of the Heidelberg Catechism recognized the power of shared experience in the communication of meaning, and sought to leverage it in their quest to unite Lutheran and Reformed into one evangelical faith. In any case, their appeal to experience had the effect of widening the potential audience of the Heidelberg for their own time and for today. It means that separated Christians who are interested in a more complete reception of recent ecumenical agreements could benefit from the catechism's testimony to the "comfort" that we all possess in Christ.

---

19. See Calvin, *Institutes of the Christian Religion* 3.2.7.

A FIRST PRESSURE POINT: THE COMMUNION OF THE SAINTS

As mentioned above, the Heidelberg explicitly condemns "prayer to the saints and other creatures."[20] It is not simply the action of prayer that is rejected, but the underlying assumption that "salvation or well-being" might be *mediated* to believers through those who have already died.[21] In other words, the authors of the Heidelberg approach the veneration of saints through the theological concept of mediation. We can hear the powerful influence of Calvin for whom mediation is a controlling metaphor for understanding the relationship between a sovereign God and a sinful humanity. "Even if man had remained free from all stain, his condition would have been too lowly for him to reach God without a Mediator."[22] Therefore Calvin's favorite title for Jesus Christ is "the One Person of the Mediator" who is "the mid-point between God and creatures, so that the life which was otherwise hidden in God would flow from him."[23] The Heidelberg writers also identify Jesus Christ as "Mediator" and from this perspective they interpret the veneration of the saints as violating the Reformation concept of *solus Christus*. For them such veneration implies "either Jesus is not a complete Savior, or those who by true faith accept this Savior must find in him all that is necessary for their salvation."[24]

Imagine a Catholic believer who is reading the Heidelberg's account of our deliverance from sin as it unfolds in Questions 12 and following. The Christology of this section is profoundly catholic. From Anselm it draws the language of sin as a debt to God's honor; from Chalcedon it takes the insistence that the mediation of Christ must be a mediation in two complete natures, human and divine; even the title of Mediator does not originate with Calvin but pays homage to I Tim 2:5 and to Augustine.[25] After affirming that we participate in the benefits of Christ through faith which is "worked in us by the Holy Spirit through the gospel," a statement with which Lutheran, Reformed and Catholic would be likely to agree (with some discussion about the meaning of the preposition "through"), the writers launch into an exposition of "the articles of our catholic and undoubted

---

20. Presbyterian Church (U.S.A.), "The Heidelberg Catechism," question 94.
21. Ibid., question 30.
22. Calvin, *Institutes of the Christian Religion* 2.12.2 (trans. Battles, 465).
23. Tylenda, "Christ the Mediator," 13.
24. Presbyterian Church (U.S.A.), "The Heidelberg Catechism," question 30.
25. Tylenda, "Controversy on Christ the Mediator," 151.

Christian faith" as it is summarized in the Apostle's Creed.[26] They lay out the doctrines of creation and providence in a winsome way, appealing to the reader's experience of "leaf and blade, rain and drought, fruitful and barren years, food and drink, health and sickness, riches and poverty."[27] Into this long sweep of catholicity comes the polemic against seeking "salvation and well-being" from creatures or from oneself, with its attendant assertion—utterly understandable in the Reformation context—that the veneration of saints represents a denial of Jesus as one's only Savior.

What do Catholic believers seek in the saints today? Is it salvation, or mediation, or wellbeing, or something else? In *Towards a Common Understanding of the Church*, Catholic and Reformed believers together declared that "Jesus Christ, the one true mediator between God and humankind, is also the unique way which leads toward pleasing God."[28] Previously, in *The Presence of Christ in Church and World*," the two parties had already agreed to describe Jesus as "our sole advocate in heaven."[29] Both of these statements reflect the work of Vatican II theologians to correct both problematic understandings of the communion of saints and the inappropriate practices which stemmed from those understandings. The following sections from *Lumen gentium* are also prefaced by an identification of Christ Jesus as "the one mediator between God and humanity":[30]

> Exactly as Christian communion among pilgrims brings us closer to Christ, so our communion with the saints joins us to Christ, from whom as from its fountain and head flow all grace and life of the people of God itself. It is most fitting, therefore, that we love those friends and co-heirs of Jesus Christ who are also our sisters and brothers and outstanding benefactors, and that we give due thanks to God for them, humbly invoking them, and having recourse to their prayers, their aid and help in obtaining from God through his Son, Jesus Christ, Our Lord, our only redeemer and Savior, the benefits we need.[31] At the same time, in keeping with its pastoral preoccupations, this council urges all concerned to remove or correct any abuses,

---

26. Presbyterian Church (U.S.A.), "The Heidelberg Catechism," question 21.
27. Ibid., Question 27.
28. WARC/PCPCU, "Towards a Common Understanding of the Church," paragraphs 78–79.
29. Ibid, "The Presence of Christ in Church and World," paragraph 80.
30. Vatican II, *Lumen gentium*, 75.
31. Ibid., 76.

> excesses or defects which may have crept in here or there, and so restore all things that Christ and God be more fully praised.[32]

In no way do the Catholic voices in these documents withdraw their support from the veneration of, or from prayer to, the saints. Yet it is clear that the word "mediation" does not describe the activity of the saints from the Catholic perspective, as Christ clearly occupies the role of the One Mediator and the "only redeemer and savior." An informed Catholic would therefore not see herself as one who seeks "salvation in the saints." But what about "well-being"? The key terms in *Lumen gentium* for what believers are seeking from those who are *in heaven* are "communion" and "intercession." The word "communion" is very interesting in that it sends us to Heidelberg Question 55, in which the communion of saints *on earth* is described:

> Q. What do you understand by the communion of saints?
> A. First, that believers, all and everyone, as members of Christ have communion with him and share in all his treasures and gifts.1 Second, that everyone is duty-bound to use his gifts readily and cheerfully for the benefit and well-being of the other members.

According to the Heidelberg it is quite correct to seek one's "well-being" in the *earthly* communion of saints, especially because such well-being is a participation in the benefits of Christ. Yet one should not seek it in the *heavenly* communion. But if there is truly a communion between believers on earth and the saved in heaven, why distinguish between what believers might seek from each? After all, the Heidelberg writers used the same term for "well-being" (German: *heil*; Latin: *salutum*) with respect to both. And this parallel usage makes perfect sense to a Catholic person, since according to *Lumen gentium* the earthly and heavenly communions are the one body of Christ, joined in a mystical union. We are dealing not with two communions, but with one. "So it is that the union of the wayfarers with the brothers and sisters who sleep in the peace of Christ is in no way interrupted; but on the contrary, according to the constant faith of the church, this union is reinforced by an exchange of spiritual goods."[33] Think of it as having brothers and sisters with Christ who want to "use their gifts readily and cheerfully" for your benefit, as the Heidelberg phrases it. Yet they are in the presence of Christ, outside the limitations of time and space, and have resources that you do not have. They are still creatures; they do not save or

---

32. Ibid., 77.
33. Ibid., 75.

mediate. But they may intercede in a similar way to those who pray for us on earth.

This understanding of the veneration of saints is, to my knowledge, a fairly accurate portrait of what contemporary Catholics believe. It is not the Lutheran or Reformed position. But the Catechism's overt condemnation of the practice in Question 30 is mitigated by the language of Question 55 regarding the communion of saints. Among Christians, there is an exchange of benefits through our union in Christ that enriches our mutual "well-being." To look for salvation from the saints is truly an error; to look for well-being may simply be an expression of Christian community across space and time. I propose that Catholic readers can receive "catholic" theology on the communion of saints from Questions 30 and 55, and not simply condemnation. Reading the Heidelberg alongside *Lumen gentium* might help them to reflect on the necessary theological difference between the intercession that members of Christ's body exercise on one another's behalf and the mediation that only Christ can provide. If they have some education in the goals and concerns of Reformation theology, they will understand why the authors of the Heidelberg were so disturbed by prayer to the saints. In fact, ecumenical reception is a powerful tool for increasing theological education among the laity of all our churches. But Question 94, which forbids "prayer to saints or to other creatures," will remain an obstacle until Lutheran, Reformed and Catholic can clarify with one voice that such prayer is properly understood as a request for intercession, rather than for mediation.

ANOTHER PRESSURE POINT: THE LORD'S SUPPER

To suggest a Catholic reception of the Heidelberg Catechism without addressing the polemical cast of its teaching on the Lord's Supper would beg serious questions. It is important to note, however, that the section on sacraments begins with a general sacramentology that is strikingly catholic. The sacraments are the work of the Holy Spirit "instituted by God so that by their use he might the more fully declare and seal to us the promise of the gospel."[34] While the recurring description of sacrament as "sign and seal" displays the influence of Calvin, it is also reflective of Luther and Augustine. Of course it is problematic for a Catholic reader that the Catechism limits the number of sacraments to two, not seven, and that this decision is stated but never explained.[35] However, in the discussion of baptism which immediately follows, a Christian's baptism is efficacious not in its own right but

---

34. Presbyterian Church (U.S.A.), "The Heidelberg Catechism," question 66.
35. Ibid., question 68.

as a participation in the one cross of Christ, by faith.³⁶ This approach is accessible to Lutheran, Catholic and Reformed because it keeps to the biblical heart of the matter and prescinds from sectarian distinctions regarding what type of sin baptism removes, and to what extent.

Not surprisingly, the Heidelberg's discussion of the Lord's Supper is more polemical than its presentation of baptism. Its content reflects the discord between Lutheran and Reformed theologians in the 16th century as well as tension between the evangelical churches and Rome. Most troubling to a Catholic would be Question 80:

> Q. What difference is there between the Lord's Supper and the papal mass?
>
> A. The Lord's supper testifies to us, first, that we have complete forgiveness of all our sins through the one sacrifice of Jesus Christ, which he himself accomplished on the cross once for all; and, second, that through the Holy Spirit we are grafted into Christ, who with his true body is now in heaven at the right hand of the Father, and this is where he wants to be worshipped. But the mass teaches, first, that the living and the dead do not have forgiveness of sins through the suffering of Christ unless he is still offered for them daily by the priests; and, second, that Christ is bodily present in the form of bread and wine, and there is to be worshipped. Therefore the mass is basically nothing but a denial of the one sacrifice and suffering of Jesus Christ, and an accursed idolatry.

We know that Question 80 was not present in the first draft of the Heidelberg, nor in the original German edition. Dreyer speculates that Caspar Olevianus, Ursinus' colleague, was instrumental in adding it to later editions with a double purpose: to refute the anathemas of the Council of Trent, and to closely echo Luther's own rejection of the Mass as an olive branch to Lutherans.³⁷ But this history may not help Catholic readers who are experiencing the text as it comes to them. To imply that the Mass and the Lord's Supper are two different events is deeply insulting, even if the Catechism were to say nothing at all about the agency of priests or the doctrine of transubstantiation. Moreover, the Heidelberg authors will later define idolatry as "having or inventing something in which to put our trust instead of, or in addition to, the only true God who has revealed himself in his Word."³⁸ This is incredibly offensive to Catholics, who treasure the Mass *because* of

---

36. Ibid., questions 69–70.
37. Dreyer, "The Heidelberg Catechism," 3.
38. Presbyterian Church (U.S.A.), "The Heidelberg Catechism," question 95.

their trust that, in the bread and wine, they receive the Son of God who is Himself the Word.

To recover the catholic content of the Heidelberg on the Lord's Supper, we will identify the valid sacramental concerns which motivated the inclusion of Question 80. Catholics can also receive and share these concerns when we recast them into more constructive language. Secondly, we will look again at a document currently available for reception—*The Presence of Christ in Church and World*—in which Reformed and Catholic believers tackled these and other legitimate concerns together. In doing so they "reached a common understanding of the meaning and purpose and basic doctrine of the Eucharist, which is in agreement with the Word of God and the universal tradition of the Church." Furthermore, they judged that "the terminology which arose in an earlier polemical context is not adequate for taking account of the extent of common theological understanding which exists in our respective churches."[39] What is this common Eucharistic understanding? Does it overlap with the positive theology of the Heidelberg, in a way that could facilitate Catholic reception of that older document?

Consider the following words or phrases in Question 80: "complete" "one sacrifice" and "once for all." The Heidelberg writers are obviously anxious to reject a view of the Supper in which Christ is "offered . . . daily by the priests." This reminder is another expression of the **solus christus** principle and, stated in its positive form, affirms "our entire salvation rests on Christ's one sacrifice for us on the cross."[40] Catholic and Reformed dialogue partners have together recognized the validity of this concern. In *The Presence of Christ in Church and World*, they agreed that the Greek term *anamnesis* does not indicate a re-enactment of Christ's sacrifice; nor does it refer only to "a mental act of recalling.'"[41] Like the Heidelberg writers, they affirmed Christ's "once-for-all self-offering."[42] They also agreed that only true host of the Lord's Table is the Lord:

> The presidence of the commissioned church office bearer at the celebration of the Meal effectively represents this unique role of Christ as the Lord and Host. The commissioned office-bearer is there to show the assembled community that it does not have disposal itself over the Eucharist but simply carries out obediently what Christ has commissioned the Church to do.[43]

39. WARC/PCPCU, "The Presence of Christ in Church and World," paragraph 91.
40. P.C. (U.S.A), "The Heidelberg Catechism," question 67.
41. WARC/PCPCU, "The Presence of Christ in Church and World," paragraph 70.
42. Ibid., paragraph 80.
43. Ibid., Paragraph 75.

A second valid concern pertains to the location of the risen Christ's physical body. Remember that Question 80 is a later, polemically motivated addition to the text. The statement that Christ's body is now "in heaven at the right hand of the Father" is controversial in two directions: with respect to the Lutheran teaching on Christ's ubiquity, and to Catholic teaching on transubstantiation.[44] But the affirmation of a bodily presence of Jesus in heaven is important to the Christian *paradosis*. In *The Presence of Christ in Church and World*, Reformed and Catholic theologians observed that "the glorified body of the Lord with which the New Testament community had fellowship in the Supper" is none other than "the risen Jesus Christ as the second Adam."[45] Theologically it is important that a glorified, but still human, body is with God at His right hand. It signals a restoration of the leadership of creation, which God originally granted to Adam but which Eve and Adam lost through sin. Moreover, according to the *PCCW* authors, this glorified human body reminds us that the risen Christ who is fully and freely present in the Eucharist is two complete natures in one Person. "The specific mode of Christ's real presence in the Eucharist," they explained, "is thus to be interpreted as the presence of the Son who is both consubstantial with us in our human and bodily existence while being eternally consubstantial with the Father and the Holy Spirit in the Godhead."[46]

In other words, the authors of *The Presence of Christ in Church and World* felt very strongly that a return to the language of Chalcedon was the remedy for polemical language regarding the Eucharist. Reformed Christians have focused on the spiritual presence of Christ, reacting to what they have perceived as an over-emphasis among Catholics and Lutherans on the physical presence of Christ in the elements. The *PCCW* writers sought to remind both their communities that Scripture affirms the presence of Jesus—whom Paul calls *both* a glorified body and a "life-giving Spirit"—in the Eucharist, without spending any time whatever defining how this can be so. What matters is that Jesus is present with us at his Table *in both of his natures*, human and divine, and present "without confusion, without change, without division, without separation."

This return to Chalcedon is "the common understanding of the meaning and purpose and basic doctrine of the Eucharist" which the *PCCW* authors believed they had recovered. In a marvelous way, their insight accords beautifully with the overall Christology of the Heidelberg. Willem

---

44. As Dreyer points out, this reference to the location of Christ's body provoked tension between Lutheran and Reformed well into the seventeenth century. See "The Heidelberg Catechism," 4.

45. WARC/PCPCU, "The Presence of Christ in Church and World," paragraph 72.

46. Ibid., paragraph 84.

Van Vlastuin has stressed that when the Catechism celebrates our union with Christ through faith, it is the risen, eschatological Christ with whom we are united.[47] The risen Lord greets us at the daily table of faith as well as at the Lord's Table. His resurrection is a physical and a spiritual triumph, and in it we are healed in both dimensions. Therefore it is fitting to end this exploration with Question 57, which speaks to all Christians:

> Q: What comfort does the resurrection of the body offer you?
>
> A. Not only shall my soul after this life immediately be taken up to Christ, my Head, but also this my flesh, raised by the power of Christ, shall be reunited with my soul and made like Christ's glorious body.

CONCLUSION

This article has enthusiastically recommended the Heidelberg Catechism as a vehicle for ecumenical reception, primarily with Catholic readers in mind. The irenic roots of the Catechism, its invitation to personally experience the *paradosis* via the work of the Holy Spirit, and the universal tone it adopts in the vast majority of its statements make it a likely candidate for the ecumenical "sharing of ideas." As Christian literature goes, the Heidelberg is a treasure that no one should miss. I have made no attempt to overlook polemical moments in the text. Instead I have suggested that one may lessen the divisive impact of such content by reading it in light of the whole Catechism, by honoring what is useful in it, and by receiving it concomitantly with more recent ecumenical documents that have dealt with the same issues.

Above all, this has been an exercise in theological empathy. It is essential that we learn to read our own traditions' theological products with our separated brothers and sisters in mind. Few of us will have the opportunity to participate in official ecumenical dialogue face-to-face, but we can critically examine our traditions through Augustine's double lens: the love of God and the love of neighbor. There is no better hermeneutic for distinguishing classical Christian theology, which builds unity, from the divisions and distractions that can and must be left behind.

---

47. Vlastuin, "The Joy of the Law," 180.

BIBLIOGRAPHY

Barth, Karl. *The Heidelberg Catechism for Today*. Edited by Shirley C. Guthrie. London: Epworth, 1964.

Calvin, John. *Institutes of the Christian Religion*. 2 vols. Edited by John T. McNeill. Translated by Ford Lewis Battles. LCC 20–21. Philadelphia: Westminster, 1960.

Denlinger, Aaron Clay. "'Men of Gallio's Naughty Faith?' The Aberdeen Doctors on Reformed and Lutheran Concord." *Church History and Religious Culture* 92, no. 1 (2012) 57–83.

Dreyer, Wim A. "The Heidelberg Catechism: A 16th Century Quest for Unity." *HTS Teologiese Studies / Theological Studies* 70, no. 1 (2014) 1–5.

George, Timothy. "Engaging John Together." *First Things*, 2016. https://www.firstthings.com/web-exclusives/2015/02/engaging-john-together.

Lutheran World Federation, and Pontifical Council for Promoting Christian Unity. "Joint Declaration on the Doctrine of Justification." Augsburg, Germany, 1999. http://www.vatican.va/roman_curia/pontifical_councils/chrstuni/documents/rc_pc_chrstuni_doc_31101999_cath-luth-joint-declaration_en.html.

Petersen Finch, Karen. "A Deeper Reception: Engaging Lay Theologians in the Outcomes of Reformed and Roman Catholic Dialogue." In *Full, Conscious and Active: Lay Participation in the Church's Dialogue with the World*. Rome: Libera Editrice Vaticana, forthcoming.

Presbyterian Church (U.S.A.). "The Heidelberg Catechism." 2014. https://www.pcusa.org/site_media/media/uploads/oga/pdf/boc2014.pdf.

Tylenda, Joseph N. "Christ the Mediator: Calvin versus Stancaro." *Calvin Theological Journal* 8, no. 1 (1973) 5–16.

———. "Controversy on Christ the Mediator: Calvin's Second Reply to Stancaro." *Calvin Theological Journal* 8, no. 2 (1973) 131–57.

Van Vlastuin, Willem. "The Joy of the Law: A Revisitation of the Usus Normativus in the Heidelberg Catechism." *Journal of Reformed Theology* 9, no. 2 (2015) 166–81.

Vatican II. *Lumen Gentium*. In *The Basic Sixteen Documents: Vatican Council II (A Completely Revised Translation in Inclusive Language)*, edited by Austin Flannery, 1–95. Northport, NY: Costello, 1996.

———. *Unitatis Redintegratio*. In *The Basic Sixteen Documents: Vatican Council II (A Completely Revised Translation in Inclusive Language*, edited by Austin Flannery, 499–523. Northport, NY: Costello, 1996.

World Alliance of Reformed Churches, and Pontifical Council for Promoting Christian Unity. "The Church as a Community of Common Witness to the Kingdom of God," 2007. http://www.prounione.urbe.it/dia-int/r-rc/doc/e_r-rc_3-contents.html.

———. "The Presence of Christ in Church and World," 1977. http://www.vatican.va/roman_curia/pontifical_councils/chrstuni/alliance-reform-docs/rc_pc_chrstuni_doc_19770301_first-phase-dialogue_en.html.

———."Towards a Common Understanding of the Church," 1990. http://www.prounione.urbe.it/dia-int/r-rc/doc/e_r-rc_2-menu.html.

John Calvin and the Construction of a Confessional Church

A Case Study for Evangelicals

SCOTT M. MANETSCH

ADDRESSING A LARGE CROWD in Philadelphia in 1740, the famous revivalist George Whitefield employed his usual theatrics to lampoon the dizzying array of denominational divisions that he encountered in America.

> "Father Abraham, Whom have you in heaven? Any Episcopalians?"
>
> "No!"
>
> "Any Presbyterians?"
>
> "No!"
>
> "Any Independents or Seceders, New Sides or Old Sides, any Methodists?"
>
> "No! No! No!"
>
> "Whom have you there, then, Father Abraham?"
>
> "We don't know those names here! All who have come are Christians-believers in Christ, men who have overcome by the blood of the Lamb and the word of his testimony..."
>
> "Then . . . God help us all, to forget having names and become Christians in deed and truth."[1]

---

1. Sweet, *The Story of Religion in America*, 141–42. This passage was called to my attention by Dockery, "Denominationalism."

This suspicion of denominations and creedal divisions was echoed a half-century later on the American frontier by the one-time Presbyterian, but now "Christian" minister Alexander Campbell. Decrying "the melancholy thralldom of relentless systems," and purporting to rescue the holy Scriptures from "the perplexities of the commentators and system-makers of the dark ages," Campbell urged his fellow countrymen to lay aside the creeds and traditions of historic Protestantism, and pursue, instead, a purified and unified Christian church modeled after the New Testament example.[2] Campbell and his company of Christian Restorationists were soon identified by their bold slogan, "No creed but the Bible!"[3]

The attitudes of Whitefield and Campbell are indicative of the pervasive suspicion that continues to exist within many corners of modern-day evangelicalism toward organized denominations, theological traditions, ancient creeds, and formal confessions of faith. A good number of evangelicals fear that confessional authorities like these necessarily undermine the unique authority of Scripture, promote an arid intellectualism, quench the work of the Spirit, sow disunity among Christians, and further fragment the universal Church, thus contravening Jesus Christ's high priestly prayer in John 17:23 that his disciples might experience "complete unity" so that the "world knows that you sent me and have loved them even as you have loved me." Each of these concerns deserves—and has received—serious consideration from evangelical scholars, who continue to explore the various ways that the essential doctrinal core of evangelical faith intersects denominational (and non-denominational) boundaries and interacts with ancient creeds and the confessional traditions of historic Christianity.[4] As Timothy George has recently noted, "Despite this aversion to credalism, evangelicals today are finding that the historic creeds of the church are a resource of faith and spiritual life. Evangelicals are engaged in a process of retrieval for the sake of renewal."[5]

With George's statement serving as my point of departure, this essay explores the various resources for faith and spiritual life that Protestant confessional theology offers to contemporary evangelical Christians. By confessional theology, I mean an approach to Christian doctrine that

---

2. Hatch, *The Democratization of American Christianity* 163, 168–69

3. In his "Remarks on Confessions of Faith," Campbell noted: "The New Testament, as respects Christian faith and practice, is our only creed, form of discipline, and the avowal of the *One Foundation* our only bond of union. I object to all human creeds as terms of communion from the following considerations," 47–48. I am grateful to my student David Ford for providing me with this quotation.

4. Packer and Oden, *One Faith, The Evangelical Consensus*.

5. George, *Evangelicals and the Nicene Faith*, xxii.

affirms formal, often historic, confessional statements (statements of faith, creeds, catechisms, liturgy) and recognizes their secondary authority (after Scripture) for the contemporary church. This essay will examine one particular case study that I know best: Geneva's reformed church during the sixteenth century.[6] I will argue that the institutional structures and formal presentation of Christian belief in Calvin's Geneva were crucial in defining the boundaries of the religious community, maintaining clerical discipline, enhancing Christian knowledge, and preserving and promoting doctrinal unity among its adherents. Admittedly, the historical and cultural distance between Genevan-style reformed Christianity and modern evangelicalism is vast, and it would be not only unwise, but impossible to impose Calvin's religious system *en toto* on modern congregations. Nevertheless, through this case study, it will be suggested that modern evangelical churches will be strengthened as they recognize their historical roots in the Protestant reformation and appropriate with discernment the fruit of confessional patterns from this heritage.

CONSTRUCTING GENEVA'S CONFESSIONAL CHURCH

On May 21, 1536, after years of political intrigue and religious conflict, the city of Geneva declared her independence from the Catholic Duke of Savoy and formally embraced the Protestant faith. On that day, a general assembly of citizens voted to "live henceforth according to the Law of the Gospel and the Word of God, and to abolish all Papal abuses."[7] Two months later, a young Frenchman named John Calvin (1509–1564) arrived in Geneva for the first time, and was immediately recruited by the fiery preacher Guillaume Farel to serve as a member of the city's pastoral company. From the start, Farel and Calvin faced a volatile religious situation where there were only a handful of qualified preachers, no church constitution, no Protestant liturgy, and no program for educating the city's young people in the tenets of the new faith. As Calvin later recalled, "When I first arrived in this church there was almost nothing. They were preaching and that's all. They were good at seeking out idols and burning them, but there was no Reformation. Everything was in turmoil."[8] Over the next three decades, Calvin and his pastoral colleagues worked tirelessly to construct a city church faithful to

6. This present essay draws upon historical details presented in my monograph *Calvin's Company of Pastors*.

7. Monter, *Calvin's Geneva*, 56.

8. Calvin, "Discours d'adieu aux ministres," in Calvin, *Ioannis Calvini opera omnia* [hereafter cited as *CO*], 9:891–94. See also Monter, *Calvin's Geneva*, 95–97.

the Christian gospel, founded upon four confessional standards that included a confession of faith, a church constitution, a catechism, and a liturgy. These confessional pillars were crucial in shaping the theology and religious culture of Geneva's reformed church for generations to come.

Confession of Faith

One of the most pressing concerns that Calvin faced in the months following Geneva's reformation was the need to set forth with clarity the republic's new religious faith. Hence, in the fall of 1536, Calvin and Farel produced a brief *Confession of Faith* that defined in twenty-one articles Geneva's public theology.[9] The first article of the *Confession* affirmed that Scripture was the only "rule of our faith and religion;" the church must receive no doctrine other than that taught in the authoritative Word of God.[10] At the outset, then, the *Confession* made clear that it was intended to be a concise statement of the chief teachings of holy Scripture—not a substitute for them. The remaining twenty articles of the *Confession* summarized important doctrines found in other Protestant confessions of the period, including human depravity, justification by grace alone through faith alone, Christ's unique mediatorial role in salvation, the nature of the two sacraments, Christian liberty and the obligations of Christian citizens. At the same time, Calvin and Farel gave accent to several doctrines that would become distinctive of reformed Christianity, including the priority of right worship (*soli deo gloria*), the continued role of God's law in the Christian life, and the necessity of church discipline for a rightly ordered church.

Calvin believed that Geneva's confessional statement was not only faithful to Scripture, but also consistent with historic Christian teaching. Hence, in article six of the *Confession of Faith*, Calvin and Farel inserted the Apostles' Creed as an authoritative summary of "all that Jesus Christ has done and suffered for our redemption."[11] In a similar fashion, in his dedicatory epistle to King Francis I, written the previous year and published with his *Institutes of the Christian Religion* (1536), Calvin defended French

---

9. Calvin and Farel, *Confession of Faith*, in Calvin, *Calvin: Theological Treatises*, 25–33. Scholars have debated the paternity of this important theological document. An older generation of scholars, including G. Baum and A. L. Herminjard ascribed the work exclusively to the pen of Farel. Most modern scholars ascribe the work to Calvin, or to the collaboration of Calvin and Farel.

10. Ibid,. 26.

11. Ibid,. 27.

Protestants against the Catholic charge of novelty by appealing not only to Scripture, but also the testimony of the early Christian fathers.

> Moreover, they [the Catholic apologists] unjustly set the ancient fathers against us (I mean the ancient writers of a better age of the church) as if in them they had supporters of their own impiety. If the contest were to be determined by patristic authority, the tide of victory would turn to our side . . . I could with no trouble at all prove that the greater part of what we are saying today meets their approval.[12]

Calvin made a similar argument three years later in his epistolary response to Cardinal Jacob Sadoleto: "Our agreement with antiquity is far closer than yours . . . In all these points, the ancient Church is clearly on our side."[13] From Calvin's perspective, Geneva's reformed faith was no sixteenth-century innovation, but was a faithful summary of biblical Christianity, consistent with the historic teachings of the one, holy, Catholic Church.

Conflict arose almost immediately over the enforcement of Geneva's *Confession of Faith*. Calvin and his pastoral colleagues insisted that all Genevan inhabitants should be required by law to subscribe to the doctrinal standard. They reasoned that, if Geneva was to be a city where the Protestant faith was "purely preached and proclaimed," and where people "lived according to the true Reformation of the gospel," then it was imperative that the pastors have final say on matters of doctrine and discipline—and that the citizens abide by these confessional standards.[14] Though the magistrates initially supported the idea of universal subscription, they soon pushed back due to its political and practical difficulties, and also out of a concern that the city's ministers were undermining magisterial prerogative. They feared that if left unchecked, the Protestant ministers would become new "bishops" and "popes" within the city. After simmering for more than a year, this disagreement exploded into a bitter public controversy in early 1538 when the Small Council began mandating changes to the church's liturgy without the consent of the pastoral company. The city ministers responded by rebuking the magistrates in their sermons and then refusing to celebrate the Lord's Supper at Easter. The magistrates' response was swift and uncompromising:

---

12. Calvin, *Institutes of the Christian Religion: 1536 Edition*, 6. For a helpful discussion of Calvin's understanding of Protestant catholicity, see Beckwith, "The Reformers and the Nicene Faith: An Assumed Catholicity," 70–73.

13. Calvin, *John Calvin-Jacopo Sadoleto: A Reformation Debate*, 62, 74.

14. These descriptions of Geneva's Reformation are found in *Registres du Consistoire*, Archiv d'État de Genève, vol. 17 (1560), fol. 121. Hereafter abbreviated as [R]. Consist.

Calvin and Farel were dismissed from their pastoral posts and commanded to leave the city.[15] Calvin never succeeded in achieving universal subscription to the city's *Confession of Faith*.

Ecclesiastical Ordinances

After a three year exile in Strasbourg, Calvin was welcomed back to Geneva in September 1541, thanks in large part to a shift in the political winds and the city's desperate need for competent religious leadership. Calvin placed two conditions on his return: the city magistrates must approve church-sponsored moral discipline and require catechetical instruction for all the city's residents. Working at a furious pace, Calvin drafted a new constitution for the Genevan church, which was approved by the city council in November 1541 under the title *Ecclesiastical Ordinances*.[16] This constitution created the religious architecture for Geneva's reformed church with the primary goals of "conserving the doctrine of the holy gospel of our Lord and rightly maintaining the purity of the Christian Church."[17] The *Ordinances* recognized four religious offices: the office of pastor, elder, deacon, and doctor. Pastors were expected to preach, administer the sacraments (the Lord's Supper and Baptism), and provide pastoral care. Elders were responsible, with the pastors, for overseeing church discipline. Deacons were assigned the role of collecting and dispensing alms as well as overseeing the public welfare hospital. Doctors or professors were given the responsibility for teaching and defending correct doctrine in the church and schools. In addition to these four offices, the *Ordinances* established daily preaching services in the city's three parish churches; mandated quarterly celebrations of the Lord's Supper[18]; created a disciplinary tribunal known as the Consistory; required children to attend weekly catechism classes; and established guidelines for marriages, funerals, and the visitation of prisoners and the sick.

The *Ecclesiastical Ordinances* created a Christian commonwealth where ministers and magistrates exercised separate, but interdependent

---

15. Gordon, *Calvin*, 78–81; Manetsch, *Calvin's Company of Pastors*, 23–24.

16. Kingdon and Bergier, "Ordonnances Ecclésiastiques," 1–13. An English translation of the first draft of the *Ordinances* is found in Calvin, *Calvin: Theological Treatises*, 56–72.

17. Kingdon and Bergier, "Ordonnances Ecclésiastiques," 1:1.

18. Calvin, *Calvin: Theological Treatises*, 66. Calvin's first draft of the *Ordinances* stipulated that the Lord's Supper should be celebrated once a month in the city or four different times of the year in each of the city's three parish churches. The final draft of the *Ordinances* required that the Lord's Supper be celebrated only four times a year: at Christmas time, Easter, Pentecost, and the first Sunday in September.

roles.[19] Geneva's pastors were responsible to teach God's Word, supervise the religious life of the community, and rebuke the magistrates when they violated divine law. The civil government, on the other hand, in addition to its temporal functions, had jurisdiction over the prosecution of heretics and moral offenders, the provision and maintenance of the city churches, the appointment of elders and deacons to their respective offices, and the financial support of the city's clergy. That Calvin and his colleagues served the church at the good pleasure of Geneva's magistrates was made clear in the oath of office, which was appended to the *Ordinances* the following year. In that oath, the ministers swore to serve God faithfully by "setting forth purely his Word for the edification of this Church," and to "guard and maintain the honor of the Seigneury" and its laws.[20]

Geneva's Catechism

For Calvin, recovering the ancient practice of catechesis was essential for cultivating Christian understanding and preserving authentic Christianity. In a letter to an English correspondent in 1548, he noted that "the church of God will never preserve itself without a catechism, for it is like the seed to keep the good grain from dying out, causing it to multiply from age to age."[21] Calvin wrote not one, but two full-length catechisms during his tenure in Geneva. His first catechism, published in 1538, was written in narrative form and arranged into thirty-three theological topics, including brief treatments of the Ten Commandments, the Apostles' Creed, and the Lord's Prayer (in that order).[22] When Calvin returned from Strasbourg in 1541, he immediately set out to write a much longer catechism that would be better suited to the pedagogical needs of Geneva's children and families.[23] The *Genevan Catechism*, which appeared in early 1542, was organized in the form of a dialogue between a minister and child, covering 373 concise questions and answers. Beginning with the foundational question "What is the chief goal of human life?" (Answer: "It is to know God"), the *Catechism* proceeds to discuss the doctrine of the Trinity, the person and offices of Christ, the atonement, the ministry of the Holy Spirit, the nature of the church, the Law, right worship, prayer, and the sacraments. As with his first catechism, Cal-

19. Gordon, *Calvin*, 126–29; Manetsch, *Calvin's Company of Pastors*, 26–31.
20. Calvin, *Calvin: Theological Treatises*, 71–72.
21. Calvin, "Calvin to Seymour," 5:191.
22. Hesselink, *Calvin's First Catechism, A Commentary*.
23. Grosse, *Les Rituels de la Cène,* 480–98; Manetsch, *Calvin's Company of Pastors*, 265–74.

vin structured his theological discussion around the Ten Commandments, the Apostles' Creed, and the Lord's Prayer—although now he discusses the Commandments *after* the Creed, most likely to emphasize the importance of God's law in guiding Christians toward holiness and obedience.[24] At the end of the *Catechism*, Calvin appended a brief prayer book, containing five model prayers intended for household use and private worship throughout the day. Calvin's goal was not merely to communicate religious information, but also to promote Christian devotion.

Though intended to supplement Geneva's *Confession of Faith*, Calvin's *Catechism* in practice replaced the *Confession* as Geneva's authoritative confessional standard.[25] During the sixteenth century, pastoral candidates and theological students in Geneva were required to affirm publicly that they believed the teaching of Scripture as taught in the *Catechism*. Likewise, before Geneva's residents were permitted to participate in the Lord's Supper in the city's churches, they were required by law to demonstrate a general knowledge of the contents of the *Catechism* and give a public profession of their Christian faith. More than a confessional statement, Calvin's *Catechism* also served as a theological curriculum helping children and adults alike to master the basic message of Protestant Christianity. Calvin and his colleagues preached from the *Catechism* every Sunday at noon, a service which children and ignorant adults were required to attend. City regulations mandated that the weekly catechetical lesson should be reviewed and recited in Geneva's Latin schools and further reinforced by parents in their households. That is not to say that ordinary townspeople were expected to memorize all 373 questions and answers of the *Catechism*. Geneva's religious constitution stipulated that all children be able to recite a *summary* of the contents of *Catechism*, and for that purpose Calvin and several of his colleagues published catechetical summaries to assist in religious formation.[26] These summaries attempted to instill basic theological literacy, the ability to recite in the vernacular the Apostles' Creed, the Ten Commandments, and the Lord's Prayer as well as provide a brief explanation of one's Christian faith. Thus, all Genevans, adults and children alike, needed to know what

---

24. Calvin, *Calvin: Theological Treatises*, 118.

25. See, Grosse, *Les Rituels de la Cène*, 438–39. Two theological developments in the 1540s and early 1550s gave even greater definition to Geneva's public theology as found in the *Catechism*. Geneva's theological concord with Zurich, known as the Consensus Tigurinus (1549), made clear that believers partake of Christ and his gifts spiritually in the Lord's Supper. So too, in the aftermath of Calvin's bitter dispute with Jerome Bolsec in 1551, the city magistrates decreed that, henceforth, all Genevan ministers must subscribe to Calvin's understanding of predestination, as articulated in his *Institutes of the Christian Religion*.

26. Kingdon and Bergier, "Ordonnances Ecclésiastiques," 1:11.

they believed, how to behave, and how to pray. In these ways, then, Calvin's *Catechism* was crucial for defining Geneva's public theology, cultivating Christian understanding, and drawing the boundaries of the city's confessional community.

Geneva's Liturgy

A final confessional pillar of Geneva's church was its Protestant liturgy, the *Forms of Prayers*, which Calvin completed in early 1542.[27] The liturgy provided the structure and theological rationale for Geneva's public religious services, including congregational worship, the celebration of baptism and the Lord's Supper, the celebration of marriage, and the visitation of the sick. The form for Geneva's congregational worship services (held on Sundays and Wednesdays)[28] institutionalized liturgical patterns that became characteristic of reformed worship elsewhere: congregational singing of the Psalms; the general prayer of confession; the recitation of the Lord's Prayer; the prayer of illumination; the sermon; the pastoral prayer; and the recitation of the Apostles' Creed.[29] In the rhythm of the liturgy, week by week, year after year, Geneva's townspeople were instructed in and confessed the central theological truths of the Christian faith, as well as such distinctive reformed beliefs as God's sovereign hand in election, God's covenant of grace, children's inclusion in the visible family of God through baptism, and Christ's real spiritual presence in the Lord's Supper. The liturgy also underlined the spiritual authority of Geneva's ministers and elders, and offered visual testimony to their respective roles and duties. In these ways, then, Calvin's liturgy served an important pedagogical function and complemented the regular recitation of Geneva's *Catechism*.

PRESERVING GENEVA'S CONFESSIONAL CHURCH

John Calvin was not an "ivory tower" theologian. As we have seen, it was Calvin's great achievement to "translate" his religious vision into a confessional church that was intended to be reformed according to the Word of God in

---

27. Calvin, *La forme des prières et chantz ecclésiastique*.

28. Although preaching services were conducted every day of the week, they were accompanied by the full liturgy only on the Day of Prayer (Wednesday mornings) and on Sunday morning services.

29. For more on Calvin's liturgy, see Grosse, *Les Rituels de la Cène*; Manetsch, *Calvin's Company of Pastors*, 152–56. For general patterns of reformed worship, see Benedict, *Christ's Churches Purely Reformed*, 491–532; Murdock, *Beyond Calvin*, 106–18.

doctrine and practice. At the same time, the reformer constructed a number of important church institutions in an effort to consolidate and preserve Geneva's confessional identity into the future. These religious institutions included the Congregation, the Company of Pastors, the Quarterly Censure, the Genevan Academy, and the Consistory.

The Congregation

Patterned after Huldrych Zwingli's *Prophezei* in Zurich, Geneva's Congregation was established in 1536 to provide a setting in which the city's ministers, professors, and interested lay people could regularly study and discuss the contents of Scripture together.[30] The *Ecclesiastical Ordinances* (revised 1561) described the purpose of the Congregation as follows:

> It will be expedient for all the ministers, in order to preserve purity and unity of doctrine among them, to meet together one day each week for a conference on Scripture, and no one will be exempt unless he has a legitimate excuse . . . And so as to assure that every-one is diligent in study and no one becomes nonchalant, each [minister] will be given a turn explaining the Scripture passage from week to week. Afterwards, the ministers will retire and each member of the Company will advise the person who explained [the text] what was wrong, so that this censure might serve to correct him.[31]

The Congregation, then, was a weekly public Bible study, led by members of the city's pastoral company on a rotating basis, in which the ministers and lay people discussed and interpreted the Scripture and applied its message to the broader church and their personal lives. Calvin believed that these Friday morning conferences were essential for the well-being of Geneva's church because they trained the city's ministers as faithful interpreters and expositors of God's Word, held ministers accountable for continued theological development, fostered biblical literacy among the lay people, and helped maintain doctrinal unity in the church. For Calvin, the theological purity and fidelity of the confessional community depended on collegial conferences like these. As he commented to the Bernese reformer Wolfgang Musculus, "the fewer discussions of doctrine we have together, the greater the danger of pernicious opinions."[32]

30. See, De Boer, *The Genevan School of the Prophets*.
31. *CO* 10:1, col. 96.
32. Calvin to Wolfgang Musculus, December 7, 1549, *CO* 13, col. 491.

The Company of Pastors

On Friday mornings, at the conclusion of the Congregation, Geneva's ministers and theological professors retired to their private chambers to conduct the business of the church. Known as the Company of Pastors, this church institution had primary (human) authority over religious life in the city. With Calvin as its moderator, the Company of Pastors examined candidates for ministry, assigned pastors to their parishes, monitored the city's pulpits, debated thorny points of doctrine, supervised diaconal ministries, approved the curriculum at the Academy, and advised Geneva's magistrates. Over time, as Calvin's reputation soared, this deliberative body gained international prominence, becoming a kind of clearing house for pastoral candidates and sound theological advice to reformed congregations as far away as Scotland, northern Germany, and Hungary. At the same time, through its extensive correspondence, the Company of Pastors strove to create a common theological front as reformed churches confronted Catholics, Lutherans and other opponents. It was this concern that prompted the Company to commission a group of city pastors to draft the *Harmony of Confessions of Faith* (1581), which catalogued and compared eleven reformed, Anglican, and Lutheran confessions (including the *variata* edition of the *Augsburg Confession*) in an effort to demonstrate the doctrinal consensus shared by these Protestant churches.[33] In all these ways, then, the Company of Pastors was instrumental both in preserving Calvin's theological vision and promoting it far beyond Geneva's city walls.

The Quarterly Censure

The Quarterly Censure was a third religious institution that Calvin established in Geneva to maintain clerical discipline and preserve right doctrine.[34] The *Ecclesiastical Ordinances* stipulated that, four times a year, on the Friday before the city's quarterly celebrations of the Lord's Supper, the city's pastors should meet behind closed doors to address their personal differences and air their theological disagreements.[35] Although the Censure

---

33. The *Harmony* included the First and Second Helvetic Confessions (1536, 1566), the Confession of Basel (1534), the French Confession of Faith (1559), the Thirty-Nine Articles (1562), the Belgic Confession (1561), the Bohemian Confession (1573), the Tetrapolitan Confession (1530), the Saxon Confession (1551), and the Confession of Württenberg (1552), see Higman, "L'Harmonia Confessionum Fidei de 1581," in *Catechismes et confessions de foi*, 243–62.

34. See Manetsch, *Calvin's Company of Pastors*, 128–29.

35. Kingdon and Bergier, "Ordonnances Ecclésiastiques," 1:5.

was conducted in secret, the minutes of the Company of Pastors provide occasional clues as to the kinds of cases it addressed: pastors were investigated and reprimanded for sexual misconduct, arrogant behavior, resentment toward colleagues, slanderous words, inflammatory sermons, and controversial writings. The Quarterly Censure was an important way that Calvin and his colleagues resolved interpersonal conflict and preserved doctrinal unity among the city's pastors.

The Genevan Academy

Already in 1541, the *Ecclesiastical Ordinances* envisioned the creation of a college to prepare young Genevans for service to the church and civil government. This proposal took institutional shape in 1559 when Calvin founded the Genevan Academy, with Theodore Beza (1519–1605) serving as its first rector. Calvin's Academy consisted of a lower school (*schola privata*) for elementary-age boys, and an upper school (*schola publica*) where more advanced students followed a humanistic curriculum that included biblical studies (based on Greek and Hebrew texts), theology, rhetoric, poetry, history and moral philosophy.[36] The Academy was not a university per se: it had no "faculties" of masters; it imposed no matriculation fees; it conferred no formal degrees. Nevertheless, under Calvin and Beza's capable leadership, the school became "one of the richest intellectual trading markets in the world" (as one alumnus enthused), famous for its outstanding professors and uncompromising commitment to reformed doctrine.[37] In the first five years of its existence, the upper school of the Academy matriculated 338 students, 98 percent of whom were foreign born. Following their studies, most of these students returned to their homes, committed to Calvin's theological vision; perhaps as many as two-thirds became Protestant ministers.[38] The confessional nature of the Academy is illustrated in the formulary that all students were required to sign at matriculation, which affirmed the theological substance of Geneva's *Catechism* and rejected the heresies condemned by the church councils of Nicaea (325), Ephesus (431), and Chalcedon (451).[39] The Academy, therefore, located Geneva's confes-

36. See Maag, *Seminary or University?*; Pettegree, Duke, Lewis, eds., *Calvinism in Europe, 1540–1620*, 35–63.

37. Maag, *Seminary or University?*, 31.

38. Ibid., 29–30.

39. Thévenaz, "L'Ancien collège de sa foundation à la fin du XVIIIe siècle, précédée d'un introduction sur l'instruction publique à Genève au Moyen-Age," 52. The preamble to the *Formulaire de confession de foy* contains the following statement: "I promise that I desire to follow and believe the doctrine of faith as it is contained in the *Catechism*

sion within the larger pattern of historic Christian belief, and played an important role in educating young men in the reformed faith and deploying them as leaders of reformed churches throughout Europe.

The Consistory

Of all the institutions that Calvin established in Geneva, none was more controversial—or important—than the Consistory.[40] As we have seen, one of the conditions for Calvin's return to Geneva in 1541 was that the magistrates permit church-sponsored moral discipline in the city. Consequently, the *Ecclesiastical Ordinances* mandated that the city's pastors, along with twelve lay elders, meet weekly on Thursday afternoons to supervise public morality and apply the spiritual "medicine" of church discipline as needed.[41] Calvin found theological justification for church discipline throughout the New Testament, but especially in the fact that Jesus gave Christian churches the "power of the keys," that is, the spiritual authority to "bind and loose" sinners (Matt 16:19; 18:19). From Calvin's perspective, church discipline in its various forms (whether spiritual counsel, admonitions, rebukes, or temporary suspension from the Lord's Supper) served three important functions: it helped maintain the purity of Christ's church; it protected Christians from the bad example of unrepentant sinners; and it helped secure the repentance of sinners and their restoration to the church. Scripture-based church discipline was therefore essential for a healthy church. As Calvin noted, "all who desire to remove discipline or hinder its restoration . . . are surely contributing to the ultimate dissolution of the church."[42]

The Genevan Consistory addressed hundreds of disciplinary cases each year, the majority of which involved various forms of misbehavior, such as drunkenness, quarrels, spousal abuse, fornication, blasphemy, gambling, and lying.[43] At the same time, the pastors and elders regularly encountered cases of religious ignorance or heterodox belief, and employed their disciplinary authority to enforce Geneva's confessional standards. The Consistory admonished and sometimes suspended from the Lord's Supper people who skipped sermons, refused to learn their *Catechism*, practiced

---

of this church, and also to submit myself to the discipline which is established in it." The use of this formulary was discontinued in 1576. See Maag, *Seminary or University?*, 16–17, 52.

    40. Kingdon, "The Genevan Consistory in the time of Calvin," 21–35.

    41. Kingdon and Bergier, "Ordonnances Ecclésiastiques," 1:11–12.

    42. Calvin, *Institutes of the Christian Religion*, 2:1230.

    43. Manetsch, *Calvin's Company of Pastors*, 201.

folk magic, or espoused Catholic beliefs. In its battle against gross ignorance, the Consistory demanded that men and women purchase Bibles, attend sermons and catechism classes, hire private tutors, and meet with their pastors for personal instruction.[44] To modern sensibilities, the ministry of Calvin's Consistory sometimes appears intrusive and heavy-handed. From Calvin's perspective, however, church discipline was a form of pastoral care that assisted sinners in their journey toward repentance, spiritual restoration, and Christian understanding.

Through the ministry of these five institutions—the Congregation, the Company of Pastors, the Quarterly Censure, the Academy, and the Consistory—Calvin and his colleagues attempted to cultivate reformed convictions and godly behavior among Geneva's residents. They recognized that the future of Geneva's confessional community depended on intentional, intensive, and consistent religious instruction and supervision, at home, in school, and in the church.

CONCLUSION: EVANGELICALS AND CONFESSIONAL THEOLOGY

It goes without saying that modern-day (evangelical) Wheaton is a considerable distance removed from sixteenth-century (reformed) Geneva! Given the vast historical, geographical, cultural, and religious differences, evangelical Christians are rightly suspicious of efforts to repristinate and reproduce Geneva's state church and its religious culture in the modern world. But at the same time, Calvin's commitment to a pattern of Christian truth, codified in formal confessions and preserved through religious institutions, deserves consideration from modern evangelicals who are weary of never-ending religious fragmentation and wary of incessant religious presentism that too easily descends to fads and gimmicks yet remains blind to the rich resources of the historic church. Timothy George's call for evangelical *ressourcement*—to retrieve Christian wisdom from the past for the sake of contemporary renewal—offers a particularly hopeful way forward.

As descendants of the Protestant Reformation and the great revivals of the eighteenth century, contemporary evangelicals have much to learn and appropriate from their Protestant heritage. In particular, evangelical Christians will find time-tested resources for teaching Bible doctrine, catechizing children, and nourishing the faith of God's people as they recover the ancient creeds as well as the confessions, catechisms, and liturgies of their Lutheran, reformed, Anglican, and Anabaptist forebears. We conclude this

---

44. Manetsch, "Discipline and Ignorance in Calvin's Geneva," 103–117.

essay, then, with ten insights for faith and spiritual life that our case study of Geneva's confessional theology offers to evangelical churches and believers.

(1) Protestant confessional theology can strengthen evangelicals' confidence in the unique authority of Scripture. In Calvin's *Confession of Faith*, Scripture was recognized as the "rule of our faith and religion." Similarly, the formulary of the Genevan Academy affirmed Scripture as the perfect rule for Christian life and faith.[45]

(2) Protestant confessional theology can help evangelicals understand the central teachings of Scripture, and recognize the dogmatic rank between primary, secondary, and tertiary doctrines. Calvin's *Catechism*—and the catechetical summaries that it spawned—provided Genevan children and adults with a succinct presentation of the central tenets of the Christian message in a memorable question-answer format.

(3) Protestant confessional theology can teach evangelicals not only the substance of the Christian gospel, but also the pattern of faithful Christian life and devotion. By using the Apostles' Creed, the Ten Commandments, and the Lord's Prayer as pedagogical aids, Calvin's *Catechism* taught Genevans what Christians must believe, how they should behave, and how they were to pray.

(4) Protestant confessional theology can provide evangelicals with standards of right doctrine by which pastors and Christian workers are examined, and to which they are held accountable. In Geneva, pastors were expected to profess and preach the city's *Catechism* and *Confession of Faith*. Ministers who's teaching violated Geneva's public theology were corrected in the Quarterly Censure or rebuked by the Consistory.

(5) Protestant confessional theology can remind evangelicals that their core religious beliefs are not unique to their individual communities, but rooted in a shared orthodoxy professed by Christians around the world over the centuries. Calvin's *Catechism* and liturgy gave prominence to the Apostles' Creed, in which adults and children confessed with Christians throughout the ages, "I believe in one holy catholic Church."

(6) Protestant confessional theology can help evangelicals distinguish orthodox teaching from heresy. The formulary of the Genevan Academy affirmed the teachings of the councils of Nicaea, Ephesus, and

---

45. Thévenaz, "L'Ancien College," 55.

Chalcedon, and recognized their value in refuting the errors of contemporary heretics such as the anti-Trinitarian Michael Servetus.[46]

(7) Protestant confessional theology can provide evangelicals with the doctrinal clarity necessary for constructive ecumenical conversations. Geneva's Company of Pastors pursued ecumenical unity by commissioning the *Harmony of Confessions of Faith* (1581), a document that demonstrated the "family likeness" between Geneva's *Confession* and other reformed, Anglican, and Lutheran confessions of faith.

(8) Protestant confessional theology, as expressed in formal liturgies, can offer evangelicals a consistent pattern of public worship that glorifies God and fosters Christian understanding and faithfulness. Calvin recognized the pedagogical importance of Christian liturgy and was passionately concerned with right worship. Consequently, he structured Geneva's public worship services in such a way that reformed theological convictions were affirmed and explained in the weekly rhythm of the liturgy.

(9) Protestant confessional theology can encourage evangelicals to create church institutions to preserve and promote biblical Christianity. Calvin appreciated the strategic importance of creating church institutions, including the Consistory, the Congregation, and the Academy, to preserve his theological vision in Geneva and throughout Europe.

(10) Protestant confessional theology can help evangelicals recover a robust and biblically faithful doctrine of the Church. It is with good reason that Calvin has sometimes been called the doctor of the church (*doctor ecclesiae*) for, at the heart of his religious vocation, was a commitment to purify and strengthen Christ's Church through ministries of theological reflection and writing, preaching, and pastoral care. Calvin recognized that a solid, biblically informed doctrine of the Church was essential for Christian assurance, identity, and mission in a troubled world. Commenting on the clause "the communion of the saints" in the Apostles' Creed, Calvin noted: "Now, it is very important for us to know what benefit we shall gain from this [article]. The basis on which we believe the church is that we are fully convinced we are members of it. In this way our salvation rests upon sure and firm supports, so that, even if the whole fabric of the world were overthrown, the church could neither totter nor fall."[47]

---

46. Ibid., 52, 54.
47. Calvin, *Institutes* 4.1.3 (trans. Battles, 2:1015).

BIBLIOGRAPHY

Beckwith, Carl L. "The Reformers and the Nicene Faith: An Assumed Catholicity." In *Evangelicals and the Nicene Faith*, edited by Timothy George, 61–73. Grand Rapids: Baker, 2011.

Benedict, Philip. *Christ's Churches Purely Reformed. A Social History of Calvinism*. New Haven, CT: Yale University Press, 2002.

Calvin, Jean. *Calvin: Theological Treatises*. Edited by J. K. S. Reid et al. Philadelphia: Westminster, 1954.

———. "Calvin to Edward Seymour, Duke of Somerset and Regent of England, October 22, 1548." In *Selected Works of John Calvin: Tracts and Letters*, edited by Henry Beveridge, 5:191 1858. Repr., Grand Rapids: Baker, 1983.

———. *La forme des prières et chantz ecclésiastique, avec la maniere d'administrer les Sacremens, & consacrer le Mariage: selon la coustume de l'Eglise ancienne*. Geneva: n.p., 1542. (English)

———. *Institutes of the Christian Religion*. Edited by John T. McNeill. Translated by Ford Lewis Battles. Vol. 2. LCC 21. Philadelphia: Westminster, 1960.

———. *Ioannis Calvini opera quae supersunt omnia*. 59 vols. Edited by E. Cunitz, G. Baum, and E. Reuss. Corpus Reformatorum. Braunschweig: Schwetschke, 1863–1900.

———. *John Calvin, Institutes of the Christian Religion: 1536 Edition*. Translated and annotated by Ford Lewis Battles. Rev. ed. Grand Rapids: Eerdmans, 1986.

Calvin, John. *John Calvin-Jacopo Sadoleto: A Reformation Debate*. Edited and translated by John C. Olin. Grand Rapids: Baker, 1987.

Campbell, Alexander. "Remarks on Confessions of Faith." *Christian Baptist* 2, no. 1 August 2, 1824.

Chute, Anthony L., Christopher W. Morgan, and Robert A Peterson, eds. *Why We Belong: Evangelical Unity and Denominational Diversity*. Wheaton, IL: Crossway, 2013.

De Boer, Eric. *The Genevan School of the Prophets: The Congregations of the Company of Pastors and Their Influence in 16th Century Europe*. Geneva: Droz, 2012.

Dockery, David S. "Denominationalism: Historical Developments, Contemporary Challenges, and Global Opportunities." In *Why We Belong: Evangelical Unity and Denominational Diversity*, edited by Anthony L. Chute, Christopher W. Morgan, and Robert A. Peterson, 209–31. Wheaton, IL: Crossway, 2013.

George, Timothy. *Evangelicals and the Nicene Faith: Reclaiming the Apostolic Witness* Grand Rapids: Baker Academic, 2011.

Gordon, Bruce. *Calvin*. New Haven, CT: Yale University Press, 2009.

Grosse, Christian *Les Rituels de la Cène*. Geneva: Droz, 2008.

Hatch, Nathan O. *The Democratization of American Christianity*. New Haven, CT: Yale University Press, 1989.

Hesselink, John, I. *Calvin's First Catechism, A Commentary*. Louisville: Westminster John Knox, 1997.

Higman, Francis. "L'*Harmonia Confessionum Fidei* de 1581." In *Catechismes et confessions de foi*, edited by Marie-Madelaine Fragonard and Michel Peronnet. Montpellier: Université de Montpellier, 1995.

Kalantzis, George, and Andrew Tooley, eds., *Evangelicals and the Early Church: Recovery, Reform, Renewal* Eugene, OR: Cascade, 2012.

Kingdon, Robert. "The Genevan Consistory in the Time of Calvin." In *Calvinism in Europe, 1540–1620*, edited by Andrew Pettegree et al., 21–34. Cambridge: Cambridge University Press, 1994.

Kingdon, R., and J. F. Bergier. "Ordonnances Ecclésiastiques." In *Registres de la Compagnie des Pasteurs de Genève au Temps de Calvin*, edited by R. Kingdon and J. F. Bergier, 1:1–13. Geneva: Droz, 1964.

Maag, Karin. *Seminary or University? The Genevan Academy and Reformed Higher Education, 1560–1620*. Aldershot, UK: Ashgate, 1995.

Manetsch, Scott. "Discipline and Ignorance in Calvin's Geneva." *Unio cum Christo* 3, no. 2 (2017) 103–17.

———. *Calvin's Company of Pastors: Pastoral Care and the Emerging Reformed Church, 1536–1609*. New York: Oxford University Press, 2013.

Monter, William E. *Calvin's Geneva*. New York: Wiley & Sons, 1967.

Murdock, Graeme. *Beyond Calvin: The Intellectual, Political and Cultural World of Europe's Reformed Churches* New York: Palgrave Macmillan, 2004.

Packer, J. I., and Thomas Oden. *One Faith, The Evangelical Consensus*. Downers Grove, IL: InterVarsity, 2004.

Pettegree, Andrew, Alastair Duke, and Gillian Lewis, eds. *Calvinism in Europe, 1540–1620*. Cambridge: Cambridge University Press, 1994.

Phillips, Richard, Philip Ryken, and Mark E. Dever. *The Church: One, Holy, Catholic and Apostolic* Phillipsburg, NJ: P&R, 2004.

Registres du Consistoire, 1551–1609. Unpublished manuscript, Archiv d'État de Genève.

Sweet, William Warren. *The Story of Religion in America*. New York: Harper & Bros., 1950.

Thévanaz, Louis J. "L'Ancien college de sa foundation à la fin du XVIIIe siècle, précédée d'un introduction sur l'instruction publique à Genève au Moyen-Age." In *Histoire du Collège de Genève*, edited by Louis J. Thévenaz et al. Geneva, 1896.

An Unacknowledged Heritage

D. Mark DeVine

> If an American church calls itself "non-denominational,"
> nine times out of ten what that means is Baptist.
> Parish Priest in the Episcopal Church[1]

> What you have as heritage,
> Take now as task;
> For thus you will make it your own!
> Goethe, *Faust*

2002. IF ANY SMALLISH flames of Southern Baptist triumphalism yet remained, they surely flickered out that year, or should have. With stark statistical bluntness Philip Jenkins measured and charted the weakening and prognosticated the decline of Christianity in North America. The release of his *The Next Christendom* marshalled too much evidence to pass over or wave off.[2] Not decline in the mainline. No news in that! But decline among evangelicals. Decline signaled even by the giant denominational juggernaut canary in the evangelical coal mine—the Southern Baptist Convention.

The undeniable reality the cold numbers revealed delivered a shock to the Baptist consciousness. For generations these Baptists had known almost nothing but numerical growth, geographical expansion, and eventually, great cultural influence, even formidable political clout. Sometimes slow and steady, more often robust or even exponential, the rise of the Baptists roared right into the second half of the twentieth century. For almost a hundred

---

1. Jonathan Mitchican, "Ask an Anglican: An Evangelical, a Baptist, and a Charismatic Walk Into a Bar . . ." *Conciliar Anglican* (blog), January 19, 2014, https://conciliaranglican.com/2014/01/19/ask-an-anglican-an-evangelical-a-baptist-and-a-charismatic-walk-into-a-bar/.

2. Jenkins, *The Next Christendom*.

and fifty years, the strengths and skillsets developed among them fit well enough the challenges of growth management, the building and sustaining of new and growing institutions and expanding global missionary frontiers.

Faced now with waning indices of health and growth and Jenkins' brutal demographic trend lines, the feel of being Southern Baptist suffered a startling, unexpected reversal. The self-assured Baptist surfers on an ever-swelling triumphant wave reduced now to passengers alternately in shock, panicky, numb and resigned, riding the deck of a sinking denominational Titanic.

For some century and quarter, from their slavery-entangled inception in 1845, Southern Baptists rose along an amazing upward arc of growth. No wonder admission that that party is over has come only slowly and grudgingly. But come it has and, with the colossal shift of the center of gravity and forecasted future vitality of the church to the global south, a fresh examination not only of Southern Baptists but of the now four century old Baptist movement itself seems especially appropriate.

THE SKY AIN'T FALLIN'

As acceptance of decline spread, certain Baptists leaders themselves joined and sometimes led a chorus of pessimism. Here and there the language of doom deepened and darkened. But once the newly minted rhetoric of "the declining church" morphed into "the dying church," statisticians, number crunchers, and trend-observers pushed back, Ed Stetzer among them.

Not only is the church in North America not dying, Stetzer insisted, it is growing. Granted, that growth lags significantly behind projected increase in total population. The "decline" Jenkins's charts and rubs in our faces apply not to raw numbers, but to market share. Embedded within this continent-wide church-growth anemia, pockets and streams of spiritual vitality yet pulsate, networks of ecclesial renewal grow and extend, and effective evangelism still occurs.

But where and through whom and how do such streams of evangelical vitality flourish among us? Two juxtaposed Stetzer findings in particular should intrigue observers and friends of the Baptist movement.[3] These show that decline in Southern Baptist affiliation coincides almost exactly with the rise of nondenominational communities of faith. That coincidence renders

---

3. Ed Stetzer, "The Rapid Rise of Nondenominational Christianity: My Most Recent Piece at CNN," *Christianity Today*, The Exchange, June 12, 2015, http://www.christianitytoday.com/edstetzer/2015/june/rapid-rise-of-non-denominational-christianity-my-most-recen.html.

the epigram header to this chapter all the more intriguing. Additional research makes clear that, far and away the most significant pockets and streams of Christian growth in North America are evangelical, nondenominational, and, in varying degrees, charismatic.

What is the relationship of the nondenominational phenomenon and the 400-year-old Baptist movement? I offer two anecdotes to help us answer this question. The first involved my own irresistible attraction to a bunch of nondenominational pastors and the communities of faith they led. The second centers on the Episcopal priest's intriguing and cocksure outing of nondenominational Christians in greater Philadelphia as Baptists.

My first encounters with what has become a significant international church-planting movement were with pastors and churches associated with or deeply influenced by Mark Driscoll, Darrin Patrick, and the Acts29 network. The attraction and repulsion these doctrine-friendly emerging churches stirred up included, from the get-go, both alien and familial dimensions.[4] Certain ostensibly *un-Baptist-like* practices flourished among them. Pronouncedly non-cessationist, they sought and expected fresh movements of God the Holy Spirit wielding the full biblical array of weapons and gifts, supernatural ones included. And not a few of them drank and cussed and ran with them that did likewise.

How Baptist can such folk be? And yet my own Southern Baptist shaping is so deep, so congenital, that I doubt turning atheist could fully undo it. Perhaps it's a bit like being a Jew? So I expect my Baptist-detecting radar ranks with the most sensitive and sure available. Though the Southern Baptist Convention I have inhabited since childhood accommodated far more diversity than is usually acknowledged, I certainly had never encountered nor even heard of Baptists like these. Some of them, though most, had never been a member of a church with Baptist in the name. Others could not remember hearing the name Lottie Moon!

And yet, the more exposure to them I gained, the more they stirred and drew my Baptist sensibilities like metal filings to a gigantic magnet. At some gut level, I knew these "non-denoms" were my spiritual siblings as no Roman Catholic, Anglican, Presbyterian, or Methodist could ever be. This realization, at first largely instinctual and unexamined, was of that not so easily dismissed, takes-one-to-know one sort.

But what about that Yankee Episcopalian? Their non-committal, non-denominational moniker notwithstanding, the priest, with the air of

---

4. For an examination of such doctrine-friendly nondenominational groups and the rationale for including them within the emerging church movement, see my "The "Emerging Church: One Movement—Two Streams," in Henard and Greenway eds., *Evangelicals*, 4–45.

an accusatory "Aha!," declared those sheep-stealing interlopers to be "Baptists!" No matter what they called themselves and no matter what their name seemed to deny or attempted to obfuscate, he knew who they were and wanted his little Episcopal flock to know and be warned.

This was no takes-one-to-know-one identification—the priest had never been nor wanted to be a Baptist. His confidence, equally impressive, sprang from long familiar acquaintance with an alien life form—the Baptist life form. The priest is the 12-year-old BB gun-toting boy in his third summer, traipsing through the woods relaxed and assured, poised to spot game. He has never been a squirrel and never shall be, but he'll recognize one consistently and with absolute accuracy till the day he dies. And he'll never mistake one for a raccoon.

BAPTISTS OR NOT?

Well squirrels and raccoons are one thing. Baptists and not-Baptists are another. Is the priest's cocksure declaration accurate? Was my visceral attraction to the nondenoms truly familial? Closer scrutiny of these nondenominational seems to yield conflicting data.

In addition to alcohol, they imbibe a fair amount of Presbyterian, Reformed Anglican and Reformed Baptist literature, resulting in a kind of Peter-John-Piper-picked-a-peck-of-J.I. Packers hermeneutics. But the penetration of paedo-baptist influence notwithstanding, adherence to believer's baptism remains strong among them. For these "nondenoms," application of water to an infant, however accoutremented with holy language, well-meaning parents, and encouraging clergy, never justifies application of the word "baptism" to the event.

The church-planting pastors among them are saturated with the Bible and answerable to it. They believe in conversion and employ a myriad array of approaches to secure them. They self-consciously rejected the most blatant seeker-sensitive accommodations of the gospel message to target audiences, but do relentlessly attempt to identify and remove unnecessary stumbling blocks to gospel advance and church growth.

Growth matters to them. Like Luke and the original church planters lionized in the book of Acts, they count conversions and disciple-makings, record them, celebrate their increase, and are sure this is what the Holy Spirit is about. And lo and behold their numbers are increasing and that's why Stetzer's graphs look the way they do.

Also striking is their recovery, whether consciously or not, of contemporarily weakened but still quintessential markers of historic Baptist identity.

The quest for regenerate church membership sought through doctrinally serious pre-baptismal and pre-membership pastoral scrutiny. Reversion to early Baptist plural male-elder leadership. And perhaps most surprising and conspicuous, pursuit of an explicitly confessional, disciplined, and "covenanted" model of congregational life. And like the Particular Baptists of the seventeenth century, they hold to Reformed soteriological views.

The careful crafting and considered employment of church covenants among these non-denominational marks an especially fascinating development. It bears upon the question of the degree of "Baptistness" with which these communities can be justifiably accused. It anchors these non--denominationals within a "covenanting" tradition far more conspicuous among Baptists than any other major historic stream of the Christian tradition. It connects them to the "believers church" tradition reaching back to the Hussites and Czech Brethren of Bohemia.[5] Predating the emergence of the Baptist movement by almost two centuries, it was from the convictional and temperamental soil of the believer's church tradition that the Congregationalists and the English Separatists and finally the Baptist movement itself would emerge.

Among these assorted progenitors and developers of the believers' church tradition, it was the Baptist movement that emerged as a veritable covenant-making machine. So what are these covenants? They are the "ethical counterparts to confessions of faith."[6] In confessions members articulate shared belief. In covenants they declare how they ought and intend to behave, toward one another and toward those outside the church. Early Baptists made formal vocal ascription to such covenants, often buttressed by annual renewals. Such practice waned almost to the vanishing point among Baptists in the twentieth century. But today, led by the Baptist nondenominationals, the practice is coming back, not just among these nondenoms, but within Southern Baptist churches as well.

BAPTIST NON-DENOMINATIONAL?

Like the word "post-modern" so "non-denominational" trumpets its own weak, makeshift, stop-gap character. But the non-denominational moniker in this case, ironically, and perhaps unbeknownst to the priest, far from undermining, may actually strengthen his outing of them as Baptists.

Recall that the Southern Baptist Convention has never been and is not now a "church" as say, the Presbyterian Church of America or the Roman

---

5. See Deweese, *Covenants*, 38; and George and George, eds., *Confessions*, 14–16.
6. George and George, eds., *Confessions*, 14.

Catholic Church undoubtedly are. The SBC is a convention of voluntarily associating local churches. The fundamental and irreducible unit of the reality called "church" for Baptists, from their early seventeenth century British beginnings, was unmistakably and emphatically the gathered local body of believers, period. Supplementation of such gathered communities with various affiliations or partnerships added precisely nothing to their status as churches, nor could the loss or severing of such external ties diminish that status in their eyes one whit.

For Baptists, the *sina qua non* of "church" includes lots of stuff—authoritative Bibles, a Reformation-shaped gospel, believer's baptism, regenerate church membership, and local church autonomy—all of which apply to these nondenoms. For Baptists, protectiveness for local church autonomy did not forestall, but rather allowed for Baptist church affiliation with other Baptist churches and entities. The most spectacular historical flourishing of such Baptist affiliation is undoubtedly the convening, rise, and growth of the Southern Baptist Convention with its supporting sub-affiliations of Baptists in local associations and state Baptist conventions. But every extra-local church connection or partnership among them remained derivative, utilitarian, explicitly voluntary, ontologically *ad hoc* and so, ultimately, dispensable. And that applies to denominational affiliation as well. So, oddly, even the non-denominational status of these communities of faith cannot, of itself, count against the priest's charge of "Baptist!"

NON-DENOMINATIONAL CREDENTIALS

The actual situation on the ground reveals that the so-called non-denominational have trouble living up to their own non-denominational posture. Scratch just below the surface of these churches boasting utterly "Baptist"—devoid websites and street signage and what do you find? With some frequency you catch them all mired-up in denominational affiliation after all.

With plans to attend for the first time the church of a former student, I asked for a bit of information about the congregation. The first thing out of the student's mouth, and without one hint of hesitance or embarrassment was "Well, it's Southern Baptist . . ." Later that day, perusing the church's website, on perhaps the fifteenth click of the mouse, I stumbled upon the single occurrence of the word "Baptist" to be found—one of the staff members was also employed at the Baptist Children's home in that state.

One conviction is shared by our Episcopal priest, the legitimately non-denominational Baptists, and the denominationally affiliated Baptists posing as non-denominational; namely, that the word "Baptist" is a downer and a turn-off. For the priest, a downer and turn-off to his own parishioners—if they knew those folks are really Baptists, fewer would stray that way. For the nondenom leaders, a downer and turn-off to those they wish to reach with the gospel. The weakness of the term non-denominational is its failure to offer positive signification. Its attraction for nondenom church planters lies in its perceived utility for the disentangling of itself from the stumbling block of Baptist denominational affiliation. But even here the nondenom church planters are tracking along with the Southern Baptist Convention, which itself has considered a change of name with "Baptist" excised.

The misleading connotations of the term non-denominational prove complex indeed. We think of the nondenoms as leaving behind Baptist sources of spiritual formation in favor of non-Baptist mentors, literature, and non-denominational networks. But, recently I was invited to give my personal testimony at one these congregations—"give your personal testimony?—already the strong whiff of Baptist vapors wafting about!

This congregation boasted five teaching elders, three of them grateful graduates of none other than The Southern Baptist Theological Seminary. It's easy as pie to track down congregation after congregation of these nondenoms led by pastors whose formal and face-to-face spiritual and theological formation occurred largely within Southern Baptist churches, seminaries, and mission agencies. The SBC, her institutions and cooperating churches are simultaneously serving as a negative foil against which these Generation X and Millennial pastors react and as sources of shaping and producers of spiritual and ecclesial resources for them.

This complex cross-pollination between the nondenoms and the denomination itself includes a very powerful feedback loop in the opposite direction as well. The chosen models and mentors for current Xer and Millennial pastors and planters of Southern Baptist churches are precisely the Xer and Millennial pastors of the nondenom churches.

What we are witnessing in the rise of Baptist non-denominational is a renewal movement within the Baptist tradition. That renewal involves significant cross-pollination between a wide and diverse array of Baptist congregations and institutions across the entire spectrum of stronger, weaker, hidden, and non-existent denominational affiliation. They are watching each other, copying each other, reading each other's books and blogs and dipping toes into each other's networks. Examination of the non-denominational phenomenon draws one into a big complex and dynamic Baptist happening boasting numerous North American bases of vitality and international church-planting tentacles.

NON-DENOMINATIONAL IDENTITY

The inability of the non-denominational moniker to signify much combined with eschewal of the Baptist name by communities bearing the characteristic marks of historic Baptist identity results in strangely stymied efforts to tell the world and themselves who they are.

Redeemer Church, Cedar Rapids, Iowa is a case in point. Their website overall and their confession of faith in particular locates them squarely among the Baptist nondenoms. The pastors' confession of faith runs onto eighteen pages and is carefully and, at times, even beautifully crafted. This confession of faith is undergirded by (I am not kidding) two-hundred and ninety-nine endnotes! These endnotes are chocked full of, not just Scripture citations, but extensive and carefully selected Scripture quotes—fifty-nine pages worth! As far as ecclesial identity is concerned, folks who feel compelled to explain themselves so formally and elaborately must be ranked among the most identity-fixated imaginable.

But the best is yet to come. The confessional section of the website boasts two appendices, the first entitled "Denials." These pastor/elders, having offered extensive positive affirmation of who they are, now insist on making clear who they aren't. In this four-page section, organized around thirty-two bullet points, the elders want all to know that they are not liberals, fundamentalists, isolationists, hyper-Calvinists, universalists, moralists, religious relativists, open theists, egalitarians, classic dispensationalists, theonomists, naturalists, evangelical feminists, or polemicists.[7] *Good Heavens!* Is it possible to successfully avoid being so many things? It seems doubtful but the attempt is impressive. These bulleted and rejected stances and views are not just listed in this "Denial" section of the website, they include clarifying, mini-explanations for the uninitiated.

Yet within this stunningly laborious exercise of identity affirming, denying and circumscribing, one word remains conspicuously absent, ostensibly un-needed, and seems especially unwelcome—"Baptist." But take note, this word is not only absent in the confessional assertions but fails to appear in the denials as well. Surely that word, though absent from the little mountains of identity-articulating verbiage, hovers like ghost above the whole "this is who we are" and "this is who we aren't" enterprise. Its absence evidences a strain of tension and ambiguity snaking through many of these non-denominational churches—communities of faith bearing unmistakable distinguishing marks, especially when they occur in combination,

---

[7] "Pastoral Statement of Faith," Redeemer Church, https://static1.squarespace.com/static/518d802ae4b05913b69c534f/t/51bf59a2e4b03b777468233a/1371494818018/Pastoral+Statement+of+Faith.pdf.

of the 400 year old Baptist movement: local church autonomy, believer's baptism, regenerate church membership, covenant congregational life undergirded by locally crafted church covenants, potent and often effective evangelical and missional zeal, theological rootedness in the Reformation and with traces of Great Awakening zeal for conversion and heart religion.

RETRIEVAL AND DEVELOPMENT

Even the ways in which the nondenoms differ from the Southern Baptist churches from which they recoil actually situates them within, not outside the Baptist movement. Their explicitly Reformed soteriological beliefs and male-elder leadership models retrieve historic Baptist conviction and practice. Likewise, in their eschewal of the worst accommodations of the gospel message by the seeker church movement they revert to more historically confident dogmatic Baptist engagement with the world. The recovery of church covenants, church discipline, a more sacramental understanding of the Lord's Supper as a spiritual banquet, the guarding of regenerate church membership more closely at the baptismal pool and in the reception of already baptized candidates for membership, retrieves a Baptist ecclesial seriousness that had attenuated during the middle decades of the twentieth century.[8] Even their dropping of Baptist tee totaling recovers historic majority practice from across the pond. There it was mainly the Methodists, not the Baptists, who traded in their port for grape juice.

Another distinction of these nondenoms, a self-conscious ecumenical cross-pollination and borrowing, may be unique in Baptist history, certainly when the scale of the phenomenon is taken into account. These Baptists are open to examination of, learning from, and ultimately adoption of convictions and practices from a wide spectrum of streams within the Christian tradition.

They are reexamining and reshaping worship and many are moving away from historic Baptist low-church suspicion of ritual, liturgy, and the sacramental. Though still privileging the ear, "faith comes by hearing," the nondenoms are designing worship experiences to engage the other four senses as well. It is hard to find one of these churches that does not celebrate the Lord's Supper weekly. And they tend to do so by intinction with every member filing forward in a visually arresting display of communion with each other and with their Lord. One does not here of glossolalia outbreaks among them, and no one seems upset that this is so. Yet they tend to be

---

8. See Fowler, *More Than a Symbol*; and Cross and Thompson, *Baptist Sacramentalism*.

pronouncedly non-cessationist in their views on the activity and gifts of the God the Holy Spirit.

TRADITION, RENEWAL, AND THE NON-DENOMS

The ecumenical openness and engagement of the nondenoms also situate them on the more Baptist (as opposed to more Restorationist or Campbellite) modes of Protestantism. Yes, early Baptists, constrained by their reading of Holy Scripture, felt so compelled to resist, reject, and rebuke so much that they found in the Church of England, that only separation offered a path forward. But their earliest confessional statements modeled themselves as much as possible upon that quintessential standard of English Presbyterianism, the Westminster Confession of 1647.

The Baptist framers of the 1679 Orthodox Creed were proud planters of separated, autonomous, local congregations, but also grateful heirs of the patristic consensus of the early church. For them, being Baptist required separating from the Church of England and saying some hard things about the Pope. It meant full-throated embrace of both the formal and material bases of the Reformation, together with all the *solas* including the one on Scripture insisting upon submission to the Bible as the *norma normans* of faith and practice. But that same commitment to Holy Scripture meant commending the Nicene, Athanasian, and Apsotles Creeds which, they said, "ought thoroughly to be received and believed."[9]

Restorationist language such as "getting back to the early church" and "no creed but the Bible" would eventually flourish among Baptists. But these catch phrases belie and mask the more fundamental anchoring of Baptists within the great Christian tradition that their confessional history confirms. Careful examination of the Baptist tradition reveals it as a renewal movement within the great orthodox tradition of the historic church. Does close scrutiny of these Baptist non-denominationals reveal a renewal movement within the 400 year old Baptist movement? I think so.

A decade ago, David S. Dockery identified multiple dimensions of Southern Baptist life in need of renewal. Is it not striking how closely many of the prominent features and stated aspirations of these non-denominational churches center on those concerns?[10] Dockery called for renewal in Baptist preaching, biblical centeredness, practice of the ordinances, worship, and Baptist confessional seriousness, acknowledgment of and embrace of Baptist indebtedness to (1) the Trinitarian and Christological consensus of

---

9. George and George, eds., *Confessions*, 120–21.
10. Dockery, *Consensus*.

the early church, (2) the formal and material bases of the Reformation, and (3) the conversion-seeking and heart-transforming emphases of the Great Awakenings. Every one of these targeted dimensions of renewal receive significant focus in various parts of the diverse phenomenon that is the Baptist non-denominational movement.

Not surprisingly, one area identified by Dockery is conspicuously absent among the nondenoms—renewal through recovery of our shared Baptist heritage. My contention is that these nondenoms, however weak or strong or non-existent their indices of Baptist denominational affiliation or disaffiliation, are in fact part of the historic Baptist movement and are both developing that movement and bringing needed and surprising elements of renewal to it. I believe, furthermore, that this renewal is being nurtured, not only by non-Baptist but also by denominationally located Baptist entities, especially certain of the SBC seminaries which are educating many of the pastor/elder leaders of these congregations. I also believe that the nondenoms are bringing renewal to Southern Baptist churches and to the SBC through various feedback channels—especially the SBC affiliated church pastors who choose the nondenom churches as models and seek mentoring from nondenom pastors. Recently, at an SBC church conference, I discovered that one of the workshop leaders serves as an elder at an ACTS29 affiliated church-plant launched and sponsored by a sister SBC church.

A cross-pollination of renewal seems strong across the ever changing Baptist landscape. Efforts by stronger churches to re-plant declining ones and the pursuit of church mergers by struggling congregations of similar strength are taking their place alongside more traditional from-scratch church planting.[11] Baptists seem particularly equipped to confront the new challenges of the increasingly post-Christian landscape that is North America. Baptist habituation to local church autonomy and thus local church responsibility welcomes multiple and changing voluntary partnerships, paths of communication, and cooperation. It seems uniquely prepared for trial and error in leadership, adjustment, and changes of direction.

IDENTITY FIXATION

The non-denominationals' obsession over their identity suggests that they long for but have not found something only heritage and name can possibly provide. This longing first expressed itself not in the current proliferation

---

11. See e.g., the replanting efforts led by Mark Jobe, lead pastor of the non-denominational New Life Community Church in Chicagoland (http://newlifecommunity.church/Ministries); and DeVine and Patrick, *RePlant*.

of verbiage filling up their "Who We Are" website links, but as a quest for what they called "authenticity" and "authentic relationships" and "authentic community." This quest found public expression during the early days of the emerging churches, before the doctrine-friendly Baptist non-denoms eschewed the "emerging" label. Because of their commitment to Christian orthodoxy, Reformation theology, and disciplined communities of faith, they rejected the doctrine-wary and doctrine-averse advancers of a "generous orthodoxy." These restless but not reformed emerging church leaders envisioned community life either devoid of doctrinal commitment altogether or one free of all but minimalist confessional requirements.[12] They exhibited keen alertness to the relational dangers strict doctrinal policing posed. "Belonging before believing" became their mantra.[13]

But make no mistake about it—the doctrine friendlies of the ACTS29 and now the Sojourn church planting networks, while recognizing the nonsensical and unworkable attenuation of belief among the doctrine-averse, still long to belong. They are sure that depth of fellowship depends, in significant measure, upon shared conviction, and that real belonging is always built upon authentic relationships. But what do they mean by "authentic?"

"Authentic" may serve as a catch-all phrase referencing relational deprivations suffered disproportionately first by Gen-Xers and now by Millennials. The first generation of nondenom leaders are the children of the Baby-boomer parents who divorced one another at unprecedented rates. These same Gen-Xers also experience the dislocations attending an increasingly more mobile populace grappling with an economy demanding more and more travel and rewarding frequent moves. Throw in the isolating effects of increased internet surfing, ubiquitous, continuous earbud usage, and the hunger for relationship and community seems easy to explain.

But neither the deprivation of relationship and community nor the hunger for both nor the pursuit of both indicate depth of understanding or potential for establishing or maintaining either. Tim Keller says the Millennial generation may well articulate deeper longing for authentic, lasting relationship than any ever seen. But, he cautions, they may also perhaps be, as a generation, especially ill-equipped for the establishing and maintaining of such relationships. Inability to trust and commit thwart and cripple their pursuit of what they say they especially desire—sustained authentic relationships in community. A major contention of this chapter is that the deepest sustainable Christian siblinghood, the birthright of every member

---

12. See McLaren, *Generous*; and Hansen, *Restless*.
13. See Gibbs and Bolger, eds., *Emerging*, 124–25.

of the Body of Christ, is only available where conscious embrace of the historically identifiable traditions to which one is heir occurs.

Many nondenom pastors and elders exhibit strong susceptibility to embrace of an historically embedded comprehension of identity. They are spiritually awake, biblically rooted, and historically engaged. They have difficulty suppressing or hiding an unrequited desire for a genuine, historically locatable and trackable lineage within the body of Christ. They seek out and find historical teachers, mentors, and models with impressive energy and consistency. From the Cappadocians and Augustine to Luther and Calvin, Edwards and Spurgeon, Packer and Piper, Stott and Keller. They periodically snuggle up to various Lutherans, Presbyterians, Congregationalists, Anglicans and yes, Baptists too.

WHAT'S IN A NAME?

Yet no name attaching to the historically embedded ecclesial homes of their teachers is allowed to materialize *in concreto* and apply to them. If the word "Baptist" is visible near their worship space it will cry out unwelcome from ineffaceable letters etched in the stone facade of an old Baptist church they now inhabit.

Rather than burden themselves with the historically "authentic" name of an historical and thus an "authentic" tradition, even their own, they choose names that seem to offer escape from that historical morass—names that seem able to soar above the historical fray. Names drawn from the Bible—Christ, Redeemer, Sojourn—or names attempting to capture some ideal ecclesial aspiration or feature of true discipleship—Mosaic, Journey. Wonderful names all. But do they not signal also a retreat from authenticity? The Episcopal priest did not need to see the actual letters B–a–p–t–i–s–t to know what was in front of him. And neither do I.

What sullied the word Baptist, what expanded its semantic range to encompass spheres of shame was the same thing that tarnishes most words taken as names—the attachment of the name to actual people, people eat-up with sin. Did not the Crusades do the same thing to the name "Christian" and "church"? But the thing about names is that they come to "embody" as they signify, authentically, the real histories of the actual peoples—the peoples of God replete with all their triumphs and tragedies. These streams of tradition record, remember, and cherish the history of our Lord's post-canonical promise-keeping as when he said "I will build my church."

As the branches of the differentiated traditions trace out the particular histories of the obediences and disobediences of particular peoples, they also bear witness to the particular and myriad faithfulnesses of God, his forgivenesses and mercies, his spankings and his deliverances. The members of these distinctive branches bear both the burden and the privilege to give authentic witness to God's faithfulness that only their branch can offer—their distinct contribution to the chorus that glorifies God. The plural "us" Jesus put into our mouths in "forgive us our trespasses" applies to and facilitates authentic Christian siblinghood not only within local congregations, but within the traditions to which they are heirs. Those who try to fly above the historical fray settle for observance of such historically embedded, authentic, family worship. Owning one's heritage opens the door to fuller, more authentic participation. Authenticity and familial bonds co-inhere. Attenuation of one diminishes both.

Angelina Jolie disowned Jon Voight, the biological father who abandoned her. She refused to take his name, refused to see him for years. But nothing she could do could undo the unique bequeathment biological parentage alone delivers—the innumerable and indelible earmarks of family, some visible and obvious, others subtle but all the more telling for being so. Her face, her gait, distinctive behavioral habits and tendencies of temperament bore the unmistakable stamp of that oh so namable lineage from which she sought extrication and escape—the physical and spiritual stamp of the Voight clan.

When the all but irrepressible urge of the adopted child to find their birth parents erupts, it is usually driven by a hunger for self-discovery and belonging of a sort biological parents alone can provide. Jaroslav Pelikan offers this advice to Christians either neglectful or wary of their "parenting" traditions in the faith:

> Maturity in relation to our parents consists in going beyond both a belief in their omniscience and a disdain for their weakness, to an understanding and a gratitude for their decisive part in that ongoing process in which now we, too, must take our place, as heirs and yet free. So it must be in our relation to our spiritual and intellectual parentage, our tradition. An abstract concept or parenthood is no substitute for real parents, an abstract cosmopolitanism no substitute for our real traditions.[14]

All human beings belong not only to the human family but to an actual biologically traceable one. The longing of the adopted child in search of that family, the quest by others to trace their family trees arises not from mere curiosity but from a deep and legitimate search for one's true self and the most authentic community of one's human belonging, not just to that

---

14. Pelikan, *Vindication*, 54.

family, but that family as the only authentic path to ones belonging within the wider human family.

However indelible is the biological inheritance that shapes us as human beings who belong to Jesus Christ, it cannot compete with, is in fact trumped by, even as it is redeemed by our incorporation into this spiritual family tree. This one alone is permanent. Here we meet our eternal siblings with whom we share our eternal Father. Here alone we find the place where the deepest, most authentic relationships in community are formed and thrive.

The attempt to fly above the Christian tradition and treat it as a treasure trove from which we may pick and choose what want according to some independent preference involves an act of self-deception. One does actually belong to a real, historically locatable and traceable branch of the family tree the triune God planted. It is along particular branches that we receive life giving water coming up from the trunk. It is along particular branches that the photosynthesized nutrients of leaves spread down that branch and feed the other branches and the tree as a whole.

Staff and I were discussing "Baptistness" just before worship at an SBC-affiliated but non-denominationally postured church. A layperson, overhearing the conversation, interrupted us with happy enthusiasm. "I grew up Southern Baptist and dropped out of church eight years ago. But two years ago I made two decisions—(1) I would find a church and (2) it would definitely NOT be a Baptist church. So I ended up here. A few months later I discovered that this is not only a Baptist church, it's a Southern Baptist Church. But it's too late now. I love it here and I feel completely at home now."

The most effective medicine for many a dissatisfied, disgruntled, disgusted, and wounded Baptist turns out to be some concoction of Baptist ecclesial elixir mixed up and served by some variety of Baptist denominational. Why might this be? Why do folks set on not being Baptist somehow find themselves chewing again the same ole Baptist cud? Partly because of the power of tradition. What Jaroslav Pelikan says of this power is true: "tradition does not have to be understood," much less self-consciously embraced "in order to be dominant."[15]

HERITAGE, TASK, AND OWNERSHIP

My desire is to see all three elements of Goethe's encouragement play out among the nondenominational for whom the Baptist shoe fits. The first

15. Ibid., 19.

order of business it seems to me, is to illumine the character and existence of the Baptist heritage in such a way that certain nondenoms see themselves as inheritors and thus bearers of that heritage. This first task is not best understood as an attempt to shame good folks who were minding their own business to admit that they are Baptist and to take on the name whether they like it or not. What we are exploring first of all are not questions of praxis or nomenclature but of ontology. Ecclesial traditions spawn and bequeath heritages and those heritages, according God's secret wisdom and meticulous providential governance of this world, shape our very beings according to the good plans he has for us, his children. I wish to illumine an unrecognized reality—the reality of one's heritage. Only then may the other questions properly and profitably claim attention.

In his little book *The Vindication of Tradition*, Jaroslav Pelikan offers the most compelling case for and exploration of the power and the significance of tradition as such and of Christian tradition in particular. I close with a few excerpts that indicate something of the path I wish not only the nondenoms but every follower of Jesus Christ would discover:

> Coming to terms with the traditions from which we are derived is, or should be, a fundamental process of growing up. Obviously, that ought to include knowledge of the contents of those traditions. . . we do not have a choice between being shaped by our intellectual and spiritual DNA and not being shaped by it, as though we had sprung into being by some kind of cultural spontaneous generation. . . We do, nevertheless, have some choices to make. One . . . is whether to understand our origins in our tradition or merely let that tradition work on us without our understanding it, in short, whether to be conscious participants or unconscious victims.[16]

It seems to me the teaching elders and pastors of any church bear special responsibilities with regard to the reality and potency of tradition on behalf of those they shape and shepherd.

Once nondenoms acknowledge the Baptist tradition as their own, then Goethe's second step becomes possible—to takes one's heritage as task. And then it becomes possible to "make [one's tradition] one's own" which is not the same things as endorsing it or succumbing to it.

The options available are not to either surrender and succumb to one's tradition or opt out of tradition all together—because "tradition demands to be served even when it is not observed."[17] But as Goethe's third step in-

---

16. Ibid., 53.
17. Ibid., 70

dicates, only as we receive tradition as our heritage and make it our task does it become possible to then "make it our own." The goal is to learn to walk down the only truly authentic and promising path open to us, where we walk as our true selves within the body of Christ, as what we are and are meant to be in relation to our tradition—"as heirs yet free." For it is only along this path with the melody of our spiritual parents and grandparents ringing in our ears as a sort of "counterpoint that we go on to compose melodies of our own."[18]

BIBLIOGRAPHY

Cross, Anthony R., and Philip E. Thompson eds. *Baptist Sacramentalism*. Colorado Springs: Paternoster, 2003.

Deweese, Charles W. *Baptist Church Covenants*. Nashville: Broadman, 1990.

Dockery, David S. *Southern Baptist Consensus and Renewal: A Biblical, Historical, and Theological Proposal*. Nashville: B&H, 2008.

Fowler, Stanley K. *More Than A Symbol: British Baptist Recovery of Baptismal Sacramentalism*. Nottingham: Paternoster, 2002.

George, Timothy, and Denise George, eds. *Baptist Confessions, Covenants, and Catechisms*. Nashville: B&H, 1996.

Gibbs, Eddie, and Ryan K. Bolger, eds. *Emerging Churches: Creating Christian Community In Postmodern Cultures*. Grand Rapids: Baker Academic, 2005.

Hansen, Collin. *Young, Restless, and Reformed*. Wheaton, IL: Crossway, 2008.

Henard, William D., and Adam W. Greenway, eds. *Evangelicals Engaging Emergent: A Discussion of the Emergent Church Movement*. Nashville: B&H Academic, 2009.

Jenkins, Philip. *The Next Christendom: The Coming of Global Christianity*. Oxford: Oxford University Press, 2007

McLaren, Brian. *A Generous Orthdoxy*. Grand Rapids: Zondervan, 2006.

Pelikan, Jaroslav. *The Vindication of Tradition*. New Haven: Yale University Press, 1984.

---

18. Ibid., 54.

Covenant
An Ecclesiology of an Undivided Christ

Paul S. Fiddes

IS CHRIST DIVIDED?

"Is Christ divided?" Dr. Timothy George echoed the question of the Apostle Paul (from 1 Corinthians 1:13) in posing this challenge in an article in *Christianity Today* in 2005.[1] He enquired whether, when Jesus declared, "Upon this rock I will build my church," he intended that the people called to bear his name in the world "would eventually be divided into 37,000 competing denominations." Noting that evangelicals certainly believe in the spiritual oneness of all true Christians—what Augustine of Hippo called the "invisible church"—he still asked whether this means we should have no concern for *visible* church unity.

That his own answer to both these questions was in the negative became clear when he went on to say, "Our visible disunity causes many unbelievers to stumble. The problem is not only division, but divisiveness, within congregations as well as between (and within) denominations." Dr. George has given us an update of his answer in his more recent remarks as a delegate of the Baptist World Alliance to the General Assembly of the Synod of Bishops on "The New Evangelization" in Vatican City in 2012. He urged his listeners to realise that "the missionary God who gave the church this commission [to evangelization] also placed before her an imperative for Christian unity. We are not only to proclaim the Good News to all peoples but to do it in a way that visibly reflects the unity and love between the

---

1. George, "Is Christ Divided?," 31–33.

Father and the Son," adding that "Where our witness is fractured, our message is unpersuasive, if not inaudible."[2]

The point of his earlier article was for us to be provoked by Paul's ironic question as much as Paul earnestly wanted the Corinthians to be. It is a virtue of his piece that, while regarding the multiple divisions of the church as a scandal, he nevertheless recognizes that an answer to Paul's question must be a nuanced one. There is bound to be *diversity*, as each communion of faith seeks to be true to the truth, as it has perceived it to be within its own life of Christian discipleship. He warns that "honest dialogue among Christians of different denominations or theological commitments must be predicated on the understanding that any unity not based on truth is a unity not worth having." There is "an apostolic mandate to speak the truth in love." Unity is thus not uniformity: "To try to impose an artificial oneness on the genuine diversity in the body of Christ is to be blind to the many-faceted, many-colored wisdom of God." But his challenge is that living under the cross of Christ, taking on the humility of Christ, means always *seeking* to come "closer" to the undivided Christ with our fellow Christian churches. He concludes "How we should proceed toward unity is a matter of healthy debate. That we should continue to move closer to one another is not."[3] We might, perhaps, paraphrase him as saying that the momentum should always be towards unity.

In this book of essays written to honor Dr. George as a pastor, scriptural exegete, historian and theologian of global distinction, it is surely right that we should rise to his challenge, which has now resounded in Baptist and evangelical ears for more than a decade. My intention in this essay, with which I make my own tribute to a good friend, is not directly to reflect on the ecumenical venture itself but to develop a baptistic ecclesiology in the light of the ecumenical imperative. I propose that—rightly understood—Baptist ecclesiology *is* the ecclesiology of an undivided Christ, though Baptists have admittedly not always been faithful to their own insights. My argument will be that a covenant ecclesiology is capacious enough to enable an overcoming of division in obedience to Christ and yet also to have room for the "many-colored wisdom of God" which Dr. George celebrates. So let us begin, as Dr. George does, with the lordship of Christ.

---

2. George, "Remarks," 73.
3. George, "Is Christ Divided?," 33.

CHRIST AS COVENANT-MEDIATOR IN THE CHURCH

In his article in *Christianity Today*, Dr. George draws a direct correlation between ecclesiology and Christology, between "the church and its heavenly head, Jesus Christ." Since Christ himself cannot be divided, it follows that the church as his body *should not be* divided. So "when we live in rancor, bitterness, and enmity with one another, we are not only sinning against one another, we are also sinning against Christ." Paul's ironic question calls, I suggest, for a nuanced answer on many levels, due to the multiple meanings of "body of Christ": in the New Testament the phrase indicates the risen and exalted personality of Jesus, the earthly community of his church and the communion bread. The first cannot be divided, the second is, but should not be, and the third is necessarily broken as the means by which we encounter Christ in his service for us. The meanings overlap and interweave, and since Christ is identified with his church, I suggest that there is a sense in which Christ is humble enough to live in a state of brokenness. I shall have more to say about that surprising answer to Paul's rhetorical question by the end of the paper, but for the moment I want to rehearse the covenant ecclesiology of early Baptists, which envisaged the church as always living under the "rule" of Christ.

Early Baptists understood a church to be formed by its members entering into a covenant together, an ecclesiology rooted deeply in the convictions and practice of English Separatists, Christian believers who had separated themselves from the newly-formed Church of England in the late sixteenth and early seventeenth centuries. Separatists had conceived of covenant, or mutual agreement, in two directions at once—vertical and horizontal. The church was gathered by the members' making a covenant or mutual agreement *both* with God *and* with each other. The founding Baptist John Smyth adopted this theology, declaring that "A visible communion of Saints is of two, three or more Saints joined together by covenant with God & themselves. . . ."[4]

But it seems that Smyth took an original step at this point. He was shaped by the Reformed theology of the time, that 'covenant' referred to an eternal 'covenant of grace' which the triune God had made with human beings and angels for their salvation in Jesus Christ.[5] Smyth thus made a leap of thought that was to be influential for Baptists to come: he saw that the intersection of the horizontal and the vertical dimensions of covenant means that God's eternal covenant of grace is fused with the covenant-making of

---

4. Smyth, *Principles and Inferences*, 1:252.
5. Calvin, *Institutes of the Christian Religion* 2.6.1–4; 3.21.6–7 (trans. Battles).

a local congregation. The everlasting covenant becomes actualized in time and history at the moment when members make covenant with each other.[6] Smyth puts it like this: "We say the Church or two or three faithful people Separated from the world and joined together in a true covenant, have both Christ, the covenant, & promises. . . "[7] Clearly, 'the' covenant referred to here is the eternal covenant of gracious salvation. Somewhat later, the model covenant of the Particular Baptist minister, Benjamin Keach, at Horsley Down (1697) begins with the pledge: 'to give up ourselves to the Lord, in a Church state . . . that he may be our God, and we may be his People, through the *Everlasting Covenant* of his Free grace, in which alone we hope to be accepted by him, through his blessed Son Jesus Christ.'[8]

Christ is the mediator of this covenant, first because the eternal covenant is made through his atoning death, and second because the risen Christ stands in the midst of the congregation as the ruler or "only lawgiver"[9] of his people who are seeking his mind in covenant together now. Taking up the Reformation theology of the threefold office of Christ as prophet, priest and king,[10] baptized disciples are given a share in the first two offices through preaching and the Lord's Supper. To these two marks of the church familiar in Reformation ecclesiology (the word rightly preached, the sacraments rightly administered) Baptists with other dissenters added a third mark—discipline, or a mutual "watching over" (*episkope*) of each other, or keeping each other up to the high call of discipleship. This was a participation in the third office of Christ, his kingly rule, and Baptist objections to Anglican bishops were that *episkope* was being exercised effectively by King and Parliament in rivalry to Christ.

It is essential then to grasp that Baptist ecclesiology is not based on any "autonomy" of the local congregation (a term which means "self-rule"), but on a freedom under the rule of Christ. It is because the local church stands under the direct rule of Christ that it has liberty and cannot be imposed upon or constrained by any external ecclesial authority. But, since the assembling of churches together in association also stands under the rule of Christ, the local church meeting must pay attention to the way that churches gathered together believe they have found the mind and purposes of Christ, and must use its freedom with flexibility and discretion. As an

---

6. White, *The English Separatist Tradition*, 128.

7. Smyth, *Paralleles, Censures*, 2:403.

8. Keach, *The Glory of a True Church*, 71.

9. *Declaration of Faith* (1611), 9, in Lumpkin, *Baptist Confessions of Faith*, 119.

10. *Confession of Faith* (1644), 10, 13, in ibid., 159–60, 166; see *Confession of Faith* (1677), 8, in Lumpkin, *Baptist Confessions*, 260.

approved document of the Baptist Union of Great Britain put it, the local church is "competent, but it is scarcely Omni competent" and needs the gifts of the Spirit distributed to other churches to discern fully the purposes of Christ and share effectively in the mission of God.[11]

The sense of one, trans-local body of Christ is prominent in early Baptist thinking. In considering the bond of covenant existing between local congregations, the (Particular Baptist) London Confession of 1644 asserts that "*although* the particular Congregations be distinct and several Bodies . . . *yet* are they all to walk by one and the same Rule . . . as members of the one body in the common faith under Christ their only head."[12] At the first general meeting of the Abingdon (Particular Baptist) Association in 1652 the churches record that "the churches of Christ do all make up one body or church in general under Christ their head."[13] From among the General Baptists, the *Orthodox Creed* (1679) affirms that the "visible church of Christ on earth is made up of several distinct congregations, which make up that one catholic church, or mystical body of Christ."[14] In line with this it refers to the representatives to general councils or assemblies of churches as making "but one church,"[15] although it must be said to be unusual among Baptists in using the word "church" to refer directly to a gathering of churches.

An achievement of the recent international theological conversations between the Baptist Alliance and the Roman Catholic Church has been to bring together the themes of "communion" familiar in the *koinonia* ecclesiology prominent in the years since Vatican II, and the covenant theology of Baptists. The report notes that both *koinonia* and covenant, both grounded in the triune God, integrate relations within the church and relations between the church and God. It also makes the affirmation that *koinonia* means that "the local fellowship does not derive from the universal church, nor is the universal a mere sum of various local forms, but that there is mutual existence and coinherence between the local and universal church of Christ." It goes on to reflect that "covenant" expresses the same simultaneity.[16] We may add that the advantage of aligning *koinoinia* with covenant is that the relation between the local and the trans local church is established

---

11. *Confession of Faith . . . Relating and Resourcing*, 2:7, esp. 4.

12. *Confession of Faith* (1644), chap. 47, in Lumpkin, *Baptist Confessions*, 168–69; my italics.

13. White, ed., *Association Records of the Particular Baptists of England, Wales and Ireland to 1660*, 3:126

14. *Orthodox Creed*, 30, in Lumpkin, *Baptist Confessions*, 319.

15. *Orthodox Creed*, 29, in Lumpkin, *Baptist Confessions*, 327.

16. "The Word of God in the Life of the Church," 11–12, 16–18.

on the basis of trust, characteristic of covenant relations, without any structure of canon law.

Thus, while the local church has "freedom" to find the purpose of Christ for its life and mission, it aims to exercise this freedom in listening to the way that churches assembled together discern Christ's mind. My point is that a rehearsal of the covenant ecclesiology of Baptists shows that it blends a seeking of unity with the maintaining of truth in the 'multi-colored wisdom' that Dr. George urges. How these dimensions hold together can, however, only be discovered in practice rather than theory, in experiments of "walking together and watching over each other."

BAPTISM INTO THE CHURCH

Dr. George links the question "is Christ divided" with the following apostolic question: "into whose name were you baptized"? He notes that, in the early church, baptism signified the transfer of loyalty from one realm to another. Baptism was far more than an initiatory rite of passage; rather, it involved a decisive transition from an old way of human life to a new and different way. Baptism, Dr. George affirms, was an act of *radical obedience* in which a specific renunciation was made and a specific promise was given.[17]

On the one hand, these observations appear to be a strong defence of believers' baptism, since "radical obedience" makes most sense where a believing disciple is being baptized and thereby commissioned to share in the mission of God in the world. Baptists, indeed, have generally associated the baptism of disciples with the making of covenant, rather than simply "inheriting" a covenant relationship through the church family, as is typical in reformed paedobaptist ecclesiology. Baptism as a believing disciple is thus inseparable from a covenant ecclesiology in a Baptist sense. But on the other hand, when Dr. George places this second question of Paul in the context of the first one ("Is Christ divided"), bearing in mind the direction of his overall argument, he seems to be setting us a challenge. Is he implying that baptism "into the name of Christ," and not into the name of a particular Apostle, means today not being baptized into any particular denomination of the church which is the body of Christ? If so, is Dr. George challenging us to find a relation between church and baptism which will *both* give substance to the vision of an undivided Christ, *and* cope with the diversity of baptismal practice among the churches—notably the difference between infant baptism and disciples' baptism?

17. George, "Is Christ Divided?," 32

In another significant article, Dr. George notes that, with regard to admission to the Lord's Table and to membership, there has been historically a tension in Baptist thinking between the extension of hospitality to all Christian people 'in the spirit and love of Jesus' and the need to "take seriously the covenantal and disciplinary dimensions of Baptist ecclesiology."[18] In these respects, he argues, the open communionists and the strict communionists were both right. His article on "The Limits of Baptist Fellowship" is thus sympathetic to the open approach of John Bunyan, Robert Hall and C.H. Spurgeon, but notes the unintentional result of an undermining of the significance of baptism.[19] We can perceive here the same tension Dr. George points to in "Is Christ Divided?," between affirming an "undivided Christ" and yet holding firm to truth as it has been perceived by particular communions—in this case Baptists seeking the mind of Christ about true baptism. In his article on "limits," Dr. George does not attempt—at least explicitly—to resolve the tension, but we might briefly review three possible ways of doing so.

The first, which was the way of Spurgeon, is to make a distinction between "open communion" (the hospitality of the table) and open membership, only membership requiring a disciples' baptism.[20] This seems, however, altogether inconsistent with a covenant ecclesiology, since the Lord's Supper is the seal of the covenant, the decisive expression of a community in which Christ's presence and rule is affirmed, both through the breaking of bread and in the bodies of all the members gathered together. Spurgeon's own "theology of presence" to which Dr. George draws attention only underlines this.[21] Moreover, this distinction breaks down even further in an age when "belonging" to a community takes flexible forms, and the idea of "church membership" is increasingly being re-thought in new ways.

A second approach to the question, and thus to an ecclesiology of an "undivided Christ," has been an attempt to define the "essence" of baptism, beyond its particular "form and subjects." Particular Baptist minister Daniel Turner, for example, insisted that baptism was essential for entrance into the church, and so contested the view of Bunyan that baptism was not a "church-ordinance."[22] However, Turner was able to welcome paedobaptists to the table and (in the case of the covenant he wrote for the Dissenters'

---

18. George, "Controversy and Communion," 58.
19. Ibid., 54–55.
20. Spurgeon, "Meeting of our Own Church," 260.
21. George, "Controversy and Communion," 56–57.
22. Bunyan, *Differences in Judgment about Water-Baptism No Bar to Communion*, 32–35.

Church in Oxford, later New Road Baptist Church) to church membership, because he found that the "essence" of baptism was in the obligation it laid upon those baptized to live a "holy life."[23] If persons baptized as an infant recognized that their baptism had given them a sense of this demand of Christ upon their life, then their own conscientious belief that they had been truly baptized should be accepted as sufficient for fellowship. They had the "essence," beyond the "form" (immersion or sprinkling) and the "subject" (young infant or disciple). We are bound today to be suspicious of the attempt, characteristic of the Enlightenment confidence in reason, to separate the "essence" of something from its social context and material forms. But Turner was reaching toward the heart of baptism as the rule of the Christ who makes covenant, also expressed more biblically in his affirmation that "as the Lord Jesus receives and owns them on both sides of the question, we think we ought to do so too."[24]

Third, a modern attempt to formulate this obedience to the covenant-rule of Christ has been the proposal, made by Baptists in a range of inter-church conversations recently, that different churches should affirm a "common process of initiation" into Christ and the church, rather than attempt to confess a "common baptism."[25] The latter phrase implies that baptism of infants and believing disciples is simply the same act, and Baptists are unlikely to accept this, understanding baptism to be a convergence of God's grace and human faith, a moment of encounter between a God who is giving God's own self to transform human life, and disciples who come with their own trust in Christ and a desire to be commissioned for the mission of God in the world. But it may be possible for Baptists to understand initiation, or the beginning of life in Christ and his church, to be a process or journey in which there are *several* significant moments. A moment of baptism as an infant, expressing the prevenient grace of God and the faith of the church community, may thus find completion in a future moment when a disciple takes the step of "radical obedience" for himself or herself, owning covenant in the church-act often called "confirmation." Another possibility for this moment of obedience, increasingly practised in paedobaptist evangelical and charismatic churches, is "renewal of baptismal vows" through

---

23. Turner, *A Modest Plea for Free Communion at the Lord's Table*, 10.

24. Turner, *Charity the Bond of Perfection*, 21; see also Turner, *A Modest Plea for Free Communion at the Lord's Table*, 6; and Bunyan, *Differences in Judgment about Water-Baptism No Bar to Communion*, 43, appealing to Rom 14:3 and 15:7. So the covenant of New Road Baptist Church of 1780.

25. See *Conversations around the World* 31–57; *Word of God in the Life of the Church*, §§101–4.

immersion in water (which is not understood as a re-baptism).[26] Baptists will have their own journey of beginnings, starting with the church's prayer for a young infant and a blessing from God, and finding fulfilment in baptism as a believer.

If churches can recognise parallel journeys into the one Christ like this, then "baptism into the name of Christ" will mark a covenant ecclesiology of an undivided Christ, which still recognizes the "many-colored wisdom of God."

THE CHURCH INVISIBLE AND INVISIBLE

One way in which Baptists have affirmed the church of an undivided Christ is through affirming a universal, invisible church, made up of all the redeemed in all periods and in places. The congregation of John Smyth affirmed in their *Propositions and Conclusions* (1612) that the "outward church visible consists of penitent persons only," and is a "mystical figure outwardly, of the true, spiritual, invisible church; which consisted of the spirits of . . . the regenerate."[27] Among Calvinistic (Particular) Baptists this has been identified as the sum total of those elected to salvation, known only to God,[28] but the idea of an invisible church itself does not require a strong doctrine of predestination. Dr. George remarks that the movement of "Landmarkism" among Southern Baptists, with its confidence in a succession of Baptist churches from primitive times, and its associated closure of the communion table and a highly limited recognition of legitimate baptism, "ran counter to the historic Baptist doctrine of the universal church, invisible and indivisible, the one Body of Christ scattered throughout time as well as space."[29]

Dr. George also, however, warns that the idea of the catholic church invisible should not result, as it regrettably has done, in a reluctance to seek any form of "visible" unity beyond the local congregation.[30] There too we must look for the oneness of the body. Here he is in tune with seventeenth-century affirmations of the "one rule" of Christ I have already mentioned: the very association principle means "visible saints" are not just a local phenomenon. A notion of "visible catholicity" is also explicitly defined in

---

26. Provided for in *Common Worship: Services and Prayers for the Church of England*, 349–50.

27. Smyth, *Propositions and Conclusions*, 64–65, in Lumpkin, *Baptist Confessions*, 136.

28. *Confession of Faith* (1677), 261, in Lumpkin, *Baptist Confessions*, 285.

29. George, "Southern Baptist Ghosts," 17–24.

30. George, "The Sacramentality of the Church," 26.

the *Orthodox Creed* (General Baptist). The article headed "Of the invisible catholic Church of Christ" affirms that "There is one holy catholic church, consisting of, or made up of the whole number of the elect, that have been, are, or shall be gathered by special grace."[31] But the accompanying article on "Of the catholic Church as *visible*," finds that "the visible church of Christ on earth" is "made up of several distinct congregations, which make up that one catholic church, or mystical body of Christ."[32] Here "*several* distinct congregations" explains the designation "visible catholic," not one congregation alone.

It is clear then that the body of Christ becomes visible, not only in *each* congregation, but in the gathering of congregations together.[33] Indeed, a little thought makes clear that the one, universal body of Christ cannot be totally invisible, as this would undermine the whole point of the metaphor of a "body," which is about visibility and tangibility. Churches have the *duty* to relate together because they are summoned in the covenant to allow Christ to become manifest through his body universally.

Conceptual clarity was brought to all this by Daniel Turner in the eighteenth century, who distinguished three forms of the church: the invisible catholic church, the visible catholic church and the visible local church. First, church in its full and proper sense means "the real or *invisible catholic* or universal *church*; part of which is triumphant in heaven, and part militant on earth."[34] This is the "*whole number of real saints and peculiar people of God* who sincerely love and obey him." Second, church means "the *apparent* or *visible catholic* church," which is "the whole body of those that make any visible profession of a religious regard to the revealed will of God," even though some may have only "the form of godliness" and not its "real power."[35] In the third place, he says, the term "church" sometimes means a "particular visible gospel church," denoting "only one particular society of Christians . . . usually meeting for divine worship in one place."[36] With this final meaning of church, Baptists are of course familiar, but they may not be so familiar with Turner's stress on the "whole body of those" who make visible profession. Turner graphically illustrated this idea of the visible church

---

31. "Orthodox Creed," 29, in Lumpkin, *Baptist Confessions*, 318.

32. Ibid., 319.

33. Ibid.

34. Turner, *A Compendium of Social Religion, or the Nature and Constitution of Christian Churches* 2.

35. Ibid., 3–4.

36. Ibid., 5, 4.

in a sermon on the occasion of the re-establishment of a Dissenters' Church in Oxford, urging that:

> We do not mean to set up this little Society in *Opposition* to *any* other Protestant Church in *particular*; nor as a *Separation* from the Church of Christ in *general*, but as an *Addition* to it, connected with it in the *Bonds of Christian* Charity—a small hallowed Porch annexed to that grand common *Temple,* which *is the Habitation of* GOD *through the Spirit*. . .[37]

It could be argued, as does Dr. George, that the notion of the church as a sacrament underplays the idea of the universal invisible church, since the whole point of a sacrament is to make invisible grace visible. He therefore suggests that to call the church a sacrament says "less about it than is true."[38] But on the other hand, identifying the church as sacrament does make clearer the visibility of the church in the catholic and local forms of visibility to which Turner draws attention. The Church makes Christ visible in the world, gathering together all the members to allow the body to stand out. It seems appropriate to associate the word "sacrament" with the church since Baptists have usually preferred the Eucharistic theology of Zwingli (not a mere memorialism), in which the congregation, eating the bread, *becomes* the body of Christ through which his presence is known.[39]

Perhaps there is not so great a difference in the end between "church as sacrament" and "church as like a sacrament" (*veluti sacramentum*) which is the form of words Dr. George prefers.[40] In any case, both the invisible and visible forms of the Catholic church can express the undivided nature of Christ, while in the local visible forms there is room for diversity and the "many-colored wisdom" of God. Dr. George has made the interesting observation that one result of "The Controversy" among Southern Baptists in recent years has been a kind of "evangelicalizing" of the Southern Baptist Convention, allowing—as it were—for the some of this "multi-coloured wisdom." The cooperation between Southern Baptists and evangelicals signals, he urges, a new day, but he warns that it may also come with a price, namely, "the diminution of Baptist identity and a sense of uprootedness from a particular tradition."[41] I hope that we have enough in our tradition of covenant to keep us rooted there.

---

37. Turner, *Charity the Bond of Perfection,* 8.

38. George, "Sacramentality," 25.

39. Zwingli, *Letter to Matthew Alber,* 16 November 1524 (trans. Pipkin, *Huldrych Zwingli. Writings,* 2:141).

40. George, "Sacramentality," 15.

41. George, "Southern Baptist Ghosts," 22.

CHURCH AS THE BROKEN BODY OF THE UNDIVIDED CHRIST

So we return to the provocative question of the Apostle Paul, re-voiced for our age by Dr. George: "Is Christ divided?" The answer, I have been suggesting, is both "no *and* yes." No, the glorious body of the risen Christ is not divided, but yes –the church as the body of Christ is divided in actuality. While division is a scandal, and Paul's rhetorical question is meant to make us see this should *not be*, we must not confuse this with a proper kind of diversity or differentiation—the "many-colored wisdom of God"—to be respected as a work of the Spirit of Wisdom. The answer, then, is a complex one: the risen and glorified body of Christ cannot be divided, but as the church the body is both divided (shamefully) and diversified (surely helpfully). Complexity inheres in a moving boundary between division and diversity, and in the use of the latter as an excuse for the former. My argument is that a Baptist ecclesiology of covenant has at least the potential for embracing this complexity.

There are ecclesiologies, which attempt to deny either division or diversity in an ideal vision of the church.[42] One is Orthodoxy, according to which the "visible church" is the whole church here on earth, composed of many specific congregations, while the "invisible church" refers to the church in *heaven*, the glorified saints and the angels. Orthodoxy strongly insists that there are not two churches but only one, and in its theology and in its liturgy it affirms one communion, one continuous reality. But since the church on earth is identical with the heavenly church, the visible church must be undivided in actuality, not only in hope and intention, and it exists as the Orthodox Church, which must be one because God is one.[43] The result of this thinking is to restrict members of the church to the Orthodox; some Orthodox thinking still allows for regenerate believers outside the boundaries of the visible church, but these are "united to her by ties that God has not chosen to reveal to her."[44] In the words of Bishop Kallistos Ware, who also takes this view, "Many people may be members of the church who are not visibly so; invisible bonds may exist despite an outward separation."[45] Ware is careful *not* to say that such make up an "invisible church" on earth, since the only invisible church is in heaven; it is the *bonds* to the one visible church that are invisible.

---

42. The following four paragraphs draw on and summarize material from Fiddes, *Tracks and Traces*, 201–7.

43. Ware, *Orthodox Church*, 245.

44. Khomiakov, "The Church is One," 2.

45. Ware, *Orthodox Church*, 308.

Baptists will agree with Orthodox thinking that each specific congregation is "the church in wholeness,"[46] but they will want to affirm that the church on earth is always a mixture of the visible and the invisible. Its visibility—whether local, regional or international—is always fragmentary, and will not be complete until the final coming of the kingdom of God. This does not mean, as Miroslav Volf maintains from a professedly free-church perspective, that the notion of the church universal is *only* an eschatological reality, and that the only link between local churches at the moment is the presence of the Holy Spirit in the hearts of believers.[47] Of course the church universal will be *partly* invisible, as we shall not see it in its glory until the eschaton; the lordship of Christ over the cosmos is only partially acknowledged at present. It is partly hidden. But this does not mean that Christ does not *want* to be visible and manifest in the world in his whole body, as far as is possible. We have already seen that this conviction lies behind the principle of association of churches among Baptists. Moreover, Baptists such as Robert Hall and Daniel Turner urged open communion because they believed it to be an imperative for the universal body of Christ to come to visible expression in some way.[48] The same sense of necessity is clearly expressed in words from the Confession of Faith of the German Baptist Union, that "it cannot be God's will for denominational barriers to hinder the visible fellowship of all believers."[49]

Like the Orthodox Church in the East, the Roman Catholic Church in the West deduces from the unity of God and the sole lordship of Christ that the one undivided church *must already exist*, in reality and visibility. A significant difference is that while the Orthodox understands the unity of the church to be guaranteed by the bishop in each region in collegial fellowship with all other bishops, the Roman Catholic Church finds the final sign and guarantor of unity to be the Bishop of Rome. So in the encyclical *Ut Unum Sint* Pope John Paul II speaks movingly of his "ministry of unity," and places weight here on Jesus' words to Peter, "strengthen your brethren."[50] Thus, the conviction that visible unity must already exist in the church leads to the belief that the true church must have a unitary structure, and the only claims on the table seem to be eastern Orthodoxy and western Catholicism. Several recent documents have followed Vatican II in affirming that "the

---

46. Zizioulas *Being as Communion*, 147–53, 235–36.

47. Volf, *After Our Likeness*, 203, 213, 250.

48. Turner, *Compendium* 120. See also Hall, *Terms of Communion*, in *Works*, 2:9–14, 105–8.

49. Parker, *Baptists in Europe. History and Confessions of Faith*, 69.

50. *Ut Unum Sint*, §§88, 90.

One Church of Christ . . . subsists in the Catholic Church, governed by the Successor of Peter and by the Bishops in communion with him."[51] Outside her own structure and the Orthodox churches of the east, there exist only "elements of the church" (*elementa Ecclesiae*), characterized by sanctification and truth, which "derive their efficacy from the fullness of grace and truth entrusted to the Catholic Church."[52]

From this situation we can see that if either the unity of God, or an undivided Christ, is the *only* basis for ecclesiology, then we must ask where the one church is *already* visible with an undivided structure. Having established that to our satisfaction, we will then see in others only "aspects" or "elements" of that way of being the church. Such a dogma may well recognize (as does *Dominus Jesus*) that "the lack of unity among Christians is a *wound* for the church,"[53] but it will not think that it is deprived of its fundamental visible unity, only that disunity hinders the *completeness* of its catholicity in history.[54] The question, then, is this: how deep are the wounds of the church, and behind these, the wounds of God?

Within a covenant ecclesiology, or the conviction that an undivided Christ makes covenant with his church, there is room for both diversity and the tragedy of division. Just as in the Hebrew Bible we catch a glimpse of different covenants which the same covenant God makes with different people in different times and places (with, for example, Abraham, David, and Moses—and with all created beings in the covenant of Noah), so we can conceive that there is a diversity of covenants in the troubled history of the church while there has been always one covenant-maker, the Christ of the new covenant. We also see from the scriptures that a covenant-making God is humble enough to bear with people who do not grasp the divine purpose, remaining faithful in either maintaining the covenant with them despite their sin, or in offering to re-make it when it has been broken by human disobedience.

The complexity of the situation is not only a moving boundary between division and diversity. There is also a blurring of the difference between two kinds of brokenness. First, the church is broken because it shares in the dying of Christ for the world, and so must always be humiliated, being broken like Eucharistic bread to nourish others. When we identify the body of Christ with the bread, it is fragmented for the sake of salvation. But

---

51. *Lumen Gentium*, §8; *Unitatis Redintegratio* §4, *Ut Unum Sint*, §§10, 86, *Dominus Jesus*, §16.
52. *Dominus Jesus*, §17; *Unitatis redintegratio*, §3.
53. *Dominus Jesus*, §17.
54. *Unitatis redintegratio*, §4.

second, the church is also broken through its own sin, divided in rivalries and power-seeking. In both kinds of fragmentation it manifests the suffering, which is inflicted upon God. Christ is willing, in humility, to live with a broken body in the world. In a covenant ecclesiology the church may be recognized precisely *through* the broken nature of the body. This is quite different from an ecclesiology where visibility is equated with indivisibility. But a vision of the undivided, risen Christ prompts us always to seek in practice to find the difference between disunity and diversity (what is often called "legitimate diversity") and between different kinds of brokenness, seeking to seek to heal the wounds that are self-inflicted by the church's own disobedience and lack of faithfulness. It is this spirit we can detect in one of John Smyth's "Propositions" (1612), reflecting that the "outward" or visible church is rent asunder:

> That all penitent and faithful Christians are brethren in the communion of the outward church, whosesoever they live, by what name soever they are known, which in truth and zeal, follow repentance and faith, though compassed with never so many ignorance's and infirmities; and we salute them all with a holy kiss, being heartily grieved that we which follow after one faith, and one spirit, one Lord, and one God, one body, and one baptism, should be rent into so many sects and schisms: and that only for matters of less moment.[55]

A covenant ecclesiology proposes that the nuanced answers to Paul's questions can only be worked through as disciples "walk together and watch over each other" under the rule of Christ, in the bonds of trust. This is an ecclesiology of the broken body of the undivided Christ.

BIBLIOGRAPHY

Bunyan, John, *Differences in Judgment about Water-Baptism No Bar to Communion.* London, 1673.

Calvin, John. *Calvin: Institutes of the Christian Religion.* 2 vols. Edited by John T. McNeill. Translated by Ford Lewis Battles. 2.6.1–4; 3.21.6–7. LCC 20–21. Philadelphia: Westminster, 1960.

Common Worship. Services and Prayers for the Church of England, London: Church House, 2000.

The Confession of Faith, of Those Churches, Which Are Commonly (Though Falsely) Called Anabaptist (1644), in W. L. Lumpkin, *Baptist Confessions of Faith.* Philadelphia: Judson Press, 1959.

---

55. *Propositions and Conclusions,* art. 69; see Lumpkin, *Baptist Confessions,* 137.

Relating and Resourcing: The Report of the Task Group on Associating. Issued January 1998, the Baptist Union of Great Britain.

Conversations Around the World. The Report of the International Conversations between the Anglican Communion and the Baptist World Alliance. London: Anglican Communion Office, 2005.

Declaration of Faith of English People Remaining at Amsterdam, 1611, art. 9, in W.L. Lumpkin, *Baptist Confessions of Faith,* Philadelphia: Judson Press, 1959, 119.

Dominus Jesus §17; *Unitatis redintegratio,* §3.

Fiddes, Paul S. *Tracks and Traces: Baptist Identity in Church and Theology* Carlisle: Paternoster, 2003.

Furcha, E. J., ed. *Huldrych Zwingli Writings: Defense of the Reformed Faith.* Allison Park, PA: Pickwick, 1984.

George, Timothy. "Controversy and Communion: The Limits of Baptist Fellowship from Bunyan to Spurgeon." In *The Gospel in the World. International Baptist Studies,* edited by D. W. Bebbington, 38–58. Carlisle: Paternoster, 2002.

———. "Is Christ Divided? And Two More Apostolic Questions Today's Church Must Answer." *Christianity Today* 47, no. 7 (2005). Accessed January 18, 2018. http://www.christianitytoday.com/ct/2005/july/23.31.html.

———. "Remarks by the Rev. Dr. Timothy George, Fraternal Delegate, Baptist World Alliance to the General Assembly of the Synod of Bishops on 'The New Evangelization for the Transmission of the Christian Faith,' Vatican City, October 16, 2012." *Christianity Today* 57, no. 1 (2013).

———. "Southern Baptist Ghosts." *First Things* 93, May 1999. Accessed January 19, 2018. https://www.firstthings.com/article/1999/05/southern-baptist-ghosts.

———. "The Sacramentality of the Church." In *Baptist Sacramentalism,* edited by Anthony Cross and Philip Thompson, 21–36 Carlisle: Paternoster, 2003.

Hall, Robert. *On Terms of Communion,* in Olinthus Gregory (ed.), *The Entire Works of the Rev. Robert Hall,* 6 volumes; London: Holdsworth and Ball, 1831, vol. II.

Keach, Benjamin. *The Glory of a True Church, and Its Discipline Displayed.* London, 1697.

Khomiakov, Alexis. "The Church Is One." In *Russia and the English Church,* edited by William J. Birkbeck, 77–82. London: Eastern Churches Association, 1895.

Lumen Gentium (21 Nov. 1964). In Flannery, Austin, ed. Vatican Council II. The Conciliar and Post Conciliar Documents. Dublin: Dominican Publications, 1977, 350-426. Lumpkin, William L. *Baptist Confessions of Faith.* Edited by Bill J. Leonard. Valley Forge, PA: Judson, 1959.

Lumpkin, W. L. *Baptist Confessions of Faith.* Philadelphia: Judson, 1959.

Parker, Keith. *Baptists in Europe. History and Confessions of Faith.* Nashville: Broadman, 1982.

Pipkin, W. P. *Huldrych Zwingli Writings.* Vol 2, *In Search of True Religion: Reformation, Pastoral, and Eucharistic Writings. Letter to Matthew Alber concerning the Lord's Supper, Nov 1524.* Alison Park, PA: Pickwick, 1984.

Pushing at the Boundaries of Unity. Anglicans and Baptists in Conversation. London: Church House 2005.

Smyth, John. *Paralleles Censures, Observations (1609).* In *The Works of John Smyth,* edited by W. T. Whitley, 2:403. Cambridge: Cambridge University Press, 1915.

———. *Principles and Inferences.* In *The Works of John Smyth,* edited by W. T. Whitley, 1:252. Cambridge: Cambridge University Press, 1915.

———. *Propositions and Conclusions concerning True Christian Religion, Containing a Confession of Faith of Certain English People, Living at Amsterdam (1612-1614)*. Art. 80. In *Baptist Confessions of Faith*, by William L. Lumpkin, 139. Valley Forge, PA: Judson, 1959.

Spurgeon, C. H. "Meeting of Our Own Church." In *Metropolitan Tabernacle Pulpit*, 8 April 1861, 7:260. London: Passmore & Alabaster, 1861–1917.

Turner, Daniel. *A Modest Plea for Free Communion at the Lord's Table; Particularly between the Baptists and Poedobaptists*. London, 1772.

———. *Charity the Bond of Perfection*. Oxford, 1780.

———. *Compendium of Social Religion, or the Nature and Constitution of Christian Churches*. London: Ward, 1758.

Ut Unum Sint: Encyclical Letter of the Holy Father John Paul II on Commitment to Ecumenism. London: Catholic Truth Society, 1995. §§88, 90.

Unitatis redintegratio. In *Vatican Council II: The Conciliar and Post Conciliar Documents*, edited by Austin Flannery, 452–70. Dublin: Dominican, 1977.

Vatican II. *Lumen Gentium*. In *Vatican Council II: The Conciliar and Post Conciliar Documents*, edited by Austin Flannery, 350–426. Dublin: Dominican, 1977.

———. *Dominus Jesus*. Congregation for the Doctrine of the Faith, August 6, 2000. www.vatican.va/roman_curia/congregations.

Volf, Miroslav. *After Our Likeness: The Church as the Image of the Trinity*. Grand Rapids: Eerdmans, 1998.

Ware, Timothy (Kallistos). *The Orthodox Church*. New ed. Harmondsworth: Penguin, 1997.

White, B. R. *The English Separatist Tradition: From the Marian Martyrs to the Pilgrim Fathers*. Oxford: Oxford University Press, 1971.

White, B. R., ed. *Association Records of the Particular Baptists of England, Wales and Ireland to 1660*. Part 3. Abingdon Association. London: Baptist Historical Society, 1974.

"The Word of God in the Life of the Church: A Report of International Conversations between The Catholic Church and the Baptist World Alliance 2006-2010." *American Baptist Quarterly* 31, no. 1 (2012) 28–122.

Zizioulas, John D. *Being as Communion. Studies in Personhood and the Church*. London: Darton. Longman and Todd, 1985

The Doctrine of the Church in Evangelical Thought

GRAHAM COLE

INTRODUCTION

A WIDELY HELD PERCEPTION is that evangelicalism lacks an ecclesiology i.e. a doctrine of the church. Leanne Van Dyk speaks for many: "It is often said that evangelicalism lacks an ecclesiology, or at least a coherent ecclesiology."[1] This idea should not surprise. Evangelicalism as the name suggests has to do with the evangel (the gospel). Ecclesiology is not its defining characteristic as Alister McGrath points out, it is a "nondenominational (or better transdenominational)."[2] It is a movement, not a polity. Michael F. Bird further suggests that "being evangelical is a *theological ethos* and not a *denominational entity*."[3] Timothy George adds "fellowship" to the list of descriptors: "Evangelicalism is a fellowship: "an international, transdenominational fellowship of some one-half billion believers around the world."[4] In this light, let's begin by making observations about the evangelical movement before considering evangelical ecclesiology.[5] Next we shall consider

1. Van Dyk, "The Church in Evangelical Theology and Practice," 125.
2. McGrath, *Evangelicalism and the Future of Christianity*, 79.
3. Bird, "Towards an Evangelical Ecclesiology"; original emphases.
4. George, "Toward and Evangelical Ecclesiology," 123.
5. In some ways it is a pity that one of the theological loci is ecclesiology. In my view over the centuries and to look no further than the Anglophone world, the English word "church" has been made to do too much theological work to the hurt of the scores of other New Testament ways of describing our corporate reality. Take 1 Peter. Here is a New Testament letter with many descriptors corporate: elect exiles, obedient children,

a prominent evangelical's ecclesiology, that of Timothy George, and how representative it is. Then, we shall consider how evangelical ecclesiology relates to different denominational polities. Lastly and from a western perspective, we shall examine how an evangelical ecclesiology may interface with the wider society.

EVANGELICALISM AS A MOVEMENT

Evangelicalism is a movement as evidenced by the fact that professing evangelicals—as yet to be defined with any precision- are to be found in numerous denominational settings. Evangelicals are to be found in independent churches, the Anglican communion, Lutheran churches, Baptist churches, Presbyterian churches to name a few. There are even professing evangelical Roman Catholics.[6] How then may a convictional evangelical be identified?[7]

Historian, David Bebbington has made four observations of British evangelicalism that have become a widely used grid for identifying the presence of the evangelical movement.[8] He observed that evangelicalism is Biblio-centric, Christo-centric, conversionist and activist. Evangelicals are people of the book. Bible people. Devotion to Christ is at its heart. There is a desire that others come to believe in and devote themselves to Christ. This means conversion. This desire leads to fervent activism as evangelicals reach out to others in evangelism and missions of mercy. Bebbington's understanding of the evangelical movement has been catalytic. A number of other scholars have engaged his thesis and sought to qualify it in this way and that.[9] Bebbington acknowledges that the weakness in his historical

---

living stones, a spiritual house, a chosen race, a royal priesthood, a holy nation, a people for his own possession, sojourners, servants of God, stewards, the household of God, a flock, and a brotherhood. The Greek word "ekklēsia," which is translated mostly as "church," is not mentioned. This is also true of 2 Peter. For the significance of other ways of describing our corporate reality and a critique of the over use of the term "church," see my "The Doctrine of the Church: Toward Conceptual Clarification."

6. See Millegan "Serious Catholics Are Evangelical."

7. I use the qualifier "convictional" because there exists a cultural evangelicalism, especially in the USA. The phrase "cultural evangelicalism," which is fading in the USA, I use to refer to those who have made decisions for Jesus in a church, camp, or parachurch settings but such decisions have proved superficial in the extreme and have little or no impact on lifestyle. For the purposes of this essay, I will simply use the term "evangelical," but have in view convictional ones.

8. See Bebbington, *Evangelicalism in Modern Britain: A History from the 1730s to the 1980s*.

9. See Haykin and Stewart, eds., *The Advent of Evangelicalism*. In the volume,

treatment of evangelicalism was the inadequate attention he gave to Methodism and its contribution to evangelical identity. Even so Bebbington notes the following agreement amongst scholars regarding evangelicalism:

> The first is that the nature of evangelicalism appears to be more or less agreed. Evangelicals believed the Bible, returning to its pages for teaching, consolation and guidance. They saw the cross of Christ as central to their faith, for the atonement saved them from their sins. They held that individuals must be converted so as to begin changed lives of allegiance to Christ. And they displayed an activism that carried the gospel to others and brought them help in their suffering. For all the enormous differences between evangelicals, emphasis on the Bible, the cross, conversion and activism are together the features they have displayed down the ages.[10]

Noteworthy is the absences of ecclesiology as a defining characteristic of evangelicalism historically considered.[11]

So from where do evangelicals get their understanding of the church?

Toward an Evangelical Ecclesiology: Timothy George

John S. Hammett maintains that when it comes to formulating an evangelical doctrine of the church: "Beyond Scripture, there seem to be two major historical resources. One is the article in the Nicene Creed of belief in 'one holy catholic and apostolic church . . . . The second resource is the Reformation description of the marks of the true church."[12] Eminent evangelical theologian and leader, Timothy George provides a sterling example in support of Hammett's contention.[13]

In an essay on evangelical ecclesiology with numerous quotations and references to the biblical witness, George also draws upon what he terms as "two classic texts from the evangelical tradition" to establish support the

---

seventeen scholars devote themselves to engaging Bebbington's thesis concerning evangelical identity. The volume concludes with a response by Bebbington.

10. Ibid., 425.

11. Bebbington's treatment of evangelicalism is that of an historian not that of a theologian. Theologically considered, given that theology is a normative discipline, a theologian would argue that evangelicals ought to be characterized by being bibliocentric, crucicentric, conversionist, and activist in gospel and mercy ministry.

12. Hammett, "The Boundaries of Evangelical Ecclesiology."

13. See Haykin and Stewart, eds., *The Advent of Evangelicalism*, 13–15.

idea of the universality of the church.[14] The first of the two is the Heidelberg Catechism of 1563 which asks the question: "What doest thou believe concerning the holy Catholic church?"[15] In part the answer runs: 'a chosen communion in the unity of the true faith."[16] The second is the Second London Confession of 1677 which refers to "the Catholic or universal Church" in terms of "the whole number of the elect."[17] The understanding of what the universality of the church means is fleshed out further with reference to George Florovsky's notion of "an ecumenicity in time as well as . . . an ecumenicity of space."[18] Here he draws on the Orthodox tradition. The Roman Catholics are not left out as his reference to Vatican II's *Lumen Gentium* shows. *Lumen Gentium* affirms universality in terms of "from Abel, the just one, to the last of the elect."[19] What is striking is that in general terms there is nothing distinctive in his notion of universality. In more specific terms, he rejects any notion that the church is an extension of the incarnation and affirms that "In the New Testament the church universal is depicted as a heavenly and eschatological reality, not as an earthly institution to be governed and grasped by mere mortals."[20] Such a church "includes the elect of all the ages: the saints of the old covenant as well as those of the new, the *ecclesia triumphans* and also the *ecclesia militans*."[21]

The priority of the gospel, for Timothy George, is a key element in an evangelical ecclesiology.[22] The priority lies in the fact that Gospel is constitutive for the church and not the reverse. In this contention, he follows Luther's understanding of justification by faith alone.[23] George elaborates: "An evangelical commitment to the priority of the Gospel means that justification by faith alone should remain the kerygmatic center of our proclamation and common witness."[24] The "church" in this part of his analysis is the visible church. George works with the traditional distinction between the visible church (the object of sight) and the invisible church (true believers

14. George, "Toward," 125.
15. Ibid.
16. Ibid.
17. Ibid.
18. Ibid.
19. Ibid.
20. Ibid., 127.
21. Ibid., Australian Anglican evangelicals have especially explored the earthly, heavenly and eschatological nature of the church. See Kuhn, "The Ecclesiology of Donald Robinson and David Broughton Knox."
22. George, "Toward," 128.
23. Ibid., 129.
24. Ibid., 130.

known only to God). Both the universal church and the invisible church are encountered in local congregations, he maintains.[25]

Timothy George's debts to the past are also on view in his drawing on the four classic notes of the church as found in the Nicene Creed of 381AD.[26] These notes are: one, holy, catholic and apostolic. George sees the oneness of the church residing in "the fact that we worship one God."[27] For the magisterial reformers, Luther and Calvin that meant seeking to reform the church in their day. They were not schismatics. However, the radical reformers "pursued a different ideal of reform, seeking not so much to purify the church as to restore it to its original, New Testament condition."[28] This pursuit, he argues has led to "the proliferation of numerous denominations and competing sects. 'separated brethren' who were often more separated than brotherly in their relations with one another."[29] He makes this astute and important observation: "Evangelicals today are heirs of both reformational and restitutive models of ecclesiology and their approach to controverted questions of church order, ministry, and ecumenism often depends on which of these two paradigms is more prevalent."[30]

Holiness is the next defining characteristic which George explores. The church on earth, he contends, is not holy in the sense of set apart. Rather, it is holy because of its relation to its head, Jesus Christ, and its animation by the Holy Spirit.[31] Even so a distinction needs to be drawn between the holiness of God and the holiness of the church: "Evangelicals insist, however, that the holiness of God be clearly distinguished from the holiness of the church. The holiness of the church on earth is entirely derived, emergent and incomplete; that of God is eternal, substantial and unbroken by the vicissitudes of imperfection and finitude."[32] The imperfections of the church need acknowledgement.

---

25. Ibid., 32.

26. Ibid., 132–41. Interestingly, George only cites the Apostles Creed with its notion of the communion of saints. The four notes from the Nicene Creed—strictly speaking, the Niceno-Constantinopolitan Creed—are refracted through a statement quoted from *Lumen Gentium* of Vatican II.

27. George, "Toward," 132.

28. Ibid., 133.

29. Ibid.

30. Ibid., The celebrated contratemp between David Martyn Lloyd-Jones and John Stott over whether Stott ought to have left the Church of England may be illustrative George's point.

31. Ibid., 134.

32. Ibid., 135.

In his discussion of the holiness of the church, George makes a somewhat curious move.[33] He discusses the marks of the church. In other evangelical formulations of the doctrine of the church, the marks are usually given a section in their own right. The marks of the church as an idea arose among the reformers. The marks are two or three in number: word, sacrament (Luther and Calvin) and for some discipline as well (Anabaptists, for example). How are these to be related to the Nicene notes of the church? George argues: "The evangelical marks—proclamation, worship, and discipline-are distinguished from the traditional Nicene attributes precisely because they are not merely descriptive but dynamic: they call into question the unity, catholicity, apostolicity, and holiness of every congregation which claims to be the church."[34] One could wish that George had been more precise here given the evangelical tradition. He could have written of the preaching of the pure word, the right administration of the sacraments, and godly discipline. These adjectives, "pure," "right" and "godly," matter to evangelicals. Thus understood the marks can also serve as ways of discerning a true congregation of Christ's people. They did so for the reformers.

Catholicity is the third classic note of the church. In George's mind this catholicity consists of the geographical extent of the church which is not restricted by any particular place or nation but has the whole world in view, as well as it inclusive membership and its indefectibility or persistence through time.[35] Importantly, he brings in to play the missionary aspect of an evangelical ecclesiology: "In contemporary evangelical life, perhaps the most notable aspect of catholicity is the worldwide missionary vision which is the heart and soul of the evangelical movement."[36] He argues: "The evangelical understanding of catholicity is nowhere better seen than in this world Christian movement."[37] This is a catholicity informed by the gospel priority.[38]

---

33. Curious because they could have been discussed and elaborated on in their own right and the logical connection with the holiness motif is not immediately obvious. Convinced evangelicals are not known for their doctrinal laxity and the need to identify the true church has been a desideratum since the Reformation.

34. Ibid., 136.

35. Ibid., 137.

36. Ibid.

37. Ibid., 138.

38. From a Roman Catholic perspective, Avery Cardinal Dulles is right to see evangelicalism embodying what he terms the herald model of the church. See his essay "Church, Ministry, and Sacraments in Catholic-Evangelical Dialogue," 103. For the herald model and five other ones, see Dulles's influential work, *Models of the Church*.

George acknowledges that there are two very different understandings of apostolicity, the fourth note:

> The church is apostolic which stands under the direction and normative authority of the apostles, whom Jesus chose and sent forth in His Name. Evangelicals, no less than Roman Catholics, claim to be apostolic in this sense, but the two traditions differ sharply on the way in which they understand the transmission of the apostolic witness from the first century until now.[39]

He elaborates: "As heirs of the Reformation, evangelicals do not define the apostolicity of the church in terms of a literal, linear succession of duly ordained bishops."[40] This is known in some circles as "the pipeline of grace" theory and is highly sacramental in its construal. So what is the evangelical claim? George maintains: "The [evangelicals] point to the primordial character of the Gospel, the inscripturated witness of the apostles, and the succession of apostolic proclamation."[41] Once more, we see the priority of the gospel informing Georges' ecclesiology. He is explicit: "For evangelicals, public preaching of the word of God is a sure sign of apostolicity for through the words of the preacher, the living voice of the Gospel (*viva vox evangelii*) is heard."[42]

George's Biblio-centrism is also in evidence in his discussion of apostolicity. He is explicit: "For evangelicals the principle of *sola Scriptura* means that all the teachings, interpretations, and traditions of the church must be subjected to the divine touchstone of Holy Scripture itself."[43] However, he also distinguishes sola Scriptura from *nuda Scriptura*. On the one hand, tradition is not co-equal with Scripture. On the other, hand tradition is not to be ignored. He argues: "The consensus of thoughtful Christian interpretation of the Word down the ages . . . .. Is not likely to be wrong, and evangelicals, no less than other Christians, have much to learn from the church fathers, schoolmen, and theologians of age past."[44] George's exploratory formulation of an evangelical ecclesiology shows his debts not only to Scripture, but also

---

39. George, "Towards," 138. Van Dyk, "The Church," 130, rightly observes: "The apostolicity of the church has perhaps been the Nicene mark most embraced by evangelical instincts, but perhaps also most open to reductionism." Happily reductionism is not true of George's ecclesiology.

40. George, "Towards," 139.

41. Ibid.

42. Ibid., 140.

43. Ibid.; original italics.

44. Ibid.

to the best Christian thinking of past generations as well as the present one. Being evangelical and being learned are not antithetical.

Lastly, the way of the cross is thematized in George's treatment of evangelical ecclesiology. He is realistic about the imperfections and failings of the empirical church: "In this life the true church is always *ecclesia in via (Kirche im Werden)*, the church in a state of becoming, buffeted by struggles, beset by eschatological 'groaning which mark those 'upon whom the ends of the world have come' (Rom 8:8–15; 1 Cor 10:11)."[45] He notes: "To the eyes of faith the church is a 'worthy maid,' the Bride of Christ, but by the standards of the world she is a poor Cinderella surrounded by numerous dangerous foes."[46] George points to instances of the martyrdom of those, "who live under the shadow of the cross and whose faithful witness is even now leading many of them to the shedding of their blood."[47] His examples include evangelical and Roman Catholics, and stretch over time from WWII to the contemporary scene. There is an ecumenical fellowship of suffering for the Name of Christ.

Timothy Georges' Evangelical Ecclesiology: Idiosyncratic or Representative?

Georges' understanding of evangelical ecclesiology is widely representative and not idiosyncratic.[48] Indeed, David Bebbington's four defining characteristics of the historic evangelical, movement are on show: biblio-centric (George uses biblical evidence throughout his treatment), Christo-centric (he makes it clear that it is Christ who heads the church), conversionist (the missionary enterprise) and activist (again, the missionary enterprise).

Other evangelical theologians draw upon both Nicene Creed for the notes of the church in framing their ecclesiology and/or the Reformation's marks of the church. Michael F. Bird's work of systematic theology is just one example. He does not use "note" as a descriptor. He uses "mark" instead.[49] In his chapter "The Marks of the Church" he employs the four traditional

---

45. Ibid., 141. The Latin phrase *ecclesia in via* means "the church on the way or road," and the German phrase *Kirche im Werden* means "the church in the making."

46. Ibid.

47. Ibid., 143.

48. Two theological themes George does not discuss, but other evangelical theologians do in discussing ecclesiology, are kingdom and Israel. For example, see Grenz, *Theology for the Community of God*, 472–79, for kingdom; and Erickson, *Christian Theology*, 964–66, for Israel.

49. As does Van Dyk, "The Church," 130.

notes: one, holy, catholic and apostolic and he acknowledges that he is drawing upon the Nicene Creed at this point.[50] He then moves to consider the Reformation contribution of "the preaching of the Word, the proper administration of the sacraments, and (for some) the application of church discipline though it was recognized by most of the Reformers that church discipline was not an essential mark of the church, but more properly, the mark of a healthy church."[51]

For Bird, "the authorizing insignia of a true church is the preaching of the gospel and the signification of the gospel by the sacraments."[52] In a chapter entitles "The Evangelical Church" Bird makes the gospel motif the organizing one:

> The evangelical churches are those that have the gospel at the center of their proclamation and practice. The evangelical church is a community created by the gospel, a church that promotes and preaches the gospel, that cultivates the gospel in its spirituality. Its members strive to live lives worthy of [the] gospel, and its center is Jesus Christ.

As noted previously, Avery Cardinal Dulles argued that an evangelical ecclesiology is informed by the herald model.[53] Bird's accent of the gospel and its proclamation bears Dulles out. Dulles also saw in evangelical ecclesiology the community of disciples model.[54] Bird's summation above exhibits that motif as well.

Other evangelicals also work with the classic distinction between the invisible and visible. One of the most famous and influential of recent evangelical leaders, John Stott makes this sweeping claim, "all evangelicals accept the difference between the visible and invisible church."[55] For him, the distinction is particularly relevant to the question of church membership. It is God who admits men and women "into his true (invisible) church," when they exercise trust in Jesus. Pastors "admit people by baptism into the vis-

---

50. Bird, *Evangelical Theology*, 735.

51. Ibid., 739. A recent, splendid evangelical monograph on ecclesiology by Gregg R. Allison does not make either the Nicene notes of the church nor the Reformers' marks of the church in his main text but refers to them in a couple of places and then in footnotes, *Sojourners and Strangers: The Doctrine of the Church*. 50–51.

52. Bird, *Evangelical Theology*, 740.

53. Dulles, "Church, Ministry, and Sacraments," 103.

54. Ibid.

55. Stott, *Evangelical Truth: A Personal Plea for Unity, Integrity and Faithfulness*, 100. All the quotations in this paragraph are found on this page. A further example of an evangelical theologian who employs the classic distinction is Erickson, *Christian Theology*, 966–69.

ible church, and they do this on the profession of faith." According to Stott, membership of the visible church "does not guarantee salvation."[56]

The distinction between the universal and local churches also has wide currency amongst evangelicals. Gregg R. Allison is representative in arguing "that the church exists in two aspects, being both 'local' and universal."[57] He expresses his point well:

> As we assemble Sunday morning with other Christ-followers in the particular church of which we ae members together, the universal church-all deceased believers now with Christ in heaven, as well as all living Christ-followers throughout the world-is being manifested. The church is local and universal; earthly and heavenly.[58]

Timothy George makes a related claim: "The invisible or universal church emerges into visibility in the form of local congregations gathered around the faithful preaching of the Word of God."[59]

What George especially adds to the evangelical discussion is the accent on suffering, even martyrdom. This is a distinctive contribution.[60]

EVANGELICAL ECCLESIOLOGY AND DENOMINATIONAL POLITIES

In standard discussions of the organization of church life its structure and its ministers, three main forms of polity emerge: episcopal (e.g. Anglican), Presbyterian and congregational (e.g. Baptist). With regard to the latter, some are in associations and some are independent (a denomination with one member church?). Evangelicals, being Biblio-centric, seek to find a biblical warrant for their particular polity or mount a biblical argument that the New Testament does not prescribe any one church order or structure of ministry, but provides principles which need to be observed in framing a polity. Thus evangelicals can be found in episcopal structures (John Stott),

---

56. Bird, *Evangelical Theology*, 732–33, argues persuasively that the invisible-visible distinction, although venerable with Augustine and Calvin as proponents, must not be employed in such a way as to undermine the importance of the visible church and its need for appreciation.

57. Allison, *Sojourners and Strangers*, 467.

58. Ibid., 467–68.

59. George, "Toward," 132.

60. Distinctive but not unique. Milne includes suffering in his evangelical ecclesiology, *Know the Truth*, 321–22.

Presbyterian (John Frame) and congregational ones (D. A. Carson).[61] This phenomenon buttresses the argument that evangelicalism is a movement that allows crystallization on more than one kind of ecclesial community.

EVANGELICAL ECCLESIOLOGY IN THE MIDST OF CULTURAL CHANGE

Evangelical church life does not take place in a cultural vacuum. We are sociologically and historically situated beings. We live outside of paradise and this has led to a paradoxical life setting for evangelicals as Gregg R. Allison points out: "The church is *in* the world, but not *of* the world. It is *for* the world, yet *against* the world."[62] Western societies are arenas of changing and clashing social values as Judeo-Christian ethics have less and less purchase on the popular moral imagination as the societal shift in thinking about same sex relations shows. The contemporary social imaginary of which Charles Taylor has written is proving an enormous challenge to evangelicals, especially in North America.[63] The moral majority has or is rapidly becoming the moral minority.[64] As intimated above, issues of human sexuality are at the forefront of the changes. Eminent moral philosopher, Alasdair MacIntyre famously concluded his magisterial book After Virtue in the words:

> If my account of our moral condition is correct [a new age of barbarism and darkness is coming], we ought also to conclude that for some time now we too have reached that turning point. What matters at this stage is the construction of local forms of community within which civility and the intellectual and moral life [and I would add the Christian life] can be sustained through the new dark ages which are already upon us. And if the tradition of virtues was able to survive the horrors of the last dark ages, we are not entirely without grounds for hope. This time however the barbarians are not waiting beyond the

---

61. Frame has severe words for the phenomenon of denominations, *Systematic Theology*, 1022, "I believe that denominationalism is an offense against God and that it has weakened the church's witness. The rise of denominations is caused by sin, either sin of those who left the original church or sin of those who forced them to leave-or, most likely both." Frame is an ordained Presbyterian minister. A robust work on the theological understanding of denominationalism remains to be written.

62. Allison, *Sojourners and Strangers*, 467; original emphases.

63. For Taylor's account of the social imaginary and how it is changed over recent centuries in the West, see *A Secular Age*.

64. See Turner, "What Happens When the 'Moral Majority' Becomes a Minority?"

frontiers; they have already been governing us for quite some time. And it is our lack of consciousness of this that constitutes part of our predicament. We are waiting not for a Godot, but foe another-doubtless very different –St. Benedict.[65]

Orthodox writer, Rod Dreher heard the call.[66]

Rod Dreher sums up the way forward in what is "a truly post-Christian civilization." It is for Christians of all stripes, including evangelicals, is to embrace what he calls the Benedict Option.[67] The Benedict in question is known to church history as St. Benedict of Nursia (480–547 AD), the inspiration for the Benedictine Order. Dreher describes Benedict "as an educated young Christian who left Rome, the city of the recently fallen Roman Empire, out of disgust with tis decadence... Eventually, he gathered around him some like-minded men, and formed monasteries."[68] In addition, "Benedict wrote his famous Rule, which became the guiding constitution of most monasteries in Western Europe in the Middle Ages."[69] Finding inspiration in the example of Benedict, Dreher argues for "the centrality of practices in shaping our Christian lives."

Importantly, Dreher is not calling for a retreat from engagement with the wider society. He notes that MacIntyre wrote of "a doubtless very different-St Benedict." What then would adopting the Benedict option look like? Dreher sums it up in these terms: "Put less grandly, the Benedict Option—or 'Ben Op'—is an umbrella term for Christians who accept MacIntrye's critique of modernity, and who also recognize that forming Christians who live out Christianly according to the Great tradition requires embedding within communities and institutions dedicated to that formation."[70] The Benedict Option is about forming intentional communities which are focused on discipleship as a way of life. Significantly, he argues *"no church can be authentically Christian without evangelizing."*[71]

---

65. MacIntyre, *After Virtue: A Study in Moral Theory*, 263.
66. Dreher quotes MacIntyre at great length in "Benedict Option FAQ."
67. Ibid.
68. Ibid., Christians often speak loosely with regard to the fall of the Roman Empire. Strictly speaking, just before Benedict's time, it was the Western Roman Empire that had fallen. Romulus Augustus was the last emperor in the West and he was deposed in 476 AD by the barbarians. The Eastern Roman Empire, also know as the Byzantine Empire, finally fell to the Ottoman Turks in 1453 AD.
69. Ibid.
70. Ibid.
71. Ibid.; original emphasis.

Dreher's Benedict Option is getting both traction and pushback in the evangelical world. With regard to traction, Phillip Cary suggests: "In the wake of *Obergefell*, I expect we'll be talking for some time about the 'Benedict Option Rod Dreher is proposing. At least I hope so. I'd like to see how it might work, for evangelical Protestants as well as for Roman Catholics."[72] Others aren't entirely convinced and Michael Gerson and Peter Wehner have proposed the Wilberforce Option instead. This option is defined as "the relentless defense of human dignity in the course of human events."[73] William Wilberforce was that evangelical English political leader so crucial to the success of the ant-slavery campaign in the nineteenth century. Gerson and Wehner fear that the Benedict Option may leave evangelical churches disengaged from the wider social context and too pessimistic about the possibility of positive social change. It may well be that evangelical Christians and gay pro-family advocates can co-operate in seeking the optimum social conditions for family life (and especially children) to flourish, even though ideological so disagreed on the propriety of same sex marriage per se. It is true that Christians are "resident aliens," but it is also true in Jeremiah's terms that the Christian is to "seek the welfare of the city (Jer 29:7)."[74]

What the debate over these options shows is that evangelical are wrestling with how to relate evangelicals to perceived cultural drift from Judeo-Christian values.[75] What needs to be observed is that Rod Dreher, who is Orthodox, thinks in ecclesial terms, but with Gerson and Wehner the individual Christian or Christians plural are on view. Once more there is evidence that evangelicalism is a movement, rather than a church per se.

CONCLUSION

Evangelicalism is a movement which finds its instantiation in a variety of denominational polities. Some, but not all, evangelicals draw on the classic

---

72. Cary, "The Benedict Option For Evangelicals." *Obergefell* refers to the Supreme Court case that in 2015 saw same sex marriage made possible by law.

73. Gerson and Wehner, "How Christians Can Flourish in a Same-Sex Marriage World."

74. Ibid., Dreher is unimpressed with the Wilberforce option and finds it flawed. See his response, "Wilberforce vs. Benedict."

75. In a previous generation, evangelical Quaker Elton Trueblood argued for the St. Columba option. St. Columba began the re-evangelization of Scotland using the Island of Iona as his base for Christian communal life and seeing Scotland as his field for missionary endeavor. The movement was from the base of Christian community to mission in the wide world. Trueblood said: "The test for the vitality of any group does not occur primarily while the group is meeting; it occurs after the meeting is over," *The Company of the Committed*, 74–75.

descriptors of the church found in the Christian past to understand the nature of the church or how to recognize a true church. With regard to the nature of the church, these evangelicals draw on the Nicene Creed of the patristic age with its accents on unity, holiness, universality and apostolicity. From the Reformation era, the marks of the church provide criteria for identifying the true church: a true church is recognized by the presence of the pure word preached, the sacraments or ordinances rightly and duly administered, and perhaps godly discipline. Biblical warrant is sought for the four notes and the two or three marks as to be expected from a Bibliocentric movement. What creates a family resemblance between the varied polities in which evangelical are to be found, if they are to be comfortable for evangelicals, is the place given to the priority of the gospel and its proclamation and promotion. Timothy George is so right about that priority for convinced evangelicals.

BIBLIOGRAPHY

Allison, Gregg R. *Sojourners and Strangers: The Doctrine of the Church*. Wheaton, IL: Crossway 2012.

Bebbington, D. W. *Evangelicalism in Modern Britain: A History from the 1730s to the 1980s*. Grand Rapids: Baker, 1992.

Bird, Michael F. "Towards an Evangelical Ecclesiology." *Patheos*. May 27, 2011. Accessed August 29, 2016. http://www.patheos.com/blogs/euangelion/2011/05/towards-an-evangelical-ecclesiology/.

———. *Evangelical Theology: A Biblical and Systematic Introduction*. Grand Rapids: Zondervan, 2013.

Cary, Phillip. "The Benedict Option For Evangelicals: The Gospel as External Authority." *First Things*. June 30, 2015. Accessed September 28, 2016. https://www.firstthings.com/blogs/firstthoughts/2015/06/the-benedict-option-for-evangelicals#print.

Dreher, Rod. "Benedict Option FAQ." *American Conservative*. October 6, 2015. Accessed September 28, 2016. http://www.theamericanconservative.com/dreher/benedict-option-faq/.

Dulles, Avery. *Models of the Church*. New York, New York: Image, 2014.

Erickson, Millard J. *Christian Theology*. 3rd ed. Grand Rapids: Baker Academic, 2013.

Frame, John M. *Systematic Theology: An Introduction to Christian Belief*. Phillipsburg, NJ: P & R, 2013.

George, Timothy. "Toward an Evangelical Ecclesiology." In *Catholics and Evangelicals: Do They Share a Common Future?*, edited by Thomas P. Rausch, 122–49. New York: Paulist, 2000.

Gerson, Michael, and Peter Wehner. "How Christians Can Flourish in a Same-Sex Marriage World." November 2, 2015. Accessed September 28, 2016. http://www.christianitytoday.com/ct/2015/november/how-christians-can-flourish-in-same-sex-marriage-world-cult.html.

Grenz, Stanley J. *Theology for the Community of God*. Grand Rapids: Eerdmans, 2000.

Grudem, Wayne. *Systematic Theology: An Introduction to Biblical Doctrine.* Leicester, UK: InterVarsity, 1994.

Hammett John S. "The Boundaries of Evangelical Ecclesiology." Lausanne-Orthodox Initiative. Accessed September 30, 2016. http://www.loimission.net/wp-content/uploads/2014/08/The-Boundaries-of-Evangelical-Ecclesiology-HammettJ.S..pdf.

Haykin, Michael A. G., and Kenneth J. Stewart, eds. *The Advent of Evangelicalism: Exploring Historical Continuities.* Nashville: B&H, 2008.

Kuhn, Chase. "The Ecclesiology of Donald Robinson and David Broughton Knox: A Presentation, Analysis and Theological Evaluation of Their Thought of Nature of the Church." PhD diss., University of Western Sydney, 2014.

MacIntyre, Alasdair. *After Virtue: A Study in Moral Theory.* 2nd ed. London: Duckworth, 1985.

McGrath, Alister. *Evangelicalism and the Future of Christianity,* Downers Grove, IL: InterVarsity, 1995.

———. *Christian Theology: An Introduction.* 5th ed. Chichester, UK: Wiley-Blackwell, 2011.

Millegan, Brantly. "Serious Catholics Are Evangelical." Review of *Evangelical Catholicism: Deep Reform in the 21st Century Church,* by George Weigel. *Christianity Today,* March 6, 2013. Accessed September 26, 2016. http://www.christianitytoday.com/ct/2013/march-web-only/weigel-counter-reformation-is-over.html.

Milne, Bruce. *Know the Truth: A Handbook of Christian Belief.* 3rd ed. Downers Grove, IL: IVP Academic, 2009.

Stott, John. *Evangelical Truth: A Personal Plea for Unity, Integrity and Faithfulness.* Rev. ed. Downers Grove, IL: IVP Academic, 2003.

Taylor, Charles. *A Secular Age.* Cambridge, MA: Belknap, 2007.

Trueblood, Elton. *The Company of the Committed.* New York: Harper & Row, 1961.

Turner, Laura. "What Happens When the 'Moral Majority' Becomes a Minority?" *The Atlantic.* September 27, 2015. Accessed 9/28/2016. http://www.theatlantic.com/politics/archive/2015/09/end-of-moral-majority/407359/.

Van Dyk, Leanne. "The Church in Evangelical Theology and Practice." In *The Cambridge Companion to Evangelical Theology,* edited by Timothy Larsen and Daniel J. Treier, 125–43. Cambridge: Cambridge University Press, 2007

Webb, B. G. "The Doctrine of the Church: Toward Conceptual Clarification." In *Church, Worship and the Local Congregation,* edited by B. G. Webb, 3–17. Homebush, NSW: Lancer, 1987.

The Church as a Resurrection Community
The Church's Identity in Late Modernity

Piotr J. Małysz

The ethos of personal autonomy and self-sufficiency, once articulated as a challenge by modernity's champions, now appears largely to be the creed of its diehard epigones, disciples of self-proclaimed disciples many times removed. Its last, tough by no means insignificant, trench is the ubiquitous genre of the self-help manual. Or so it might seem. The picture is not quite so simple. A protracted agony is obviously not a death knell. On the one hand, what for Immanuel Kant was a task that elevated one above the mundane, in a posture at once critical and profoundly respectful of universal rationality, today is frequently only an occasion for a gnostic flight into a realm of seemingly free-range personal preference. On the other hand, quite apart from ideological temptations, those whose feet are planted more firmly on the ground do find themselves, as Zygmunt Bauman has observed, doomed to resolve structural-societal, indeed global, issues and uncertainties in our own personal biographies.[1] "We are—most of us—free to enjoy our freedom, but unfree to avoid the consequences of that enjoyment."[2] This late modern predicament, with its undaunted assumption—and, for all the posturing, glaring lack—of individual autonomy, shows no signs of final demise. This twilight zone of neither here nor there may be our home for the foreseeable future, or so it would seem.

---

1. Bauman, "Freedom and Security: The Unfinished Story of a Tempestuous Union," *The Individualized Society* 47.

2. Bauman, "Modernity and clarity," 69.

Christians, with their sobering understanding of the world's fallenness, have had every reason to refuse the path of defeatism. This refusal, in our late modern context, takes the form of what Roman Catholics have generally taken for granted, and what Protestants are now also beginning to appreciate in today's global, yet hopelessly (or so it would seem) fragmented, world: being Christian is *irreducibly* communal. The strength of this claim should not be overlooked. The community is neither a felicitous byproduct nor a contingent support structure—neither a perk nor a prop—but the very *public and counter-cultural* reality of Christian existence in the world. This, one might argue, is the import of St Cyprian's adage that outside the church there is no salvation (*salus extra ecclesiam non est*).[3]

This said, mere recovery of the communal, ecclesiological mindset among today's heirs of the Reformation may not yet, as such, be the sought—after panacea for our late modern ills or the radiance to dispel the intractable twilight of our existence. For the question remains: *How is the community to understand itself?* Much hinges on how one answers this question, and not every answer will make the community into the beacon of light it was called to be (Matt 5:14; Eph 5:8). My goal, accordingly, is to defend St Cyprian's maxim precisely by inquiring into the self-understanding of the Christian community which both sets it apart from, and places it in service of, the world. This approach, we may note, will sidestep the issue of authority or Petrine succession; as a Protestant (and that of a particular sort, namely, a Lutheran), I remain skeptical of orienting the question in this manner. Rather, the inquiry pursued here will turn its critical attention to communal self-understandings, put forth by some Protestants, as ultimately unable to rise above our late modern milieu and so inevitably hampered in their understanding of the gospel and the community it seeks to give rise to.

STRENGTH IN NUMBERS?

How then ought the Christian community to understand itself? Of course, by asserting the irreducibly communal character of being Christian in the world, we have not simply ended up where St Cyprian brought us already two millennia ago—a position and a place we occupied rather unproblematically (or so the story goes) until the dawn of the modern era, from which we then foolishly strayed, and in which we now, thank God, seem to find ourselves again. We are wiser. To contextualize Bauman's analysis of the late modern burden of freedom, we know now, better than ever, that it is a rather tall order, *pace* Bultmann, to require each and every one of us, as "those who

---

3. Cyprian of Carthage, *Epistle* 72.21.

have the modern world view [to] live as though [we] had none," to "believe . . . in spite of experience," to go through life with the interminable and unmitigated burden of "a new understanding of [my] personal existence";[4] or, for that matter, industriously to cultivate a personal relationship with Jesus. Moreover, we also now realize that being a Christian hardly accords with outward conformity to the power structures of the age, while quietly enjoying an oasis of inner freedom (a Kantian view that is sometimes, and largely unfairly, ascribed to Luther).[5] Not to mention such a posture is surely downright impossible, unless "freedom" is the guise with which self-deception clothes bondage. To put things another way, Christianity is not a matter of a ceaseless dialectic between the seen and unseen which I must constantly *resolve in my own existence*; nor is it true to form when relegated to the private sphere, the private life, the deeply cherished in the soul. For all its emphasis on each believer's standing, first and foremost, *coram Deo*, Christianity is not essentially individualistic, such that the sole rationale for the community, though its importance is by no means played down, is strength in numbers, or something akin to a book club, designed to edify otherwise disparate and largely self-sufficient members.

With the disastrous implications of the modern turn to the subject as his target, Peter Leithart's *Against Christianity*[6] charges us to reclaim robust Christendom over against tepid Christianity. The latter Leithart considers, virtually by definition, to be "biblical religion disemboweled and emasculated by (voluntary) individualization and/or privatization."[7] In a distant echo of Schleiermacher's critique of state hijacking of the church's rites, in order to punctuate and give expression to its own rhythms,[8] Leithart, too, calls on the church to reclaim what belongs to it. To be sure, Leithart's goal is not to make the church more palatable to its cultured despisers but rather to put an end to further embarrassment: if there has to be cause for offence, let it be a legitimate one, and let it be visible! The church must be an unapologetic community, confident with its own language,[9] unabashed in its affirmation of the miraculous[10] and, above all, disciplined and thus able to reassert its own jurisdiction of morals.[11] Only in this way can it emerge

---

4. Bultmann, *Jesus Christ and Mythology*, 85, 84, 73.
5. Marcuse, "A Study of Authority: Luther, Calvin, Kant," 115–45.
6. Leithart, *Against Christianity*, 17.
7. Ibid.
8. Schleiermacher, *On Religion*, Speech Four, esp. 86–90.
9. Leithart, *Against Christianity*, 57.
10. Ibid., 90.
11. Ibid.,131.

as a public community in a public terrain,[12] a community whose goal is no less than Christendom.

Stanley Hauerwas and William Willimon's vision, articulated in their 1989 volume, *Resident Aliens: A provocative Christian assessment of culture and ministry for people who know that something is wrong*,[13] may seem, at first glance, to be diametrically antithetical to Leithart's Constantinian nostalgia. Hauerwas and Willimon reject stagnant and self-complacent Christendom in favor of "a movement, a people,"[14] "resident aliens, an adventurous colony through a society of unbelief."[15] But Leithart is not as naively optimistic as he may sound, and neither is Hauerwas resigned to pessimism. Both projects, in the end, are equally predicated on the opposition between the culture of the wider society and the culture of the church as a *communal task in the world*, and not simply an insoluble opposition in the believer's soul. This is not to say Hauerwas's vision is reducible to moralism or social gospel. He certainly stresses "the necessity of the church being a community of people who embody our language about God, where talk about God is used without apology because our life together does not mock our words."[16] But if we press further the question of the church's language about God, this language, Hauerwas reminds us, is eschatological. It points not to the perdurance of the world, burdening us with making history come out right; it insists, instead, that "God has already made history come out right."[17] It is thus language with unparalleled social-critical capacity. Still, for this capacity to become operative, the church must first live up to its own language before it turns its dissecting blade to the outside. The church must be "the visible, political enactment of our language of God by a people who can name their sin and accept God's forgiveness and are thereby enabled to speak the truth in love."[18] If the church fails to model its language, it is then that its language atrophies into gimmicky sentimentality,[19] self-fulfillment recipes and "suffocating moralism,"[20] all of which, in blissful ignorance, chip away at the rationale for its existence.[21]

12. Ibid., 63.
13. Hauerwas and William Willimon, *Resident Aliens*, 87, 90, 120, 171.
14. Ibid., 21
15. Ibid., 49
16. Ibid., 171.
17. Ibid., 87.
18. Ibid., 171.
19. Ibid., 120.
20. Ibid., 90.
21. Ibid., 120.

Beyond Affinity and Enacted Ethos

More recently, Paul Hinlicky has also taken a stab at articulating the public and communal character of the church in the form of what he calls the "Beloved Community."[22] Hinlicky's *Luther and the Beloved Community: A Path for Christian Theology after Christendom* opens with an acknowledgement, following Josiah Royce, that "Life is essentially, in its ideal, social"[23]; thus one should not be surprised that, as Bonhoeffer already observed, "all the basic Christian concepts" likewise have a "social intention."[24] The gospel, in its exposure of humans' self-preserving violence, is, among other things, a public irruption of a non-violent economy in the world's midst. Hinlicky extends this Girardian theme by offering a historical analysis of Christian commitment to non-violent action in the figures of Luther, Reinhold Niebuhr and Martin Luther King. Non-violence, Hinlicky concludes, cannot remain without social impact which must be described in terms of moral coerciveness and spiritual confrontation.

All this being said, Hinlicky critiques René Girard for ultimately reducing Christ to a "unique individual" to be imitated. Taking his cue from John Milbank, Hinlicky insists on our *participation* in Jesus' violence-refusing sacrifice (99–103; 337–354).[25] Crucially, it is this emphasis that shows the initial opposition between a privatized Christianity and its communal alternative to be at best a half-diagnosis. Such is also the view that Christianity has to do with a divinely established blueprint—moral-political or even eschatological—for a new order for the ages. For what is at stake in the notion of participation is not simply the manner of *our* being, as Christians, in the world, or of this or that communal self-expression. What participation brings into view is *divine action and its availability*. To be sure, "the Spirit does not make our choices for us," as Hinlicky duly notes, but rather "sets the conscience free to make moral choices."[26] But more is at play than our choices, and this "more" makes true imitation of Christ not into an *imitatio operis* but, first and foremost, into an *imitatio mentis*.[27] When St Paul appealed to the Philippians to have "the same mind in you that was in Christ Jesus," he was already insisting on the precedence of transformation which

---

22. Hinlicky, "Luther and the Beloved Community: A Path for Christian Theology after Christendom," 5, 11.

23. Ibid., 11.

24. Ibid., 5.

25. Ibid., 99–103; 337–54. This should not be taken as a *tout court* endorsement of Milbank's views.

26. Ibid., 336

27. Ibid.

proceeds from the Spirit and is rooted in God's gracious privilege (Phil 1:29; 2:5).

The question of divine action and its availability is, I believe, the crux of the matter. It deserves even more attention and an explicitly trinitarian articulation. It is, I submit, none other than the question of the gospel, both as such, and as it must be articulated in today's society. For what confronts us is not simply that modernity is anti-, or at best tangentially, communal; and that Christianity has nearly self-destructed by drinking the individualistic Kool-Aid, which accounts for much emotional agitation and social indifference, lethargy, not to say impotence. Late modernity, some have argued, is actually strongly communal in its outlook and makes much of a sense of belonging. The real problem is that the vast majority of our communities are, to borrow Benedict Anderson's term, "imagined communities." We are inhabitants of our neighborhoods and participants in our congregations, hipsters, members of professional guilds, Facebook users, champions of the church's catholic tradition, Americans, even husbands and wives—but each of these is predicated on a founding act of choice. "The choice," writes Bauman, "is restated daily and ever new actions are taken to confirm it"[28]–if only through maintained awareness that there always are other options. What characterizes late modern communities, Bauman continues, is that they are held together by bonds of *affinity*. Affinity, to be sure, boasts "the intention to make the bond like that of *kinship*," but, even as it works assiduously to cement it, affinity can never quite shrink from keeping some options open. (The phenomenon of imagined communities is not, of course, unrelated to the former fetishization of an isolated and self-sufficient self; arguably, what we have here is a particularly insidious case of survival-through-adaptation by assuming the form of the opposite.)

If the above is indeed an accurate picture of our society, then *mere* insistence on the recovery of the communal, on collective deployment of an economy of grace to oppose this world's relentless individualism and nauseating violence—even in imitation of Jesus and in sincere devotion to the Sermon on the Mount—may actually make the church more cultural than ever. The church, in spite of itself, becomes a purveyor of an ethos in the marketplace of meaning: a protest ethos, to be sure, but for this very reason only another communal *task* in the world, either appealing or off-putting to all those who are in search of an intellectually and affectively compatible home. This makes the church—*even in its own self-understanding*—no different from how society itself operates. Society, as Peter Berger observes, is a collective undertaking that, through intellectual and material production,

---

28. Bauman, *Liquid Love: On the Frailty of Human Bonds*, 29.

orders the physical world into a meaningful whole.[29] So ordered, the whole, or what Berger calls the *nomos*, confronts us, as those who have been socialized into it, as an apparently inviolable and sheltering objectivity. Against its backdrop, underwritten, further, by appeals to the ultimate, we can then verify the meaningfulness of our own lives, and the lives of countless generations before and yet to come. Berger stresses the sense of liberation that comes from "self-denying submission to the power of the collective nomos."[30] Religion, according to Berger, is particularly effective in legitimating a nomos "because it relates the precarious reality constructions of empirical societies with ultimate reality."[31] But the social production of meaning is not always foolproof. It is threatened by irruptions, such as senseless pain and death, which cannot be readily given meaning. Those irruptions expose the world's coherence as a matter of cultural production and maintenance of meaning; they expose the world's very fragility. What we know as reality is shown to hang only "on the thin thread of conversation."[32] Confrontation with other, rival *nomoi* may have the same, literally earth-shattering, effect. In all such marginal situations, the perdurance of a nomos depends crucially on its capacity persuasively to integrate disturbing encounters. All in all, society, for Berger, is at bottom a theodicy, "a community in the face of death,"[33] sustaining itself through memory, ritual, and speech.[34]

The church can, of course, never avoid the appearance of religion as a socially posited phenomenon. It is also a community in the face of death, sustained through its own memory, speech and broadly understood ritual. But if that is how it understands itself, as a communal undertaking for the sake of a more authentic social vision, then, in today's late modern milieu, the church is no more than another group that may win our allegiance, at least for as long as we are not confronted with something drastic, or a competitor does not come along with a better take on things. What both Bauman and Berger help clarify is the need for the church to understand itself in distinction from communities based on affinity and thus, fundamentally, in distinction from communities whose center is the human enactment of a vision, however divine the latter is held to be. Now, this may seem like an *ad hoc* ecclesiology, with the church keeping just a step ahead of its detractors.

29. Berger, *The Sacred Canopy: Elements of a Sociological Theory of Religion*, 17, 32, 40–41, 57, 80.
30. Ibid., 57.
31. Ibid., 32.
32. Ibid., 17.
33. Ibid., 80.
34. Ibid., 40–41

But it is not. What is at issue here is that which confronted Augustine in the Milanese garden—before Berger theorized the human production of the world and Bauman its late modern fragmentation. That night, the spotlight was suddenly drawn away from Augustine's own quest for meaning to a transformation that was the work of another: God. Augustine's intellectual journey to Christianity had been a resounding success, but it was not enough. It was not yet the gospel. Something else was needed than a compelling comprehensive picture of the world and an overwhelming desire to commit to it.[35]

All this is to illuminate the urgent need to recover a sense of the gospel as *God's ongoing action* for the *self-understanding* of that community which aspires to be God's church. No mere communal outlook, or culture-challenging ethos will do the trick. Even Hauerwas's admonition to remember that in Jesus's crucifixion and resurrection God has made "history come out right" and that, therefore, we should have no fear "to become citizens of a new Kingdom, a messianic community where the world God is creating takes visible, practical form"[36] is not enough. It is not enough if the emphasis falls on our enactment of the Kingdom for the sake of its credibility, on persuasion rather than the gospel.

Resurrection Community

How then do we announce the gospel, the action of God that transcends even the best we can offer—that is, the togetherness of living together, the togetherness of best intentions and a shared worldview—and conforms our minds to Christ and transforms our embodied existence into a togetherness of kin? Hauerwas gives us a clue when, in passing, he speaks in the present tense of God creating. We must follow this clue, but, as we do so, we must also make sure we do not dilute the reality of God's creation in a monochrome account of divine providence and mere conservation. When the Bible speaks of creation—new creation, to be specific—it understands by it the *present* reality of the resurrection. It is in the resurrection, I believe, that we must seek our further clue to Christian being in the world and communal identity.

In the witness of the New Testament, the resurrection of Jesus of Nazareth is inextricably bound with the resurrection of all flesh. Crucially, in this the resurrection is no mere announcement of what the future will bring, of what awaits when God at long last wraps all history up. It is, in other words,

35. Augustine, *Confessions*, book 8.
36. Ibid., 87.

not a foretaste of what will come, with the implicit understanding that one sparrow assuredly points to, but does not yet *make*, a spring. The resurrection is not just a declaration of what God will *one day* bring to pass in all of his creation. It declares what already is the case! The choice between the future tense 'will' and the present (perfect) may seem a trivial one, merely a matter of rhetoric. But no less than the nature of God's action in history, and with it biblical ecclesiology, is at stake.

Jesus' resurrection—we must affirm!—is evidence of what God *has already begun* to do to all of his creation. Consider, first, the alternative: If the import of the resurrection is merely a hope in the future, then the church emerges as a fundamentally human reality, a phenomenon of the interim. Confined to an anthropological plane, the church is only a negative community, set against the world by its own story, which means simply the refusal of other available stories. With this founding story the church comforts itself—in words spoken and symbolized through practice. The church may even be tempted to engage in explicit competition and seek to make a case for the superiority of its story. Ulrich Zwingli's ecclesiology, espoused by many evangelicals today, betrays this ecclesial self-understanding. "All celebrations . . . give historical faith," Zwingli insists, "they remind us of some event, refreshing the memory." If God's work is discerned at all, it is only as the Spirit's secret bestowal of faith on the heart quite apart from "external things,"[37] or it is acknowledged as equally secret, undifferentiated providential instigation of all that takes place (what Hinlicky aptly refers to as pantheistic determinism).[38]

By contrast, an altogether different reality comes into focus if the import of the resurrection is that, *beginning with the risen man Jesus*, the new creation *is already underway*.[39] So understood, the resurrection certainly does not obviate the need for human speech and practice, yet it fundamentally reorients those. For now the gospel is not a mere message but, above all, bears tangible witness to *God's present action*. Here we must be even more specific: the gospel attests to God's redemptive-creative work. It is, in fact, God's own self-attestation. And this takes place not merely in the hidden and rather treacherous recesses of the believer's heart, but in the midst of creation, breaking into history's flow and showing, in the here and now, the futility of death's grip, the absurdity of sin, and the obsolescence of the demonic.

---

37. Zwingli, *An Exposition of the Faith*, 260.
38. Zwingli, *A Sermon on the Providence of God*, 128–234.
39. Prenter, *Creation and Redemption*, 427–28.

How does all this take place? It is *already in the present* that we truly are buried into Christ's death and raised with him to newness of life (Rom 6) in a public act where Christ himself, in the words of Luther, "is present at baptism and in baptism, in fact is himself the baptizer."[40] And it is already in the present that grain and grapes yield not only bread and wine, but a heavenly feast, as Irenaeus states so eloquently.[41] It is likewise in the present that the word of absolution is sounded forth, which relives one of the tyranny of one's past and of the need still to make something of oneself and then cement that identity at all costs lest it dissolve. Through the word of forgiveness, which carries no less than heavenly implications (Jn 20:21–23; Mt 18:18), the believer's new life is hidden with Christ in God (Col 3:3). God at work in the here and now—the self-same God who has already raised his servant Jesus from the dead—is our comfort and our hope. Precisely this is the gospel, the good news of the new creation already being called into being. Through and around this gospel, we too are being gathered as a people made by God unto himself. God's unceasing work on behalf of his creation transforms us from our former nothingness, rescues us from our empty ways, and renews us in our minds; it is our new birth which will find its completion in no less than bodily incorruption.

The significance of the sacraments as God's *public* acts of new creation, openly exhibiting the already inaugurated reality of the resurrection, can hardly be overstated. In order properly to appreciate the sacraments' public nature, a word must be said here about John Calvin's doctrine of the Lord's Supper. It, too, is characterized by a strong sense of divine action—yet in a way that disregards its public dimension and, in the final reckoning, compromises it altogether. On the one hand, we have Calvin's laudable insistence, *contra* Zwingli, on "the true and substantial partaking of the body of the Lord . . . not . . . solely by imagination or understanding of mind, but to enjoy the thing itself as nourishment of eternal life" (IV.xvii.19).[42] But, on the other hand, Calvin endeavors to argue away, as impossible, a union of the bread and Christ's body. The ascension, as Calvin understands it, has effected a spatial removal of Jesus's body from earth.[43] To make an allowance for it, Calvin subordinates the validity, that is, reality and integrity, of the Sacrament to its efficacy. Efficacy pertains only to believers. The Sacrament's reality thus becomes predicated on personal faith, which elevates the

---

40. Luther, *Concerning Rebaptism*.
41. Irenaeus, *Against Heresies* 5.2 (*ANF* 1:527–28).
42. Calvin, *Institutes of the Christian Religion* 4.17.19.
43. Ibid., 4.17.27.

individual believer to heaven, there to partake of Christ's body.[44] One must certainly question, as we briefly and implicitly shall, whether Calvin fully grasps the theological import of the ascension. All that needs to be noted here is that he ends up burdening the individual believer with the fundamental task of soul-searching. The believer must, first and foremost, assure not worthy reception of what is antecedently established and already provided by God—where worthiness lies simply in faithful recognition of God at work in supplying the gifts of the new creation, as is the case for Luther and the church catholic. Rather, for Calvin, the believer must personally determine and establish access to God's gifts, for only as elevated to heaven by faith can one partake of Christ's body and blood. Despite his avowed sacramental realism, Calvin is thus unable to get beyond an individual's conscience as the theater of the dialectic between seen and unseen. Preoccupied as he is with an attempt to mediate between Luther and Zwingli, he fails to grasp the *creation-like, public* character of God's sacramental action which conveys the heart of the gospel.[45]

What sets the church apart from the world—in distinction from both modernist individualism and, especially, its late modern communitarian, affinity-based avatar—is not simply the church's communal character. For the church does not re-present yet another intellectually apprehended and socially enacted theodicy (à la Berger), or some other umbrella of self-salvation. Rather, through the church, in creation's very midst, God *publicly* displays his faithfulness and enacts his promise. With Christ as its head, the church is thus the *reality of the resurrection*—whose subject is God—between the resurrection of the One and the assured rising of all. It is decidedly not a community where the individual mediates an unseen reality.

This is exactly what Luther had in mind when he insisted that grace was fundamentally divine favor.[46] He thus challenged the medieval view of grace as a quality infused in the soul, a quality that gave rise to a disposition,

---

44. Ibid., 4.17.31.

45. Lutheran theology of the Lord's Supper, while maintaining a non-negotiable emphasis on the objective reality of the sacrament, has been historically constricted by its own strongly polemical focus: the real presence of Christ's body and blood is understood as grounded in the divine promise and related only to the conveyance of individual forgiveness. But, beyond a narrowly understood scriptural mandate, little attempt is generally made to construe this sacramentally embodied and underwritten promise, as well as the individual's forgiveness, against the broader, creation-wide tapestry of God's redemptive work. The same criticism could, in point of fact, be made of the broader Western theological tradition, preoccupied as it has been rather narrowly with the metaphysics of the real presence.

46. Małysz, "Spiritualty, Ontology, and the Church: A Response to Jared Wicks," 21–44.

which it was up to the believer to exercise in works of charity. But, at the same time, Luther's insistence on grace as *favor Dei* in no way implied that grace was only in the mind of the divine beholder, or that its outcome was a mere judicial pronouncement on God's part. Rather, the favor of God was, for Luther, God's continued public action in the midst of his people. This action, to be sure, took place outside the believer (the famous *extra nos*), thus possessing a completeness and integrity of its own. But into this action the believer was decisively caught up, justified according to its communal co-ordinates, defined and remade according to its logic of kinship. With this view of grace, Luther rejected two individualisms: the medieval individualism of a Christian consumed by his or her own virtue and the Protestant individualism of a justified believer tasked with now converting his or her justification into a sanctified life, whether individually or communally.

None of this is, of course, to suggest that the church does not also have a story to tell, a story which believers truly take to heart. But the church is no mere rhetoric, or, even worse, a language game, a "thin thread of conversation" in the gap between what was and what is to be, or may be. Rather, the church is God's own people in the vivifying, re-creating, sacramental presence of their Risen and now ascended Lord. The church is God's people who, raised with Christ to newness of life, repeatedly find their sustenance in his body and blood and, precisely *in* doing so, "proclaim the Lord's death until he comes" (1 Cor 11:26). As such the church is—it assuredly is!—the very embodiment and conduit of salvation, even if, just as certainly, it is not salvation in, of, and by itself.

As a people gathered by divine favor and caught up into the orbit of God's public re-creative acts, the church is a community both set apart from, and placed in service of, the world. The church offers no escape, either individual or communal, into a gnostic region of ever-morphing personal preference where the sky alone is the limit. Rather, as hidden with Christ in God—defined by his resurrection work—the church lives in openness to the world. The character of this openness can now be spelled out with more precision. Since the church is a community of kinship, rather than an imagined community of affinity, it goes into all the world and reaches to all. It does not seek those of a like mind, or wonder how to include others without compromising its own identity. Rather, for the church to live out of God's resurrection is to realize that it would compromise its own identity without openness to those who, by the church's own judgment (if it actually had that power!), do not belong. As Linn Tonstad has recently argued, "The logic of the kingdom in many of Jesus' parables, and in early church debates over Gentile inclusion, is less about who I (the presumptive insider) get to include than about the danger I run in seeking to weed out others (Gentiles, those of lesser faith, the tares, the least of these) from 'my' righteous, holy community, thereby using my own presumed piety as a weapon against them."[47]

That it should be so brings us back to the God-at-work. God is he at whose right hand now sits the risen Jesus of Nazareth. Resurrection theology is inextricably bound with the theology of the ascension as a theology not of mere absence but of anticipatory presence.[48] The ascension makes clear that the one whom the community follows is "God of God" and "Light from Light"; and that God, who in Jesus of Nazareth has united to himself human nature, has now made himself the safe-keeper of the humanity of all. The ascension thus underscores God's prevenience in the history of salvation; and it clarifies human action in the world not as mere imitative communitarianism but as participation in the loving self-communication, in the very triune life and missions, of God: the Father's re-creation through the sending of the Son and the bestowal of the Holy Spirit. What is more, in this endeavor, precisely as ascended, Jesus is now close to *all of us* with the presence of the triune God himself. He remains the Good Shepherd of his people, for the Trinity repeatedly "opens the doors of heaven," so that "mortals may eat of the bread of angels" (cf. Ps 78:23, 25). The ascended Christ, with whom our resurrection being is hidden, *is* our manna, springing from the desert floor, until the day he "comes again with glory."

CONCLUSION

Talk of Christian community and Christian being in the world begins with the ceaselessly creating God. It begins with Baptism, the Lord's Supper, and the absolving word of the gospel—all understood through the lens of the resurrection of all flesh and the divine renewal of all things. Stefan Alkier's warning is quite *à propos*: "Without the theology of the resurrection, the community of the Lord's Supper does not celebrate the in-breaking of the kingdom of God, but rather situates itself in the hell of its own self-righteousness or self-pity for the duration."[49] Without the theology of the resurrection, it remains—even in its own self-understanding—only a community of affinity, when it is, in fact, called to be God's household (1 Tim 3:15; cf. 1 Cor 12), participating in the wonders of God's "making all things new" (Rev 21). But when it understands itself as participating, mind and body, in God's

---

47. Tonstad, *God and Difference: The Trinity, Sexuality, and the Transformation of Finitude*, 256.

48. Farrow *Ascension Theology*, 16.

49. Alkier, *The Reality of the Resurrection: The New Testament Witness*, 263.

unfolding of his new creation, it then with renewed mind and body justifies God (*iustificat Deum*) as the true Redeemer and Creator.[50] That is, those who were once doomed to self-sufficiency and autonomy now depart from the altar into the world as God's own people, gathered around the Father's good gifts and, therefore, also ambassadors and participants in the divine renewal and its ever new possibilities.[51]

BIBLIOGRAPHY

Alkier, Stefan. *The Reality of the Resurrection: The New Testament Witness*. Translated by L. A. Huizenga. Waco: Baylor University Press, 2013.

Arendt, Hannah. *The Origins of Totalitarianism*. San Diego: Harvest, 1968.

Bauman, Zygmunt. "Freedom and Security: The Unfinished Story of a Tempestuous Union." In *The Individualized Society*, 41–57. Cambridge: Polity, 2001.

———. "Modernity and Clarity." In *The Individualized Society*, 51–70. Cambridge, UK: Polity, 2001.

———. *Liquid Love: On the Frailty of Human Bonds Liquid Love: On the Frailty of Human Bonds*. Cambridge: Polity, 2003.

Berger, Peter. *The Sacred Canopy: Elements of a Sociological Theory of Religion*. New York: Anchor, 1967.

Bultmann, Rudolf. *Jesus Christ and Mythology*. New York: Scribner's Sons, 1958.

Calvin, John. *Calvin: Institutes of the Christian Religion*. 2 vols. Edited by John T. McNeill. Translated by Ford Lewis Battles. LCC 20–21. Philadelphia: Westminster, 1960.

Cyprian of Carthage. *To Jubaianus, Concerning the Baptism of Heretics* [Epistle 72]. Translated by Ernest Wallis. In *ANF*, edited by Alexander Roberts and James Donaldson, 5:379–86. Buffalo, NY: Christian Literature, 1886.

Farrow, Douglas. *Ascension Theology*. London: T. & T. Clark, 2011.

Hauerwas, Stanley, and William Willimon. *Resident Aliens: A Provocative Christian Assessment of Culture and Ministry for People Who Know That Something Is Wrong*, Nashville: Abingdon, 1989.

Hinlicky, Paul. *Luther and the Beloved Community: A Path for Christian Theology after Christendom*. Grand Rapids: Eerdmans, 2010.

Irenaeus of Lyons. *Against Heresies* [5.2]. In *ANF*, edited by Alexander Roberts and James Donaldson, 1:527–28.

Kant, Immanuel, *An Answer to the Question: What Is Enlightenment?* (1784). In Immanuel Kant, *Practical Philosophy*, edited by Mary J. Gregor. Cambridge: Cambridge University Press, 1996.

Leithart, Peter. *Against Christianity*. Moscow, ID: Canon, 2003.

Luther, Martin. *Concerning Rebaptism* [1528]. Translated by Conrad Bergendoff. In *Luther's Works* [*LW*], edited by Jaroslav Pelikan et al., 40:225–62. American ed. Philadelphia: Fortress, 1955.

---

50. Luther, *Lectures on Galatians*; LW 26:227.
51. Malysz, "Exchange and Ecstasy," 294–308.

———. *Lectures on Galatians* [1535]. Translated by Jaroslav Pelikan. *LW* 26:227.St. Louis: Concordia, 1962.

Małysz, Piotr J. "Spiritualty, Ontology, and the Church: A Response to Jared Wicks." *Luther Refracted: The Reformer's Ecumenical Legacy*, edited by P. J. Małysz and D. Nelson, 21–42. Minneapolis: Fortress, 2015.

———. "Exchange and Ecstasy: Luther's Eucharistic Theology in Light of Radical Orthodoxy's Critique of Gift and Sacrifice." *Scottish Journal of Theology* 60, no. 3 (2007) 294–308.

Marcuse, Herbert. "A Study of Authority: Luther, Calvin, Kant" [1936]. In *The Frankfurt School on Religion,* edited by Eduardo Mendieta, 115–48. New York: Routledge, 2005.

Prenter, Regin. *Creation and Redemption*. Translated by T. I. Jensen, Philadelphia: Fortress, 1967.

Schleiermacher, Friedrich. Edited and translated by Richard Crouter. *On Religion: Speeches to Its Cultured Despisers* [1799]. Cambridge: Cambridge University Press, 1996.

Tonstad, Linn Marie. *God and Difference: The Trinity, Sexuality, and the Transformation of Finitude*. New York: Routledge, 2016.

Zwingli, Ulrich. *An Exposition of the Faith* [1531]. In *Zwingli and Bullinger*, edited and translated by G. W. Bromiley, 239–79. LCC 24. Philadelphia: Westminster, 1953.

———. *A Sermon on the Providence of God* [1530]. Translated by S. M. Jackson. In *The Latin Works of Huldreich Zwingli*, edited by W. J. Hinke, 2:128–234. Philadelphia: Heidelberg, 1922.

Vatican II and "Evangelicals and Catholics Together

A Roman Catholic Perspective"

THOMAS G. GUARINO

CHUCK COLSON AND RICHARD John Neuhaus founded Evangelicals and Catholics Together (ECT), an ecumenical initiative, in 1994. I have been blessed to work closely with Dean Timothy George on this bi-lateral dialogue since 1995, and in particularly close collaboration since 2009 when we were elected as co-chairmen of ECT. For as long as I have known Timothy, he has been a resolutely committed Christian. He has been firmly committed, as well, to continuing dialogue with those who share his faith in Jesus Christ and in biblical truth. Before addressing a specifically theological topic, I would like to relate, if I may, a few personal memories from my collaboration with Dean George over the past two decades.

First, allow me to say that Timothy has been a driving force behind the success of Evangelicals and Catholics Together almost since the beginning of this ecumenical enterprise. Most importantly, he has been fully supportive of the affirmation made in the very first ECT statement: "All who accept Christ as Lord and Savior are brothers and sisters in Christ. Evangelicals and Catholics are brothers and sisters in Christ."[1]

This was a bold and controversial claim, one that was not universally accepted in the Evangelical world. As Professor J. I. Packer has recently written, this statement was met with "howls of negativity" from certain Evangelical precincts.[2] And yet Timothy has ardently insisted on this fraternity in the Lord Jesus Christ—despite our differences—for some twenty years.

---

1 George and Guarino, eds., *Evangelicals and Catholics at Twenty*, 9.
2 Packer, "Preface," vii.

Second, let me also say that Dean George is the master of the theological *mot juste*—no small talent in ecumenical endeavors. Whenever ECT was engaged in discussion on a selected theological topic, the dynamic often went like this: Fr. Richard Neuhaus would state the Catholic position on an issue in strong terms—understatement was never one of Richard's gifts—with a papal citation or two thrown in for good measure. The Evangelical brethren, led by Chuck Colson, would remain unimpressed and would push back in a gentlemanly way—seeking clear biblical warrants for some Catholic claim. While we were groping for a way forward, Dr. George, in his slight Southern accent, would say, "Now this is a contentious topic but I think that, together, we can say something like this. . .." And then Timothy would present a smartly worded statement in which there was always something of the Catholic position, but now refined and strained by having passed through the evangelical filter proper to Timothy's mind.

On prayers to the saints, for example, Timothy would gently say: Now, we Evangelicals think Catholics go too far here, saying more than the Bible allows. But I think we can affirm together that "no true Christian, living or dead, can be outside the *communio sanctorum*." All of us share fellowship in the crucified and risen Lord.[3] It takes a decided talent to see positive value in two positions, and then offer an alternative, which respects both.

Third, Timothy is a formidable theologian, one who has published an important book on Reformation thinkers, and who is presently editing a Reformation commentary on the Bible. But he possesses, as well, a deep and sympathetic knowledge of the entire tradition of the Church. During our years together on ECT, I have always admired his ability to enter into the theological logic of the Catholic Church, even if not fully agreeing with it.

In that sense, Timothy possesses the true ecumenical temperament. That temperament, needless to add, should never be confused with a spineless malleability that seeks weak compromises and eschews forceful positions. That's a cartoon caricature of ecumenism and one that certainly does not characterize either Dean George or ECT. The ecumenism represented by Timothy is this: Listen to your interlocutor's position with utmost seriousness; treat it with respect; learn from it when possible; and correct it when necessary. These are excellent ecumenical postures, but Dr. George did not develop them during his time on ECT; he possessed them from the first moment I met him in 1995.

It should also be said that during our time on Evangelicals and Catholics Together there has never been a moment when we have ignored differences. As ECT clearly asserted in its first statement of 1994, *The Christian*

---

3 See George and Guarino, eds., *Evangelicals and Catholics at Twenty*, 71.

Mission in the Third Millennium: "We reject any appearance of harmony that is purchased at the price of truth." And again, "The only unity to which we would give expression is unity in the truth. . .."[4] Indeed, our method has been to face our theological disagreements head-on, examining them honestly and carefully.

VATICAN II AND ECUMENISM

Vatican II's Decree on Ecumenism (called *Unitatis redintegratio*) was the *magna carta* for Catholic involvement in the ecumenical movement. The many Protestant observers at the council were heartened by this decree and, in fact, were in constant dialogue with the theologians and bishops who composed it. As Dean George and I wrote in the introduction to the recent volume collecting all nine ECT statements, Vatican II was not just a Catholic event, but, given its marked accent on ecumenical dialogue, an important event for the entire Christian world.[5]

The council made several advances when speaking about the relationship between Catholic and Protestant Christians. In the Dogmatic Constitution on the Church (*Lumen gentium*), for example, the council taught that Protestant churches truly, formally and substantially participate in the Church of Christ.[6] To the "separated brethren," that may seem like a small admission—and perhaps a grudging one at that. But it represented a sea-change in the official position of the Catholic Church which had been avoiding ecumenical activity for decades. In his 1928 encyclical, *Mortalium animos*, Pope Pius XI had spoken of ecumenical work as purveying a "false Christianity, entirely foreign to the one Church of Christ." And he warned Catholics, in strong terms, against taking part in ecumenical meetings because these "pan-Christians" (as he called ecumenists) are searching for a lowest-common-denominator form of Christianity, absent specific Catholic beliefs.

Vatican II's recognition of Protestant churches as formally participating in the Church of Christ-given their possession of determinate "*elementa ecclesiae*" (that is, elements of sound Christian doctrine and sacraments)– was a major step forward. It indicated a clear acknowledgement that Catholics share—to take Evangelicals as an example—significant dimensions of unity with the separated brethren: Belief in the one Triune God; in Jesus Christ, the Eternal Word made flesh and the Redeemer of the world; and in

4 Ibid., 8–9.

5 Ibid., xx.

6. See Guarino, "Analogy and Vatican II," 44–58.

the Holy Scriptures as the divinely inspired, written Word of God. These are only a few of the most significant areas of common faith.

A second important advance at the council had to do with divine revelation. The first schema on revelation presented at Vatican II, entitled *De fontibus revelationis*, had little interest in ecumenism. And for this reason (among others), it came under heavy attack by the conciliar bishops. For example, on November 19, 1962, Bishop Emile De Smedt of Bruges, Belgium said that the schema—lacking an ecumenical character—represents a "step backwards."[7] This schema was ultimately rejected by a large number of bishops, and was remanded to a mixed commission (composed of members of both the Theological Commission and the Secretariat for Christian Unity) for re-drafting.

The re-written schema sought to balance carefully the relationship between Scripture and tradition. As Joseph Ratzinger has stated, the redrafted constitution on Revelation (ultimately entitled *Dei Verbum*), included several formulations which "were the product of the attempt to take into account, to the widest possible extent, the points made by the Reformed Churches and were intended to keep the field open for a Catholic idea of *sola scriptura*...."[8] Ratzinger points out that these attempts were not always successful. Nonetheless, it remains the case that Vatican II left open the possibility of speaking of the material sufficiency of Scripture in matters of salvation—a significant ecumenical step forwards.

In order to assuage those bishops who were concerned that "tradition" was not given its proper due in *Dei Verbum*, Pope Paul VI communicated to the Theological Commission a few improvements that would be "opportune" to make prior to the final conciliar vote on the document. The pope offered several suggestions and, as Ratzinger notes, the Commission decided to accept the third of the formulations offered by Paul. It reads: *quo fit ut Ecclesia certitudinem suam de omnibus revelatis non per solam Sacram Scripturam hauriat*. ("It is not from Sacred Scripture alone that the Church draws her *certitude* regarding all that has been revealed." *Dei Verbum*, no. 9, emphasis added).

Ratzinger affirms "from the ecumenical point of view there can be no objections to it [this sentence]." He cites in support of this claim the Swiss theologian, Heinrich Ott who stated that Protestant Christians who are attentive to the Reformation recognize that *certainty* about God's revelation

---

7 See *Acta synodalia* 1/3:184–87, esp. 186.
8 Ratzinger, "The Transmission of Divine Revelation," 192.

comes not just from Scripture, but also through preaching and from the inner testimony of the Holy Spirit.[9]

Why did Paul VI insist on this change to *Dei Verbum*? The pope clearly feared (and was attentive to others who feared) an individualist reading of Scripture, apart from the community and the Church. Paul was also preoccupied with the unity of the council and with ensuring that a significant minority did not reject any conciliar document. So while Vatican II intended to accent the material sufficiency of the Bible for the truths of salvation, this sufficiency could not be affirmed apart from the role of the church, its tradition, and its continuing life.

It is with regard to just this point—the relationship between Scripture and tradition—that I would like to mention the work of Dr. George, who has frequently insisted at ECT meetings that the *sola Scriptura* of the Reformation cannot be taken as equivalent to *nuda Scriptura*. The Reformation maxim should be understood, rather, in the sense of *prima Scriptura* or *suprema Scriptura*.[10] Scripture cannot be understood entirely apart from tradition and the community, even if the Word of the Lord must ultimately judge both the tradition and the community.[11]

A third important ecumenical advance by Vatican II, found in its ground-breaking Decree on Ecumenism (*Unitatis redintegratio*), was its affirmation that in Catholic teaching there exists a "hierarchy of truths." To quote the passage in its entirety:

When comparing doctrines, [theologians] should remember that in Catholic teaching there exists an order or 'hierarchy' of truths, since they vary in relationship to the foundation of the Christian faith (*UR*, no. 11). Important theologians, Oscar Cullmann among them, saw this as one of the most significant passages of Vatican II.[12] The concept of "hierarchy

---

9. Ibid., 194–95. It is worth noting that, as a much older man, Joseph Ratzinger (at this point Benedict XVI and just two weeks away from his retirement from the papal office) recalled these days of the council and how Paul VI, with the "delicacy of a father," made this decisive intervention in *Dei Verbum*. See Benedict's speech, "Meeting with the Clergy of Rome."

10. See George and Guarino, eds., *Evangelicals and Catholics at Twenty*, 38–52, esp. 48–49.

11. Ibid., xxiii–xxvi.

12 Cullmann remarks, "But I should like . . . to stress a point which has not as yet been adequately emphasized, and which seems the most important in the whole Schema [Decree on Ecumenism] for the future of our dialogue: it is para. 11, which recommends Catholic theologians to 'remember that there is *an order or hierarchy of truths* in Catholic doctrine, by reason of their differing relationship to the bases of the Christian faith.' I consider this passage the most revolutionary to be found, not only in the Schema *de oecumenismo* but in any of the schemas of the present Council." See "Comments," 94.

of truths" allowed for a distinction between a doctrine's content (or *centrality*) and the *certainty* with which a particular teaching is proposed. So, for example, the Catholic dogma of the bodily Assumption of Mary, the Mother of God, is certain (according to Catholic teaching), but it is clearly not as *central* as the Incarnation. This distinction led Cullmann to say that the "hierarchy of truths" makes it. . .possible to place dogmas concerning the primacy of Peter or the ascension of Mary (without denying them, of course) on a different plane from dogmas concerning Christ and the Trinity. To me this seems to be a first step, foreshadowing a third Vatican Council, and as such it may from now on become a point of departure for ecumenical developments which justify every hope.[13] I think Professor Cullmann was correct in seeing "hierarchy of truths" as a point of departure for future ecumenical developments, even if this "strategy" has not yet been fully exploited. Recently, Pope Francis echoed Cullmann when he stated that

All revealed truths derive from the same divine source and are to be believed with the same faith, yet some of them are more important for giving direct expression to the heart of the Gospel. In this basic core, what shines forth is the beauty of the saving love of God made manifest in Jesus Christ who died and rose from the dead. In this sense the Second Vatican Council explained, "in Catholic doctrine there exists an order or a 'hierarchy' of truths, since they vary in their relation to the foundation of the Christian faith." This holds true as much for the dogmas of faith as for the whole corpus of the Church's teaching, including her moral teaching.[14] And then Francis offered a practical application for this "hierarchy":

Missionaries on [various] continents often mention the criticisms, complaints and ridicule to which the scandal of divided Christians gives rise. If we concentrate on the convictions we share, and *if we keep in mind the principle of the hierarchy of truths*, we will be able to progress decidedly towards common expressions of proclamation, service and witness. The immense numbers of people who have not received the Gospel of Jesus Christ cannot leave us indifferent. Consequently, commitment to a unity, which helps them to accept Jesus Christ, can no longer be a matter of mere diplomacy or forced compliance, but rather an indispensable path to evangelization.[15]

---

13. Ibid., 94–95.
14 Pope Francis, *Evangelii gaudium*, no. 36.
15 *Evangelii gaudium*, no. 246; emphasis added.

Although many have argued that this phrase remains replete with unfulfilled potential, it has already borne good fruit for the ecumenical movement.[16]

The Decree on Ecumenism was pivotal for Catholicism in entering the ecumenical movement, and in treating Protestant Christians as true brothers in Christ. But we should also acknowledge that serious ecumenism is never carried out without difficulty, precisely because it entails wrestling with important theological differences. Dr. George has always engaged in these careful discussions with abundant good will, even while eschewing the doctrinal indifference and "false irenicism" that the Decree on Ecumenism itself condemns.

In just this regard, it is worth examining certain last-minute changes made to *Unitatis redintegratio* in November 1964. These changes were mandated by Pope Paul VI and caused pain to the Protestant observers and to many of the Catholic participants at the council. In retrospect, I believe it can be said that the alterations ordered by the pope had little long-lasting effect on Catholic theology. But we can see in these changes—in both those making them and those reacting to them—the kind of courage it takes to engage in serious ecumenical dialogue.

Let us proceed to examine one specific alteration mandated by Paul VI, a change that is now largely forgotten, but which, at the time of the council, caused much consternation among both Catholic and Protestant theologians.

LATE CHANGES TO THE DECREE ON ECUMENISM

Journalists covering Vatican II dubbed the third week of November, 1964, as "*la settimana nera*" or "the black week" of the council. Why this doleful designation? Because of three actions of Pope Paul VI which, in the eyes of some, were injurious to the council's freedom and fundamental intentions. First, the pope sustained the decision of the council presidents to postpone the voting on the declaration on religious liberty, *de libertate religiosa* (ultimately, *Dignitatis humanae*) until the final conciliar session in the fall of 1965. This postponement was required, so argued the conciliar presidents, because the text had been substantially rewritten. According to Vatican II's rules, the bishops needed time to study and debate a significantly re-drafted text before any voting could take place.[17] In retrospect, this was a reasonable

---

16 For a recent article on the "hierarchy of truths," reviewing much of the literature, see Echeverria, "Hierarchy of Truths," 11–35.

17 See *Il Concilio Vaticano II*, 4:476–78.

decision since the text had been deeply altered and the declaration clearly moved Catholic teaching in a new direction, affirming the objective right of men and women to follow their conscience in worshipping God other than in Jesus Christ. But the postponement was considered a disaster, particularly in the eyes of the American bishops who ardently desired to depart the council in 1964 with a strong endorsement of religious freedom.[18]

A second reason for the designation of the "black week" of the council was that Paul VI asked that a "Note" be written explaining episcopal collegiality in more juridical terms. This request resulted in the well-known *Nota praevia explicativa* that appears at the end of the Dogmatic Constitution *Lumen gentium*. The point of this Note was to allay the fears of some (including Paul himself) that since "episcopal collegiality" was a *novum* in the recent history of the Church, it needed to be expressed with juridical, as well as theological, clarity. At stake here was the relationship between the authority residing in the college of bishops as compared with the authority resting in the Petrine office—a debate that had roots going back centuries. Was supreme authority in the Catholic Church now divided between two "parties"? How was this authority to be properly exercised? To clarify these matters, the pope insisted on an explanatory note. But this papal intervention was deeply regretted by many who saw it as an unnecessary juridical imposition on *Lumen gentium*.[19]

A third reason for the "black week" designation—and most importantly for our purposes—was that Paul VI made several last-minute changes to the Decree on Ecumenism even though the document was ready for a final vote. What motivated these alterations?

Paul himself was a strong proponent of ecumenism, as may be seen from his speech opening the second session of the council on September 29, 1963.[20] John XXIII had died in June, just a few months earlier. Paul VI's speech was carefully monitored for clues to determine the direction in which he would take Vatican II. Would the new pope "pull back" on the council's ecumenical intentions? In fact, in Paul's addresses and actions, one sees very strong support for ecumenism from the outset of his pontificate.[21]

---

18. See Grootaers, "La crayon rouge," 321–24. Also see O'Malley, *What Happened*, 240–42.

19. On the other hand, Douglas Horton, one of the Protestant observers at the council, stated that the Note reminded him of those committee face-saving devices that, in fact, "change nothing." See his *Vatican Diary*, 163. Cited in O'Malley, *What Happened*, 367n140. Similarly, Yves Congar said of the *Nota Praevia*, "as far as I can see, it changes nothing." See *My Journal*, 682.

20. See Thurian, "Paul VI," 253.

21 See Duprey, "Paul VI et le Decret," 230–32.

Although a vigorous supporter of ecumenism, Paul also recognized that this constituted a new direction for Catholicism. As we have seen, the encyclical *Mortalium animos* of 1928 had expressed decided reservations about the ecumenical movement and had banned Catholics from participating in it. The memory of this encyclical was so strong that on the eve of council, Yves Congar, a significant conciliar theologian, wrote in his journal that he had low expectations for ecumenism at Vatican II. The bishops were not prepared for this moment. Indeed, Congar ruminated, the council might be coming 25 years too early as far as Christian unity is concerned.[22] As we know, however, Vatican II made significant progress, committing the Catholic Church to the ecumenical enterprise. The fruit of this progress is to be found, primarily, in the council's Decree on Ecumenism.

But on November 19, 1964, a day before the scheduled final vote on the decree, Paul VI mandated nineteen last-minute changes to the document. Pierre Duprey, who was a staffer at the Secretariat for Christian Unity (SCU), said the pope wanted the changes to be presented to the conciliar bishops in an elegant way, but without naming him directly. The formula chosen was that these changes were "*suggestiones benevolas auctoritative expressas.*"[23] The general secretary announced them to the gathered bishops just one day before the final vote.[24]

Most of the nineteen changes, Duprey relates, were acceptable, not touching the essence of the text.[25] But number eighteen was certainly the most important—and caused an immediate storm of controversy. One clause in the original text of article 21 of the Decree on Ecumenism read: "*Spiritu Sancto movente in ipsis sacris Scripturis Deum inveniunt. . . .*" (By the movement of the Holy Spirit, [the separated brethren] discover God in these very Scriptures. . ..)

The last-minute change mandated by Paul VI: "*Spiritum Sanctum* invocantes *in ipsis Sacris Scripturis Deum* inquirunt. . ..*" (*Invoking* the Holy Spirit, [the separated brethren] *seek* God in these very Scriptures. . .. Emphasis added.)

Duprey notes that the pope, in his own hand, had replaced the Latin word "*inveniunt*" with "*inquirunt.*"[26] This served, of course, to weaken the straightforward affirmation that Protestant Christians, through the movement of the Holy Spirit, *discover* God through their reading of the sacred

---

22. Congar, *My Journal*, 4.
23. Duprey, "Paul VI et le Decret sur L'Oecumenisme," 244.
24 See *Acta synodalia*, 3/8:422–23; Caprile, *Il concilio Vaticano II*, 480n22.
25 See Feiner, "Appendix," 159–60.
26. Duprey, "Paul VI et le Decret sur L'Oecumenisme," 242

Scriptures. And the pope let it be known that this alteration was not a matter for discussion; he was insisting that *"inquirunt"* replace *"inveniunt"* in article 21 of the decree. Johannes Willebrands, the secretary of the SCU, deeply regretted this alteration—not because the word "seek" could not be explained—but because the change from "discover" to "seek" would make "a detestable impression."[27] Why was this change made?

Duprey claims that by this alteration, "[Paul VI] wished to avoid saying that all reading of Scripture is made under the inspiration of the Holy Spirit and that in every case the reader encounters the Word of God." He continues, "It seems that [the pope] has in view here certain Protestant positions which would affirm that the individual reading of Scripture suffices, apart from the community and apart from its tradition."[28] To say *"inveniunt,"* without qualification, would be too absolute and definitive. Perhaps the change can also be explained by the fact, noted earlier, that Paul VI always sought (and succeeded in achieving) virtually unanimous support for the conciliar documents. Accomplishing that goal demanded that he remain sensitive to the concerns of the (traditionalist) minority. A large number of *"non-placet"* votes for *De oecumenismo* would indicate that a significant number of conciliar bishops dissented from this document. Paul no doubt reasoned that a judiciously worded alteration would win the support of many bishops who otherwise had reservations about the Decree and, indeed, about ecumenism in general.

The *theological* issue at stake in the alteration from *"inveniunt"* to *"inquirunt"* was, once again, the role of tradition in the life of the Catholic Church. Could one "find" God by searching the Sacred Scriptures alone? Did this formulation not risk the conciliar endorsement of a *nuda Scriptura*? Did not one need the further complement of the Church's life and tradition to understand the Scriptures fully? As we have seen, an appropriate understanding of tradition was an ongoing issue in the conciliar debates. As one author has stated, "the problem of the relationship between Scripture and Tradition is found, from the very beginnings of Vatican II, to be at the center of ceaseless controversies."[29] It was precisely in order to protect the role of tradition that Paul VI added to *Dei Verbum* the sentence noted above: "It is not from Sacred Scripture alone that the Church draws her certainty about all that has been revealed."

The changes to the Decree on Ecumenism mandated by Paul VI came at a tense time for Vatican II. On the same day (November 19, 1964) that

---

27. Ibid., 243.
28. Ibid., 246–47
29 Grootaers, "La crayon rouge de Paul VI," 328.

the council Fathers received the nineteen *"suggestiones benevolas"* for the Decree on Ecumenism, they were told that the vote on the schema *De libertate religiosa* was being postponed until the following year. As earlier noted, this text had been substantially revised and so would once again be subject to debate. But there was no time for such prolonged discussion during the third session of the council, which was rapidly drawing to a close. Duprey reports that the announcement of the postponement caused a spirited reaction in St. Peter's basilica. Some bishops were indignant at this turn of events while others were simply saddened.[30]

Given this widespread frustration, several council Fathers wondered whether they should still vote in favor of the Decree on Ecumenism, especially given the nineteen changes mandated by the pope absent conciliar debate. But the members of the Secretariat for Christian Unity urged the restive bishops to take the long view of matters. The Decree was the result of unending hours of serious work. Despite the changes introduced by Paul VI, the document's substance remained untouched; it would establish a strong foundation for Catholic ecumenism for decades to come. If the Decree were not promulgated, the Secretariat for Christian Unity would receive a blow from which it would be difficult to recover. The staffers of the Secretariat argued that the Decree remained entirely acceptable; they urged the bishops to vote *placet* without reservation.[31]

On that very same afternoon (November 19th), there was a regularly scheduled meeting with the Protestant observers at the offices of the SCU, the last one scheduled for the third session of the council. The agenda for the meeting was the draft schema on the missionary activity of the Church. At the very outset, however, the distinguished theologian, Oscar Cullmann, asked if he could speak on a theme unrelated to the subject at hand. Cullmann expressed his concern about the change from *"inveniunt"* to *"inquirunt"* in article 21 of the decree, stating that while the new word is not objectionable, it is the change itself that makes a bad impression.[32] Cullmann further stated that he was well aware of the saying of Blaise Pascal: one can only seek what one has already found. And he graciously added that *"inquirere"* is perhaps a more clearly Protestant word than *"invenire."* Nonetheless, he regretted the change, thinking it would be difficult to explain to those who were not present at the council. The other observers applauded Cullmann's remarks (245).[33] Willebrands thanked Cullmann for his sincerity and frankness, say-

---

30. Duprey, "Paul VI et le Decret sur L'Oecumenisme," 244.
31. Ibid.
32. Ibid., 245.
33. See Cullmann, "Comments," 94.

ing that he, too, regretted the alterations mandated by the pope, particularly the change to no. 21.[34] He asked the observers for their prayers.

The vote on the Decree on Ecumenism took place on Friday, November 20, 1964. Duprey says that waiting for the result caused tension. But the vote was overwhelmingly in favor of the Decree: 2054 *placet*; 64 *non placet* (246). Given this extraordinary majority, it was clear that Paul VI would certainly promulgate *De oecumenismo*.[35]

Yves Congar wrote in his journal that it was "for a mystical reason" that he went to St. Peter's on the morning of November 21, 1964, when Paul VI formally promulgated both *Lumen gentium* and *Unitatis redintegratio*. Unlike at Vatican I, there was no dogma to be defined that morning. Nonetheless, there were "two great acts of proclamation of the *De ecclesia* [*Lumen gentium*] and the *De oecumenismo* [*Unitatis redintegratio*]." As he had participated in the sweat and tears of composing the documents, Congar wanted to participate in the joy of their proclamation as well.[36]

Despite this sense of gratitude, Congar thought that the last few days of the third session of the council had been unfortunate from an ecumenical point of view. Paul VI had mandated important alterations to the Decree on Ecumenism, absent conciliar debate. Further, on the very day of the promulgation of *Lumen gentium* and *Unitatis redintegratio*, the pope announced a new title for the Blessed Virgin Mary, *Mater ecclesiae* [Mother of the Church]. In Congar's mind, these gestures showed little "of a true ecumenical sensibility" on the pope's part. Indeed, he thought that these high-handed papal actions could cause the Protestant observers to lose trust in the Catholic Church.[37]

While acknowledging Congar's reservations, I think one can say, in retrospect, that Duprey, Willebrands, and the other members of the SCU saw clearly that, despite some late turmoil, the Decree on Ecumenism was built on a solid foundation and would have lasting importance for the ecumenical movement. The members of the Secretariat agreed that Paul VI's last-minute alterations, particularly the change from "find" to "seek," were unfortunate and unnecessary. But they recognized that the essence of the decree had been untouched, and would contribute to the success of the ecumenical movement far into the future.

Unitatis redintegratio remains a sterling affirmation of the Catholic Church's commitment to ecumenism. With the change from "*inveniunt*" to

34. See Congar, *My Journal*, 690.
35. See *Acta synodalia*, 3/8:636–37, 781–83.
36. Congar, *My Journal*, 695.
37. Ibid., 696–97.

"*inquirunt*" Paul VI unnecessarily weakened the text. But one can understand his desire that the Decree receive the support of the entire council. A sizeable minority of bishops remained concerned that the interpretative light offered by the Church's tradition had not been affirmed in the document with sufficient clarity; the pope altered this sentence to make that point more lucidly. Paul VI no doubt thought he was responsible for unifying the entire Church behind what was surely a new direction for Catholicism and, indeed, what was, at least in some sense, a reversal of earlier magisterial teaching.[38]

The difficult decisions made by Paul VI indicate that serious ecumenism is never painless. True ecumenism requires fortitude and courage. It demands a commitment to one's own position even while listening sympathetically to the commitments of one's interlocutor, trying to understand, and enter into, his theological reasoning. I can attest from two decades of participation in Evangelicals and Catholics Together that Dean Timothy George is a model of that method and ecumenical posture. While fully committed to his Baptist heritage and to biblical truth, Dr. George has always been an ecumenist of the first rank: listening, seeking to understand, learning and, when necessary, disagreeing and offering alternatives. ECT has been blessed by both his theological learning and by his *humanitas*.

CONCLUSION

Vatican II decidedly changed the optic through which other Christian churches were theologically evaluated by Catholicism. The council approached the issue of the "separated brethren" not by concentrating on differences, but by examining the analogical similarity between Catholicism and Protestantism. The separated brothers were clearly committed to faith in the Holy Trinity, to Christ Jesus as the Eternal Son of God sent for our redemption and salvation, and to the written Word of God as normative for Christian belief and action. For the council, then, other churches participate in the means of sanctification and truth which characterize the Church of Christ. Neither Evangelicals nor Catholics were particularly enthusiastic about ecumenism when it burst upon the scene with the International Missionary Conference convened in Edinburgh in 1910. Catholics were fearful that the ecumenical movement would lead to a weak-wristed, lowest-common-denominator form of Christianity. Evangelicals thought ecumenism might unacceptably trim a full-throated commitment to biblical truth. Yet

---

38 I have explained how this reversal may be understood in "Evangelicals and Catholics Together: On the Twentieth Anniversary of an Ecumenical Initiative," 238–51n13.

both Catholics and Evangelicals have entered into the ecumenical movement and, together, have achieved a great deal in terms of Christian witness both within the Church and in society at large. I can attest that much of that progress is directly attributable to the incisive foresight, theological learning, and Christian discipleship of Dean Timothy George. *Ad multos gloriosque annos.*

BIBLIOGRAPHY

Acta synodalia sacrosancti concilii oecumenici Vaticani II. Vatican City: Typis Polyglottis Vaticanis, 1971.

Caprile, Giovanni. *Il Concilio Vaticano II.* Vol. 4, *Terzo periodo, 1964–1965.* Rome: La Civiltà Cattolica, 1966.

Congar, Yves. *My Journal of the Council.* Translated by Mary John Ronayne and Mary Cecily Boulding. Collegeville, MN: Liturgical, 2012.

Cullmann, Oscar. "Comments on the Decree on Ecumenism." *Ecumenical Review* 17 (1965) 93–95.

Duprey, Pierre. "Paul VI et le Decret sur L'Oecumenisme." In *Paolo VI e I Problemi Ecclesiologici al Concilio*, 225–48. Brescia: Edizioni Studium, 1989.

Echeverria, E. J. "Hierarchy of Truths Revisited." *Acta Theologica* 35 (2015) 142–53 and 157–64.

Feiner, Johannes. "Appendix." In *Commentary on the Documents of Vatican II*, edited by Herbert Vorgrimler, various translators, 2:159–64. New York: Herder and Herder, 1968.

Francis, Pope. *Evangelii gaudium.* Apostolic Exhortation. Vatican City, November, 2013 no. 36.

George, Timothy, and Thomas G. Guarino, eds. *Evangelicals and Catholics Together at Twenty: Vital Statements on Contested Topics.* Grand Rapids: Brazos, 2015.

Grootaers, Jan. "La crayon rouge de Paul VI." In *Les commissions conciliaires à Vatican II*, edited by M. Lamberigts, Cl. Soetens and J. Grootaers, 317–35. Leuven: Bibliotheek van de Faculteit Godgeleerdheid, 1996.

Guarino, Thomas G. "Analogy and Vatican II: An Overlooked Dimension of the Council?" *Josephinum Journal of Theology* 22 (2015) 44–58.

———. "Evangelicals and Catholics Together: On the Twentieth Anniversary of an Ecumenical Initiative." *Josephinum Journal of Theology* 23 (2014) 238–51.

Horton, Douglas. *Vatican Diary 1964.* Philadelphia: United Church Press, 1965.

O'Malley, John, W. *What Happened at Vatican II.* Cambridge, MA: Belknap, 2008.

Packer, J. I. "Preface." In *Evangelicals and Catholics Together at Twenty*: *Vital Statements on Contested Topics*, edited by Timothy George and Thomas G. Guarino, vii–xii. Grand Rapids: Brazos, 2015.

Ratzinger, Joseph. "The Transmission of Divine Revelation." In *Commentary on the Documents of Vatican II*, edited by Herbert Vorgrimler, 3:181–98. New York: Herder and Herder, 1969.

———. (Benedict XVI). "Meeting with the Clergy of Rome." *Acta apostolicae sedis* 105 (2013) 283–94.

Thurian, Max. "Paul VI et les Observateurs au Concile Vatican II." In *Paolo VI e I Problemi Ecclesiologici al Concilio*, 249–58. Brescia: Studium, 1989.

Vanhoozer, Kevin, J. "Scripture and Tradition." In *The Cambridge Companion to Postmodern Theology*, edited by Kevin J. Vanhoozer, 149–69. New York: Cambridge University Press, 2003.

Timothy George and Evangelicals and Catholics Together

An Evangelical Perspective

JOHN D. WOODBRIDGE

EVANGELICAL PROTESTANTS AND ROMAN Catholics constitute two of the largest religious communities in the United States. For this reason alone, taking stock of the twenty-year old history of a dialogue between Evangelicals and Roman Catholics is a worthwhile enterprise. In some regards, it is surprising that Roman Catholics and Evangelicals have engaged in a meaningful ecumenical dialogue, given their former wariness if not overt hostility towards each other.

Timothy George and Thomas G. Guarino list statements by ECT [Evangelicals and Catholics Together] drawn up during a two-decade period of dialogue. The volume includes informative prefaces by J. I. Packer, a distinguished ECT Anglican participant, and Timothy Cardinal Dolan, a distinguished Roman Catholic supporter of ECT.[1]

In a Foreword, George Weigel, an influential Roman Catholic political commentator, provides a first-hand account of the creation of ECT in 1994—a dialogue initiated by the late Father Richard John Neuhaus (1936–2009) and the late Mr. Chuck Colson (1931–2012). Stimulated by a conversation with Herbert Schlossberg, Weigel arranged for Father Neuhaus and Mr. Colson to meet each other and to discuss the various ways Evangelicals and Roman Catholics might commence beneficial conversations. Weigel proposes that Pope John Paul II's commitment to a "New Evangelization" (1990) set the stage for such conversations. Weigel believes the heuristic value of ECT has been stunning: "But I don't think I risk a charge of untoward

---

1. George and Guarino, eds., *Evangelicals and Catholics Together at Twenty*.

boasting when I suggest that there has been nothing quite like Evangelicals and Catholics Together for seriousness, for depth of theological encounter and for genuine results."[2]

Timothy George and Thomas Guarino offer a robust theological introduction to the volume in which they unpack the theological parameters, the goals, and import of ECT. Owing to their intimate knowledge of ECT, George and Guarino are choice commentators to reflect upon this religious dialogue: "The ecumenical initiative known as Evangelicals and Catholics Together (ECT) began more than two decades ago with a stroke of insight by Chuck Colson and Richard John Neuhaus. Their bold intention was to advance unity and fellowship among Christians by establishing a serious theological dialogue between Evangelicals and Catholics, the two largest Christian groups in North America. Both men were concerned that religion in general and Christianity in particular were being increasingly relegated to the margins of public life in the United States. Religious faith, the most comprehensive and foundational of all realities, was being consigned to the provincial areas of private devotion and sectarian belief. Colson and Neuhaus argued, however, that the Christian faith is indispensable to understanding and addressing the great issues of the day. Evangelicals and Catholics needed to be fully engaged in the complex social, cultural, and political questions that the nation faced—illuminating them with the truth of the gospel." George and Guarino propose that a "fraternal union in Christ was the cornerstone on which ECT was founded."[3]

The purpose of the present essay is to proffer personal reflections upon the influential role Timothy George has played in ECT over the last two decades. George, a brilliant essayist, church historian, and theologian, has been one of the principal Evangelical participants in ECT. It is quite difficult to imagine the existence of the ECT enterprise without his significant irenic involvement.

A SURPRISING PHONE CALL FROM THE U.S.

It was a beautiful Spring day in Paris. The year was 1996. The phone suddenly jangled in the apartment where I was residing. I picked up the receiver and then heard a stentorian voice ask, "May I please speak with John Woodbridge?" I responded, "This is he." The speaker then identified himself as Father Richard John Neuhaus, the editor of the magazine *First Things*. He

---

2. George Weigel, "Foreword," xvi.

3. George and Guarino, "A Theological Introduction," in George and Guarino, eds., *Evangelicals and Catholics Together at Twenty*, xvii.

was calling from New York City in the United States. He indicated that Mr. Chuck Colson, the founder of Prison Fellowship, had suggested to him that I should be invited to join the roster of "Evangelicals and Catholics Together (ECT)." At the time, I really did not know much about ECT, except that controversy hovered over the publication of the first ECT joint statement, "Evangelicals and Catholics Together: The Christian Mission in the Third Millennium" (1994). I also understood that Mr. Chuck Colson and Mr. Bill Bright both of whom I greatly admired were the subjects of serious criticism for having signed the document. I enquired from Father Neuhaus what my engagement in "Evangelicals and Catholics Together" might represent. I then asked Father Neuhaus if I might have a few days to think over my decision. He replied, "Certainly."

At the time my hesitancy was not due to a total unfamiliarity with Roman Catholicism. In the Spring of 1996, I was teaching in the Roman Catholic division of Hautes Etudes, the Sorbonne [The University of Paris]. I had pursued doctoral studies in history in France at the University of Toulouse and post-doctoral studies at the Sorbonne. I had co-edited a book with a distinguished French Roman Catholic scholar, Professor Jacques LeBrun. Some of my closest academic acquaintances in France were Roman Catholics. They were generally of quite a "liberal" theological stripe. I had regularly attended retreats in which they with a few Protestant scholars presented academic papers on the history of religion in France.

Despite a certain familiarity with Roman Catholicism, I was a convinced evangelical Protestant Christian who was teaching at Trinity Evangelical Divinity School. I believed with Luther that the church stands or falls with its commitment to the doctrine of justification by faith alone and viewed Holy Scripture as the inerrant written Word of God. I believe in Scripture norms and tradition (including Roman Catholic church tradition), creeds, and all academic disciplines.

Owing to the small amount of information I had regarding ECT except for the troubling controversy regarding its first publication (one I could not have signed), I felt no overbearing pressure to accept Father Neuhaus' kind invitation. I decided the best thing to do would be to call Dr. Kenneth Kantzer, a trusted mentor and close friend and to seek his counsel. With many others, I viewed Dr. Kantzer as a model of what an evangelically faithful Christian scholar might be.

I dialed the home of Dr. Kantzer in the United States. He graciously entertained my call. He proposed that he did not think it was a judicious decision for me to become a member of ECT. And he proffered persuasive reasons to back up his perspective. I thanked him sincerely for his wise advice. After hanging up the phone, however, I felt quite conflicted regarding what to do. A few days later and after considerable soul-searching, I called Father Neuhaus in New York City and accepted his invitation. As much as I appreciated Dr. Kantzer's sage counsel, I could not shake a growing sentiment. Perhaps given my study of the history and theology of Roman Catholicism, I might serve even if in a very minor way as a resource person for Dr. Bright and Mr. Colson in their exchanges with seasoned Roman Catholic interlocutors. I deeply appreciated Campus Crusade for Christ [now Cru] and Prison Fellowship. It pained me that both organizations were presently suffering financial losses. The ostensible reason for these losses: the involvement of Dr. Bright and Mr. Colson in ECT.

A TENSE ECT EXCHANGE (FALL 1996 MEETING)

The first meeting I attended of ECT took place in the Fall of 1996 at the famous Union Club in New York City. Representing the Evangelical side were Chuck Colson, J. I. Packer, Tom Oden, Timothy George, and others. Representing the Roman Catholic side were Father Richard John Neuhaus, Father Avery Dulles, soon to be Cardinal Avery Dulles, Father Francis Martin, George Weigel, and others. I had never met Father Neuhaus, the leader of the Roman Catholic contingent. He immediately impressed me as a powerful personality—remarkably charming and gregarious and a marvelous wordsmith. As the saying goes, he could take over a room. Father Neuhaus had formerly been a Missouri Synod Lutheran pastor. In time, Father Neuhaus and I were to become friends.

After Mr. Colson and Father Neuhaus had introduced the new participants at the ECT meeting, the atmospherics of the session suddenly turned tense. Father Neuhaus launched blistering salvos directly at the Evangelicals present. Father Neuhaus proposed that, while Roman Catholics enjoyed unanimity in their doctrinal beliefs, Evangelicals were a doctrinally divided and disparate group of people. Moreover, their origins were very recent. They allegedly emerged from nineteenth century American revivalism. What is more, they upheld the doctrine of justification by faith alone, which Father Neuhaus characterized as a Calvinist doctrinal aberration.

This first verbal volley aimed squarely at the Evangelicals stunned me. The spell of ecumenical cordiality dissipated rapidly in the meeting room. I replied to Father Neuhaus that his claim Roman Catholic doctrinal unity throughout the world was an illusion. I had just returned from teaching in the Roman Catholic division of Hautes Etudes, the University of Paris, and my colleagues there were "Liberal Catholics." They did not share the more theologically conservative beliefs of the Roman Catholic participants in ECT. What's more, I turned to the various Evangelicals seated in the room and asked if their respective churches upheld the doctrine of justification by faith alone. One after the other, the Evangelicals whether Methodist or Anglican, Southern Baptist or Presbyterian volunteered that their denominations affirmed the doctrine of justification by faith alone. Father Neuhaus's assertion that the doctrine of justification by faith alone constituted a uniquely "Calvinist" doctrinal aberration was simply not the case.

Father Neuhaus immediately and graciously reversed course. In fact, he agreed there were Roman Catholic "liberals" scattered throughout Roman Catholic universities worldwide. He bemoaned their power and extensive influence in Roman Catholic academia. He alluded to an initiative of the Papacy to regain a greater conservative Roman Catholic presence in Roman Catholic schools. Nor did he attempt to argue again that the doctrine of justification by faith alone was a "Calvinist" doctrinal innovation. A sense of cordiality once again began to permeate conversations.

MEETING WITH TIMOTHY GEORGE AND CHUCK COLSON

At various coffee breaks I had the opportunity to chat with Dr. Timothy George, the Dean of Beeson Divinity School. I had never met Dr. George before. Dr. Kantzer had described him to me as an outstanding evangelical church historian who specialized in the Protestant Reformation. And indeed Dr. George is that. Dr. George had not signed the first ECT document.

Little did we realize in our first meeting, we would both become engaged with ECT for the next twenty years plus. In the year 2016 we were the only remaining Evangelical ECT veterans of the Fall 1996 meeting at the Union Club. We became friends and worked on multiple projects together. We shared a determined commitment to uphold and promote the Evangelical faith in ECT discussions.

During the 1996 meetings, Chuck Colson invited the two of us out for a breakfast chat in a local. bustling New York City restaurant where servers rushed about. Both Timothy and I thought the world of Chuck. We greatly admired his big-hearted concern for down and outers and up and outers ("the least, the last and the lost"), his defense of religious liberties for people of all faiths, his espousal of social justice and advocacy of the sanctity of life (for the elderly, the infirm and the unborn child). Chuck's love for Christ, the Gospel and Scripture, the written Word of God, was infectious and exemplary. Here was a Christian who without fear would witness for Christ equally in the front seat of a taxicab ride to New York's La Guardia

Airport or on an ABC Television set in the Big Apple. Having spent time in prison for a Watergate associated offence, Chuck was especially moved by Jesus' words, "I was in prison and you visited me." Chuck embraced a special evangelistic mission to preach the Gospel to prisoners so they might be "born again," just as he had been. They needed to accept Jesus Christ as their Lord and Savior. Chuck indicated that when he visited prisons, he could not help but tear up a little while listening to prisoners sing their "National Anthem"—the song "Amazing Grace." He also wanted to care for the families of prisoners—especially their children. Despite his remarkable accomplishments including service as President Richard Nixon's Special Counsel and as founder of Prison Fellowship, a worldwide ministry, Chuck was a humble man. In many regards, Chuck was a modern day social reformer like William Wilberforce, a man whom he greatly esteemed.

Seated across the table from us at the restaurant, Chuck reflected upon the ins and outs of the ECT meeting in which we were presently engaged. And then he said: "I need your help. I would like to invite you two to become my theological advisors in ECT." Quite surprised by this generous offer, both Timothy and I nonetheless replied almost in unison: "Chuck, you can do better than us in finding some people who would be more accommodating in ecumenical discussions. We are convinced Evangelical Christians who will not compromise or accommodate our evangelical convictions." Chuck replied, "No, No, you are just the persons I need because you will not do this."

Sensing the deep earnestness of Chuck's request, neither Timothy nor I could refuse his offer. We both agreed to become his advisors. Little did we realize at the time what awaited us including some very good moments and some very difficult moments. Nor did we fully understand Chuck's firm conviction that any statement issuing from ECT would gain greater credibility if its signees were known as staunch defenders of their respective theological traditions. Chuck did not want "lowest common denominator statements" in which co-signers had sacrificed their theological beliefs to gain an ecumenical accord. The first ECT statement re-enforces this point: "We reject any appearance of harmony that is purchased at the expense of truth." We were to learn soon enough, however, that some evangelical critics of ECT, a number of whom were our good friends, sincerely doubted we were in fact faithful in upholding evangelical beliefs. Their criticisms were quite sincere and pointed.

There were Important take away's from the first 1996 session of ECT: 1. The Roman Catholics made it clear that Holy Scripture should serve as an important warrant for any ECT document. 2. The Roman Catholics were worried about evangelical Pentecostal advances in Latin America and in

North American inner cities like New York and Chicago. The Pope had recently warned about the presence of "wolves" in the sheepfold of Latin America. In a private meeting with Timothy and Chuck, we reckoned that the Pope was referencing as "wolves" our evangelical brethren, the Pentecostals of Latin America. It also dawned on us that we were perceived in some regards as "wolves." The Roman Catholics were worried about Evangelicals "evangelizing" or "proselytizing" Roman Catholics. 4. Father Neuhaus emphasized the point that members of ECT spoke as individuals *from and to, but not for* their respective communities. Nonetheless, Father Neuhaus let it be known that the Papacy in Rome was closely following our ECT discussions. 5. Our Roman Catholic participants were generous in spirit and quite cordial in personal relations. Moreover, Father Neuhaus often stepped in to honor our evangelical convictions during the drafting process of certain ECT Statements—especially "The Gift of Salvation". 6. The amicable resolution of the initial dust-up between the Roman Catholics and Evangelicals signaled that both parties could articulate their positions with frankness and not risk thereby scuttling the ECT enterprise. ECT participants dined together in a convivial spirit after each working day's session. Father Neuhaus and Chuck Colson induced light-hearted bantering and encouraged marvelous story-telling. On occasion, Father Neuhaus invited us to his apartment to chat in an even more relaxed environment.

After this first session of ECT, I was not certain what helpful role, if any, I could play. I now realized that my own knowledge of Roman Catholicism [especially American Catholicism] was less substantial than I had supposed. For example, as one ECT Roman Catholic friend later privately informed me, the way we Evangelicals do theology and the way Roman Catholics do theology are quite different.

Timothy's role as a trusted advisor for Chuck expanded rapidly and dramatically. Timothy joined the Board of Prison Fellowship and served as a theological advisor. He provided Prison Fellow Board members with thoughtful discussions of evangelical doctrines. Timothy became the principal Evangelical writer on various sub-committees, which drew up first drafts for ECT statements. Timothy also served Chuck as a masterful theological guide and astute resource person in ECT discussions. The evening before ECT meetings, Chuck, Timothy, and I sometimes met for dinner to catch up on life and to discuss the present ECT topic. Sometimes the three of us had breakfast with Tom Oden and J. I. Packer as well. On very rare occasions such as at Amsterdam 2000 after Timothy and I had rendered opposing verdicts on the theological value of a potential ECT Statement, Chuck called us to his hotel quarters to talk things out. He listened carefully to both of our perspectives, made a decision about what to do, and then told us to have coffee together and work out our differences. In the ground floor restaurant of Chuck's Amsterdam hotel, we happily did so.

TIMOTHY GEORGE: A CONVINCED SOUTHERN BAPTIST ENGAGED IN ECT

Early on, Timothy and I were seated in the specious living room of Prison Fellowship in Reston, Virginia. At the time, I did not know Timothy well. Chuck had called us to Washington D.C. for an important meeting to address pointed concerns of a few of ECT's strongest Protestant critics. We had some time on our hands before meeting with Chuck. I asked Timothy why he became involved in ECT. For starters, Timothy made it very clear he engaged in ECT as a convinced and faithful Southern Baptist. He was committed to Gospel preaching and to the promotion of first-class Christian theological education especially for pastors. He was committed to seeking the unity of the church in obedience to Jesus' prayer in John 17:21–"that they may all be one; even as thou, Father, art in me, and I in thee, that they also may be in us, so that the world may believe that thou hast sent me." What Timothy said to me privately on this occasion, he consistently reiterated in ECT meetings and in other public venues.

Like Chuck Colson and Father Neuhaus, Timothy recognized the need for a strong Christian public witness in an increasingly secular American society. In this regard, Timothy wrote: "Here is an ecumenism of the trenches born out of a common struggle to proclaim and embody the Gospel of Jesus Christ in a culture of disarray."[4] For example, Evangelicals should continue to work together with Roman Catholics in the Pro-life movement defending the lives of unborn children. Timothy urged Evangelicals and Roman Catholics to stand together regarding the defense of religious freedom, the defense of Christian marriage (defined as a marriage between one man and one woman). In time ECT statements appeared that did address these specific issues and others: "That They May Have Life,"[5] "In Defense of Religious Freedom,"[6] "The Two Shall Become One Flesh: Reclaiming Marriage."[7]

---

4. George, Introduction to "Unity," in George and Guarino, eds., *Evangelicals and Catholics Together at Twenty*, 2.

5. "That They May Have Life," in George and Guarino, eds., *Evangelicals and Catholics Together at Twenty*, 89–103.

6. "In Defense of Religious Freedom," in George and Guarino, eds., *Evangelicals and Catholics Together at Twenty*, 136–150.

7. "The Two Shall Become One Flesh: Reclaiming Marriage," in George and Guarino, eds., *Evangelicals and Catholics Together at Twenty*, 151–164.

Timothy was also worried about religious antagonisms between Protestants and Roman Catholics in Latin America. Neuhaus and Colson had expressed their joint concern that "animosities between Evangelicals and Catholics threatened to mar the image of Christ by turning Latin America into a Belfast of religious warfare."[8] Was it possible that the modeling of Evangelicals and Roman Catholics getting along together in North America might encourage Latin American Pentecostals and Roman Catholics to emulate this example and eschew the dangerous path of tragic religious warfare?

It is one thing to sense the need for Evangelicals and Roman Catholics to engage in meaningful ecumenical conversations, it is quite another to entertain any realistic hope that such conversations would be worthwhile. Had not the Roman Catholic Church fulminated harsh anathemas against Protestants at the Council of Trent (1545–1563)? Had not Protestants returned the favor and on occasion castigated the Pope as the anti-Christ? As a leading expert on the Protestant Reformation, Timothy George was well versed on touchstone doctrinal beliefs like *Sola Scriptura* and *Sola fide* that separated Protestants from Roman Catholics. Timothy was also well apprised of the socio-political/ religious wars, which had stoked hatred between Protestants and Roman Catholics during the sixteenth and seventeenth centuries and beyond. But he also rejoiced that fresh theological winds had been especially blowing since Vatican II (1962–1965). They had greatly influenced the Roman Catholic Church to appreciate more fully the value of ecumenical dialogue. Timothy also recognized that by the 1990s some Evangelicals had become less hostile towards Roman Catholics owing in particular to the influence of Billy Graham and Harold John Ockenga.

In "A Theological Introduction" to the book *Evangelicals and Catholics Together at Twenty*, co-editors George and Guarino describe these developments that rendered ecumenical conversations more promising. They did so under the rubric: "Three Themes at the Heart of Ecumenism and of ECT" 1. The Content of the Christian Faith; 2. Scripture and Tradition; 3. Ecclesia semper reformanda/purificanda.[9]

TIMOTHY GEORGE: AN INDISPENSABLE PARTICIPANT IN ECT

After Father Neuhaus passed away in January 2009, Tom Guarino and Rusty Reno, editor of *First Things*, assumed the Roman Catholic leadership of

---

8. Colson and Neuhaus, eds., *Evangelicals and Catholics Together*, xviii

9. George and Guarino, "A Theological Introduction," in George and Guarino, eds., *Evangelicals and Catholics Together at Twenty*, xvii.

ECT. After the death of Chuck Colson in 2012, Timothy George assumed the leadership of the Evangelical contingent.

For Chuck Colson, the most significant of ECT declarations was clearly "The Gift of Salvation."[10] He viewed its historical importance as nothing less than epochal. Why so? Chuck believed that the doctrine of justification by faith alone resided at the heart of the Gospel. The Protestant Reformers had described the doctrine of justification by faith alone (*sola fide*) as the lynch-pin doctrine upon which the church rises or falls. Chuck thought the statement "The Gift of Salvation" drafted and approved by both Roman Catholics and Evangelicals provided vital evidence that both Evangelicals and Roman Catholics could affirm the doctrine of justification by faith alone. The statement reads: "The New Testament makes it clear that the gift of justification is received through faith. 'By grace you have been saved through faith; and this is not your own doing, it is the gift of God' (Eph 2:8). By faith, which is also the gift of God, we repent of our sins and freely adhere to the gospel, the good news of God's saving work for us in Christ. By our response of faith to Christ, we enter into the blessings promised by the gospel. Faith is not merely intellectual assent but an act of the whole person, involving the mind, the will, and the affections, issuing in a changed life. We understand that what we here affirm is in agreement with what the Reformation traditions have meant by justification by faith alone (*sola fide*) (pp. 34–35)."[11]

Tom Oden, a renowned patristic scholar, presented persuasive documentation that a number of early church fathers espoused the doctrine of justification by faith alone. In his introduction to "The Gift of Salvation" in the George-Guarino volume, Oden writes: "For the Reformers, of course, justification was the benchmark by which they evaluated all Christian teaching. *The Gift of Salvation* gives expression to our agreement that ancient Catholic teaching confirms justification by faith alone (*sola fide*). For evangelicals who might doubt that this is ancient Catholic teaching, we need only quote a few leading voices, Christian teachers who express this conviction from the beginning. Key texts from Clement of Rome, Augustine, and others demonstrate the patristic anticipation of Reformation teaching on justification."[12] A number of Roman Catholics agreed with Evangelical exegetes that Paul taught forensic justification in the book of Romans.

---

10. Colson and Neuhaus, eds., *Evangelicals and Catholics Together*, "The Gift of Salvation."

11. Ibid., 34-35.

12. Thomas C. Oden, Introduction to "Justification," in George and Guarino, eds., *Evangelicals and Catholics Together at Twenty*, 24–27.

As for Father Neuhaus's openness to the doctrine of justification by faith alone, George and Guarino relate the following colorful vignette: "We remember well Richard John Neuhaus leaning back in his chair and lighting a cigarette at the very beginning of our discussion in 1996. He opened the conversation by saying that, as a former Lutheran pastor, he had no problem with justification by faith alone (p. xxx)." Timothy George, Tom Oden, Father Neuhaus and others helpfully crafted the Statement, "The Gift of Salvation."

Edward Iris Cardinal Cassidy, President of the Pontifical Council for Promoting Christian Unity, attended the October 6-7, 1997 meeting at which time ECT members approved the "The Gift of Salvation" Statement. He greatly appreciated the document. Nearly two years later, on September 17, 1999, Cardinal Cassidy delivered an important address entitled, "The Meaning of the Joint Declaration on Justification. " In this discourse, he sought to interpret "The Joint Declaration" approved by some Lutherans and Roman Catholics in February of 1997. Whereas many Lutherans approved "The Joint Declaration," others (particularly German Protestant theologians) criticized it sharply.

A second meeting followed immediately upon the heels of the ECT "Gift of Salvation" gathering in October 1997. And what an amazing meeting it was! Cardinal Cassidy also attended this meeting. Roman Catholic Cardinals and Archbishops from Latin America had flown to New York City to conduct church business and to interact with ECT participants. Some of the Latin American clergy who met with us previously had little contact with any Evangelicals whatsoever. In their own countries relations between Evangelicals and Roman Catholics were quite frayed—sometimes completely fractured.

One of the first topics discussed between the Latin American prelates and North American Evangelicals was this: how did Evangelicals view the Virgin Mary? Timothy George addressed this question in a magnificent manner. He explained to the Latin American clergy that Evangelicals hold Mary in very high esteem. Some Evangelicals do in fact deem her the "Mother of God." At the same time, they affirm that Mary was a sinner in need of a Savior, the Lord Jesus. Timothy's eloquent explanation of Evangelicals' attitudes towards Mary was well received by the Latin American clergy. Timothy would later serve as the principal Evangelical draftsman for the ECT Statement, "Do Whatever He tells you: The Blessed Virgin Mary in the Christian Faith and Life."[13] This document explicates the shared beliefs

---

13. "Do Whatever He Tells you: The Blessed Virgin Mary in Christian Faith and Life," 109–30.

as well as the continuing disagreements Evangelicals and Roman Catholics have regarding the Virgin Mary.

One of the pressing concerns the Latin American clergy articulated in the October 1997 meeting was the continuing advance of secularism, materialism and communism in Latin America. They discussed among themselves various strategies to help halt and reverse these developments. In this context, Father Neuhaus intervened and urged that they should spread the Gospel of Jesus Christ in Latin America as expressed in the ECT Statement, "The Gift of Salvation." Father Neuhaus's admonition was warmly welcomed.

Immediately after the session with the Latin American clergy, I spoke with Chuck Colson. He was more than elated by what he had just witnessed. Had not one of the original motivations for ECT been to encourage Evangelicals and Latin American Roman Catholics to establish and maintain more cordial relations? Perhaps the amical exchanges which had just taken place might contribute to that worthy goal, at least in some measure. Then again, the approval of "The Gift of Salvation" Statement might advance the cause of Evangelicals and Roman Catholics working together in greater harmony and fellowship.

Little did we realize at the time that a number of Evangelical critics would be less than enthusiastic about "The Gift of Salvation" Statement. Some faulted us for not emphasizing the imputation of Christ's righteousness and the forensic nature of justification (we are declared righteous) in the document. We assumed that these teachings had been covered by the notation in the "Gift of Salvation" that the definition of justification by faith alone articulated was in accord with the Reformation traditions of *Sola Fide*. Our critics were thoughtful well-respected Evangelical Christians. Over the next few years we met with them several times behind closed doors. In time, we crafted a document together which made clear our common commitment to the doctrine of justification by faith alone. Timothy George participated in these helpful discussions. Timothy was quite simply an indispensable participant in ECT.

TIMOTHY GEORGE'S INSPIRING HOMILY AT THE MEMORIAL SERVICE FOR CHUCK COLSON

On April 21, 2012, Chuck Colson passed away. The news of Chuck's death was almost too much to believe. After all, Chuck had seemed like such a vital, bigger than life person. Moving tributes began to pour into Chuck's family and Prison Fellowship. Individuals by the thousands expressed their love for Chuck and their gratitude to the Lord for Chuck's life and ministry. Even for those who had never met Chuck personally and perhaps only heard him on the radio program *Breakpoint*, they somehow felt they knew him and they cared very much about him.

On May 16, 2012, a Memorial Service for Chuck Colson was held in the National Cathedral of Washington, D. C. The expansive Washingtonian audience which filled the cathedral for the service attested to the great respect and esteem in which many held Chuck.

As the marvelous service unfolded, a figure dressed in a red and black gown climbed the stairwell up to the ornate pulpit of the National Cathedral, the nation's church. The figure was Timothy George, Chuck Colson's beloved friend and long-time associate. Timothy then proceeded to give one of the most beautiful and Christ centered homilies that some of us in the audience had ever heard. It was entitled, "Be Not Afraid!" Timothy observed: "Charles Wendell Colson was once the youngest captain in the United States Marines and, at his request, he was laid to rest several days ago at Quantico National Cemetery. He loved his country fiercely and served it well. But we are here today, in this the nation's church, to celebrate the life of one who ended his days as a soldier in another army, the *militia Christi*, a battalion without bullets, soldiers of Christ, arrayed in truth, wielding weapons of faith, prayer, and love."

Timothy noted in his homily Chuck's special commitment to and involvement in ECT: "Chuck Colson was a Baptist but he had a passion for Christian unity that reached far beyond his own denomination. In the early nineteen nineties, Chuck and his close friend, the late Father Richard John Neuhaus, brought together a group known as Evangelicals and Catholics Together—not a mere coalition but a fellowship of earnest Evangelicals and faithful Catholics who recognized that beyond the differences that continued to separate us, we shared a fundamental unity as brothers and sisters in Christ, a vision for reconciliation that continues still." Timothy also mentioned very favorably the 2009 Manhattan Declaration, which was likewise dear to Chuck's heart.

For persons grieving Chuck's death, Timothy offered these genuinely consoling words of comfort and hope in the Gospel of Jesus Christ: "It has been said that this life is a chasm of light suspended between two eternities of darkness. But the Gospel Chuck Colson believed and proclaimed tells a different story: this life is the real shadow land, and often a vale of tears, suspended between two eternities of light. We come into this world, each of us, from the hands of the invisible God who dwells in light inaccessible. And we leave this world, trusting in Jesus Christ to go into what the African American preacher calls the land of "no more," no more sorrow, no more crying, no more pain or death, no more crime or violence, no more prison and no more night, for we go into that land beyond the shadows, where we shall have no need of candles, nor light of the sun, for the Lord God will give light to all those gathered around his throne and that of the Lamb."

A card bearing Chuck Colson's likeness in a painting was distributed at the time of the Memorial Service. On the reverse side of the card were these powerful words: "Remain at your post and do your duty—for the glory of God and His Kingdom—Chuck Colson. For to me to live is Christ, and to die is gain. (Phil 1:21)"

CONCLUDING REFLECTIONS

Today Timothy George is one of America's most respected church historians, theologians and Christian educators. The influence of his marvelous ministry for Christ is extensive indeed. Timothy George's involvement in ECT and his endeavors with Chuck Colson are not the only theatres of his expansive ministry. But certainly, even by themselves, they constitute a very important chapter in the oft times inspiring story of American Evangelicalism.

BIBLIOGRAPHY

Colson, Charles W., and Richard J. Neuhaus, eds. *Evangelicals and Catholics Together: Toward a Common Mission*. Waco, TX: Word, 1995.
"Do Whatever He Tells You: The Blessed Virgin Mary in Christian Faith and Life." *First Things*, November 2009, 109–30.
George, Timothy, and Thomas G. Guarino, eds. *Evangelicals and Catholics Together at Twenty: Vital Statements on Contested Topics*. Grand Rapids: Brazos, 2015.
"The Gift of Salvation." *First Things*, January 1998. https://www.firstthings.com/article/1998/01/001-the-gift-of-salvation. Accessed Feb. 22, 2018.
Weigel, George. Foreword to *Evangelicals and Catholics Together at Twenty: Vital Statements on Contested Topics*, edited by Timothy George and Thomas G. Guarino, xii–xvi. Grand Rapids: Brazos, 2015

Section Three

Ministry and Engagement

The Church and Pastor-Theologians

R. Albert Mohler Jr.

THE PASTOR IS THE only theologian most Christians will ever know. Most believers will never sit in a seminary classroom, will never know an academic theologian, and will never read a systematic theology. They are dependent upon the theological vocation of pastors.

Therein lies the problem. The separation of the pastoral and theological vocations in the long history of the church has produced churches that are deprived of theology and pastors who assume that theology is someone else's responsibility.

Now, in what intellectual historians call the late modern age, the church is no longer able to linger under the illusion that the divorce between theological and pastoral vocations can continue. Congregations will become more theologically defined because they are more theologically led, or they will simply secularize before our eyes—or wither and die.

THE GREAT DIVORCE

As we will see, it was not always so. The separation of theology from the pastoral calling is not a recent reality, and it emerged from multiple developments, each of which must be understood as contributors to this reduction of the pastoral ministry. Something we can rightly call a Great Divorce has taken place. Theology retreated to academic settings and the pastorate was redefined so that theology became someone else's responsibility. As is the case with any divorce, the entire community was weakened.

One of the first major developments in the separation of the theological and pastoral callings was the emergence of a largely, if not exclusively, sacerdotal conception of the ministry. By the fourth century, a priesthood, ordained for a sacerdotal ministry, focused on the performance of the sacraments. The Donatist controversy and debate over the Latin formula, *ex opere operato*, underscored the growing definition of the priesthood in largely sacramental terms. In this sacerdotal understanding of ministry, therefore, the pastor was not expected to be a theologian resident among Christ's people, but a priest charged with pastoral care and sacramental worship. Over centuries, the teaching ministry was marginalized and theological vocation was largely lost.

In the medieval centuries, theology became central to the university—the Queen of the Sciences. Theology developed as an essentially academic enterprise, though under the supervision of the church. The model Christian scholar became a monk, keeping knowledge alive and treasuring texts, or the university scholar, lecturing within the university. In this tradition, theologians often only addressed themselves to fellow theologians, not to the laity. In many respects, this tradition still continues even into today. For over a millennium now, theology has been primarily identified with the university and, later, with the seminary—not within local congregations.

Theology, once the vocation of pastors and bishops, became a formal academic discipline which, though later displaced within the university in modern times, was seen as increasingly disconnected from the lives of believers and local congregations.

In more modern times the trajectories of theology and ministry have diverged even more dramatically. Here, the blame falls on both theologians and congregations.

In the Modern Age, the rise of the modern research university came at a great cost to the theological vocation of the church. The ideal of theology changed radically, conforming to the secular norms of other academic disciplines. The rise of academic guilds and the redefinition of the university not only left theology dethroned as Queen of the Sciences—it was redefined as a *Wissenschaft*, a project for academic research conducted according to the secular norms of the academy.

In 1875, Old Testament scholar August Dillmann at the University of Berlin pointed to a "contradiction between traditional doctrine and modern knowledge," pleading for an "atmosphere of science" in which theology could alone survive as and intellectual enterprise.[1] The singularly most influential German Protestant academic of his age, Adolph von Harnack, as

---

1. Howard, *Protestant Theology and the Making of the Modern German University*, 15.

Thomas Albert Howard explained, "even argued that theology conducted under ecclesiastical auspices was positively injurious to true *Wissenschaft*."[2]

> Howard draws a very helpful distinction between theology as understood by the ancient church and theology as a modern academic discipline:
>
> In other words, from the vantage point of premodern Christianity, or at least influential strands thereof, normative theology was regarded as essentially suprascientific, wary of worldly political powers and integrally tied to the doctrinal, spiritual, and practical concerns of the church, the *ecclesia*. By contrast, numerous nineteenth-century German theologians, mirroring Harnack, Dillmann, and others, wound up holding an almost fundamentally opposite view: to avoid succumbing to ecclesiastical obscurantism, theology, in step with secular academic disciplines, should be rigorously scientific, intentionally aloof from church direction, and incapable of thriving in a state-supported university environment.[3]

George Marsden, describing the loss of what had remained as a tradition of religious studies within the American university in the early twentieth century, noted: Part of the reason why the religious dimensions of American higher education in the first half of the twentieth century have been so thoroughly forgotten is that even by then they had become peripheral, if not necessarily unimportant, to the main business of the universities. Then, under the heat of new cultural pressures in the 1960s and beyond, most of what was substantial in such religion quickly evaporated, often almost without a trace and seldom with so much as a protest.[4]

But it was the German university in the nineteenth and early twentieth centuries that set the pattern. As Michael Legaspi states plainly, "In the nineteenth century, there were two kinds of universities: German universities and those that wanted to be German."[5]

> He describes the larger dynamic as driven by the perceived need to survive within the larger secular academic culture:
>
> Over the course of the nineteenth century, academic theologians succeeded in assimilating theology to the realities of the modern state in order to ensure the continued survival of their discipline. The fate of theology at the university contains

2. Ibid., 15.
3. Ibid., 17.
4. Marsden, "The Soul of the American University."
5. Lagaspi, *The Death of Scripture and the Rise of Biblical Studies*, 28.

the paradox: by innovating, the Germans conserved. Striking a Faustian bargain with the growing power of the state, they maintained their religious and cultural inheritance by folding the authority of the Bible and of the Protestant theological tradition into the larger programs of *Verwissenschaftlichung* (scientization), *Entkonfessionalisierung* (deconfessionalization), *Professionalisierung* (professionalization), and *Verstaatlichung* (nationalization)–all programs centered at the University. The end result of these programs, as the success of hard knocks defensive academic theology in the early twentieth century shows, was the firm establishment of theology among the scientific disciplines at the modern university.[6]

A high a cost indeed! Theology moved further and further into the embrace of the academy and away from the church. In even more recent decades, the academic study of theology has come to include virtually anything that could be described, even remotely, as religious studies and the theological spectrum has exploded into a kaleidoscope of competing theological variants and identities, mirroring the larger university context.

And yet, even as theology was moving further from the church, the pastoral calling was being redefined in accord with larger cultural currents. The most dominant of these currents included the rise of a managerial culture and the redefinition of the pastorate as a profession, as well as the emergence of a culture driven by both entertainment and therapeutic concerns.

A debate over whether the pastor should be considered a professional was a fixture of nineteenth century Protestantism. By the twentieth century, however, the debate was largely over and professionalization reigned supreme. This came even as the rise of a new professional class in the larger society was a hallmark of the twentieth century and was understood to be central to the project of modernity. Pastors, in order to maintain professional status and standing within the community would have to be seen as professionals themselves. At the same time, the larger culture was both adopting and emulating a new managerial ideal. Trends in corporate America and in the nation's largest institutions quickly influenced American Protestants and their understanding of the role of the pastor.

Simultaneously, the process of suburbanization and the rise of much larger churches within both urban and suburban contexts raised the expectations concerning the managerial expectations of pastors. Pastors now had to be executives equipped to administer staff and to take on the larger responsibilities of the managerial class. In that class, pragmatism reigned

---

6. Ibid., 29.

supreme and the ministry was thus transformed so that managerial and pragmatic concerns were paramount.

This was also the era described by Philip Rieff as "the triumph of the therapeutic." The rise of psychiatry and psychology as major medical professions also came as pop psychology and therapeutic themes came to dominate the culture. By the second half of the twentieth century, the more liberal Protestant denominations had moved to a model of pastoral counseling as a way of professionalizing the role of pastors in counseling and, simultaneously, bringing expectations in line with contemporary psychiatric and psychological understandings. Evangelicals followed by adapting many therapeutic themes to modern ministry.

As if all this were not enough, the rise of modern media and an entertainment culture also brought new expectations of the pastor in local church ministry. Preaching, in many churches, was reconceived as communication to be accompanied by necessary entertainment. Prominent television ministries also raised expectations among church members, transforming both worship and pastoral ministry.

David Wells describes the new reality clearly: "Whereas ministers once focused on such staple interests as brokering God's truth, caring for the sick and ailing, and building up Christian character and understanding, they now have to extend their energies to a whole new line of responsibilities, which in some cases eclipses the older and more foundational responsibilities."[7] Further: "In this new clerical order, technical and managerial competence in the church have plainly come to dominate the definition of pastoral service. It is true that matters of spirituality loom large in the churches, but it is not at all clear that churches expect the pastor to do anything more than to be a good friend. The older role of the pastor as broker of truth has been eclipsed by the newer managerial functions."[8]

In many churches (and in their pulpits) theology simply disappeared. In others, it has been displaced. Wells describes this in terms of two models of ministry—an older model with the minister as theologian and "broker" of truth, and the second with the pastor as a newly defined religious professional. He wrote of this displacement with lament: "The difference between the two models is not that theology is present in first but not the other. Theology is professed and believed in both. But in the one, theology is the reason for ministry, the basis for ministry; it provides the criteria by which success in ministry is measured. In the other, theology does none of these things; here the ministry provides its own rationale, its own criteria, its own

---

7. Wells, *No Place for Truth: Or What Happened to Evangelical Theology?*, 232.
8. Ibid., 233.

techniques. The second model does not reject theology; it simply displaces it so that it no longer gives the profession of ministry its heart and fire."[9]

THE GRAND TRADITION: THE PASTOR-THEOLOGIAN IN THE CHURCH

The vision of the pastor as theologian is hardly an eccentric or recent conception. In the New Testament, we see the clear expectation that a pastor is to be a shepherd to the flock of God, and that vocation, though clearly encompassing an entire range of pastoral responsibilities, is inescapably theological. The apostle Paul instructed Timothy concerning his responsibility as a steward of the faith, maintaining the pattern of sound words and the theological articulation of biblical truth. I would define the pastor's calling as the stewardship of the mysteries of God, and the New Testament conception of the pastor is inherently theological.

Similarly in the early church we find that robust theological debate and the deepest doctrinal conversations of the church were conducted by pastors and bishops. The early church fathers were, almost without exception, devoted churchmen who held the pastoral office. A distinction between the role of the pastor and the theologian would have been foreign to these early Christian theologians. As we have seen, this divide would come all too quickly, but until the rise of the university in the medieval period, the only theologians of the church were churchmen. The towering theological figures of Christian antiquity—Ambrose, Gregory, Basil, and the Cappadocian fathers, as examples—were pastor-theologians. Among them, no one towered over the landscape like Augustine of Hippo.

Augustine was the great pastor-theologian of the early church. His theological writings spill over into dozens of volumes and remain classics for theological inquiry even today. His monumental works, like *De Trinitate*, are evidence of a first-rate mind and intellect at work. In his own time, no other thinker rivaled Augustine for long-term influence and his sophistication as a theologian sets him apart even today.

Augustine, however, was first and foremost a churchman. In his most dominant years he was both pastor and bishop in Hippo. There is no way to separate Augustine into two separate lives, one theological and one pastoral. This is nowhere more apparent than in his catechetical works and in his own pastoral ministry. Peter Brown, the most influential biographer of Augustine of our times, has helped to make this pastoral dimension of Augustine's ministry abundantly clear.

9. Ibid., 255.

Most interestingly, as Brown has updated his work, he has taken advantage of recent manuscript discoveries that have revealed the pastoral dimensions of Augustine's ministry in new light. Brown writes of the "voice" of Augustine and how it appears different to him now, decades after he wrote his magisterial biography:

> But what exactly is that voice like, and how does it differ from the voice I had strained to catch in Augustine's writings when I wrote my biography of him in the 1960s? It is not the voice of Augustine the theologian or of Augustine the thinker. Rather, it is the living voice of Augustine the bishop, caught, in turns, at its most intimate and at its most routine. In sermons preserved as they were preached by stenographers, we can literally catch the voice of Augustine as he spoke face to face with Catholic congregations in the first decade of his episcopate. Almost twenty years later, in the Divjak letters, we find Augustine, now an old bishop, caught up in the seemingly endless, day-to-day business of the Catholic Church in Africa.[10]

Augustine struggled with all the demands a pastor knows. He was responsible for pastoral counsel, for organizational management, and a range of practical concerns. But he was foremost a preacher and a teacher. And that meant being a theologian and pastor. In a very moving passage, Brown writes of Augustine's determination to feed his flock. "As a bishop of Hippo, depressed by human weakness, he will turn his creativity into a form of giving food: he will always present it as 'feeding' men as much in need of nourishment now as he now felt himself to be."[11]

This is not the Augustine imagined by many today. Augustine was not just the theological giant of his epoch; he was also a pastor for whom theology was anything but a mere *Wissenschaft*. Theology, as every true pastor knows, is a matter of life and death.

The medieval centuries are marked by an eclipse of the pastor as theologian. The nature of the medieval priesthood and the rise of the university, as we have seen, implied and defined a separation of theology and ministry. In the Reformation of the sixteenth century, we see the re-emergence of the pastor-theologian in a new context.

Like Augustine, Martin Luther was both a pastor and a towering theologian in his era. Having received Holy Orders as a young man, Luther showed academic potential that impressed his teachers. By the time he arrived on the scene in Wittenberg, Luther was an "ordinary professor

---

10. Brown, *Augustine of Hippo: A Biography*, 445.
11. Ibid., 275.

of theology," as well as a priest of the Augustinian order. Shortly thereafter, he was both professor and preacher for a local congregation. Luther would work out his theology of the cross and lead the Reformation from both pulpit and lectern. He was equally at home in the dock of a theological disputation and in the pulpit. His theological writings and his sermons continue to speak powerfully, even as this very year (2017) marks the 500th anniversary of the theological act for which he is most remembered—the nailing of the famous Ninety-Five Theses to the castle church door in Wittenberg.

Today, few seem to remember that the first of the theses on Luther's list had to do with penance and the priestly office. From beginning to end, Luther was a pastor-theologian with both dimensions of his ministry so intertwined that no one, Luther first of all, could have divided them.

As with Augustine and his catechetical works, we see the pastoral Luther in his doctrinal teaching, his hymns, his attention to biblical worship, and his preaching. Similarly, we see his theological vocation realized in his pastoral mentoring, his counsel, his leadership of an expanding Reformation, and his writings. Furthermore, we see Luther the theologian even in his famous "Table Talk"—the *Tischreden*. These sayings attributed to Luther by those who sat at his table still speak through the centuries, serving as full evidence that Luther was a pastor-theologian even at the dinner table.

Luther would declare that the theologian is not made by "understanding, reading, or speculation, but by living, nay, dying and being damned." Thus, Luther was not only a theologian of the cross, he was a preacher of the Gospel and a pastor to those who, like him, were sinners desperately in need of a Savior.

In Geneva, John Calvin was even more systematic and comprehensive than Luther in his theological project. At the same time, he was no less a pastor. The same man who produced the *Institutes of the Christian Religion* was the man who preached several times a week in Geneva, who oversaw an academy for pastors, and who met regularly with other pastors to learn from one another and to deal with pastoral issues within congregations. The church in Geneva recognized four offices: pastor, doctor, elder, and deacon. Calvin was both pastor and doctor. As Scott Manetsch notes:

> The church office of doctor or teacher is a unique feature of Geneva's ecclesiastical constitution and a distinctive characteristic of Calvin's ecclesiology. Doctors, like pastors, were charged to interpret the Scriptures and teach sound doctrine. Their mandate extended beyond the local congregation to the larger church, however, and included the responsibility to teach future pastors and protect the church from doctrinal error. The *Ecclesiastical Ordinances* anticipated the creation of a college in

which these doctors would prepare Geneva's youth for service to the church and state. This vision took institutional shape with the founding of the Genevan Academy in 1559, consisting of a lower-level Latin school (*schola privata*) and an upper level 'seminary' or 'university' (*schola publica*) to train students for Christian ministry law and medicine.[12]

Writing in his Commentary on Ephesians, Calvin made the distinction between pastors and doctors clear: "Pastors, to my mind, are those to whom is committed the charge of a particular flock. I have no objection to their receiving the name of doctors, if we realize that there is another kind of doctor, who superintendents both the education of pastors and the instruction of the whole church. Sometimes he can be a pastor who is also a doctor, but the duties are different."[13]

The point here is that Calvin understood that all pastors have an essentially theological ministry—but that some, the doctors, have a special responsibility for the theological education of other pastors. In this scheme, the distinction is not between an order of ministers who are not theologians and an order who are, but rather a common theological calling that, in the case of the doctors of the church, is extended to the preparation of pastor-theologians.

Like Luther, Calvin towered over his contemporaries. His theological influence was vast and lasting. His theological works, all written within decades of Luther's, seem even more contemporary. Calvin was a master exegete and a powerful expositional preacher. His theological writings represent a library unto themselves, but Calvin never saw himself as a theologian in any sense disconnected from the ministry of the church and his role as a pastor. Furthermore, his example was infectious. As Manetsch states: "Calvin believed that this was true of his own vocation: God had called him to be both pastor and teacher in the Genevan church.... In the half century after Calvin's death, this paradigm of the pastor-doctor was reflected in the ministries of a number of Geneva's most notable religious leaders, including Theodore Beza, Lambert Daneau, Bonaventure Bertram, Antoine de La Faye, Jean Diodati, and Theodore Tronchin."[14]

In Calvin's view, every pastor is a theologian and every theologian should be a pastor—though some have a special theological vocation to other pastors. This serves as a very helpful model when we consider the role of theological education in the life of the church today.

12. Manetsch, *Calvin's Company of Pastors: Pastoral Care and the Emerging Reformed Church, 1526–1609*, 28.

13. Ibid., 29.

14. Ibid.

Leaving Calvin and Luther, we find another example of the pastor-theologian in Charles Spurgeon. The famed London pastor of the Victorian era was hardly recognized as a theologian by the academic theologians of the day, but his theological works continue to influence long after their works have been forgotten. By some estimates, Spurgeon remains the most published individual author in the history of the English language. By any estimation, he was the most influential preacher of his day—in a London filled with prominent preachers and pulpits.

What many miss is that Spurgeon was also a theologian, modeling what it means to be a pastor-theologian in the early modern age. Spurgeon was constantly dealing with an entire range of theological controversies, and, like Augustine, Luther, and Calvin, he was also engaged in the regular teaching ministry of the church, right down to the categorizing of children.

In the words of Christian T. George, Spurgeon "re-animated classical Reformed theology."[15] He defended classical Reformed theology and preached it in a pastoral key. His sermons are deeply pastoral, covering the full range of pastoral concerns, but they are also deeply theological. Spurgeon defended Protestant orthodoxy as theological liberalism was steadily gaining ground in Great Britain and throughout Europe, and he steadfastly insisted upon a careful articulation and confession of central evangelical doctrines. Beyond this, he oversaw a vast evangelical empire including everything from tract and publication societies to an orphanage and a school for preachers. And yet, Spurgeon never cease to be anything less than a theologian in any of these roles.

Spurgeon's distinctive role as a theologian-pastor in his own age is often overlooked today, even by those who admire him. Christian T. George explains, "Chalcedonian in creed, Alexandrian in style, Spurgeon's Christology developed within the milieu of a complex Victorian religious context."[16] The most interesting dimension of this description is the language linking Spurgeon, an evangelical preacher in Victorian London, to ancient Chalcedon and Alexandria. All this underlines Spurgeon's role as a pastor-theologian.

In the United States, the towering pastor-theologian is Jonathan Edwards. Paul Ramsey once described Edwards as "the greatest philosopher-theologian yet to grace the American scene."[17] George Marsden described him as "the most acute early American philosopher and the most brilliant of

---

15. Christian T. George, "Jesus Christ, The 'Prince of Pilgrims,'" 7.
16. Ibid., 11.
17. Ramsey, "Introduction," viii.

all American theologians."[18] While Edwards is thus recognized for his stature here as theologian and philosopher, he was also a pastor whose theological and philosophical contributions grew out of a most remarkable (if controverted) ministry.

The range of Edward's interests was extraordinary. A true son of the Scottish Enlightenment, Edwards was interested in both spiders and substitutionary atonement. Marsden points out that America has produced many notable philosophers in its history, but Edwards was the last to be philosopher, theologian, and pastor. It is still worthy of note that the most famous single work by Edwards remains a sermon preached to a congregation: "Sinners in the Hands of an Angry God."

Edwards saw theology as a science, though he preferred to speak of "divinity" as the theological science that leads, not to mere knowledge about God, but to the knowledge of God. In Edwards's own words:

> God himself, the eternal Three in one, is the chief object of this science; and next Jesus Christ, as God-man and Mediator, and the glorious work of redemption, the most glorious work that ever was wrought: then the great things of the heavenly world, the glorious and eternal inheritance purchased by Christ, and promised in the gospel; the work of the Holy Spirit of God on the hearts of men; our duty to God, and the way in which we ourselves may become . . . like God himself in our measure. All these are objects of this science.[19]

Edwards saw himself as both a theologian of divinity and, for most of his life and ministry, as a preacher and pastor. He united theological instruction and pastoral ministry and serves as the model of the pastor-scholar.

THE WAY OF RECOVERY

The separation of the pastoral and theological callings—the "Great Divorce" that has so divided the theological academy from the church—can only be overcome by an intentional and comprehensive recovery of the pastor-theologian within the church. There is no excuse for this divorce, and the results of this divide have been nothing short of catastrophic. The church is endangered by a definition of pastoral ministry that continues to focus on managerial and theological concerns. David Wells is absolutely correct in affirming that, unless the pastor is affirmed once again as a "broker of truth," the church will continue to be woefully malnourished.

18. Ibid., 1.
19. "Christian Knowledge," 2:159.

In a radically secularizing culture, when evangelical Christianity is losing its privileged posture within the larger culture, the need for a new generation of pastor-theologians has never been more acute. All needed resources are close at hand. The history of the Christian church is replete with examples of those who combined the pastoral calling with deep theological passion, acumen, and intentionality. Congregations desperately need for a new generation of pastor-theologians to arrive, armed with the deep resources of the Christian tradition, inspired by the examples of pastor-theologians in the past, committed to the fullness of Christian truth, and able "rightly to divide the word of truth."

A PERSONAL WORD

When I arrived as a seminary student, now almost four decades ago, my own vocation as a pastor and theologian was encouraged and immeasurably deepened through the influence of one professor above all others. That professor was Timothy F. George. It was Timothy F. George who introduced me to the riches of Christian history. In his classroom, history comes alive and students are taken to the front lines of church history, reading the original sources and engaging the issues both historically and theologically. My own trajectory as theological educator, theologian, and minister is unknowable to me apart from the formative experiences of reading Augustine, Calvin, Luther, and so many others under the direction of Timothy F. George in the classroom, in the doctoral seminar, and, most importantly, in personal conversation. I am thankful that Timothy was not only my teacher, but has been for so many years my friend. Even when we disagree—and Timothy is not intimidated by disagreement—I continue to be instructed by the model of Christian scholarship that Timothy George has represented for over a half century. In his own way, he is himself a pastor-theologian. More than that, through his influence, many pastors have become theologians through his teaching and example. I can think of no more fitting chapter than this as I gladly honor Timothy George.

BIBLIOGRAPHY

Brown, Peter. *Augustine of Hippo: A Biography*, New ed. Berkeley: University of California Press, 2000.

Edwards, Jonathan. "Christian Knowledge: Or the Importance and Advantage of a Thorough Knowledge of Divine Truth." In *The Work of Jonathan Edwards*, 2:159. Edinburgh: Banner of Truth Trust, 1974.

George, Christian T. "Jesus Christ, The 'Prince of Pilgrims': A Critical Analysis of the Ontological, Functional, and Exegetical Christologies in the Sermons, Writings, and Lectures of Charles Haddon Spurgeon (1834–1892)." PhD diss., St. Andrews University, 2012.

Howard, Thomas Albert. *Protestant Theology and the Making of the Modern German University.* New York: Oxford University Press, 2006.

Lagaspi, Michael C. *The Death of Scripture and the Rise of Biblical Studies.* Oxford Studies in Historical Theology. New York: Oxford University Press, 2010.

Manetsch, Scott M. *Calvin's Company of Pastors: Pastoral Care and the Emerging Reformed Church, 1526–1609.* Oxford Studies in Historical Theology. New York: Oxford University Press, 2013.

Marsden, George M. "The Soul of the American University." *First Things,* January 1991. https://www.firstthings.com/article/1991/01/005-the-soul-of-the-american-university.

Ramsey, Paul. "Introduction." In *Freedom of the Will,* by Jonathan Edwards, viii. New Haven: Yale University Press, 1957.

Wells, David F. *No Place for Truth: Or What Happened to Evangelical Theology?* Grand Rapids: Eerdmans, 1993.

Preaching and the Church

Robert R. Smith

INTRODUCTION

This chapter will express the timeless and inextricable relationship between preaching and the church[1] as revealed through the 21st-century church, the lens of the German pastor-preacher and theologian, Helmut Thielicke, and Scripture. It will offer a diagnosis (the assessment of preaching in the life of the church), prognosis (the prediction of the future state of preaching and the church) and prescription (the redeeming values of preaching for the life of the church). Like the prophet-preacher Ezekiel, Thielicke preached authentically, proclaiming the gospel as an eyewitness and not simply a secondhand reporter. Thielicke capably and effectively relayed biblical *sitz im leben*[2] to the church of his day moving seekers to go to great lengths to hear biblical preaching applied instructionally, beneficially and Christologically to their lives.

DIAGNOSIS: THE ASSESSMENT OF PREACHING IN THE LIFE OF THE CHURCH

Preaching provides a vital service to the church that should not be discarded or relegated to a minor role in ministry since hearers must receive Jesus Christ in order to be saved. Of this pertinent act Paul asked how believers

---

1. The church will be defined as the people of God—children of Abraham by faith whether physical and/or spiritual descendants. Rom 9:6–7; Gal 3:6–9.
2. The context in which a text was written.

can come to faith without a preacher who has been sent.[3] Martin Luther also grasped the saliency of preaching and the preacher. He said, "If I could today become king or emperor, I would not give up my office as preacher."[4] However, in 2012 the Barna Group asked over 600 pastors to rank their priorities for the upcoming year and only 22% definitely planned to assess the spiritual growth of the church.[5] Such lack of focus given to the purpose for which we live reveals itself in widespread lack of concern for God, others and self. Thielicke wrote, "The trouble with preaching lies deep in our spiritual condition, in a pathological condition of our Christian state."[6] In my book, *Doctrine that Dances*,[7] I offered a diagnosis of the preaching of the contemporary pulpit. What is the matter with preaching today? First, there is *the dilution of grace*. Paul in his writings always put a theology of grace before a theology of works. Doctrine always preceded deeds. In Rom 1–11 he talks about the grace of justification, sanctification, glorification, adoption, and the like. When he comes to Rom 8:31 he asks: "What shall we say to these things?" "These things" refer to all the doctrines of grace preceding this verse. And then he goes on to talk about election and predestination in chapters 9–11. In chapter 12 he opens up, "Brethren, I beseech you by the mercies of God," mercies that are visible in the first eleven chapters. Furthermore, he discusses the service gifts from the end of chapter 12 through chapter 16. These are ethical deeds and responsibilities.

Martin Luther lifted up the indicative above the imperative. The indicative is who I am; the imperative is what I must do as a result of who I am. It is not the imperative first: I must do this in order to become a Christian. Rather, it is the indicative first: because I am a Christian, I do what I do. I do not work for salvation; I work from salvation. The love of Christ constrains me.

Dietrich Bonhoeffer in his book *The Cost of Discipleship*[8] mentions "cheap grace"; this is grace without any accompanying ethical and social responsibility. There is something worse than cheap grace; it is perverted grace, grace that is stretched so that it is no longer grace. Too often in our preaching we start off with justification by grace; then after people get saved, we move on to preaching sanctification by works. If I am saved by grace,

---

3. Rom 10:14.
4. Luther, cited by Meuser, *Luther the Preacher*, 39.
5. Barna Group, "How Pastors Plan to Improve Their Churches."
6. Thielicke, *Trouble*, 18.
7. Smith Jr., *Doctrine That Dances: Bringing Doctrinal Preaching and Teaching to Life*, 80–91.
8. Bonhoeffer, *The Cost of Discipleship*, 45.

then I am sanctified by grace. I cannot add anything to it. It is grace plus nothing—*not* grace plus my achievement, merits, works, or credentials; it is grace plus nothing.

Second, there is *the eclipse of the cross*. In Heb 5:8, Jesus the Son of God learned "obedience from what he suffered." The Son of God had to experience discipline to be obedient through suffering. This is the sinless and infinite One. We are not allowed to skip a theology of the cross and move immediately to a theology of glory. The cross is so central in salvation history that the only thing Elijah and Moses talked about as heavenly delegates to the summit meeting at the transfiguration of Christ was the *exodon,* or death at Jerusalem (Luke 9:31). Elijah, who represented the prophets, and Moses, who represented the law, appeared with Christ to declare that Christ was the fulfillment of both the law and the prophets.

Third, there is a *demise of doctrine*. The greatest divorce to take place in the church in the last fifty years is the divorce between the minister of music and the minister of Christian education. And what is so sad is that the pastor has officiated over the ceremony. The minister of Christian education and the minister of music need to be remarried. They were not divorced in the early church. In Acts 2:41 we learn that about three thousand souls were added to the church, and God continued to add to the church daily those who were being saved. Verse 42 states, "And they continued steadfastly in the apostles' doctrine." This is Christian education. Verse 47 adds that they continually praised God. This is Christian worship.

The pastor is the resident theologian and must inform the minister of Christian education and the minister of music that regardless of the meter and the rhythm of a song, the message must be theological and biblical. In our churches we sing more heresies than the early church councils ever condemned during the patristic period. Worshippers may do musicological flips and liturgical calisthenics, but heaven will not bless untheological and unbiblical songs. There is no antithesis between musical inspiration and biblical lyrics. The minister of Christian education prepares students for the sermon and the minister of music prepares worshippers to worship God biblically and intelligently.

Fourth, there is *the disconnection between traditional theological language and contemporary relevant imagery*. Theology is not the faith; it is talk about the faith. Harry Emerson Fosdick said, "Astronomies change while stars abide."[9] God never changes, but our studies and perspective about God do change. So we have to come to the place where we talk about God differently today from the way God was referred to fifty years ago.

---

9. Fosdick, quoted in Sweet, *Evangelical Tradition in America*, 297.

How does the preacher talk about the concept of depravity or Adamic sin in the twenty-first century? How does one talk about redemption? I am an African American, but experientially I do not know anything about slavery. How do we talk about redemption when we do not know what slavery is? But people know what a hostage is.

Fifth, there is *the dissemination of anthropocentric preaching*. We have been affected by the past. During the Renaissance, there was an emphasis on the inversion of a human being. In human thought God was replaced by a human being as the center of the universe. This is particularly true in the thinking of the seventeenth-century scientist René Descartes, whose dictum was, "I think, therefore I am" (cogito ergo sum). Our preaching is becoming more human centered than God centered. Bryan Chapell decries the rise of humanism in a concept he calls *sola bootstrapsa*: "Pull yourself up by your own bootstraps."

> Humpty Dumpty sat on a wall,
> Humpty Dumpty had a great fall.
> All the king's horses and all the king's men
>   Could not put Humpty together again.

But I know a King who can! He is the King of kings and the Lord of lords. Bryan Chapell challenges preachers to look at their congregations as a piece of swiss cheese when they stand before them to preach the Word of God. Both the preacher and the people have holes in them, and only the Word of God can fill the holes and make them complete. Second Timothy 3:16–17 says, "All Scripture is given by inspiration of God, and is profitable for doctrine, for reproof, for correction, for instruction in righteousness: that the man of God may be perfect, thoroughly furnished unto all good works." Only God can reach farther in and go deeper down to put the interiority of the human state in order.

Sixth, there is *detachment of the mystery of God from the revelation of God*. Martin Luther referred to the concealing of God as *deus absconditus* and the revealing of God as *deus revelatus*. God made humans in His own image and after His likeness. Some modern preaching is attempting to reverse the process so that the mystery of God is demystified and the inscrutability of God is unscrewed. God reserves the right to reveal Himself and to be inconspicuous. God is the God of the beyond. Too many of our modern-day preachers pose as if they were so familiar with God that they receive advance heavenly bulletins that notify them of what His next move will be. Only when faith yields to sight, the hitherto surrenders to the henceforth, and the "more" of devastation embraces the "no more" of eternity's delights will we no longer see through a glass darkly, but rather see face-to-face. Until then preachers must keep them in tension, for what God has joined together is not to be separated!

The prophet Ezekiel lived among rebellious people who were disobedient to God. God called Ezekiel to serve as a prophet to the people by eating the word of God and delivering it to his people. In essence God required Ezekiel to faithfully preach to the people while living among them and assessing their spiritual condition. In Ezekiel 3:15 the prophet sits with the Jewish exiles in Babylon for seven days by the river Chebar. He sits there for seven days without uttering a word—he simply listens to their laments and concerns. Think of it—a preacher listening for seven days without uttering a word. He listens so he can specifically address their concerns as he tries to ascertain the trouble with the exilic community. Ezekiel did what many preachers do not exercise and churches suffer the consequences. In the German church, Thielicke noted "There is no meeting today between the real consciousness of sin in the depths of the soul, on the one side, and the proclamation of the church, on the other."[10] Thielicke addressed the trouble with the church and especially its preaching in his work, *Trouble with the Church*. He recognized the passive social consciousness that allowed the Holocaust to happen while "good people" idly stood by perhaps unwittingly helping an unchristian cause. Thielicke attributed the failure of Christian growth and life values to the church and her preaching stating, "All great crises of preaching have always come out of a false theology."[11] Like Paul in Gal 1:6–10, Thielicke could question why the publicly displayed behavior of the German church did not show evidence of faith in the gospel through its social action. A quick survey of the 21st century confirms what Thielicke wrote about in 1965 could with integrity and honesty be an accurate assessment of preaching in America today. The twenty-first century is tainted by genocide while Christians watch without getting involved. News reports in the first half of 2016 are replete with stories of name-calling, murder, racism, classism, disregard for neighbor and complete ignorance of God's call for his people to be separate from the world.[12] Also among the many causes for the failure of preaching is the church's lack of trust in God. Much preaching in the contemporary church focuses on meeting the budget—keep the people happy and they will pay—instead of focusing on complete reliance on God—preach the truth. If it is God's will, then it is God's bill. Contrary to what appears to be a socially-accepted new social strata wherein a preacher is celebrity and not servant and believers are servants of celebrity and not

---

10. Quoted in Bohren, *Preaching and Community*, 36.
11. Thielicke, *Trouble*, 65.
12. Jer 51:45; 2 Cor 6:17; Rev 18:4.

of one another, the office of the preacher is not a social class of its own and believers are not relieved from the Great Command to love our neighbor as ourselves. The preacher does not stand over against the congregation with separate rules and a randomly applied understanding of the unchanging Word; rather, the preacher should be established in the midst of the congregation living with the same biblical mandates with which believers are guided toward maturation of their faith in Jesus Christ.

While diagnosing the German church, Thielicke became convinced that "Actually preaching itself has decayed and disintegrated to the point where it is close to the stage of dying."[13] The blindness of the preacher and the church to the acts of the Lord in the here and now is due to the absence of the Holy Spirit in our preaching. Just as God charged and challenged Ezekiel to see the Valley of Dry Bones, preachers today can look past well-dressed congregants and hear past well-formed colloquialisms to accurately diagnose the church and her preaching as weak, ill and in desperate need of life support. In his work, *Harry Emerson Fosdick: Preacher, Pastor, Prophet*, Robert Moats Miller noted, "A Roman Catholic observer once predicted that if Protestantism ever died with a dagger in its back, the dagger will be the Protestant sermon."[14] Thielicke's preaching effectiveness could not be separated from his relationship to the congregations in which he preached. In preaching in the bombed out churches and buildings in Ravensburg and Stuttgart during WWII, he experienced the same crises that members of his congregations experienced. Thielicke spent nights with members of his parish in air raid shelters. He spoke to them about the meaning of suffering in relation to God as he faced disaster with his congregations. Helmut Thielicke knew his people when he preached and mingled with them during the week. Pastors who mingle with their people know their story and can enflesh it with relevance and life when they relate the Sunday morning message to their lives. When the people heard Thielicke's sermons, they undoubtedly felt like he was thinking through their problems with them. However, Thielicke did not believe cleverly worded sermons, good public speaking skills or charisma contributed to healthy Christian lives. He relied upon the Holy Spirit. Like John Calvin, Thielicke believed the Holy Spirit speaks and applies the message of the gospel to the hearts of the hearers. John Calvin refers to this as the internal witness of the Spirit—that is, the Holy Spirit taking the words from the Word of scripture through the mouth of the preacher and applying and convicting the hearer through them. Thielicke believes the barometer for measuring life or death in a church

---

13. Thielicke, *Trouble*, 2.
14. Miller, *Harry Emerson Fosdick: Preacher, Pastor, Prophet*, 334.

is dependent upon its proclamation and argues, "The valley of dry bones is waiting on the awakening Spirit."[15] The church is limping because of her *Spiritless* preaching, but there is a wind waiting to blow again to give life to the dry bones.

THE PROGNOSIS OF PREACHING AND THE CHURCH

Throughout Israel's history, God has offered a choice and a consequence: obedience yields blessings and disobedience yields curses. The prognosis of preaching and the church cannot stray from God's immutable plan: obedience in response to the Word yields blessings. Disobedience yields curses. God instructed Ezekiel to speak God's truth regardless of the people's response. The preacher has a heavy responsibility. God's clear message to Ezekiel—Speak what I tell you to speak and you will be fine. If hearers choose life then they shall live. If hearers choose death then they shall die. If you do not deliver my message and hearers die for their iniquity, then the blood is on your hand.[16] Preachers, like Ezekiel, must deliver the message so vividly, truthfully and biblically that even if hearers close their eyes the picture still speaks. The responsibility is the same in the twenty-first century as it was in the fifth for Ezekiel. Preachers still must give an account for their shepherding of souls Christ bought with his blood.[17] Consequently, preaching must be critical of the church and yet take its stand within the church because of its love for the church. Preachers must love the church enough to speak God's truth without compromise. If a preacher fails to hold fast to God's instructions then the church will suffer even if it seems prosperous by worldly standards.

William Sloane Coffin stated, "There are three kinds of patriots, two bad, one good. The bad are the uncritical lovers and loveless critics. Good patriots carry on a lover's quarrel with their country. A reflection of God's lover's quarrel with all the world."[18] Relating patriots of a country to preachers in the Christian church, *uncritical lovers* are ones who love the church to the extent they declare, "My church right or wrong." They love the church too much to criticize it. *Loveless critics* are those who liberally criticize the church but have no love for it. Both of these stances lead to a dysfunctional and dying church. However, those preachers who are involved in a *lovers quarrel* do so because they love the church so much that they cannot fail

---

15. Thielicke, *Trouble*, 128.
16. Ezek 3:17–21.
17. Heb 13:17
18. Coffin, *Credo*, 84.

to criticize and/or guide it—their guidance is to the end they assess the church in an effort to present a church body that is honorable before God and humanity. Helmut Thielicke is this third type of lover. Thielicke was convicted to preach the whole counsel of God to the whole person every time. He stated, "It [the sermon] must really constitute a whole for someone who may be present today who will never come back again and I must give him his emergency rations."[19] He realized the salience of preaching and the role of the preacher—"How shall they hear without a preacher?"[20] Thielicke preached to people who were despondent and disillusioned with the church. He said, "Must I not show these disillusioned and sometimes despairing people who have become disaffected from the church that what appears to them to be dead and outworn is perhaps a corpse having not only been rendered obsolete and thrown on the scrap heap by history, as they imagine, but actually murdered by *lovelessness* and idolatry in its own ranks?"[21] The preacher must move the church from a hopeless existence devoid of love and life to the glorious, set-apart and victorious position bought by Jesus Christ—"By this all people will know that you are my disciples, if you have love for one another."[22]

In Ezek 37, the Spirit of the Lord carried Ezekiel to the Valley of Dry Bones. After Ezekiel thoroughly surveyed this valley of hopelessness—a dire prognosis—God asked Ezekiel, "Can these bones live?" Ezekiel pondered the question. Forty years ago Gardner C. Taylor gave a message on Ezek 37 at The Southern Baptist Theological Seminary in Louisville, KY. He colorized Ezekiel's response to God's question, "Can these bones live? Taylor claims Ezekiel did not say, "Yes," too quickly to avoid being presumptuous. Neither did he answer, "No" because it would have been a response of cynicism which would have canceled out his future ministry. The exiles are in Babylon for 70 years. Of course they need hope. Ezekiel said, "Sovereign LORD, you alone know." Relying on charisma, alliteration, rhyme and rhythm might get a good response from the hearers. Feel good self-help stories and encouragement with a poem might get a good response from the hearers. However, preaching is not designed to get a good response; preaching is designed to get a God response hearers are to be moved to be godlier, more like Jesus. Without a biblically founded partnership with God, preaching fails to achieve its purpose. Biblically grounded sermons developed from time spent in the Word, with the Triune God, and with

19. Thielicke, *Trouble*, 24.
20. Rom 10:14
21. Thielicke, *Trouble*, 128.
22. John 13:35

the people will point to Jesus and move from earth to the eschaton. These sermons can effectively use rhythm, rhyme, charisma, alliteration, poems and stories as useful tools. Theology says, "Only you know, oh God. Only you can bring the dead to life through words you give me to utter."

Thielicke considered the weight and responsibility of a loving preacher and declared, "The only man who can assume such a bold and hazardous task is one who is convinced that he need not bear the responsibility for its success and that *Another* is there interceding for him. He knows that not he but only the Spirit of God himself is able to reach and open the hearts of his hearers. Only to the degree that he is assured of this will he mount the pulpit consoled and strengthened."[23] Helmut Thielicke believed the Holy Spirit is the instrument, which brings closure to the salvific message of the gospel. Our preaching today tends to be binarian rather than Trinitarian—oftentimes there is no room for the Spirit in our preaching. Greg Heisler in *Spirit-Led Preaching* posited preaching's failure to connect "the discipline of homiletics with the doctrine of pneumatology, and as a result we find ourselves 'surprised' by the 'Spirit' when he does move."[24] To have a positive prognosis for preaching and the church, the Trinitarian God must be worshipped and heard, preached and believed, honored and obeyed.

PRESCRIPTIONS FOR PREACHING IN THE LIFE OF THE CHURCH

In Ezek 3:22 the Lord calls Ezekiel to the plains where the Lord addresses the exiles' present state. Ezekiel has spent time among the exiles listening to them. From Ezek 3:22 to 11:24 Ezekiel listens to God. He knows he has nothing to say to the exiles until he has listened to the Eternal. Finally he is told by the Eternal to return to the exiles and tell them to hear the Word of the Lord.[25] The people could identify with this prophet because like them he was also in exile, experiencing the same crisis. In Ezek 37, the prophet is called to preach the Word of God in the Valley of Dry Bones. He preaches until there is harmony (a rattling noise in the valley), unity (bone united with the proper bone), beauty (the skeleton is covered with flesh) and vitality (the Spirit comes into the corpses and brings life). He preached until earth reached out for heaven and heaven responded with love. Contact with the heavenly and earthly is vital to healthy preaching and a healthy church.

23. Thielicke, *Trouble*, 24–25.

24. Heisler, *Spirit-Led Preaching: The Holy Spirit's Role in Sermon Preparation and Delivery*, 3.

25. Ezek 11:25

Thielicke lamented, "The German preacher often begins in heaven and never comes down to our living earth. The American preacher just because he remains in vital contact begins with downright earthly life and its social and psychological problems and often enough never reaches heaven."[26] Preaching must be in contact with heaven and earth—a feat that cannot be achieved without a relationship with the Triune God and his people.

Thielicke's messages were geared to preaching in the *sitz im leben*. Helmut Thielicke preached so the gospel was not just good news for first century humanity but also for those in the twentieth century. Helmut Thielicke's preaching enables his hearers to identify with the biblical character in the text so that the message makes the eighteen-inch connection from the cranial to the cardiological possible. This is a movement from mere information to transformation. The hearers not only understand the biblical text—they begin to understand themselves. Helmut Thielicke managed to keep in his preaching an ongoing dialog between biblical exegesis and life experience with his 'homiletical eye' to see the text and a 'homiletical ear' to hear its message for the contemporary context in which he would be preaching. Crowds came to hear Thielicke preach over and over again. Sometimes they came to hear the same sermon. Why? Because through his style of preaching and use of story, an experience was created for them, which unearthed some experiences, which had, been buried for many years. The people would identify with his message as he moved through the sermon. Thielicke succinctly described his process: "The aim of the sermon, after all, is to create something living and set in motion. Consequently, it should be directed—not only at the intellect, but must at the same time also be aimed at the conscience, will and imagination. It is addressed to the whole person."[27]

Paul Scherer provides an accurate prescription for the seriously dire preaching diagnosis: "Nothing can do them [the hearers] good without disturbing them. And nothing will disturb them to any lasting effect unless it disturbs them deeply. It is therefore of less value than is commonly supposed week in and week out simply to address those needs which lie around on the surface of human life, needs of which everybody is conscious: how to keep from feeling lonely; what it takes to be brave; the way to bear up under disappointment; the secret of success. Jesus said astonishingly little about any of that. Instead, he addressed himself to those needs so often unconscious which lie at the root of a man's sense of bewilderment, alienation, and anxiety. He was forever getting farther in and deeper down; and that

---

26. Thielicke, *Trouble*, 30.
27. Thielicke, *Notes from a Wayfarer*, 291–92.

is never likely to be painless."²⁸ On September 11, 2001, the Twin Towers in New York City were destroyed leaving America in a state of shock. The puzzling matter for the preacher was that the attendance in the American church one month before 9/11 was greater than the attendance after 9/11. Why? Because people came to the church depressed following 9/11 and did not return because they did not hear a relevant message. On June 12, 2016 forty-nine people were killed and fifty-three were injured in the Pulse Club massacre in Orlando, FL. Undoubtedly, many family members and friends turned to the church for comfort and answers many wondering why a good God allows evil deeds. The same set of circumstances was put to the German pulpit in WWII. Walter A. Elwell asserted, "The church did not find the message for the hour. Failing to preach repentance and salvation, offered instead a proclamation of a collective guilt and a hysteria of self-accusation..."²⁹ Preaching must present the answer—Jesus Christ—not just from the womb to the tomb, but risen, reigning, praying, and coming again as King! Preaching must be alive and relevant because Jesus Christ is alive and relevant. The living Word released through preaching must inherently have the power to feed and fill hearers who eat at the table with the kerygma of Jesus Christ—his life, death, resurrection, ascension, enthronement, sending of the Holy Spirit, repentance and the eschaton.³⁰ It is the lifeline.

> Jesus is able! To you who are driv'n
> Farther and farther from God and from Heav'n,
> Helpless and hopeless, o'erwhelmed by the wave,
> We throw out the lifeline—'tis, "Jesus can save.³¹

Thielicke's sermons were Christological, cross-oriented, instructive in atonement and in the plan of salvation while also addressing the needs of maturing believers. Thielicke was not simply interested in providing a diagnosis of the church but a prognosis and a prescription for the church regaining its power and influence in the country of Germany and throughout the world. Thielicke embraced preaching as the center and not the circumference of church life. His sermons were devotional, personal, spiritual and practical. Preaching is not an avocation for Thielicke, but a vocation that needs the prophetic Spirit to unapologetically proclaim the present acts of the Lord. Thielicke's sermons reverberate with an air of 'risk ' and 'boldness.'

28. Scherer, "Preaching as a Radical Transaction," 70.

29. Elwell, *Handbook of Evangelical Theologians*, 225.

30. Sermons should be developed for the needs of the hearers and all listed elements might not be present in every sermon, but all should inform the preparation of every sermon.

31. Ufford, "Throw Out the Life-Line," 1968.

Thielicke was not afraid to take risks in the pulpit. He stated, "The man who will not utter anything that is not guarded and safe is not reckoning with him who is able to raise up children to Abraham from stones. The witness must venture something and dare not be afraid of the chips that fly as he hews."[32] Similarly, preaching must boldly declare Jesus as the only way to salvation. Preaching must enhance Christian faith continuously enabling hearers to engage in and penetrate the world without being taken over by the world or having the Word in them diminished by the world's message. Helmut Thielicke was passionate about social justice that emerged from the gospel. He believed in gospelizing the social and not socializing the gospel. Like Thielicke our preaching must have a social justice and action trajectory; it must also penetrate the spheres of cross-culturalism and racial reconciliation. In order to address these varied needs of the church, the preacher must live life among and not above the people. Caring for the church in word and deed is the price preachers pay to earn the right to be heard and trusted.

Preaching, in the homiletic of James Earl Massey, must have certain components: Proclamation—initiating the hearers into the faith (salvation); Teaching—instructing the believers about the faith (maturation) and Therapy—inspiring the saints to keep the faith (exhortation). In this way, preaching leads to more disciples of Jesus Christ. The Bible is a *Him Book*—it is all about Jesus. Doctrinal, expositional sermons offer the Savior to seekers through unpredictable sermons capable of capturing hearers' attention and moving hearers to grasp the lifeline being thrown. As it relates to the prescription for efficacious preaching and the church gleaned from the needs of the 21st century, Ezekiel and Thielicke can be summarized as follows: First we can strive to speak the language of the people so that our sermons will be understood. Secondly, we can discipline ourselves to leave our homiletical and technical tools in our study and mount the pulpit with the fruit of our labor. Thirdly, we can learn to involve ourselves with our people. Once they know how much we care, then they will care how much we know and be ready to listen to our sermons. Our care for the church is an example for the church to care for the world. We demonstrate justification by the grace of God through faith and not sanctification through works. Gratefulness for salvation compels us to serve our neighbors—members of the household of faith and those who are not. Fourthly, we must determine to never compromise the gospel truth. Fifthly, we must believe that the Word we preach is efficacious in its saving work. Sixthly, we must believe God's plan—God is real, Jesus is real, the Spirit is real and the eschaton is real. There is a divine reason we suffer for the sake of the cross and celebrate

---

32. Thielicke, *Encounter with Spurgeon*, 40.

while carrying it. Preaching and the church—healthy and thriving—must embody the love Timothy Dwight wrote about in his hymnic rendition, "I Love Thy Kingdom Lord"[33]–

> I love thy kingdom, Lord! The house of Thine abode–
> The Church our blest redeemer saved With his own precious blood.
> I love Thy Church, O God! Her walls before Thee stand
> Dear as the apple of Thine eye and Graven on Thy hand
> For her my tears shall fall, for her my prayers ascend–
> To her my cares and toils be giv'n Til toils and cares shall end.

CONCLUSION

There is a chapter in Stephen Covey's book, *Seven Habits of Highly Effective People*,[34] titled "Beginning with the End in Mind." Preaching must begin with Christ who is the Alpha of preaching and end with Christ who is the Omega of preaching, the one who will bring all things to an eschatological ending which will inaugurate an eternal doxological beginning. The ultimate goal of preaching is to paint the future portrait of believers on the present canvas of a text that points to Christ. This is authentic sermonic eschatonics. Sermonic eschatonics does not mean we grant it only the function of an appendix. The eschatonics must be implicitly inserted in the introduction of a sermon like yeast is covertly put in to dough and proceeds to evolve throughout the sermon causing it to rise to its fullest expression in the conclusion. God is the eternal eschatologian because he is the only one who knows the end before the beginning (Isa 46:10). One of the marks of twenty-first century preaching is its suspicious lack of unrealized, *not yet* eschatology. Healthy preaching is preaching that is marked by the *preservation* of the *presence* of eschatology, which enables believers to *persevere*. Preaching permeated with the eschaton is not to be equated with an utopia in our present time as in the Marxist system of an utopian vision of a classless society. Rather, it is Jurgen Moltmann's theology of hope, which offers hope to oppressed people. The ultimate hope believers have is in Christ.

> My hope is built on nothing less than Jesus' blood and righteousness;
> I dare not trust the sweetest frame, but wholly lean on Jesus' name.

33. Dwight, *New National Baptist Hymnal*, 384.
34. Covey, *The 7 Habits of Highly Effective People*.

> On Christ, the solid Rock, I stand—All other ground is sinking sand,
> All other ground is sinking sand.[35]

Eschatology that abandons the gospel has lost its reason for existence and is therefore theologically unemployed. Eschatology—that is openness to God's future for believers—is an integral part of the Christian message. Future and hope must be revived in our preaching if we want to expect a real hearing from people. Many people come into our churches without hope. What is missing in the eschatological trajectory of our preaching is not the *parousia*, but rather the expectation of it. Jesus articulated the reality of his second coming when he said to his disciples at the Lord's Supper, "I will not drink of this fruit of the vine from now on *until* that day when I drink it anew with you in my father's kingdom" (Matt 26:29). At the end of the Eucharist, worshippers in the Episcopal tradition respond by saying, "Christ has died, Christ is risen, Christ will come again." The pendulum needs to swing back to an eschatological emphasis and trajectory in preaching. Eschatology is not an epilogue or appendix. Rather, it is a prologue of the *already* awaiting the promise of the fulfillment in the eschaton of the *not yet*. In the *already* we live in the prelude of that land in which there will never be the postlude of the *not yet*. Our preaching must hold in tension the theology of the cross (*theologia crucis*) and theology of future glory (*theologia gloria*). The eschaton must be preached in such a way the *already* and *not yet* are complimentary parts of the indissolubility of the whole—it must not be one-sided. The church has forgotten its eschatological future and has become like the five foolish virgins of Matt 25 who used the oil of their lamps to light up their own present festivities instead of keeping the oil in their lamps for the future coming of their lord. The essence of preaching the eschaton is embodied in the first question of The Westminster Confession, which is, "What is the chief end of man?" The answer, "To glorify God and enjoy Him forever." Helmut Thielicke preached with a sense of the eschaton—the blessed hope. It informed all of his preaching and should inform the preaching of the twenty-first century pulpit. His preaching had an intratrinitarian presence. The closing words of his autobiography revolve around and point to the eschatological reality of the fellowship of the saints with the sovereign God in eternity. It reads, "We are admittedly only guests on this beautiful planet, wayfarers on call and with sealed orders in which the day and hour of our departure are recorded . . . As Christians we are certain that the lifespan allotted us is only the advent of a still greater fulfillment. The land to which we are called is a *terra incognita*—and unknown,

---

35. Mote, *New National Baptist Hymnal*, 223.

even inconceivable land. There is only one voice that we will recognize there because it is already familiar to us here: the voice of the Good Shepherd."[36]

BIBLIOGRAPHY

Barna Group. "How Pastors Plan to Improve Their Churches." Barna, February 26, 2012. Accessed June 22, 2016. https://www.barna.org/barna-update/congregations/560-how-pastors-plan-to-improve-their-churches#.V3T9LzdwOOo.

Bohren, Rudolf. *Preaching and Community*. Richmond, VA: Knox, 1965.

Bonhoeffer, Dietrich. *The Cost of Discipleship*. Translated by Reginald H. Fuller. New York: Collier, 1973.

Coffin, William Sloane. *Credo*. Louisville: Westminster John Knox, 2004.

Covey, Stephen R. *The 7 Habits of Highly Effective People: Powerful Lessons in Personal Change*. Anniversary ed. New York: Simon & Schuster, 2013.

Dwight, Timothy. *New National Baptist Hymnal*. Nashville: National Baptist, 1977.

Elwell, Walter A., ed. *Handbook of Evangelical Theologians*. Grand Rapids: Baker, 1993.

Heisler, Greg. *Spirit-Led Preaching: The Holy Spirit's Role in Sermon Preparation and Delivery*. Nashville: B&H Academic, 2007.

Meuser, Fred W. *Luther the Preacher*. Minneapolis: Augsburg, 1983.

Miller, Robert Moats. *Harry Emerson Fosdick: Preacher, Pastor, Prophet*. New York: Oxford University Press, 1985.

Mote, Edward. *New National Baptist Hymnal*, Nashville: National Baptist, 1977.

Scherer, Paul. "Preaching as a Radical Transaction." In *The Word God Sent*, by Paul Scherer, 70. Harper & Row, 1965.

Smith, Robert, Jr. *Doctrine That Dances: Bringing Doctrinal Preaching and Teaching to Life*. Nashville: B&H Academic, 2008.

Sweet, Leonard. *The Evangelical Tradition in America*. Macon, GA: Mercer University Press, 1997.

Thielicke, Helmut. *Encounter with Spurgeon*. Philadelphia: Fortress, 1963.

———. *Notes from a Wayfarer*. Translated by David R. Law. New York: Paragon, 1995.

———. *The Trouble with the Church: A Call for Renewal*. Thielicke Library. Grand Rapids: Baker, 1978.

Ufford, Edward S. "Throw Out the Life-Line." Hymn, 1968. http://library.timelesstruths.org/music/Throw_Out_the_Lifeline/

---

36. Thielicke, *Notes*, 419.

The Church, Preaching, and Christian Music

JAMES EARL MASSEY

WHY IT TOOK TWENTIETH-CENTURY theologians so long to begin seriously theologizing about the arts remains a question until one recognizes that during the 20s and 30s serious thinkers in the church were preoccupied with denominational issues and the existential concerns of war and the need for peace in the world. All along, however, visual arts, literature, and music were in constant use in celebrating the Christian faith. Since ancient times, art had been subserviently used to religious ends: to teach, to remind, and to assist worshippers in their devotions. When the arts were finally given their due theologically, a variety of theologies were on the scene, offering different treatments due to the complexities associated with speaking either about "art" or "theology." I am not about to review the continuing debate among theologians concerning art—whether it is work done by Christian artists, work done to further the Christian mission, or creative work unrelated to religion.[1] Nor do I intend to offer a theological defense of art.[2] I want rather to share with you some of what three theologians, two of whom I knew, have had to say about the deep religious significance they discovered in great music. Listening to their message will help us to appreciate anew how great music serves heart and mind and life in the way it engages us, opens us, speaks to us, and helps us speak back to the inner self, to each other, and to God.

Like speech, music is a form of communication. Rightly understood, music is dialogical: it is personally made, created, and composed to show forth and share something worthy of a response. Music is potentially

1. Jarrett-Kerr, "Theology and the Arts," in *The Scope of Theology*, 199–214.
2. Hazelton, *A Theological Approach to Art*, 9–32.

revelatory by embodying what it seeks to share and by what it uses to evoke.³ Unlike speech, however, music is not immediately representational, by which I mean that it does not state facts or convey information in the same way that straightforward language does.

Music communicates by means of the functions it can serve. As sound, music can serve to imitate some of the many sounds of nature. As sound, it can be used to stimulate thought, it can move one to dance, and it can influence the mood to weep or rejoice. Much depends upon the way the sounds (notes, tones) are organized and utilized. The communication that music allows and generates, however, is best experienced when it results in a felt sense of order, when it inspires feelings that positively affect one's judgment about life and living, when it grants a psychological and spiritual sense of meaning.

Great music communicates. It speaks to us personally, arousing our emotions, but it also speaks about something beyond us by giving us a framework by which to order our lives. Igor Stravinsky voiced it well in his Norton Lectures at Harvard (1939–1940) when he stated that the profound meaning and aim of music are best experienced and understood when music "promote[s] a communion, a union of man with his fellow-man and with the Supreme Being."⁴

With this in mind, we turn now to listen to three theologians who understood and experienced this as they encountered composers whose music spoke clearly and deeply to them.

KARL BARTH (1886–1968)

Considered by all as one of the most important theologians of the twentieth century, Karl Barth, the Swiss theologian, was considered by many as the most influential one. The long-time professor of systematic theology at the University of Basel, Switzerland, founder of neo-orthodoxy, and author of the erudite and demanding multi-volume *Church Dogmatics*, Karl Barth is credited with rescuing theology from the throes of a sterile liberalism by his emphasis on divine transcendence. Thinking of Barth as a teaching theologian, Daniel Jenkins commented in print that "Barth [was] incomparable at uncovering for us again the peaks of theology in their full majesty."⁵ Thinking of Barth as the pastoral preacher he continued to be even after he left the pastorate, David G. Buttrick commented that, "[m]ore than any

---

3. See Hazelton, *A Theological Approach to Art*, esp. 50–87.
4. Stravinsky, *Poetics of Music*, 18.
5. Jenkins, "Karl Barth," 106.

thinker in the century, Barth linked theology and preaching: He proposed that theology should be 'nothing other than sermon preparation.' Thus, to enter his deliberations on preaching is to enter his theological world."[6]

Barth was not only a preacher with passionate conviction, and a theologian who uncovered "the peaks of theology in their full majesty" as a teacher, he was also a listener of great music and an enthusiastic advocate for the music of Wolfgang Amadeus Mozart (1756–1791), whose music he thought angels could rightly play for their enjoyment.

In a little book published to celebrate the two-hundredth anniversary of Mozart's birth, Karl Barth included a testimonial to Mozart's greatness, a letter of thanks to Mozart, a brief biographical treatment of Mozart, and an address he delivered on the occasion of a commemorative celebration of Mozart. In the testimonial to Mozart's greatness, Barth explained that Mozart's music was the first he remembered hearing as a child, and that for years, as an adult, he had begun each day with listening to that master. Why? Because in Mozart he heard a beautiful and masterful art of playing that "presupposes an intuitive, childlike awareness of the essence or center—as also the beginning and the end of all things. It is from this center," Barth stated, "from this beginning and end, that I hear Mozart create his music." "And when I hear him, it gladdens, encourages, and comforts me as well."[7] In his "Letter of Thanks to Mozart," Barth wrote:

> What I thank you for is simply this: Whenever I listen to you, I am transported to the threshold of a world which in sunlight and storm, by day and by night, is a good and ordered world ... with an ear open to your musical dialectic, one can be young and become old, can work and rest, be content and sad: in short, one can live.[8]

In his address for the commemorative celebration honoring Mozart's music, Barth stated: "Mozart's music always sounds unburdened, effortless, and light. This is why it unburdens, releases, and liberates us."[9] Barth later extolled Mozart's music as "free from all exaggeration, of all sharp breaks and contradictions. The sun shines but does not blind, does not burn or consume." He continued:

> Heaven arches over the earth, but it does not weigh it down, it does not crush or devour it. Hence earth remains earth, with no need to maintain itself in a titanic revolt against heaven.

6. Buttrick, "Foreword," to Karl Barth, *Homiletics*, 8.
7. Barth, *Wolfgang Amadeus Mozart*. 16–17.
8. Ibid., 22
9. Ibid., 47

Granted, darkness, chaos, death and hell do appear, but not for a moment are they allowed to prevail. Knowing all, Mozart creates music from a mysterious center, and so observes limits to the right and the left, above and below.[10]

As for that Mozartean "center" from which the music issued, Barth explained that "What occurs in Mozart is rather a glorious upsetting of the balance, a turning in which the light rises and the shadows fall, though without disappearing, in which joy overtakes sorrow without extinguishing it, in which the Yearnings louder than the ever-present Nay."[11] Hearing Mozart's music on a daily basis strengthened Barth as he dealt with the opposing aspects of life, from a center faith in which God's "Yes!" always rang louder in his soul than Satan's "No!"

HOWARD THURMAN (1900–1981)

Howard Thurman's gifted witness was nationally recognized in 1953 when he was cited by *Life* Magazine as one of America's twelve greatest preachers. His identity as an influential clergyman, educator, and theologian had long been proverbial within African American circles. Dean of Andrew Rankin Chapel at Howard University from 1932–1944, Thurman had gone west to co-pastor (with Alfred G. Fisk, a white minister) the Church for the Fellowship of All People in San Francisco, California, which was the first interracial, intercultural, interfaith congregation of its kind in the nation. His later leadership at Boston University as dean of Marsh Chapel (1953–1964) allowed him to model racial inclusiveness in an even more diverse setting and gave him another base from which to share his message of reconciliation and human unity. Several of the twenty-one books Thurman authored present with clarity his penetrating insights on religious faith and public life. His was a prophetic spirituality that drew from the universal in handling the particular, a spirituality that seeks relation to both God and others in genuine trust. It was Thurman's view that authentic religious experience infuses life with meaning, and that it enables one to go beyond the claims of custom, convention, culture, and race, acting always with concern to see deeply, live vitally, and to share one's life and findings with others.

Like Karl Barth, Howard Thurman grew up with an expressed love for one particular composer. His preferred composer was Ludwig van Beethoven (1770–1827). Although interested in Beethoven's musical

---

10. Ibid., 53
11. Ibid., 55

creations, Thurman was interested as well in what those creations reflected and in the life issues that helped to spawn them. Thurman was not as interested in musical theory as his wife Sue, a graduate of Oberlin Conservatory, but he discovered that to understand Beethoven's unique musical output he needed the help of musical analysts and strategic reference works. Here is how he spoke about the quest to understand Beethoven:

> For years I have worked at unlocking the doors to understanding the late quartets. One of the private ambitions of my life is to feel as much at home with them as I do now with the Seventh and Ninth symphonies.[12]

Thurman had learned to play a musical instrument—a B-flat clarinet—while dean of Rankin Chapel at Howard University, but from childhood he had always wanted to make music, and to make it complete with all the subtle nuances possible to someone gifted and trained to do so, but alas, he was not thus gifted; he had no "active companionship," as he put it, "with the tools needed to be a composer."

His wife, Sue Bailey Thurman, considered Mozart as *the* composer, and Mozart's birthday was celebrated annually in the Thurman home. As regards Mozart, Howard Thurman explained, "I revel in Mozart's music, but he is not the angel who soothes troubled waters. Now Beethoven! That is a different matter." He went on to say, "There is a massive vitality in Beethoven's music that consumes all foibles and mediocrities, leaving only an irreducible reality."[13] And notice this admission: "If I could share the mystery of the lonely giant Beethoven I would have the clue to my own solitariness."[14] That statement is very revealing.

Beethoven said that he composed music in keeping with a *Bild* in his mind.[15] The word *Bild*, in German, can be understood generally to mean, "picture," but Beethoven understood and used it as denoting a conception, a construct, a *realization*.

Listening avidly to the music of Beethoven's late period, particularly the quartets, Thurman sensed depths in them that bespoke such realizations. In his late works Beethoven was exploring deep regions of human consciousness; he was unbarring his soul, speaking openly and uniquely from his inward center to express to the world what he now realized. Deaf then, and emotionally isolated from the world, Beethoven was not nourished

---

12. Thurman, *With Head and Heart*: 248.
13. Ibid., 248.
14. Ibid.
15. Dahlhaus, *Nineteenth-Century*, 364.

by human speech and contacts but by personal ruminations and granted realizations. He had reached new levels of awareness, and he composed to express what he had inwardly realized.

Howard Thurman trembled inwardly at times while listening to Beethoven's revolutionary cadences move slowly along, as they sometimes hovered before rushing forward in a surge of sound that transfixed him. When the last chords subsided, the forcefulness of a felt silence continued to speak to his soul. It all meant so much: the shocking accents spoke to Thurman about suddenness in life; the indeterminate chords reflected the uncertain ties in life; fragmentary phrases reflected experienced limitations; throbbing drum beats pin-pointed instances of dread; gathering crescendos highlighted the expected experience of breaking free. There was nothing aimless in such music, nothing pointlessly self-absorbed, nothing without meaning. Trills were understood as more than the prolonged and rapid alternation of two neighboring tones, they were often a gesture of longing, questing; they were footprints of a devotional journey, a ceremonial progression to finality, an affirmation of a realization achieved.

Strangely, but uniquely in the quartets, Beethoven stretched out on a form so creatively as to link differing styles and even contrasting elements to serve his purpose. In his listening, particularly to the B-flat, Op. 130 quartet complete with the *Grosse Fuge,* Thurman was challenged yet comforted and centered through Beethoven's achievement in linking and unifying melancholy with merriment, caprice with order, laughter with tears, assertion with submission, movement with stillness, inward weariness with spiritual rest. Thurman understood what John W. N. Sullivan wrote about Beethoven's spiritual development as reflected in his late music, that the music "radiate[s], as it were, from a central experience."[16] According to Sullivan, "This is characteristic of the mystic vision, to which everything in the world appears unified in the light of one fundamental experience."[17] Small wonder, then, that Howard Thurman confessed, "If I could share the mystery of the lonely giant Beethoven I would have the clue to my own solitariness."

When he was scheduled to preach, Howard Thurman sometimes listened to something by Beethoven, something with "intimations of the sacred," to help get him ready. Thurman felt blessed by Beethoven's final way with music, and he, in his preaching, blessed others by his way with words and pauses. Just as Beethoven expands a musical line, offering small harmonic shifts and sequences, deferring action to give the hearer a sense of

---

16. Sullivan, *Beethoven: His Spiritual Development,* 154.
17. Ibid., 198–212.

space, forcing an introspective attitude, so did Howard Thurman preach: he offered an idea-flow, using a substance-style approach, and his word-pause-thought tension helped hearers to experience a realization of truth.[18] I can warmly witness to this, having known Dr. Thurman at close range across more than thirty years.

III. JAROSLAV PELKAN (1923–2006)

I remember well the time I met Jaroslav Pelikan, and the place. We were at the Seattle airport, seated on the same row of an airplane about to depart to San Francisco. I had just fulfilled an engagement in Seattle and was on my way to San Francisco to visit Mrs. Sue Thurman, who was now a widow: Dr. Pelikan had also fulfilled an engagement and was on his way to fulfill another.

I had boarded earlier, and was seated in the bulkhead row at the window, reading a book. As the plane was preparing for take off, I noticed that the passenger sitting one seat over also had a book propped up in his hands, and the title on the book jacket identified the contents as theological. I realized that I had seen the man's face before, so I leaned over and politely ventured a question: "Pardon me, Sir, but aren't you Dr. Jaroslav Pelikan?" He turned humanely toward me, and with a polite voice he quietly answered, "Yes, I am."

That was how I met Dr. Jaroslav Pelikan, *Doctor Ecclesiae*. I knew that I had interrupted his reading, but the impact of the occasion of meeting emboldened me to voice my thanks for the many books of his, which were in my personal library. Dr. Pelikan graciously thanked me for my comments and briefly shared himself in talk. Mindful of the book in his hands, and the book in mine, I did not wish to disturb him further, so I readily apologized for having interrupted him earlier, and we each returned to our reading.

There, seated near me on the plane, was a noted scholar, the Sterling Professor of Ecclesiastical History at Yale Divinity School; a distinguished theologian whose life was devoted to teaching Christian doctrine, one who across his career had been sharing from his vast learning about how Christian doctrine has been transmitted, developed, interpreted, questioned, opposed and defended.

Dr. Pelikan died some years later. Robert Louis Wilken, a history of Christianity professor at the University of Virginia and a former student of Pelikan's, commented in a memorial article that "More than any other scholar, [Pelikan] gave the history of Christian thought a public face in the

18. Massey, "Thurman's Preaching: Substance and Style," 110–21

United States."[19] A polymath, Pelikan had the rare and enviable record of going successively and successfully beyond the boundaries of any one particular period or language in church history, and he could trace in writing the continuities and discontinuities of all the subjects connected therewith. His *Christian Tradition: A History of the Development of Doctrine*, a five-volume work, is a monumental and magisterial accomplishment.

Jaroslav Pelikan loved the music of Johann Sebastian Bach (1685–1750). Bach was a musical genius, an intellectual giant, a zealous student, a master in the Baroque form, and a man with firm religious beliefs. He viewed his musical creations as an expression of his devotion to God, and he wrote on his scores "Soli Deo Gloria " because each composition was prepared with the glory of God as its goal. Given his upbringing in the Lutheran Church, his reading of Luther's German Bible, and his fondness for chorales, it has been said "Bach would not have achieved greatness without his Christian faith."[20] While that statement is arguable, what we can say for sure is that Bach's greatness did not spoil his faith. Jaroslav Pelikan, like many others, was deeply impressed by faiths significance in Bach's life. Using an historian's accuracy and a theologian's sensibility, Pelikan deftly traced Bach's path, examined his productivity, and wrote about the profundity of Bach's music as it reflects and speaks to faith, especially the Christian faith. Bach's music was informed not only by his compositional abilities but also by his theological insights. Johann Sebastian Bach was a musician equipped with theological competence.[21]

Jaroslav Pelikan wrote a book about Bach and it was published m 1986, in time to celebrate the three-hundredth anniversary of Bach's birth. The study was of Bach and the theological message reflected in his work in the context of his time, which was the first half of the Eighteenth Century. Speaking about his interest in Bach's sacred music, and particularly the Passions and the B-Minor Mass, Pelikan stated:

> "As a historian of the development of Christian doctrine, I have taken a greater scholarly interest than many of my predecessors in its liturgical and biblical context. Having now come, in my work on the fifth and final volume of *The Christian Tradition*, to the period of Bach, I have, here in *Bach Among the Theologians*, employed the texts of his sacred music as a case study in the methodological problem of how to handle the liturgical and biblical setting of Christian thought. My underlying conviction

---

19. Wilken, "Jaroslav Pelikan, Doctor Ecclesiae," 202–6, respectively.
20. Vaughan, Foreword, xii.
21. Wolff, Johann Sebastian Bach: The Learned Musician 240–241.

is that both the Christian tradition and the music of Bach can be understood better through such scholarly investigation."[22]

That slim but weighty volume was Pelikan's scholarly tribute to one whose music he loved, a musician whose life blended the sacred and the secular since he knew that God is both Creator and Redeemer; a musician whose faith inspired him to begin each musical composition with the written plea "Jesu Juva [Jesus, help]" and to close it by penning "Soli Deo Gloria [to God alone be glory]." In his memorial article about Jaroslav Pelikan, Robert Wilken reported about visiting with him a few weeks before Pelikan died in May 2006. Pelikan was gravely ill from terminal lung cancer, and Wilken had traveled from Virginia to visit him at his home in Connecticut. The two scholars talked of several things, but especially about scholarship in the Church Fathers, the strange ways of God, and music. Pelikan mentioned that he was spending time listening to Bach's music, and in particular to Bach's B-minor Mass (BWV 232). As they talked about Bach, Pelikan told Wilken about the occasions when conductor Robert Shaw had invited him to give a theological lecture in connection with the performance of some great religious choral work Shaw was to conduct at Carnegie Hall in New York. There was one occasion, Pelikan reported, when Shaw conducted Bach's St. Matthew Passion, but "before he lifted his baton to begin the performance, "[Shaw] addressed the audience. He said that for some in the audience this evening, this would be the first time you will hear the St. Matthew Passion; for others, it will be the last time. Then he turned to the orchestra and choir to begin the opening chorus."[23] Johann Sebastian Bach's Mass in B-minor (BWV 232) was that God honoring composer's last choral composition— and the last musical work to which Jaroslav Pelikan consciously gave his listening ear. That choral work is a mighty setting with breadth of styles and theological depth, and it summarizes in an artistically polished fashion Bach's writing for voice. That Pelikan was listening to that work during his last days throws light on how great music assisted his worship and faith as he awaited an imminent death.

I have examined, albeit briefly, testimonials from three preacher theologians about the role and effects of great music in their life. As for referring to them as "preacher-theologians": Karl Barth was an ordained Swiss Reformed Church minister; Howard Thurman was an ordained American Baptist minister; and Jaroslav Pelikan was an ordained minister in the Lutheran Church before his late move to the Orthodox Church. Both Barth and Thurman continued pulpit work throughout their careers, but Pelikan

---

22. Pelikan, *Bach*, x.
23. Wilken, "Jaroslav Pelikan, Doctor Ecclesiae," 21.

is remembered mainly as an academician. Martin E. Marty, a former student of Pelikan's, commented in his memorial article honoring the learned historian: "Some Christian scholars wanted Pelikan to show his churchly and 'ordained' sides more. But his vocation, he always said, was 'arts and sciences' and the place of theology among them. "[24] However one ranks Jaroslav Pelikan, whether as a preacher-theologian or mainly as a teacher-theologian, the witness he gave concerning the effects of great music in his life remains. Great music communicates. It speaks to us personally, and it speaks to us about something more than ourselves. Thomas Carlyle understood this, and wrote: "Who is there that, in logical words, can express the effect music have on us? A kind of inarticulate unfathomable speech, which leads us to the edge of the Infinite, and lets us for moments gaze into that!"[25]

BIBLIOGRAPHY

Buttrick, David G. Foreword to *Homiletics* by Karl Barth, edited by Geoffrey W. Bromiley and Donald E. Daniels, 8. Louisville: Westminster John Knox, 1991.

———. *Wolfgang Amadeus Mozart*. Translated by Clarence K. Pott. Grand Rapids: Eerdmans, 1986.

Buttrick, David G. *Homiletics*. Translated by by Geoffrey W. Bromiley and Donald E. Daniels. Louisville: Westminster John Konx, 1991.

Carlyle, Thomas. *On Heroes, Hero Worship, and the Heroic in History*. Edited by Archibald MacMecham. Boston: Ginn, 1901.

Dahlhaus, Carl. *Nineteenth-Century Music*. Berkeley: University of California Press, 1989.

George, Timothy. *Theology of the Reformers*. Rev. ed. Nashville: Broadman & Holman, 2013.

———. "Delighted by Doctrine: A Tribute to Jaroslav Pelikan," *Christian History* 91 (Summer 2006) 43-45.

Hazelton, Roger. *New Accents in Contemporary Theology*. New York: Harper & Row, 1960.

———. *A Theological Approach to Art*. Nashville: Abingdon, 1967.

Jenkins, Daniel. "Karl Barth." In *A Handbook of Christian Theologians,* edited by Dean G. Peerman and Martin E. Marty. Cleveland: World, 1965.

Jarrett-Kerr, Martin. "Theology and the Arts." In *The Scope of Theology,* edited by Daniel T. Jenkins. Cleveland: World, 1968.

Massey, James Earl. "Thurman's Preaching: Substance and Style." In *God and Human Freedom: A Festschrift in Honor of Howard Thurman*, edited by Henry James Young, 110–21. Richmond, IN: Friends United, 1982.

Marty, Martin E. "Head Cases: The Mental Health of Sanits and Presidents." M.E.M.O., *Christian Century* 123, no. 17 (2006). https://www.christiancentury.org/article/2006-08/head-cases

---

24. Marty, "M.E.M.O.," 47.
25. Carlyle, *On Heroes, Hero-Worship, and the Heroic in History*, 95.

Pelikan, Jaroslav. *Bach among the Theologians*. Philadelphia: Fortress, 1986.
Solomon, Maynard. *Late Beethoven: Music, Thought, Imagination*. Berkeley: University of California Press, 2003.
Stravinsky, Igor. *Poetics of Music: In the Form of Six Lessons*. Translated by Arthur Knodel and Ingolf Dahl. Cambridge, MA: Harvard University Press, 1970.
Sullivan, John W. N. *Beethoven: His Spiritual Development*. New York: Vintage, 1960.
Thurman, Howard. *With Head and Heart: The Autobiography of Howard Thurman*. New York: Harcourt Brace Jovanovitch, 1979.
Vaughan, David J. Foreword to *Glory and Honor: The Musical and Artistic Legacy of Johann Sebastian Bach*, by Gregory Wilbur, xi–xiii. Nashville: Cumberland House, 2005.
Wilken, Robert Louis. "Jaroslav Pelikan, Doctor Ecclesiae." *First Things* 165 (2006). https://www.firstthings.com/article/2006/08/jaroslav-pelikan-doctor-ecclesiae.
Wolff, Christoph. *Johann Sebastian Bach: The Learned Musician*. New York: Norton, 2000.

Engagement, Constitutional Structures, and Civic Virtues

Robert P. George

Those of us who are citizens of liberal democratic regimes do not refer to those who govern as "rulers." It is our boast that we rule ourselves. And there is truth in this, inasmuch as we participate in choosing those who do rule. So we prefer to speak of them not as our rulers, but as servants—public servants, or at least as people being in "public service." Of course, these so-called servants are nothing remotely like the servants in "Downtown Abbey" or "Upstairs Downstairs" or "The Duchess of Duke Street." The extraordinary prestige and usually the trappings attaching to public office, in just about all times, and in just about all places, would by themselves be sufficient to distinguish, say, the Governor of New York or the President of the United States from Carson the Butler. But that prestige signals an underlying fact that discomfits our democratic and egalitarian sensibilities, namely, the fact that even in liberal democratic regimes high public officials are rulers. They make rules, enforce them, and resolve disputes about their meaning and applicability. To a very large extent, at the end of the day, what they say goes.

Of course, our rulers rule, not by dint of sheer power, the way the mafia might do in a territory over which it happens to have gained control, but rather lawfully.[1] Constitutional rules specify public offices and settle procedures for filling them. Whether the constitution exists in the form of a specific document, such as the Constitution of the United States or of the Constitution of Commonwealth of Massachusetts or Virginia, or in some other form, as in the United Kingdom and New Zealand, it constitutes, in a sense, the set of rules governing the rulers—rules that both

---

1. Rule of Law in "Reason, Freedom, and the Rule of Law," 249–56.

empower office-holders to make and execute decisions of various sorts and limit their powers. So, though they are rulers, they are not absolute rulers. Constitutional rules set the scope, and thus the limits, of their jurisdiction and authority. They are rulers who are subject to rules—rules they do not themselves make and cannot easily or purely on their own initiative revise or repeal. They rule in limited ways, and ordinarily for limited terms (which may or may not be indefinitely renewable at the pleasure of voters). They rule by virtue of democratic processes by which they came to hold office. They can be removed or significantly disempowered at the next election if the people are not happy with them. Still, they rule.

Now, my point is not to hoot at the idea of government, and those holding governmental offices and controlling the levers of governmental power, as "servants." On the contrary, I want, in the end, to defend the idea that rulers truly can be servants. I want to establish, however, that if these people we call public servants are, indeed, servants, they are servants in a special sense, a sense that is compatible with them at the same time being rulers. They are people who serve us by ruling. They serve us well by ruling well. If they rule badly, they serve us poorly—indeed, they disserve us.

There are, of course, lots of ways that rulers can disserve those whom they have a moral obligation to serve by ruling well. Most obviously, there is incompetence. Then, of course, there is corruption. And at the extreme, there is tyranny. So what does it mean for the ruler to truly be a servant? What does it mean for someone holding political office and exercising public power to rule well?

It means making and executing decisions for the sake of the common good. Such decisions will necessarily be compatible with the requirements of justice and at the same time embody justice. If we understand the concept of the common good properly—and I will say a word about that in a moment—then we will see that no decision that violates a requirement of justice is truly for the common good; and no decision that genuinely upholds and serves the common good will fail to advance the cause of justice.

It is also important to note that decisions can fail to serve the common good and can, indeed, damage the common good, even when they are not unjust. Even honorably motivated and well-intentioned people, including rulers, can make decisions that harm the common good because they are inexpedient, imprudent, or unwise. Holders of public office, like anyone else, can make poor, even disastrous, decisions even when acting on the purest and best of motives. Poor decisions by well-intentioned public officials can trigger or prolong a great depression; lead a nation into an unnecessary and even disastrous war, or prevent a nation from going to war to protect its people and their vital interests when it should have done; undermine or weaken the marriage culture and with it family life and everything in a society that depends on the health and vibrancy of marriage and the family.

It is worth adding here that reasonable people of goodwill can, and obviously do, disagree about what the common good requires and forbids, and what is, in truth, just and unjust.[2] Honorable people exercising public power can commit injustices—even grave injustices—while seeking, in good faith, to do justice, and believing in good faith that they are doing it. So, just as not all violations of the common good are injustices, not all injustices are the result of malice, ill-will, or like vices. Still, all injustices, even if committed by officials who are sincerely trying to do the right thing, harm the common good. For justice is itself *a* common good and a central aspect of *the* common good of the political community. It is to the benefit of each and every citizen to live in a just social order; and harm to that order is therefore a loss for everyone, and not merely for the immediate and obvious victims of any particular injustice. Indeed, it is a loss even for the ostensible beneficiaries of injustices, and, indeed, even for their perpetrators—though, naturally, true evildoers don't see it that way. Corruption of character narrows their vision of the good, blinding them to the profound respects in which wrongdoing harms what is, in truth, *their* interest in living in a just society, as well as everyone else's.

The common good requires that there be rulers and that they actually rule. To grasp this is to begin to see the sense in which good rulers are also servants. Members of societies face a range—sometimes a vast range—of challenges and opportunities requiring both means-to-ends and persons-to-persons coordination, including, in the case of complex societies, coordination problems presented by the large number and the complexity of other coordination problems. Since such problems cannot, as a practical matter, be addressed and resolved by unanimity, authority—political authority—is required.[3] Institutions will have to be created and maintained, and persons will need to be installed in the offices of these institutions, to make the choices and decisions that must be made, and to do the things that need to be done, for the sake of protecting public health, safety, and morals, upholding the rights and dignity of individuals, families, and non-governmental entities of various descriptions, and advancing the overall common good.

This would be true even in a society of perfect saints, where no one ever sought more than his fair share from the common stock, or violated the rights of others, or deliberately acted in any manner that was contrary to the common good. Even in such a society, effective coordination for the

---

2. "Law, Democracy, and Moral Disagreement," 1388–1406.
3. Finnis, *Natural Law and Natural Rights*, chap. 9.

sake of common goals, and, thus, for the good of all, would be required; and seeking unanimity, assuming a large and fairly complex society, would not be a practical option.[4] So, authority would be required, and that means persons exercising authority—rulers, ruling.

But the moral justification for the rulers' ruling is service to the good of all, the common good. And the common good is not an abstraction or platonic form hovering somewhere beyond the concrete well-being-the flourishing-of the flesh-and-blood persons constituting the community. It just *is* the well-being of those persons and of the families and other associations of persons—Burke's "little platoons" of civil society—of which they are members. The right of legitimate rulers to rule is rooted in the duty of rulers to rule in the interest of all—in other words, the basis of the *right* to rule is the *duty* to serve. And the realities that constitute the content of service are the various elements of the common good. By doing what is for the common good, and by avoiding doing anything that harms the common good, rulers fulfill their obligations to the people over whom they exercise authority—thus, serving their interests, their welfare, their flourishing, in a word, *them*.

I don't know how to improve on the definition of the common good proposed by John Finnis in his magisterial book *Natural Law and Natural Rights* (which Oxford University has now put out in a 2nd edition and published alongside five volumes of his collected essays). The common good, Finnis says, is to be understood as *"a set of conditions which enables the members of a community to attain for themselves reasonable objectives, or to realize reasonably for themselves the value(s) for the sake of which they have reason to collaborate with each other (positively and/or negatively) in a community."*[5] Now every community—from the basic community of a family, to a church or other community of religious faith, to a mutual aid society or other civic association, to a business firm—will have a common good. The common good of some communities is fundamentally an intrinsic good rather than an instrumental good. That is true, for example, of the community of the family. Although families serve many valuable, and some indispensable, instrumental purposes, the point of the family is not exhausted by these purposes, nor do they define what the family is. The most fundamental point of being a member of the family is, simply, being a member of the family—enjoying the intrinsic benefit of being part of that distinctive network of mutual obligation, care, love, and support. The same is true, in Christian and Jewish thought, at least, of the common good of the

---

4. Finnis, "Law as Co-ordination," 97–104.
5. Finnis, *Natural Law and Natural Rights*, 155.

community of faith. Though communities of faith characteristically serve many valuable instrumental purposes, the most fundamental purpose of Israel or the Church is to be the people of God. Things are obviously different when it comes to, say, business firms. Although there are ordinarily many opportunities for principals and employees of companies to realize intrinsic or basic human goods (including goods that are fundamentally social, such as the good of friendship) in their collaborations in pursuit of the firms' objectives, those objectives are the ends to which the firm and the cooperation of those working in and for it are means.

Now, what about the common good of the political community—the common good served by good rulers (and to which citizens also have responsibilities)? Is it fundamentally an intrinsic good or an instrumental good? There is, in what Sir Isaiah Berlin referred to as the central tradition of western thought[6] about morality, including political morality, a powerful current of belief that the common good of political society is an intrinsic good. This seems clearly to have been the view of Aristotle, and many self-identified Thomists are firmly convinced that it was the view of Aristotle's greatest interpreter and expositor, St. Thomas Aquinas. Finnis, however, argues that the common good of political society, though, to quote Aristotle, "great and godlike" in its range and importance, is nevertheless fundamentally an instrumental, not an intrinsic, good.[7] And he further argues that the instrumental nature of the common good of political society entails limitations of the legitimate scope of governmental authority—limitations that, though not in every case easily articulable in the language of rights, are requirements of justice. Although I have a difference, at the margins, with Professor Finnis, who (along with Joseph Raz) was my graduate supervisor in Oxford, on the question of just what the limits are (and, in particular, whether they exclude in principle moral paternalism), I agree that the common good of political society is fundamentally an instrumental good and that this entails moral limits on justified governmental power.[8]

The way we have come to think of these limits is in terms of what is usually called the doctrine of subsidiarity. This is a sound doctrine, though the label has now been appropriated by some people who, for whatever reason, want the use of the word without actually signing on to the doctrine. Without implying bad faith on anyone's part, this amounts to an abuse, and destabilizes the word's meaning in a way that may eventually render

---

6. Berlin, *The Crooked Timber of Humanity: Chapters in the History of Ideas*, 208.

7. Finnis, "Is Natural Law Theory Compatible with Limited Government?," 1–26, esp. 5–9.

8. George, "The Concept of Public Morality," 17–31.

it useless. Still, we have no better word or label at the moment, so let's just try to be clear in our minds about what the doctrine actually holds. Eighty years ago, Pope Pius XI, in the encyclical letter *Quadragesimo Anno* (1931), explained the basic idea:

> *"Just as it is wrong to withdraw from the individual and commit to a group what private initiative and effort can accomplish, so too it is wrong . . . for a larger and higher association to arrogate to itself functions which can be performed efficiently by smaller and lower associations. This is a fixed, unchanged, and most weighty principle of moral philosophy . . . . Of its very nature the true aim of all social activity should be to help members of a social body, and never to absorb or destroy them."*

Now, this principle of justice and the common good reflects a particular understanding of the nature and content of human flourishing. Flourishing consists in *doing things*, not just in getting things, or having desirable or pleasant experiences, or having things done for you. The good, as Aristotle taught, consists in activity.[9] Human goods are realized by acting—one *participates* in them—thus enriching one's life and even ennobling oneself as one exercises and fulfills one's natural human capacities (for example, one's capacities for friendship, knowledge, critical aesthetic appreciation).

And so, the common good, is, as Finnis remarked, best conceived as a *set of conditions*. But, we must ask, conditions for what? Well, let's recall Professor Finnis' definition: conditions for enabling members of a community to attain *for themselves* reasonable objectives, or to realize reasonably *for themselves* the value(s) for the sake of which they have reason to collaborate with each other in a community. The common good is, in this sense, facilitative. Its elements are what enable people to do things, individually and in cooperation with others, the doing of which to a significant degree constitutes their all-round or integral flourishing. Under favoring conditions, people can more fully and more successfully carry out reasonable projects, pursue reasonable objectives, and, thus, participate in values—including some values that are inherently social in that they fulfill persons in respect of capacities for non-instrumental forms of interpersonal communion—that are indeed constitutive of their well-being and fulfillment.

Properly understood, then, the common good requires, as a matter of justice, limited government—government that respects the needs and rights of people to pursue objectives and realize goods *for themselves*. The fundamental role of legitimate government, and thus the responsibility of legitimate rulers—rulers who serve—is not to be doing things for people

---

9. Suppes, "The Aims of Education," 110–26.

that they could do for themselves; it is, rather to be helping to establish and maintain conditions that favor people's doing things for themselves, and with and for each other. Governments should do things *for* people (as opposed to letting them do things *for themselves*), only where individuals and non-governmental institutions of civil society cannot do them, or cannot reasonably be expected to do them for themselves. Finnis used the word "enable," and it is the right word here: Government's legitimate concern is with the establishment and maintenance of the *conditions* under which members of the community are *enabled* to pursue the projects and goals by and through which they participate in the goods constitutive of their flourishing.

Now, this facilitative conception of the common good does not require a doctrinaire libertarianism either in the domain of political economy or social morality; but it clearly excludes corporatist and socialist policies that, to recall those words from Pius XI, "withdraw from the individual and commit to the group what private individual and effort can accomplish," or which remove from the family or religious or civic association and commit to government what can be accomplished by non-governmental collaborative effort. Surely a conception of the common good that is serious about the principle of subsidiarity will respect private property and take care to maintain a reasonably free system of economic exchange—that is to say, a market economy. "Social" (i.e., comprehensive or even widespread state) ownership of the means of production is plainly incompatible with subsidiarity's concerns and objectives, as is anything resembling a command economy. And this would be true even if the record of socialist states were benign when it came to respect for civil liberties and political freedom—which, on the whole, it certainly is not.

And it would be true even if, again contrary to the historical record, private property and the market system were not necessary as checks against the excessive concentration and abuse of power in the hands of public officials. But, as I've noted, the historical record demonstrates that private property and the market system, while not sufficient as guarantees against the concentration and abuse of political power, are for all intents and purposes necessary conditions for civil liberty and limited government. And there is a profound lesson in this for those of us who are interested in ensuring that rulers remain servants, ruling in the interest of citizens, and do not reduce citizens to a condition of dependency or servitude. For it is critical to the effective limitation of governmental power that there be substantial non-governmental centers of power in society. Private property and the market economy not only provide the conditions of social mobility, which is important to the common good in any modern or dynamic society, but also ensure that there are significant resources (and thus opportunities for people and the private associations they form) that are not in the control of governmental officials or the apparatus of the state. This diffusion of power benefits society as a whole, and not only those who immediately benefit economically from the possession of property or the ability to profit in the market. And I am not simply here talking about general prosperity, though that is yet another benefit of private property and the market system. I am talking about the benefit to all—in terms of liberty, opportunity, and security—of the diffusion of power.

This goes well beyond economics. If we understand the common good, if we have a grasp of what constitutes or is conducive to the flourishing of human beings and what is not, we will recognize that limited government is also important because it permits the functioning and flourishing of non-governmental institutions of civil society—those little platoons again, families, churches, etc.–that perform better than government could ever conceivably do the most essential health, education, and welfare functions and which play the primary role in transmitting to each new generation the virtues without which free societies cannot survive—basic honesty, integrity, self-restraint, concern for others and respect for their dignity and rights, civic mindedness, and the like.[10] These non-governmental authority structures represent another crucial way in which power is properly diffused and not concentrated in the hands of the state and its officials. They can play their role only when government is limited—for unlimited government always usurps their authority and destroys their autonomy, usually recruiting or commandeering them into being state functionary organs—and where they are playing their proper role they help to create conditions in which the ideal of limited government is much more likely to be realized and preserved, and its benefits enjoyed by the people.

I will return to the role of these institutions of civil society towards the end of my remarks, but now let me shift the discussion to the question of constitutional structural constraints on the powers of government. Historically, political theorists have focused on the need for such constraints as the most obvious and important way to ensure that governmental power remains limited and that rulers serve the people and do not become tyrants. And I myself think that constraints of this nature are important in this cause, though I will eventually get round to saying that they are likely to be effective only when they are a part of a larger picture in which they are supported by, and in turn support, other features of social life that help to keep government within its proper bounds, for the sake of the common

---

10. Berger and Neuhaus, *To Empower People.*

good. So, as important as they are, I would warn against placing too great an emphasis on constitutional structural constraints. The danger there is ignoring the other essential features.

The Constitution of the United States is famous for its "Madisonian system" of structural constraints on powers of the central government. More than 200 years of experience with the system gives us a pretty good perspective on both its strengths and its limitations. The major structural constraints are: 1) the doctrine of the general government as a government of delegated and enumerated, and therefore limited, powers; 2) the dual sovereignty of the general government and the states—with the states functioning as governments of general jurisdiction exercising generalized police powers (a kind of plenary authority), limited under the national constitution only by specific prohibitions or by grants of power to the general government, in a federal union; 3) the separation of legislative, executive, and judicial powers within the national government, creating a so-called "system of checks and balances" that limits the power of any one branch and, it is hoped, improves the quality of government by making the legislative and policy-making processes more challenging, slower, and more deliberative; and 4) the practice (nowhere expressly authorized in the text of the Constitution, but lay that aside for now) of constitutional judicial review by the federal courts.

Now, I often ask my students at the beginning of my undergraduate course on civil liberties how the framers of the Constitution of the United States sought to preserve liberty and prevent tyranny. It is, alas, a testament to the poor quality of civic education in the United States that almost none of the students can answer the question correctly. Nor, I suspect, could the editors of the *New York Times* or other opinion-shaping elites. The typical answer goes this way:

> Well, Professor, I can tell you how the framers of the Constitution sought to protect liberty and prevent tyranny. They attached to the Constitution a Bill of Rights to protect the individual and minorities against the tyranny of the majority; and they vested the power to enforce those rights in the hands of judges who serve for life, are not subject to election or recall, cannot be removed from office except on impeachment for serious misconduct, and are therefore able to protect people's rights without fear of political retaliation.

Now, this is about as wrong as you can get; but it is widely believed, and, as I say, not just by university students. None of the American founders, even among those who favored judicial review and regarded it as implicit in the Constitution, which not all did, believed that it was the central, or even a significant, constraint upon the power of the national government. Nor did they believe that the enforcement of Bill of Rights guarantees by courts would be an important way of protecting liberty. The Federalists—in the original sense of those who supported the proposed Constitution—generally opposed the addition of a Bill of Rights because they feared it would actually undermine what they regarded as the main structural constraints protecting freedom and preventing tyranny, namely, (1) the conception and public understanding of the general government, not as a government of general jurisdiction, but as a government of delegated and enumerated powers; and (2) the division of powers between the national government and the states in a system of dual sovereignty.[11] When political necessity forced the Federalists to yield to demands for a Bill of Rights (in the form of the first eight amendments to the Constitution), they took care to add two more amendments—the ninth and tenth—designed to reinforce the delegated powers doctrine and the federalism principles that they feared would be obscured or weakened by the inclusion of a Bill of Rights.

As for the way judicial review has functioned as a structural constraint in American history, suffice it to say that the practice has given Oxford University legal and political philosopher Jeremy Waldron, a fierce critic of judicial review, plenty of ammunition in making his case around the world against permitting judges to invalidate legislation on constitutional grounds.[12] The federal courts, and the Supreme Court in particular, have had their glory moments, to be sure, such as in the racial de-segregation case of *Brown v. Board of Education* in the 1950s, but they have also handed down decision after decision—from *Dred Scott v. Sandford* in the 1850s, which facilitated the expansion of slavery, to Lochner v. NewYork, which struck down state worker protection laws limiting working hours in industrial bakers to 20 hours per week, to *Roe v. Wade* in the 1970s, which legalized abortion throughout the United States—in which the justices have drawn severe criticism for overstepping the bounds of their own authority and unconstitutionally imposing their personal moral and political opinions on the entire nation. Quite apart from whatever one's views happen to be on slavery or worker protection laws or abortion, these decisions are widely regarded as usurpations of the authority of the democratically constituted people to govern themselves.

Moreover, since the 1930s, the courts have done very little indeed by way of exercising the power of judicial review to support the other

---

11. Hamilton, *Federalist Papers*, 84.
12. Waldron, "The Core of the Case Against Judicial Review," 1345–1406.

constitutional structural constraints on the exercise of central governmental power. A very small number of isolated decisions have struck down this or that specific piece of federal legislation as exceeding the delegated powers of the national government or trenching upon the reserved powers of the states, but that is about it.[13] Most recently, and spectacularly, the Supreme Court found a way, by a bare majority, to uphold what seemed to many to be a rather obvious case of constitutional overreaching by the national government—the imposition of an individual mandate requiring citizens to purchase health insurance coverage as part of President Obama's signature "Patient Protection and Affordable Care Act."[14] The government defended the mandate as a legitimate exercise of the expressly delegated power to regulate commerce among the several states. The trouble, of course, is that on its face the mandate does not appear to *regulate* commerce at all; it seems to force people into commerce—a particular kind of commerce—on pain of a financial penalty. Now, the Court's four liberal justices were willing to stick to what has become longstanding tradition for those in their ideological camp, namely, counting virtually anything the national government proposes to do as a legitimate exercise of the power to regulate interstate commerce if that's what the government says it is. The five more conservative justices were willing to say that whatever is going on with the imposition of a mandate to purchase health insurance, it is not regulating interstate commerce. One of the five, however, Chief Justice Roberts, decided to reinterpret the penalty as a *tax*. He then joined the four liberals to uphold the mandate and the legislation as a whole as constitutionally permissible.

That's odd, to say the least, in view of the fact that the Obama administration and its supporters in Congress had repeatedly and vociferously denied that the penalty was a tax during the debate leading up to the passage of the "Patient Protection and Affordable Care Act." And there are other constitutional questions that arise, and that were not addressed by the Chief Justice, if one regards the penalty as a tax.

Many critics of the decision say that the matter should not have ended up in the courts at all. Congress itself, and the President, they say, should have recognized and honored the fact that the Constitution does not empower the national government to impose a mandate on the people to purchase products, including health care coverage. Whether one agrees with that position or not, it should remind us that one of the problems with judicial review in general is that its practice tends to encourage the belief among legislators (and, worse still, among citizens more broadly) that the

---

13. See, for example, *United States v. Lopez*, 514 U.S. 549
14. *National Federation of Independent Business v. Sebelius*, 567

constitutionality of proposed legislation is not the concern of the people's elected representatives; if a proposed piece of legislation is unconstitutional, they say, then it is up to the courts to strike it down. But this is a travesty. For structural constraints to accomplish what they are meant to accomplish, for them to constrain the power of government as they are meant to do, the question of the constitutionality of legislation in light of those constraints is *everybody's* business—judges exercising judicial review, yes, but also legislators, executives, and the people themselves.

And that brings me to the critical, yet oddly neglected, subject of political culture. I mentioned Professor Waldron earlier. A few years ago, he visited his native New Zealand to read his countrymen the riot act about what he condemned as the abysmal quality of that nation's parliamentary debate. The bulk of his lecture was devoted to an analysis and critique of a range of factors leading to the impoverishment of legislative deliberation, warranting the stinging title he assigned to his lecture: "Parliamentary Recklessness." Its penultimate section, entitled "Parliamentary Debate," and offers thoroughly gloomy appraisal. But instead of ending there, offering no grounds for hope, he concludes with a section entitled "The Quality of Public Debate," in which he points to the possibility that the deficiencies of parliamentary debate may be at least partially compensated for by a higher quality of public debate, and even hints that a higher quality of public debate could prompt the reforms necessary to at least begin restoring the integrity of parliamentary debate. But he warns that things could also go the other way. The corruption of parliamentary debate could "infect [] the political culture at large," driving public debate down to the condition of parliamentary debate. A condition he chillingly described in the following terms:

Parliament becomes a place where the governing party thinks it has won a great victory when debate is closed down and measures are pushed through under urgency; and the social and political forum generally becomes a place where the greatest victory is drowning out your opponent with the noise that you can bring to bear. And then the premium is on name-calling, on who can bawl the loudest, who can most readily trivialize an opponent's position, who can succeed in embarrassing or shaming or if need be blackmailing into silence anyone who holds a different view.

So, in a sense, it is up to the people to decide whether they will rise above the corruption that has demeaned parliamentary politics or permit it to "infect the political culture at large." But "the people" are not some undifferentiated mass; they are *people,* you and me, individuals. Of course, considered as isolated actors there is not a lot that individuals can do to affect the political culture. But individuals can cooperate for greater effectiveness in prosecuting an agenda of conservation or reform, and they can create associations and institutions that are capable of making a difference—pressure groups, think tanks, even tea parties."

A critical element of any discussion of the quality of democratic deliberation and decision-making that amounts to anything more than hot air will be the indispensable role of non-governmental institutions of civil society—those little platoons, yet again—in sustaining a culture in which political institutions do what they are established to do, do it well, and don't do what they are not authorized to do. And so we must be mindful that bad behavior on the part of political institutions—which means bad behavior on the part of the people who exercise power as holders of public offices—can weaken, enervate, and even corrupt these institutions of civil society, rendering them for all intents and purposes impotent to resist the bad behavior and useless to the cause of political reform.

My point, and this is why I promised to return at the end to the importance of institutions of civil society, is that this is true generally, and it is certainly true with respect to the bad behavior of public officials who betray their obligations to serve by transgressing the bounds of their constitutional authority and the limits embodied in the doctrine of subsidiarity. Constitutional structural constraints are important, but they will be effective only where they are effectually supported by the people—that is, by the political culture. The people need to understand them and value them—value them enough to resist usurpations by their rulers even when unconstitutional programs offer immediate gratifications or the relief of urgent problems. This, in turn, requires certain virtues—strengths of character—among the people. But these virtues do not just fall down on people from the heavens. They have to be transmitted through the generations and nurtured by each generation. Madison said that "only a well-educated people can be permanently a free people." And that is true. It points to the fact that even the best constitutional structures, even the strongest structural constraints on governmental power, aren't worth the paper they are printed on if people do not understand them, value them, and have the will to resist the blandishments of those offering something tempting in return for giving them up or letting violations of them occur without swift and certain political retaliation. But it is also true that virtue is needed, and that's not merely a matter of improving civics teaching in homes and schools. The Constitution of the United States was famously defended by Madison in Federalist Paper Number 51 as "supplying, by opposite and rival interests, the defect of better motives." He made this point immediately after observing that the first task of government is to control the governed, and the second is to control itself. He allowed that "a dependence on the people is, no doubt the primary control on the government, but experience has taught mankind the necessity of auxiliary precautions"—hence, the constitutional structural constraints, among other things. But even in this formulation they do not stand alone; indeed, they are presented as secondary. What is also necessary, and, indeed, primary, is healthy and vibrant political culture—"a dependence on the people" to keep the rulers in line.

But that brings us back to the role and importance of virtue. John Adams understood as well as anyone the general theory of the Constitution. He was the ablest scholar and political theorist of the founding generation. He certainly got the point about "supplying the defect of better motives," yet he also understood that the health of political culture was an indispensable element of the success of the constitutional enterprise—an enterprise of ensuring that the rulers stay within the bounds of their legitimate authority and indeed be servants of the common good, servants of the people they rule. He remarked, "our Constitution is made for a moral and religious people" and "is wholly inadequate to the government of any other."[15] Why? Because a people lacking in virtue could be counted on to trade liberty for protection, for financial or personal security, for comfort, for being looked after, for being taken care of, for having their problems solved quickly. And there will always be people occupying or standing for public office who will be happy to offer the deal—an expansion of their power in return for what they can offer by virtue of that expansion.

So the question, then, is how to form people fitted out with the virtues making them worthy of freedom and capable of preserving constitutionally limited government, even in the face of strong temptations, which inevitably come, to compromise it away. Here we see the central political role and significance, I believe, of the most basic institutions of civil society—the family; the religious community; private organizations (such as the Boy Scouts) that are devoted to the inculcation of knowledge and virtue; private (often religiously based) educational institutions; and the like that are in the business of transmitting essential virtues. These are, indeed, as is often said, mediating institutions that provide a buffer between the individual and the power of the central state. It is ultimately the autonomy, integrity, and general flourishing of these institutions that will determine the fate of limited constitutional government. And this is not only because of their primary and indispensable role in transmitting virtues; it is also because their performance of health, education, and welfare functions is the only real alternative to the removal of these functions to "larger and higher associations," that is, to government. When government expands to play the primary role

---

15. Adams, *Message to the Officers of the First Brigade of the Third Division of the Militia of Massachusetts.*

in performing these functions, the ideal of limited government is soon lost, no matter the formal structural constraints of the Constitution. And the corresponding weakening of the status and authority of these institutions damages their ability to perform all of their functions, including their moral and pedagogical ones. With that, they surely lose their capacity to influence for good the political culture which, at the end of the day, is the whole shootin' match when it comes to whether the ruler can truly be a servant.

BIBLIOGRAPHY

Adams, John. *Message to the Officers of the First Brigade of the Third Division of the Militia of Massachusetts.* 1798. "From John Adams to Massachusetts Militia, 11 October 1798," *Founders Online*, National Archives, last modified November 26, 2017. http://founders.archives.gov/documents/Adams/99-02-02-3102. [This is an Early Access document from *The Adams Papers*. It is not an authoritative final version.]

Berlin, Isaiah. *The Crooked Timber of Humanity: Chapters in the History of Ideas.* New York: Knopf, 1991.

Berger, Peter L., and Richard John Neuhaus. *To Empower People.* Washington, DC: American Enterprise Institute, 1977.

Finnis, John. "The Concept of Public Morality." *American Journal of Jurisprudence* 45 (2000) 17–31.

———. *Fundamentals of Ethics.* Oxford: Oxford University Press, 1983.

———. "Is Natural Law Theory Compatible with Limited Government?" In *Natural Law, Liberalism, and Morality: Contemporary Essays*, edited by Robert P. George, 1–26. Oxford: Oxford University Press, 2001.

———. "Law as Co-Ordination." *Ratio Juris* 2 (1989) 97–103.

———. *Natural Law and Natural Rights.* 2nd ed. Oxford: Clarendon, 2011.

George, Robert P. *Natural Law, Liberalism, and Morality.* Oxford: Clarendon, 1996.

Hamilton, Alexander. "No. 84: Certain General and Miscellaneous Objections to the Constitution Considered and Answered." In *Federalist Papers*, by Alexander Hamilton, James Madison, and John Jay, edited by Mary Carolyn Waldrep, and Jim Miller, 417–25. Mineola, NY: Dover, 2014.

"Law, Democracy, and Moral Disagreement," *Harvard Law Review* 110 (1997).

National Federation of Independent Business v. Sebelius, 567 U.S. 2012.

Rasmussen, Douglas B. "Human Flourishing and the Appeal to Human Nature." In *Human Flourishing*, edited by E. F. Paul, F. T. Miller, and J. Paul, 1–43. New York: Cambridge University Press, 1999.

"Reason, Freedom, and the Rule of Law." *American Journal of Jurisprudence* 46 (2001) 249–56.

Suppes, Patrick. "The Aims of Education." In *The Philosophy of Education 1995*, edited by Alven Neiman. Urbana, Illinois: Philosophy Education Society, 1996.

United States v. Lopez. 514 U.S. 549. 1995.

Waldron, Jeremy. "The Core of the Case against Judicial Review." *Yale Law Journal* 115 (2006) 1346–1406.

Recovering the Faith
Timothy George's Theology Embodied in Beeson Chapel

WILLIAM H. WILLIMON

IN THE EARLY TWENTIETH Century, American Christians had divided into two intellectual camps—orthodoxy and liberalism.[1] While liberalism was a rather loose conglomeration of ideas and practices, its advocates saw it as a Christian response to some of the challenges presented by modernity by placing the faith in dialogue with modern philosophy, culture, and social movements. Charles Hodge and Benjamin Warfield mounted an able defense of Protestant orthodoxy and fundamentalism declared war on liberalism. Fundamentalism attempted to be the reverse image of liberalism yet fundamentalism with its thoroughly modern stress upon biblical literalism, detachment from the full sweep of ecclesial tradition, personal decision and free will, was itself a curious progeny of modernity.

It became difficult for liberalism in Christianity to defend itself against the charge that it had moved beyond a conversation with secular modernity to a full capitulation to the spirit of the age. For liberals *Creed* meant an illiberal restriction of the noble individual conscience. *Liturgy* meant the humanly contrived enforcement of religious affections. *Church* meant a stolid, thoroughly optional human institutional limitation on faith that was meant to be individual and personal.

As early as 1939 Yale theologian Robert Calhoun called for a third way between waning liberalism and rigid orthodoxy, Christian theology that was "resourced," nourished again by the wellsprings of Christian tradition. Later, other Yale theologians like Hans Frei, George Lindbeck, and

---

1. See Freeman's "Beyond Fundamentalism and Liberalism," 1–5.

David Kelsey (and Yale-produced theologians like Hauerwas and Willimon) would form what would be known as "postliberal theology." Postliberalism sought to re-center the plot of Christianity within the parameters of the ancient ecumenical creeds, to interrogate and to retrieve the ancient sources as valuable contemporary resources, and to refocus upon the Christological and Trinitarian core of the faith, evangelical and catholic.[2]

BAPTIST LIBERALS

Curtis Freeman's rather surprising insight in his *Contesting Catholicity* is to demonstrate how, by the mid-Twentieth Century, even Baptists had been overtaken by good old American liberalism, though mostly inchoately and unconsciously. Many Baptists, especially those down South, would have been horrified to be classified as "liberal," inchoate or otherwise. Yet historic Baptist emphases—such fear of formalized, ritualized worship, anti-catholicism, conversion, and the presumption that to be Baptist is to have miraculously lifted oneself free of centuries of tradition so that one now participates in New Testament Christianity purified of fifteen hundred years of ecclesiastical error—left Baptists vulnerable to servitude to certain American liberal tendencies. E. Y. Mullins' individual "soul competency," too easily morphed into the same sort of "atomistic individualism"[3] that characterized some of those self-confessed liberal denominations from which the whole notion of "church" had been disastrously fragmented and weakened by the ravages of American self-help, introspective, self-derived faith.

Among Baptists, born in a protest against state-enforced, established religion, it would have been particularly painful to realize that rather than being a protest against established norms, the church had capitulated to those Enlightenment-engendered norms.

Freeman shows how a small group of Dixieland liberals like Carlyle Marney, Warren Carr, and James McClendon began movement "toward an emerging theology that looked something like the generous liberal orthodoxy described by the Yale School."[4] They found themselves turning away from popular liberal questions like "Is the church transforming society?" or "How can the church get in step with the progressive march of modernity?" and asked penetratingly how the church can more faithfully be the church, the Body of Christ, in this time and place on the basis of its core commit-

---

2. Copenhaver et al.,"Up From Liberalism."

3. Freeman, Baptists and Protestant liberalism, *Contesting Catholicity: Theology for Other Baptists*, 193.

4. Ibid., 386.

ments to the Lordship of Christ? In their concern for the visible, gathered, distinctive community of the baptized, these postliberals seem to me to be wonderfully Baptist.

In calling himself and his cohorts, "recovering Baptists," Curtis Freeman points to what he sees to be the urgent task for contemporary North American Baptists—retrieval and recovery of "a sense of continuity with the one, holy, catholic, and apostolic church."[5] Baptists must demonstrate how they are valid expressions of the church catholic or they are no church at all.

Sadly, too many Baptists (like most of us Methodists!) have lapsed into a liberal theology of personal preference. When an American Christian says that, "I'm not all that religious but I am very spiritual," or "I don't need the church or some preacher to tell me what to think; I have a personal relationship with Jesus Christ," that too often means, "God is whomever I conceive God to be." In a post-Christendom, disestablished environment, Baptists were in danger of becoming another religious affinity group of like-minded individuals who share personal experiences and lean toward the political right.

Those who would seek recovery and retrieval have their fellow Baptist critics to be sure, those who charge them with being most un-Baptist in their affection for ossified creeds and in turning their backs upon the Protestant faith with their nostalgic, romantic road trip to Rome. Freeman charges that these critics, "Having lost any memory of ecclesiality become content to live a sectarian existence that rejects the reform of the church and leads to a religious autism without a connection to historic Christianity."[6]

TIMOTHY GEORGE AS RETRIEVALIST

Although I would not label Timothy George a "postliberal" (he has never been a liberal) or one of Freeman's "Other Baptists" (I label him as more a "post conservative" but I marvel at his ability to leap over, or disregard some of the fundamentalist controversies that have wreaked havoc in his beloved church). Timothy has marked affinities with both postliberals and "Other Baptists" in his lifelong attempts not to invent but rather to retrieve and to recover the fullness of faith for contemporary Baptists from the ancient traditions of the church. From what I observe, Timothy is uncomfortably comfortable at Shades Mountain Baptist Church in Birmingham.

Surely Timothy would not reject Curtis Freeman's definition of "Other Baptists," as a "radically reforming community of contested convictions

5. Ibid.
6. Ibid., 388.

within the church catholic."[7] Timothy's intention is not to make Baptists more catholic in style or substance but more vibrantly apostolic, that is, more particularly *Christian*. Timothy has been among those who have led Baptists in taking up again that very Baptist project of critique, retrieval, and renewal of rebellion against conformity to the world by the transformational renewal of the mind (Rom 12:2).

Timothy is ever the teacher, in his writing and teaching calling us back *ad fontes*. His unabashed enthusiasm for the witness of the *communio sanctorum* is infectious. Luther, Zwingli, Calvin, Simons, and Tyndale were all featured with his blessing in Timothy's *Theology of the Reformers*.[8] I found his biography of William Carey to be downright exciting—a rare response to a work of church history.[9] In *Baptist Theologians*, Timothy and David Dockery make a case for vibrant, biblically faithful, uniquely Baptist, contemporary theology (though I couldn't help thinking that the present day theologians treated in their essays lacked the substance of their Baptist theological forebears). Timothy has frequently railed against the "heresy of contemporaneity" and the "imperialism of the present." He has criticized those fellow Baptists who presume to "leapfrog over the centuries to some mythological New Testament church."[10] Though Baptists haven't been widely noted for their theological contributions to the church catholic, Timothy demonstrates how the Baptist movement was historically driven in great part by invigorating ideas and fresh readings of Christian doctrine.[11]

HODGES CHAPEL

To enter Hodges Chapel is to be lifted out of the mire of purely personal experience, subjectivity, and the make-up-my-faith-as-I-go damage that has been done to the faith through Twentieth Century liberalism. This sacred space is bigger than my ego, densely populated by those who have walked the path of faith more nobly and at greater risk than I. Figures push out from their chapel niches and murals and, whether they mean to or not, provide a demanding canon of judgment for my merely contemporary, diminished, trimmed-down-to-the present age personal faith.

Of all of Timothy's impressive scholarly and popular publications, perhaps his greatest gift to the church and school he loves is Hodges Chapel.

---

7. Ibid., 389.
8. George, *Theology of the Reformers*.
9. George, *Faithful Witness: The Life of William*
10. George's 2016 "Drummond Lectures" on Tyndale.
11. George and Dockery, eds., *Theologians of the Baptist Tradition*.

To paraphrase the epitaph on Christopher Wren's tomb in London, if you are looking for a monument to Timothy George and to his unique gifts to the church, enter Hodges Chapel and look around you.[12] He is the best informed, most vibrantly enthusiastic "Baptist Catholic" whom I know. I mean that as high theological compliment.

The chapel is a wonder, especially in the context of an ecclesial heritage shaped by fierce antagonism to religious formalism and by an iconoclastic suspicion of religious art. The vision for the Chapel is said to have been born in a 1990 breakfast conversation between Samford president, Thomas Corts, Samford Trustee Andrew Gerow Hodges (who had been a close friend of Ralph Waldo Beeson, the school's benefactor—the school is named for Beeson's father, Methodist lay preacher, John Wesley Beeson), and architect Neil Davis. Consecrated in 1996, the architectural design of the cruciform building is by Neil Davis of Davis Architects. The wood used throughout the interior is northern Alabama cherry whose wood grain was enhanced by soaking the lumber with water for three years. At the end of each pew is a carved medallion, the Christian symbol, the Agnus Dei, "the Lamb of God."

Davis is reputed to have drawn inspiration for the chapel's plan from a variety of sixteenth and seventeenth-century sources: the coffered ceilings inspired by Robert Adams's Kettlestone Hall in England, the moldings by Christopher Wren, the stone floor by The Church of San Giovanni Crisostomo in Venice, and the overall design by Andrea Palladio's Il Redentore in Venice.[13]

As a first time worshipper in the chapel, my Baptist stereotypes were challenged by witnessing the congregation stand and enthusiastically,

---

12. Wren's epitaph, *si monumentum requiris circumspice*: "If you seek a monument, look around you." This is an epitaph on the tomb of the founder of my alma mater, Wofford College. An online guided video tour of Hodges Chapel is available at http://www.beesondivinity.com/chapel.

13. Beeson Divinity School, *Journal*, 4.

unreservedly affirm the Apostles' Creed.[14] These are Baptists? The creed, surrounded on a bed of ivy (symbolizing Christ) is engraved in stone on a tablet with gold relief above the balcony on the west wall of the chapel. I know of no contemporary churches of any denominational tradition where the creed is so prominently, visibly enshrined.

I wonder if John Leland can see the creed so beautifully venerated from his perch below the chapel's dome. Timothy could teach us that Leland, notorious critic of confessionalism, admitted to the usefulness of creeds as long as they are demonstrably "synchronized with the Bible."[15] In his Drummond Lectures he reminded his fellow Baptists that the slogan, "No creed but the Bible" was first asserted, not by Baptists but by Campbellites." Timothy argues that Baptists are best thought of, "not as creedalists who are guilty of creedalism but as Christians who are creedal."[16]

The ubiquity of Trinitarian symbols (the triquetra and circles in each of the ceiling coffers, the image of a triangle superimposed on three interpenetrating circles above the Apostles' Creed, as well as the angelic figures and hand of God the Father surrounding the creed) suggest the planning of an exuberant Trinitarian. Martin Dawes of Cherrylion Studios produced the chapel's stonework.[17]

However, it's not the chapel's symbols that impress the viewer, it's the saints. Surely more than one Baptist has winced at being welcomed to worship by a panoply of 16 saints staring down from the balustrades. A great cloud of witnesses watches us (Heb 12:1), a uniquely Baptist, generously catholic collection of spiritual forebears. Beeson's school hymn is, "For All the Saints;" surely Timothy had a hand in choosing *Sine Nomine*.

In 2010, in his sermon at the rededication of the Andrew Gerow Hodges Chapel in its fifteenth year, Timothy George took as his text Psalm 127, "Except the LORD built the house, their labor is but lost. . .." (Coverdale).[18] The historian's sermon cited Ralph Waldo Beeson and Thomas E. Corts as well as Hodges, then recalled stirring tidbits from Luther, Wesley, and dear Prayer Book-tossing Jenny Geddes, telling the congregation that "what God did at Wittenberg, and Edinburgh, and Aldersgate he may do yet again in Birmingham. . .here in Hodges Chapel."

---

14. George, *Evangelicals and Nicene Faith: Reclaiming the Apostolic Witness*.
15. George, "Drummond Lectures."
16. Ibid.
17. Dawes used a compound made by mixing polyester with marble dust.
18. George, "This Sacred Space," a sermon preached by Timothy George on January 26, 2010 in Hodges Chapel, Beeson Divinity School.

In his sermon, Timothy drew attention to the saints who "look down upon us from the mural of this dome," hedging a bit on the *communio sanctorum* in adding, "Perhaps from the balcony of heaven they look down upon us as well."

He gives thanks for the Chapel's gathering of saints: "Perpetua, Felicitas and Thomas Cranmer whose baptism in blood was the seed for the church. For Athanasius and Augustine, who by word and witness, stood unflinchingly against the world for the faith once delivered to the saints. For Thomas Aquinas and Jonathan Edwards, who knew that all truth is God's truth, and who held together the love of learning and the desire for God. For Luther and Calvin and Wesley. . ... Bunyan and Leland. . ...William Carey and Lottie Moon. . ... Spurgeon and Seymour and Kagawa" who all aid in the task for the church "forever building, and always decaying, and always being restored" (T.S. Eliot).

Timothy also noted that staring down at the pulpit are the statues of six martyrs—Romulo Sauňe, May Hayman, Bishop Haik Hovsepianmehr, Archbishop Janani Luwum, Dietrich Bonhoeffer, and Bill Wallace. Baptist missionary outreach is honored as Timothy comments that, "Each of them represents one of the six continents of the earth where countless Christians have given their lives for the sake of the Gospel in the past 100 years." Missionaries are prominent, embodiments of that thoroughly Baptist sense of urgency to take the good news to the whole world. (Having preached from that pulpit half a dozen times I can testify that it is a salubriously disarming experience to be gazed upon by contemporary martyrs when one is preaching!)

In a nice turn before the sermon's end, Timothy notes that the Chapel has numerous other niches that are empty, saying, "They are waiting for you and me, and for those who will come after us to follow Jesus Christ wherever his love may lead."

During the sermon Timothy asserted "we do not come here to *escape* from the world but to be *changed* by God's grace. . .[through] business with God." What is the change that Timothy hoped to work in worshippers in this sacred space? Judging from the iconography, I would think that a major expectation for change is for retrieval and recovery.

Shields of the apostles (carved by J. Wippell Company of Exeter, England) have been placed on the wall of the nave rather than the more typical placement in the chancel, said to signify the "church militant." Symbolism abounds, requiring interpretation to make sense of the symbols. Four large, circular pendentives at the four corners of the dome depict the traditional symbols of each of the four gospels.

Timothy has described the murals and paintings, by Romanian-born muralist Petru Botezatu as "a spectacular demonstration of Protestant sacred art."[19] Petru began studying Byzantine and Renaissance muralists in 1977. After being imprisoned by the Communists and having his work banned, he fled Romania.

Some Protestant places of worship are noted for the art of their stained-glass windows; none that I know of are distinguished for their murals. True to the Baptist-Puritan aesthetic aspiration for clarity, simplicity, and lucidity, the chapel's windows are clear, thus assuring, on most days, that the chapel's art is always bathed in sunlight.[20]

Seven large murals in the chancel apses are scenes from the life of Christ throughout the Christian year. The Methodist in me wants to know, why is John's baptism of Jesus not considered worthy to appear in these murals? To these episodes from Christ's earthly ministry are added Pentecost, and two that are labeled "Proclamation" (Paul preaching on Mars Hill and believers baptized by immersion as a trefoil symbol of the Trinity hovers) and "Reformation" (Luther nailing his 95 Theses on the Wittenberg door in 1517– an image that the murals place on par with moments from Jesus's life).

Above all, the risen Christ hovers over the center of the sanctuary, in the dome. When the Christ *pantocrator* was unveiled, Timothy noted that Christ's hands had no nail prints. Botezatus went back up the scaffold to paint Christ's wounds. Christ peers down from heaven, hands outstretched in blessing and embrace, Christ surrounded by the heavenly host who are rendered more as putti rather than cherubim and seraphim. Looking more closely at the golden cloud that surrounds Christ one sees thousands of faces of the faithful throng whom Christ has gathered to him in eternity. As in nearly all the murals, pastel blue background predominates.

A ring of sixteen witnesses look down from a painted balustrade—Perpetua and Felicitas, Athanasius, Augustinus (with mother Monica peering

---

19. "Andrew Gerow Hodges Chapel."
20. Wolsterdorf, *Art in Action: Toward a Christian Aesthetic.*

from behind him), Thomas Aquinas, Martin Luther (whose image appears more frequently in the chapel than anyone), Thomas Cranmer, John Calvin, John Bunyan, Jonathan Edwards, John Wesley, John Leland, William Carey, Charles Spurgeon, Lottie Moon (embodiments of that thoroughly Baptist sense of urgency to take the good news to the whole world), William J. Seymour, and Toyohiko Kagawa. No Martin Luther King, Jr., arguably the greatest Baptist of the Twentieth Century?

I find that Botezatu's overuse of pastel gives the chapel murals a sweet, cheerful, at times too sweet (for my taste) naiveté. Most of the figures lack depth. Some of the pictures, such as the scenes in the apse from Christ's life, are thoroughly conventional ecclesiastical art quoted from the late Italian Renaissance, many of them more illustration than fine art. True, their purpose is the nurturing of piety in those who gather in the chapel, but their uniformly childlike, pastel, sunny quality does not seem equal to the substantial theological statement to which the chapel aspires.

Most of the figures, even the putti, have a kind of static, posed quality. The rendering of energy and movement are not Botezatu's strong suit. That's unfortunate for art housed among missionary-focused, energetic Baptists who, at their best, have always been more a mission-movement, the Body of Christ in motion, rather than a sedate, located institution.

There is a beautifully rendered cross and crown atop the Létourneau Organ casing and a cross on the exterior, topping off the copper-covered dome, 110 feet from the Chapel floor. The case displays various Christian symbols including the monogram of J. S. Bach and, most prominently, the Luther rose. Baptists have come a long way from the days when crosses inside or out of a church were considered signs of alien "popery."

The pulpit is the most recent addition to Hodges Chapel. The imposing cherry wood pulpit stands at the center of the chancel, towering over the table. The pulpit's centrality and dominance seems thoroughly appropriate for a school in the Baptist tradition. Four great preachers—John Chrysostom (347–407), Jan Hus (1372–1415), John Knox (1513–1572), and George Whitefield (1714 1770)—stand around the base, every one of them holding a Bible.

They were carved by artists of the Létourneau Organ Company of Quebec. The pulpit figures, like much of the sculpture in Hodges Chapel, is an enthusiastic history lesson. All of the pulpit's sculptured figures are labeled with their names and dates, just the sort of sculptural program one might expect from a church history professor like Timothy.

In his lecture at Union University Timothy became a self-identified "contrarian" and warned his fellow Baptists that, "There is a fine line between retrieval for the sake of renewal and a projection of a 'Baptocentricity' (that's a word that I'm inventing), an egocentricity that is self-satisfying and self-promoting."[21] I find nothing in the iconography of Hodges Chapel that suggests "Baptocentricity," indeed my overall impression is that the chapel and its art are not nearly as self-promoting of Baptist heritage and identity as it could be.

HODGES CHAPEL AS THE PERFORMANCE AND EMBODIMENT OF TIMOTHY GEORGE'S THEOLOGY

I interpret Hodges Chapel is in great part the architectural, artistic embodiment of Timothy's lifelong work of retrieval for the sake of renewal. Its retrieval from the Great Tradition of Protestant Christian orthodoxy is generous and comprehensive, that charitable quality that pervades Timothy's personality and scholarly work. Although it is wonderful to see exemplars of the Baptist free-church, missionary tradition, these personages rendered in wood, paint, and stone surprise, delight, and educate the viewer, but also make one wonder if the chapel's iconography has adequately represented the unique character of Baptist life and Baptist contributions to the church catholic. The chapel's art has borrowed from mostly ecumenical, specifically catholic sources. That is understandable since the vast majority of Christian art was produced within the catholic tradition. Perhaps there is no way to

---

21. George, Lecture "Baptist Identity II" (Timothy said his actual title was "Was Jesus a Baptist?").

utilize Western Christian art and architecture without the medieval/renaissance catholic expression predominating. I wondered why the world-wide, passionately missional Baptist tradition had nothing to offer this contemporary Baptist embodiment of the faith.

The chapel makes me wonder how historical retrieval avoids becoming superficial archaism, appropriation of this and that from an iconographic tradition that does not easily mesh with a witness as uniquely formed as that of Baptists. I suppose there is no baptistry in the chapel because it's not a Baptist congregation. However, I found it strange that there is only one representation of baptism (in the "Proclamation" mural in the apse showing Paul on Mars Hill). While the chapel is a creative placement, a bold rearranging of the Western church's artistic tradition, do Baptists really have so little to offer to the ongoing artistic/architectural expression and reformation of the faith?

Still, Hodges Chapel is a remarkable achievement, the distinctive creation of a warm, brilliant scholar who has given his life to helping Baptists renew themselves by theological/historical returning, renewal, and retrieval. While Timothy George has repeatedly asserted that the chapel is *Soli Deo Gloria*, a phrase which his beloved Bach frequently inscribeds on his works, I also believe that Hodges Chapel is a glorious example of what God can do through a consecrated, passionate servant, intelligent servant of Jesus Christ.

BIBLIOGRAPHY

"Andrew Gerow Hodges Chapel." Brochure. Samford Office of Marketing and Communication. Texas: Baylor University Press, 2014.

Copenhaver, Martin B., Anthony B. Robinson, and William H. WIllimon. "Up From Liberalism." In *Good News In Exile: Three Pastors Offer a Hopeful Vision for the Church*, by Martin B. Copenhaver, Anthony B. Robinson, and William H. Willimon, 27–32. Grand Rapids: Eerdmans, 1999.

Freeman, Curtis. "Beyond Fundamentalism and Liberalism." In *Contesting Catholicity: Theology for Other Baptists*, 53–92. Waco, Baylor University Press, 2014.

George, Timothy. *Theology of the Reformers*. Nashville: B&H, 2013

———. "Drummond Lectures." March 1–2, 2016. Midwestern Baptist Theological Seminary. http://www.mbts.edu/video-category/drummond-lectures/.

———. "This Sacred Space." A Sermon on January 26, 2010 in Hodges Chapel, Beeson Divinity School.

———. "Baptist Identity II." Lecture. Feb. 17, 2007. Union University. http://www.uu.edu/audio/detail.cfm?ID=291.

———. *Evangelicals and Nicene Faith: Reclaiming the Apostolic Witness*. Hoboken, NJ: Wiley & Sons, 2014.

———. *Faithful Witness: The Life of William Carey* Birmingham, AL: New Hope, 1991.

George, Timothy, and David S. Dockery, eds. *Theologians of the Baptist Tradition.* Nashville: Broadman, 1990.

Beeson Divinity School. *Journal*, Spring 2010.

Wolsterdorf, Nicholas. *Art in Action: Toward a Christian Aesthetic.* 2nd ed. Grand Rapids: Eerdmans, 1995.

Evangelicals and the Global Church

RICHARD J. MOUW

THE PRESIDENT OF A mainline seminary had invited me to talk about "educating for multi-culturalism" at a trustee-faculty retreat. My presentations were well received—except for one trustee, who expressed his dissatisfaction with the subject in the concluding Q&A session. "All this diversity stuff is fine for a school like yours—you evangelical folks have all these international connections and get students from a lot of different cultures," he said with an irritated tone. "But it does not apply to this school. We are here for one reason: to put ordained leaders in our denomination's congregations in this part of the country. Being 'multi-' is not a part of our mission!"

I could tell that most of the other people present were not happy about his comment. Part of their distress, though, was due to the fact that what he was saying was factually correct. Their denomination's congregations in that region were not very "multi-," nor was their seminary being pressured by those congregations to help them alter the situation. But the president had rightly sensed a desire on the part of many faculty and trustees to thinking about working for change.

While that trustee was aware of the fact that he was representing a minority position in that room, he also knew that he was expressing a view that was widely shared in the seminary's larger consistency. His assessment of the prevailing mood of the evangelical movement was also fairly accurate. An awareness of our connectedness to the global church comes quite naturally to the evangelical community in North America. This was certainly true of the evangelical environs in which I was raised.

CALLED TO "TELL"

"Bible conferences" were a big part of my upbringing in the evangelical world. They were, to use the term that has become popular in recent years, a big factor in my *spiritual formation*. I also went to "Bible camps," but they were designed for youth, where spiritual activities were mixed with nature studies, crafts and recreation. The Bible conference, on the other hand, was a family affair, with extended Bible study sessions and worship services.

Our family made the rounds over many summers to several different conferences in the eastern states. For me, one of the most memorable ones was Camp-of-the-Woods, a conference center in the Adirondacks in New York state. The major worship service on Sundays featured a spirited singing of "We've a Story to tell to the Nations," with a procession of staff members, some of them wearing the garb of a specific country, with each carrying a nation's flag. I found that inspiring as a child, and in retrospect I see those services as one my earliest experiences of the multi-national character of the Christian faith.

The reality of God's concerns about all of the nations of the earth was also impressed upon me by frequent visits to our local congregation by missionaries who had returned to the United States for a furlough year. They spoke with enthusiasm about their efforts in native villages and urban centers, and they issued many "fields are white to harvest" calls for us to support them in bringing the Gospel to the nations.

Missionary events in local churches were also an occasion for encouraging young people to consider a call to missionary service. I was not yet a teenager when I made my promise to the Lord at one of those services that I would be "a missionary to the jungles of Brazil." This led me to pray regularly for people in Brazilian jungles. The images that I had in my mind when I prayed about them were informed by "slides" that a missionary couple had shown in our church, supplemented with photos from a feature on Brazilian tribal villages in *National Geographic*.

It is obvious that I did not keep my specific promise to the Lord about going to Brazil as a missionary. Indeed, for several years, during my college and university studies I wrote off that vow as a piece of childhood fantasy. But after I was into my teaching career I came to see that there was something in the spirit of that promise that I needed to honor in my academic calling.

The "We've a Story to Tell to the Nations" processional at Camp-of-the-Woods would play well in just about any evangelical congregation. Evangelicals are committed to an aggressive "telling." The story of the Gospel is not something that we can keep to ourselves. To have appropriated this story in one's own life—and in the collective life of local Christian communities—is to accept an obligation to support, not only local evangelism efforts, but the evangelistic outreach to "the nations."

To be sure, mainline denominations also accept an obligation to some form of global connectedness. In many more liberal church settings, however, "missions" has increasingly come to mean primarily a social outreach, in the form of programs dealing with poverty, education, peace-making and justice, with the efforts to sustain this kind of global mission being facilitated by denominational leaders' participation in conciliar ecumenical networks.

While the commitment to international missions on the part of grass roots evangelicals may have been stronger in the past than it is presently, it is still the reality. It is important, however, to be clear about the nature of this bonding with the international church in the evangelical movement. For one thing, the ties between North American evangelicals and Christians in other national contexts have largely been shaped by *evangelistic* concerns. We have an obligation to bring the Gospel to "the ends of the earth," and we have an obligation to give sacrificially to make this evangelistic mission possible.

Unfortunately, though, this sense of the importance of the evangelistic mission of the church does not mean that evangelicals have been especially knowledgeable about the places where the Gospel has been proclaimed. What evangelical church members know about "the mission field" has largely been *anecdotal* in nature, in the form of stories about missionary successes and failures. And missionaries pleading for financial support have told many of these stories.

I am going to explain here why the strong emphasis on the evangelistic task has often kept evangelicals from reaping all of the benefits made available to us as members of a global Christian community. I have to be clear, though, that this is not in any way to denigrate the evangelistic task, and the passionate commitment that has often characterized the missionary enterprise. To say that our global commitments require more than evangelism is not to say that they require less.

To make the case in personal terms: I love being an evangelical, and I am grateful to the Lord to have had the privilege of many decades of engagement in evangelical higher education. This engagement has been greatly enhanced for me by the opportunity of working alongside of other scholar-educators whose love for the evangelical movement has taken the shape of promoting a deeper grasp of the biblical, historical, systematic and practical dimensions of "the faith once delivered." Timothy George has been a model—and a hero!—for me in this regard, and I am pleased to offer these thoughts here, with gratitude for his contribution to my own theological formation.

AN EXPANDED SCHOLARLY AGENDA

I said earlier that while I never followed through on my vow, made in my younger years, to be a missionary to Brazil, I do see myself as having honored something in the spirit of that vow. It took a while for me to realize the connection between being a Philosophy professor and having a missionary consciousness, but the connection did come to impress itself upon me.

One of the occasions that helped me to recognize the connection actually occurred in a missionary setting. Phyllis and I had been invited to Haiti, during my first decade on the Philosophy faculty at Calvin College, to lead a retreat for a group of missionary families who were working in a rural area in northern Haiti. One evening I took a walk with one of the missionaries. He had been my student at Calvin and we reminisced about my Introduction to Philosophy course. He enjoyed reading some of the classical philosophers, he said, mentioning Plato and Descartes. Then he singled out David Hume's *Dialogues Concerning Natural Religion* as one of his favorite readings in the course. "A lot of fascinating stuff in there about the problem of evil," he said. After a brief pause he added: "Of course, much of that is irrelevant to the kind of evil we experience here in these Haitian villages." And then this: "You should teach a Philosophy course sometime on voodoo and the problem of evil!"

His comment was, at best, only half-serious. But it caught me up short, and I continued to think about it. Voodoo and philosophy—why not? A few years later I came across a nice distinction that Arthur Holmes made in a fine book that he wrote about world views, where Holmes distinguished between "theologians' theology" and "philosophers' philosophy" on the one hand, and "world-viewish theology" and "world-viewish philosophy" on the other. The first set of terms, said Holmes, points to the kinds of topics that professional theologians and philosophers talk about when they are addressing people within their own disciplines. The second set refers to the kinds of topics that come up when scholars wrestle with questions that are posed to them by people engaged in practical real-life contexts.[1]

Holmes was not meaning to denigrate the more guild-oriented discussions in philosophy and theology. Such analyses, although difficult for the uninitiated to grasp, have an intrinsic value. But he was highlighting the importance of a somewhat different kind of discussion, where intelligent folks

---

[1] Holmes, *Contours*, 34–40.

grapple with basic philosophical and theological questions as they emerge for people immersed in variety of vocations and life-situations.

Holmes had in mind topics such as work and leisure, technology and the natural order, friendship and sexuality, education and politics. But in that evening walk in a Haitian village my former student was actually pushing the agenda a little further. This missionary had enjoyed being introduced to the kind of philosophical issues raised by the academic guilds: Plato's body-soul dualism, the Cartesian *cogito*, the Cosmological Argument for God's existence. But he was also puzzled about how someone from an intellectual culture in which those discussions are taken seriously can think about, and address, a cultural context in which animism informs the patterns of everyday life. And his puzzles made an impact on me.

Around the same time as my visit to Haiti, I began to discover what were for me new dimensions to the classic Christian teaching about the atoning work of Christ. These dimensions had not been completely ignored in the Christian tradition, but evangelicals had not emphasized them in significant ways. At the heart of evangelical piety and theology is a strong emphasis on what I think of, and firmly endorse, as the intra-Trinitarian "transactional" aspects of Christ's atoning work.

In my studies of Christian social-political thought, however I had begun to wrestle with the subject of the Pauline "principalities and powers, as it had been developed in new ways by the "biblical theology" movement in post-World War II European scholarship. Many folks in the "evangelical social action" movement that had emerged in the 1970s had become enamored with this topic, particularly as John Howard Yoder had introduced it into the evangelical theological conversation about politics in his influential book, *The Politics of Jesus*.[2]

I found much that is helpful in those studies, but I worried about a tendency to see the work of the cross—primarily in terms of a decisive encounter with social-political-economic structures. Yes, Christ was put to death by the "powers" that control the patterns of sinful culture. By refusing to accept their strategies for social change—by, in Yoder's much-quoted term, "accepting powerlessness—Jesus defeated the powers, thus providing us with what it means for us, as his disciples, to his mission of redemptive suffering."[3]

There are important insights in highlighting this dimension of Christ's atoning work. There are indeed ways in which we are called to imitate the work of the cross. But there are also, important dimensions of the atonement

---

2. Yoder, *Politics of Jesus*, 135–62.
3. Ibid., 111–12.

that are *in*imitable. Jesus did for us what we could not, as lost sinners, do for ourselves. And here the intra-Trinitarian aspects rightly loom large. He paid the debt. He stood in our place. He offered himself up as the supreme sacrifice for sin.

All of this has been central to the evangelical understanding of the New Testament message. And rightly so. The folks who want to emphasize the societal dimensions of Christ's redemptive mission, though, have correctly expressed the need for a more expansive understanding. What I became sensitive to, however, was that this expansiveness is also inextricably connected to the more traditional "transactional" conceptions. Not only did Jesus pay the debt for my individual sins, but he also paid the debt for our collective racism and our shared reliance on military solutions to international tensions.

Again, my emphasis here is on *expansion*. The goal is to build on the strengths that have long characterized the evangelical commitment to the global mission of the church. Working out the scope of that expansion is an important task, which requires extensive exploration. In what follows I will focus briefly on three areas where the work of expansion has begun to bear fruit in evangelicalism in the past few decade, and needs to continue: Christian identity, sensitivity to cultural context, and a learning posture.

A NEW IDENTITY

It is encouraging these days to hear many evangelical Christians employ eschatological categories in making the case for a more robust understanding of the nature of the Kingdom. That there are solid biblical grounds for making the case in this way is clear from, for example, the wonderful passage in Revelation 7, where John reports this heavenly scenario:

> I looked, and there before me was a great multitude that no one could count, from every nation, tribe, people and language, standing before the throne and before the Lamb. They were wearing white robes and were holding palm branches in their hands. And they cried out in a loud voice:
> "Salvation belongs to our God,
> who sits on the throne,
> and to the Lamb." (vv. 9–10, NIV)

The fullness of the Kingdom will occasion the gathering in of the believing community from the "multi-" diversity of humankind. The 19th century Dutch theologian Herman Bavinck took this a step further theologically.

The gathering in of the eschaton, he argued, will be the completion of God's purposes in the very creation of humanity. The creation of first man and woman in the divine image in the Genesis story, Bavinck said, "is not the end but the beginning of God's journey with mankind." God wanted the human pair to be "fruitful and multiply" because it is "[n]ot the man alone, nor the man and the woman together, but only the whole of humanity together is the fully developed image of God. Human nature, then, is "is not a static entity but extends and unfolds itself" in the rich diversity of humankind spread over diverse cultures and times. In the coming Kingdom, then, "all the glory of the nations will be brought" into the New Jerusalem. It is only when this rich human diversity enters into the fullness of the Kingdom that we will see the many-splendored *imago dei* in its fullness.[4]

This speaks directly to the issue of human identity. Learning to think about ourselves in "multi-" terms is not just an highly desirable option for the Christian community. It is to understand who we are in Jesus Christ, what we have become because of the blood shed on Calvary. In the Body of Christ, God is restoring the unity of the human race. The celestial hymn to the Lamb in Revelation 5, puts it clearly:

> You are worthy to take the scroll
> and to open its seals,
> because you were slain,
> and with your blood you purchased for God
> persons from every tribe and language and people and nation.
> You have made them to be a kingdom and priests to serve our God,
> and they will reign on the earth. (vv. 9–10)

This is why the dissenting trustee at the seminary where I spoke was seriously mistaken. Christian formation—not just evangelical formation, but Christian formation as such—requires growing into an awareness that our identity in Christ is essentially a "multi-" identity. National, ethnic, racial and class identities no longer define who we truly are. We have been incorporated into "a chosen race, a royal priesthood, a holy nation" (I Peter 2: 9)–a reality that supercedes all other understandings of what it means to have a racial, priestly or national identity. Congregations that are not very "multi-" need to made aware of what they are professing when they sing: "Elect from every nation, yet one o'er all the earth."

---

4. Bavinck, *Reformed Dogmatics*, 577–78.

ATTENDING TO CONTEXT

Given the global character of the Christian community, the Gospel must be addressed to a rich variety of human cultural situations, speaking to those situations our the rich and many-faceted storehouse of divine truth in God's Word. The recognition of this fact has led to considerable emphasis on "contextualization" in recent years by thinkers who have wanted to draw our attention to the different ways in which the Christian message is received, appropriated and interpreted in a variety of cultural contexts. It is not uncommon for such thinkers to ask that we take an honest and critical look at the ways in which the transmission of the Gospel to the non-Western world has been weighted down by a close association with colonialist programs, as well as with the values of a technocratic-scientific worldview.

There is nothing in this emphasis that has to be seen as hostile to the core beliefs of traditional Christian communities. Indeed, contextualization issues have received much positive attention from scholars who represent the more orthodox theological perspectives, especially evangelicals and Roman Catholics. Since these two communities have continued to be in the forefront of "conversionist" missionary activity has necessitated the focus on contextualization issues, often because of the challenges presented to them by their own converts, who often combine a deep interest in cross-cultural questions with a strong commitment to theological orthodoxy.

Nor does the message of contextualization simply mean that we can, if we so choose, translate Gospel themes into the terms of a specific cultural context. The point is a much stronger one: *all* of our preaching and theologizing are inevitably contextualized. None of us escapes the formative influence of our cultural situation in our understanding of the biblical message. To recognize that the Bible's message is a many-faceted thing helps to guard against a relativistic version of multiculturalism. God's Word speaks authoritatively to a variety of different cultural contexts, but it must not be seen as "captured" in a special way by any one of those contexts. The black South African theologian Allan Boesak put it helpfully when he warned against seeing historical embodiments of "the black experience" as "*within themselves* hav[ing] revelational value on a par with Scripture." These contexts are simply "the framework within which blacks understand the revelation of God in Jesus Christ. No more, no less."[5]

This last comment is an important one. The black experience, Boesak says, is not itself divine revelation; rather it is no more than the situation in which blacks have received that revelation. But neither is it *less* than a

---

5. Boesak, *Farewell to Innocence*, 12.

situation to which God has revealingly spoken. This means that while the black historical experience is not on a par with Scriptural revelation, it is at least on a par with various *white* historical experiences, which must also be denied revelatory status.

So what we evangelicals have been learning—or at least we should have been learning—from this kind of focus in recent decades is that all theology is contextualized. It is not that black and feminist and Third World theologians have recently started to contextualize theology. Rather, we are being asked to to recognize that the contextualization has been going on all along. In practical terms, this sensitizes to that the fact that human beings hear different things in the biblical message, from context to context. The plantation slave, the urban housewife, the Russian peasant, the worker in a rice paddy, the tribal chief—each receives the gospel in terms of contextualized frameworks, questions, and anxieties. The awareness of this fact gives new occasions for celebrating the riches, and the universality, of the Christian gospel.

But for some of us there is also a word of judgment to be heard in this emphasis on contextualization. We have often been closed to other perspectives on the gospel. We have too quickly absolutized the cultural trappings that have accumulated around our understanding of the Christian faith. And this is especially unfortunate for those of us who are white Westerners, because we are, as a group, numbered among the rich and powerful of the earth; we consume a disproportionate amount of the world's goods. And many of us have a degree of control over our own destinies that would be unthinkable in other parts of the world. Unfortunately, this privileged position has influenced the way in which we have received and understood the gospel. We have often filtered out crucial elements of the biblical message. We have often distorted the Gospel so as to make it into a message with which we can live comfortably.

I must quickly add, having emphasized here the importance of the contextualization perspective, that none of this simply renders irrelevant the kinds of theological topics that have long occupied those of us who are deeply grounded in Western confessional traditions. As one who, like my friend Timothy George, loves the Calvinist tradition, I am not prepared to treat the grand themes of John Calvin's theology—our total inability to contribute anything to our own, or by God's sovereign electing grace alone, the preserving power of a love that will not let us go—as comprising only one among many cultural embodiments of biblical thought. The issues debated in Western theology—soteriological, ecclesiological, eschatological, and the like—have serious application for global Christianity. I am certainly convinced that a theology for South Korea must take its own cultural context with utmost seriousness—but there will still be important topics to be debated among Korean Pentecostals, Korean Wesleyans and Korean Calvinists. This is why our willingness to learn from cross-cultural dialogue about the Gospel means an expansion of, and not a replacement for, the theological concerns that have long occupied the minds and hearts of those who adhere to the historic Christian faith.

LEARNING FROM DIVERSITY

Taking seriously our participation as evangelicals in an international community of followers of Christ should cultivate in us a spirit of humility. We are finite and culturally situated human beings. In addition to that we are also fallen creatures, a sinful condition that often distorts the ways in which we interpret reality. So we certainly have good reasons to be rather cautious about what we can claim to know with certainty. God alone knows all things; but we his human creatures are limited, both individually and collectively, to the cultural locations that we occupy in the larger scheme of things. None of this calls for an endorsement of relativism. But it does require that we approach cross-cultural discussions in a *learning* posture.

As we all should know by now, the global south is the growing portion of Christianity in today's world, with believers in Asia, Africa and Latin America now comprising the majority of Christians in contemporary life. For evangelicals, this affords a wonderful learning opportunity, given our access to] a cross-cultural conversation undergirded by a spiritual bonding that is seldom available to Christians whose global contacts are primarily through secular academic and political networks. The privilege of participating in this extensive Christian network can nurture in us the attitudinal and communal resources that can help us to wrestle effectively with the realities of cultural diversity.

Indeed, the fact that we have a faith in Christ that we hold in common with people from many different cultures is a good place for us to begin in our exploration of what might be for us new and strange ideas. When we engage in dialogue with believers from other cultural contexts—whether in personal encounters or writings and films—we can welcome their ideas, showing an intellectual hospitality, without being fearful that those ideas will be a corrupting influence. Acknowledgement of a spiritual unity can be a profound basis for spiritual and theological exploration.

A key ingredient in learning from others is *empathy*. In an important sense, this is precisely what gave strength to the missionary movement of the past, at least when it functioned at its best. The missionaries exegeted the hopes of hearts of the human beings to whom they wanted to bring the Gospel. In many ways, our own service to the Kingdom also means encountering what may seem at first as strange new realities in areas of life and thought that we once thought we understood quite well.

This empathetic learning requires patience, an unwillingness simply to be put off by our first impressions. And it also requires a willingness to receive whatever gifts God may have in store for us in our encounters with the views of others. To be sure, we must be careful in all of this to hold on to that which is truly basic to our faith in Christ. Mere experimentation, a fascination with anything that challenges long-standing evangelical convictions.–these are patterns that we must work to avoid. But we must be willing take on new theological challenges.

The issues to be wrestled with in the theological challenges that emerge as we engage other cultural contexts are complex. The challenges are put on display nicely for us, however, in a 2014 book by Simon Chan, *Grassroots Asian Theology: Thinking the Faith from the Ground Up*. Chan, a Singaporean theologian with solid evangelical credentials, argues that there is often a theological disconnect between the methodology of Western theologians and the spiritual and theological concerns that Asian Christians wrestle with in their local contexts.

The disconnect that Chan has in mind is very clear, he argues, among liberal thinkers, who typically view a specific Asian cultural context with a stress on working for political-economic justice, or who critique what they see as the oppressiveness of patriarchy, or who want to promote interfaith dialogue. If local Christian communities do not see those approaches as meeting their needs, these theologians assume, it is because they are victimized by "false consciousness." Grassroots believers, then, need to be brought to an awareness of the realities that actually plague their lives.[6]

What this perspective fails to see, says Chan, that grassroots Christians in Asia have their own profound grasp of their cultural contexts, and it is a very different reading of the cultural context than what is offered by "elite" theologies. Following the lead of the evangelical missiologists Paul Hiebert, Daniel Shaw and Tite Tienou, Chan observes that Asian believers live spiritually in the "middle zone"—a region of engagement that falls between that which is defined by the topics of "high theology" (Trinity, atonement, eschaton) and the questions addressed by the sciences. Local communities define their lives with reference to "the realm of spirits, demons, and witch doctors," struggling in their daily existence with issues of fertility, economic wellbeing, familial relations, health, and relations with

---

6. Chan, *Grassroots*, 27.

"the living dead."[7] These believers seek out ecclesial communities in which these cultural realities are taken seriously in the light of the Gospel.

Chan's proposed program for how evangelical theologians can best serve these communities is an excellent exercise in learning from, to use the wonderful phrase in Catholic thought, the *sensus fidelium*—"the sense of the faithful." To discern the genuine core concerns of grassroots Christian communities in Asia, we must engage in, to use Chan's subtitle, "thinking the faith from the ground up." This means making the starting point of local ecclesial communities our own. Following the lead of the evangelical missiologists Paul Hiebert, Daniel Shaw and Tite Tienou, Chan observes that Asian believers live spiritually in the "middle zone"—a region of engagement that falls between that which is defined by the topics of "high theology" (Trinity, atonement, eschaton) and the questions addressed by the sciences. Local communities define their lives with reference to "the realm of spirits, demons, and witch doctors," struggling in their daily existence with issues of fertility, economic wellbeing, familial relations, health, and "the place of the dead among the living."[8]

It is a mistake, Chan argues, to judge these preoccupations on the part of Asian Christians as expressions of syncretism and superstition. To issue that verdict is to fail to see the close theological connections between primal religion and biblical Christianity. To be sure, simply to assume those connections uncritically can lead to dangers. Evangelicals will best serve these fellow believers by carefully reflecting upon, in the light of biblical revelation, the "lived theology" of these local Christian believers.

Chan not only encourages that kind of careful theological reflection, but he engages in it himself. The result is a robust discussion of some significant theological topics, many of them also vitally important for our own Western contexts as well as for Asia. He explores at some length, for example, the relevance of the kind of honor and shame culture in Asia for an evangelicalism that has typically concentrated primarily on the concepts of sin and guilt. To be sure, the Bible does tell us that we are guilty sinners who have rebelled against our Creator. But the disobedience of our first parents in the Garden was an affront to God's honor, resulting in their hiding in shame from their Lord. To ignore these honor-and-shame themes is to miss much of what the Bible tells us about our shared humanity,

Chan also addresses the topic of the veneration of ancestors, a subject seldom touched upon among Western evangelicals, but a crucial concern for Christians who struggle with what coming to faith in Jesus Christ means

---

7. Ibid., 31–35.
8. Ibid., 31, 70.

for understanding the state of their ancestors' souls. Chan's probing of issues relating to the doctrine of purgatory and Christ's "descent into hell" are provocative.

Needless to say, I want to argue back on some of the positions, which Chan explores. But Chan is a wise evangelical thinker who points to spiritual concerns that require our creative engagement. His observation that "[a]ncestor veneration underscores the unsurpassed value placed on the family in Asia"[9] is an obvious case in point. On several conversations I have had with young people in China who have recently come to Christ the question of the eternal destiny of their ancestors has come up. One young woman spoke pleadingly on the subject. Her Buddhist parents were deeply disturbed about her newfound faith in Christ, not because they are hostile to Jesus, she said—"they actually admire him as a moral teacher." But they see her becoming a Christian as her consigning her ancestors to hell. "Revering my ancestors means much to me, " she said, "and I want to assure my parents that I do not want to dishonor my family heritage. So please tell me what I as a Christian can say to my parents about this!"

I did not have a clear answer to give her. But I know that we have to wrestle with the question on her behalf. She is not just an interesting conversation partner, she is our sister in Jesus Christ. The context out of which she asks urgent questions has to become our questions as well. She reminds us in a poignant manner what it means to take up the challenges—and the exciting opportunities—of reflecting with utmost seriousness on what it means to belong to the global church for whom Christ died.

BIBLIOGRAPHY

Boesak, Allan Aubrey. *Farewell to Innocence: A Socio-Ethical Study on Black Theology and Power*. Maryknoll: Orbis, 1977.
Bavinck, Herman. *Reformed Dogmatics*. Vol. 2. Edited by John Bolt. Translated by John Vriend. Grand Rapids: Baker Academic, 2004.
Chan, Simon. *Grassroots Asian Theology: Thinking the Faith from the Ground Up*. Downers Grove, IL: IVP Academic, 2014.
Hiebert, Paul G., et al. *Understanding Folk Religion*. Grand Rapids: Baker, 1999.
Holmes, Arthur F. *Contours of a World View*. Grand Rapids: Eerdmans, 1983.
Yoder, John H. *The Politics of Jesus: Vicit Agnus Noster*. Grand Rapids: Eerdmans, 1972.

---

9. Chan, *Grassroots Asian Theology*, 189.

Index of Names

Aaron, 50
Abel, 220
Abraham, 32, 51, 122, 165, 213, 292n1, 303
Abraham, William, 113, 113n10
Adam, 27, 37, 162
Adams, John, 331, 331n15
Adams, Robert, 337
Ahimelech, 49
Akin, Daniel L., 6
Alkier, Stefan, 244, 244n49
Allen, Michael, 123n19, 124n22
Allison, Dale C., 68n10
Allison, Gregg R., 225n51, 226, 226n57, 227, 227n62
Ambrose, 82, 84, 140, 141, 284
Ampliatus, 77
Anderson, Benedict, 237
Andronicus, 76
Anselm, 156
Aquila, 76
Aquinas, Thomas, 18, 322, 339, 341
Aristotle, 77, 322
Asaph, 62
Asyncritus, 77
Athanasius, 134n20, 146, 339, 340
Augustine of Hippo, 82, 84, 98, 131, 139, 139n55, 140, 141, 142–46, 144n79, 144n80, 144n82, 150, 152, 156, 159, 163, 195, 200, 226n56, 239, 239n35, 271, 284–85, 286, 288, 290, 339
Augustinus, 340
Augustus, Romulus, 228n68

Bach, Johann Sebastian, 314–15, 341, 343
Baptist, John the, 69, 340
Barclay, John M. G., 65n1
Barrett, C. K., 73n17
Barrett, Matthew, 115n13
Barth, Karl, 18, 152, 152n7, 153, 153n12, 308–10, 309n7, 315
Basil, 132, 133, 137–38, 146, 284
Basil (Sr.), 132
Bauckham, Richard, 67n5, 69n11
Baum, G., 168n9
Bauman, Zygmunt, 232, 232n1, 232n2, 233, 237, 237n28
Bavinck, Herman, 124, 124n21, 350–351, 351n4
Beale, G. L., 71n13
Bebbington, David W., 84n11, 87, 87n28, 218n8, 218–19, 219n9, 219n11, 224
Beckwith, Carl L., 169n12
Beeson, John Wesley, 337
Beeson, Ralph Waldo, 337, 338
Beethoven, Ludwig van, 310–313
Benedict, Philip, 173n29
St. Benedict of Nursia, 228, 228n68
Pope Benedict XVI, 20, 251n9
Berger, Peter L., 237–39, 238n29, 242, 325n10
Bergier, J. F., 170n16, 170n17, 172n26, 175n35, 177n41
Berlin, Isaiah, 322, 322n6
Berry, Wendell, 93, 93n4, 93n6, 96, 96n17
Bertram, Bonaventure, 287

Beza, Theodore, 176, 287
Bird, Michael F., 217, 217n3, 224–25, 225n50, 225n52, 226n56
Block, Daniel I., 48, 48n1, 55n5
Blunt, A. W. F., 73n20
Boesak, Allan Aubrey, 352, 352n5
Bohren, Rudolf, 296n10
Bolger, Ryan K., 194n13
Bolsec, Jerome, 172n25
Bonar, Andrew, 45n1
Bonhoeffer, Dietrich, 19, 236, 293, 293n8, 339
Botezatu, Petru, 340, 341
Bowersock, G. W., 132n9
Boyce, James Petigru, 2n4, 5
Bradford, William, 85
Bradley, Ian, 84, 84n9
Bray, Gerald L., 9, 23
Bridges, Charles, 35
Bright, Bill, 264, 265
Broadus, John A., 2n4
Brown, Peter, 84, 84n14, 284–85, 285n10
Bucer, Martin, 154
Buckley, James, 100
Bullard, Scott W., 101n27
Bultmann, Rudolph, 233, 234n4
Bunyan, John, 79, 79n1, 81–82, 85, 206, 206n22, 207n24, 339, 341
Burdette, Staunton S., 103n36
Burke, Edmund, 321
Butler, Joseph, 94–95
Buttrick, David G., 308–9, 309n6

Caiaphas, 70
Caird, G. B., 67n6
Caldecott, Stratford, 96n15
Calhoun, Robert, 333
Calvin, John (Jean), 3, 4, 5, 6, 18, 19, 122, 123, 124, 153, 155, 155n19, 156, 156n22, 159, 167n8, 167–80, 168n9, 169n12, 169n13, 170n16, 170n18, 171n20, 171n21, 172n24, 172n25, 173n27, 174n32, 177n42, 180n47, 195, 202n5, 221, 222, 226n56, 241, 241n42, 242, 286–87, 288, 290, 297, 336, 339, 341, 353
Campbell, Alexander, 166, 166n3
Cantlow, W. H., 86
Cappadocians, 195
Caprile, Giovanni, 255n24
Carey, William, 5, 6, 81, 85, 336, 339, 341
Carlyle, Thomas, 316, 316n25
Carr, Warren, 334
Carson, D. A., 227
Carter, Charles, 89
Cary, Phillip, 229, 229n72
Cassidy, Edward Iris Cardinal, 272
Cavanaugh, William, 98n22, 102, 102n30, 102n31
Chalcedon, 156, 162
Chan, Simon, 355n6, 355–57, 357n9
Chapell, Bryan, 295
Christ, 26, 27, 29, 32, 33, 40, 41, 42, 45, 46, 62, 63, 71, 72, 74, 84, 88, 94, 96, 97, 98, 99, 100–101, 102, 103, 104, 111, 112, 114, 119, 120, 121, 122, 126, 145, 146n93, 153, 155, 156, 158, 159, 161, 162, 163, 168, 171, 201, 202–5, 207, 208, 211, 212, 213, 214, 218, 224, 236, 239, 241, 242, 243, 247, 252, 259, 266, 270, 271, 273, 294, 304, 305, 335, 338, 340, 341, 349, 350, 354, 355, 357. *See also* Jesus
Chrysostom, John, 341
Chryssavgis, John, 134n22
Church, 4n9
Chute, Anthony L., 84n11
Clement of Alexandria, 132
Clement of Rome, 271
Coffin, William Sloane, 298, 298n18
Cole, Graham, 217
Colson, Charles Wendell (Chuck), 8, 247, 248, 262, 263, 264, 265, 266–69, 270, 270n8, 271, 271n10, 273–75
St. Columba, 229n75
Congar, Yves, 254n19, 255, 255n22, 258, 258n34, 258n36
Copenhaver, Martin B., 334n2
Corts, Thomas E., 337, 338

Covey, Stephen R., 304, 304n34
Cranfield, C.E.B., 65n3
Cranmer, Thomas, 339, 341
Crisostomo, San Giovanni, 337
Cross, Anthony R., 86n20, 86n21, 92n2, 100n25
Cullmann, Oscar, 251, 251n12, 252, 257, 257n33
St. Cyprian, 233

Dahlhaus, Carl, 311n15
Dale, James W., 89, 89n33
Daley, Brian, 102n34
Daneau, Lambert, 287
David, 39, 49, 53, 60, 61, 62, 81, 213
Davies, W. D., 68n10
DaVinci, Leonardo, 93
Davis, Neil, 337
Dawes, Martin, 338, 338n17
De Boer, Eric, 174n30
de La Faye, Antoine, 287
De Smedt, Emile, 250
Demetrescu, Camilian, 53n3
Denlinger, Aaron Clay, 154n15
Descartes, René, 295, 348
Deusen, Nancy Van, 143n77
Dever, Mark E., 9, 35
devil, 29. *See also* Satan
DeVine, D. Mark, 183, 193n11
Deweese, Charles W., 187n5
Dillmann, August, 280, 281
Diodati, Jean, 287
Dockery, David S., 1, 2n3, 2n5, 5n15, 7n36, 192, 192n10, 193, 336, 336n11
Dolan, Timothy Cardinal, 262
Dreher, Rod, 228n66, 229, 229n74
Dreyer, Wim A., 153, 153n11, 153n13, 160, 160n37, 162n44
Driscoll, Mark, 185
Dulles, Avery Cardinal, 222n38, 225, 225n53, 265
Dunn, James D. G., 71n14
Duprey, Pierre, 254n21, 255, 255n23, 255n26, 257, 257n30, 258
Dwight, Timothy, 304, 304n33

Echeverria, E. J., 253n16

Eck, Johann, 116
Edwards, Jonathan, 195, 288–89, 339, 341
Elijah, 294
Eliot, T. S., 339
Ellis, Christopher, 100n24
Elwell, Walter A., 302, 302n29
Emerson, Matthew Y., 110n4
Emmelia, 132
Erickson, Millard J., 6, 224n48, 225n55
Ethan, 62
Eunice, 130, 146
Evagrius of Pontus, 133–34, 134n17, 134n21
Eve, 27, 139, 162
Ezekiel, 39, 53, 292, 296, 297, 298, 299, 300, 303

Falwell, Jerry, 3
Farel, Guillaume, 167, 168, 170
Farrow, Douglas, 244n48
Father in heaven, 34, 63, 66, 70, 104, 112, 121, 134, 160, 162, 197, 244, 245. *See also* God
Featley, Daniel, 88, 88n29
Fee, Gordon D., 72n15, 74n22
Feiner, Johannes, 255n25
Felicitas, 339, 340
Feuerbach, Ludwig, 101
Fiddes, Paul S., 200, 211n42
Finch, Karen Petersen, 149, 149n1
Finn, Nathan A., 84n11
Finnis, John, 320n3, 321, 321n4, 321n5, 322n7, 323
Fisk, Alfred G., 310
Florovsky, George, 220
Ford, David, 166n3
Fosdick, Harry Emerson, 294, 294n9
Fowler, Stanley K., 191n8
Frame, John M., 227, 227n61
Pope Francis, 252, 252n14
King Francis I, 168
Frederick III, 153
Freeman, Curtis, 333n1, 334, 334n3, 335–36
Frei, Hans, 333

Index of Names

Garrett, Leo, Jr., 4n8
Garrison, Greg, 9n49
Geddes, Jenny, 338
George, Christian T., 9, 79, 288, 288n15
George, Denise, 3, 4, 5, 9, 84n8, 187n6, 192n9
George, Mary Elizabeth, 129
George, Nancy Norman, 129
George, Robert P. (Robby), 8, 9, 318, 322n8
George, Timothy, 1–17, 18–20, 46, 64, 84n8, 85n18, 88n31, 88n32, 89n35, 109–10, 110n1, 110n5, 127, 129n1, 129–30, 149, 149n2, 166, 166n5, 178, 187n6, 192n9, 200, 200n1, 201, 201n2, 201n3, 202, 205n17, 205–6, 206n18, 206n21, 208, 208n29, 208n30, 210, 210n38, 210n40, 210n41, 211, 217, 217n4, 218, 219–24, 220n14, 220n22, 221n26, 221n27, 223n39, 223n40, 224n48, 226, 226n59, 247n1, 247–48, 248n3, 249, 251, 251n10, 253, 259, 260, 262n1, 262–63, 263n3, 265, 266–69, 269n4, 269n5, 269n6, 269n7, 269–75, 270n9, 290, 335–36, 336n8, 336n9, 336n10, 336n11, 337, 338, 338n14, 338n15, 338n18, 339, 340, 342n21, 342–43, 347–48, 353
Gerson, Michael, 229, 229n73
Gibbs, Eddie, 194n13
Gill, John, 85, 85n15
Girard, René, 236
God, 26, 27, 28, 32, 34, 35, 36, 37, 38, 39, 40, 41, 42, 44, 45, 46, 49, 50, 51, 52, 53, 54, 55, 56, 59, 60, 61, 62, 63, 65, 66, 67, 69, 70, 71, 72, 77, 97, 98, 99, 100, 103, 104, 111, 112, 113, 115, 118, 119, 120–21, 122, 123, 126, 129, 130, 131, 132, 133, 134, 135, 137, 138, 143, 144, 145, 156, 159, 163, 168, 196, 198, 200, 201, 202, 209, 213, 214, 221, 225, 235, 239, 240, 241, 242, 242n45, 243, 244, 245, 252, 255, 256, 271, 274, 284, 289, 294, 295, 296, 298, 299, 300, 302, 303, 305, 307, 315, 335, 338, 339, 343, 349, 351, 355, 356. *See also* Father in heaven; Yahweh
Godot, 228
Goethe, 183, 197, 198
Good Shepherd, 306
Gordon, Bruce, 170n15, 171n19
Gosnell, Peter W., 75n24
Graham, Billy, 270
Greenway, Adam W., 185n4
Gregory, Brad S., 112, 112n9
Gregory of Nyssa, 131, 132, 132n10, 133, 134, 134n19, 135, 135n23, 135n27, 135n29, 136–37, 138, 144, 146, 146n93, 284
Grenz, Stanley J., 224n48
Grootaers, Jan, 254n18, 256n29
Grosse, Christian, 171n23, 172n25, 173n29
Guarino, Thomas G., 9, 247, 247n1, 248n3, 249n6, 251n10, 262n1, 262–63, 263n3, 269n5, 269n6, 269n7, 270, 270n9, 272

Hall, Robert, 206, 212, 212n48
Hamil, Bessie Jane, 130
Hamilton, Alexander, 327n11
Hammett, John S., 84n10, 86, 86n24, 219, 219n12
Hansen, Collin, 194n12
Harnack, Adolf von, 280, 281
Harvey, Barry, 97n20, 101, 101n27, 101n28
Hatch, Nathan O., 166n2
Hauerwas, Stanley, 102, 102n32, 235, 235n13, 239, 334
Haykin, Michael A. G., 84n11, 218n9, 219n13
Hayman, May, 339
Hazelton, Roger, 307n2, 308n3
Heisler, Greg, 300, 300n24
Heman, 62
Hemming, Laurence Paul, 102n33
Henard, William D., 185n4
Henry, Carl, 7, 7n44

Hermas, 77
Hermes, 77
Herminjard, A. L., 168n9
Herodion, 77
Hesselink, John I., 171n22
Hezekiah, 61
Hiebert, Paul, 355, 356
Higman, Francis, 175n33
Hinlicky, Paul, 236, 236n22, 240
Hodge, Charles, 333
Hodges, Andrew Gerow, 337, 338
Holmes, Arthur F., 348n1, 348–49
Holmes, Stephen R., 83, 83n5, 85, 86n19
Holy One, 49
Horton, Douglas, 254n19
Hosea, 38
Hovsepianmehr, Haik, 339
Howard, Thomas Albert, 280n1, 281
Hugenberger, George, 119n16
Hume, David, 348
Humphreys, Fisher, 6
Hus, Jan, 341

"Immanuel," 69. *See also* Christ; Jesus
Irenaeus, 241

Jacob, 39
James, Robison, 2n3
Jarrett-Kerr, Martin, 307n1
Jeduthun, 62
Jenkins, Daniel, 308, 308n5
Jenkins, Phillip, 183, 183n2, 184
Jeremiah, 53
Jesus, 27, 41, 62, 68–69, 70, 83, 89, 93, 94, 97, 101–2, 103, 111, 115, 121, 150, 152, 157, 162, 177, 196, 200, 206, 212, 223, 225, 234, 236, 239, 240, 241, 243, 269, 272, 294, 299, 303, 305, 315, 340, 350, 357. *See also* Christ
Jesus Christ, 23, 24, 25, 26, 28, 32, 34, 35, 43, 44, 63, 66, 77, 80, 81, 83, 89, 114, 121, 122, 127, 156, 160, 166, 168, 197, 198, 202–5, 221, 247, 249, 252, 254, 267, 273, 274, 289, 292, 297, 299, 302, 303, 335, 339, 343, 351, 352, 356, 357

Jesus of Nazareth, 69, 244
Jewett, Robert, 76n25
Jobe, Mark, 193n11
Pope John Paul II, 97, 97n21, 150, 212, 262
John the Apostle, 44, 67, 68, 69, 70, 350
John the Baptist, 69, 340
Pope John XXIII, 254
Johnson, Adam, 62, 63n9
Jolie, Angelina, 196
Jorgensen, Cameron H., 110n3
Joshua, 55
Josiah, 61
Judson, Ann and Adoniram, 81
Junia, 77
Justin Martyr, 73, 74

Kagawa, Toyohiko, 339, 341
Kannengiesser, Charles, 134n20
Kant, Immanuel, 93n7, 232
Kantzer, Kenneth, 264, 265, 266
Keach, Benjamin, 203, 203n8
Keener, Craig S., 73n16
Keller, Tim, 35, 194, 195
Kelsey, David, 334
Khomiakov, Alexis, 211n44
Kierkegaard, Sören, 19
King, Martin Luther, Jr., 236, 341
Kingdon, Robert, 170n16, 170n17, 172n26, 175n35, 177n40, 177n41
Knox, John, 341
Korah, 62
Kuhn, Chase, 220n21

Laing, Sefana Dan, 129
Lampe, Peter, 77n27
Lash, Nicholas, 94n9
LeBrun, Jacques, 264
Legaspi, Michael, 281, 281n5
Leithart, Peter, 234, 234n6, 234n9, 235
Leland, John, 338, 339, 341
Lewis, C. S., 95, 95n11, 96n14, 96n16
Lindbeck, George, 333
Linkous, Ollie, 3, 4
Lloyd-Jones, David Martyn, 221n30
Lohfink, Gerhard, 101n26

Index of Names

Lois, 130, 146
Longenecker, Richard N., 71n12, 130n6
Luke, 73–74, 186
Lumpkin, W. L., 203n9, 203n10, 204n12, 204n14, 204n15, 208n27, 208n28, 209n31, 214n55
Luther, Martin, 4, 5, 111, 112, 113, 116, 120, 122, 123, 124, 155, 159, 160, 195, 220, 221, 222, 234, 236, 241, 241n40, 242–43, 245n50, 264, 285–86, 287, 288, 290, 293, 293n4, 295, 314, 336, 338, 339, 340, 341
Luwum, Janani, 339

Maag, Karin, 176n36, 176n37
MacIntyre, Alasdair, 227–28, 228n65
Macrina, 131–39, 144, 146, 147
Madison, James, 330-331
Małysz, Piotr J., 232, 242n46, 245n51
Manetsch, Scott M., 165, 173n29, 175n34, 177n43, 178n44, 286–87, 287n12
Manly, Basil, Jr., 2n4
Marcuse, Herbert, 234n5
Marney, Carlyle, 334
Marsden, George, 281, 281n4, 288–89
Martin, Francis, 265
Marty, Martin E., 316, 316n24
Mary. See Virgin Mary
Massey, James Earl, 9, 303, 307, 313n18
Mathews, Kenneth A., 48
Mathison, Keith, 123, 123n18
Matthew, 69
McClendon, James, 334
McGrath, Alister, 7n41, 113, 217, 217n2
M'Cheyne, Robert Murray, 44–45
McLaren, Brian, 194n12
McNeill, John, 123, 123n20
Melanchthon, Philip, 153
Melmoth, William, 74n22
Messiah, 40
Meuser, Fred W., 293n4
Milbank, John, 236, 236n25
Millegan, Brantly, 218n6

Miller, Robert Moats, 297, 297n14
Milne, Bruce, 226n60
Milton, John, 19–20
Miriam, 77
Mitchican, Jonathan, 183n1
Mohler, R. Albert, Jr., 7, 279
Moltmann, Jurgen, 304
Monica, 131, 139–46, 147, 340
Monter, William E., 167n7, 167n8
Moody, Dwight L., 6
Moon, Lottie, 185, 339, 341
Moses, 39, 50, 53, 55, 61, 62, 74, 118, 119, 213, 294
Mote, Edward, 305n35
Mouw, Phyllis, 348
Mouw, Richard J., 345
Mozart, Wolfgang Amadeus, 309–10, 311
Mullins, E. Y., 2n4, 334
Murdock, Graeme, 173n29
Musculus, Wolfgang, 174, 174n32

Nafzger, Peter H., 118n15
Nash, Hattie Ann, 129
Nathanael, 69
Naucratius, 137
Nehemiah, 61
Nereus, 77
Nero, 67
Neuhaus, Richard John, 247, 248, 262, 263–64, 265, 266, 268, 269, 270, 270n8, 271n10, 273, 325n10
Neuhaus, Richard John., 272, 274
Newman, Elizabeth, 92
Nicomachus the Pythagorean, 135n26
Niebuhr, Reinhold, 236
Nixon, Richard, 267
Noah, 213
Noll, Mark, 20

Obama, Barack, 328
Oberman, Heiko, 7
Ockenga, Harold John, 270
Oden, Thomas C., 166n4, 265, 268, 271, 271n12, 272
O'Donnell, James J., 145n88
Olevianus, Caspar, 160
O'Malley, John W., 254n18, 254n19

Index of Names 365

Oncken, Gerhard, 85
Ott, Heinrich, 250

Packer, J. I., 6, 86, 112, 112n7, 166n4, 195, 247, 247n2, 262, 265, 268
Pal, Krishna, 85
Palladio, Andrea, 337
Parker, Keith, 212n49
Parsons, Susan Frank, 102n33
Pascal, Blaise, 257
Patricius (Patrick) [Monica's husband], 139–40, 143
Patrick, Darrin, 185, 193n11
Paul (apostle), 24–26, 29, 30, 31, 32–33, 35, 40–41, 42, 43, 46, 64–67, 70–72, 74–77, 82, 99, 100, 109, 115, 118, 130, 141, 149, 162, 200, 201, 202, 205, 211, 214, 236, 250, 271, 284, 292–93, 296, 340, 343
Pope Paul VI, 250, 251, 251n9, 253, 254, 255, 256, 257, 258, 259
Pelagius, 152
Pelikan, Jaroslav, 196, 196n14, 197, 198, 313, 315, 315n22
Perpetua, 339, 340
Persis, 77
Peter (apostle), 73, 212, 252
Peter (brother of Gregory and Macrina), 132, 137, 138, 146
Philip, 125
Philologus, 77
Phlegon, 77
Piper, John, 195
Pope Pius XI, 249, 323, 324
Plato, 348, 349
Poteat, William H., 93, 93n3, 93n5, 93n8
Prenter, Regin, 240n39
Prisca, 77

Ramelli, Ilaria, 135, 135n22, 135n28
Ramm, Bernard, 121, 121n17
Ramsey, Paul, 288, 288n17
Ratzinger, Joseph, 250, 250n8, 251n9
Raz, Joseph, 322
Reno, Rusty, 270
Richardson, Cyril C., 73n21

Rieff, Philip, 283
Roberson, Lee, 7
Roberts, Chief Justice, 328
Roberts-Donaldson, 84n13
Robertson, A. T., 2n4
Robinson, Anthony B., 334n2
Rose, Devin, 114n12
Ross, Allen P., 60, 60n8
Ross, Mark, 40
Royce, Josiah, 236

Sadoleto, Jacob, 169
Samuel, 36
Satan, 67, 68. *See also* devil
King Saul, 36, 37, 38, 39, 49, 60
Sauñe, Romulo, 339
Schaff, Philip, 125, 125n23
Scherer, Paul, 301, 302n28
Schindler, David L., 95, 95n12, 95n13
Schleiermacher, Friedrich, 234, 234n8
Schlossberg, Herbert, 262
Schmemann, Alexander, 99n23, 101, 101n29
Schreiner, Thomas R., 88, 88n30
Seymour, William J., 339, 341
Shakespeare, 43
Shaw, Daniel, 355, 356
Shaw, Robert, 315
Sibbes, Richard, 41
Simons, Menno, 5, 336
Slater, Peter, 131, 131n7, 143n78, 144, 144n81
Smith, Christian, 113, 113n11, 114
Smith, Robert R., Jr., 5n13, 7, 7n37, 9, 292, 293n7
Smyth, John, 202n4, 202–3, 203n7, 208, 208n27, 214
Solomon, 52, 53, 54, 61
Son of God, 104, 121, 161, 294
Spinoza, Baruch, 113
Spurgeon, Charles H., 6, 47, 82, 86n25, 86–87, 87n27, 195, 206, 206n20, 288, 339, 341
Stamps, R. Lucas, 110n4
Steinmetz, David, 7
Stennett, Samuel, 103n36
Stetzer, Ed, 184, 184n3, 186
Stewart, Kenneth J., 218n9, 219n13

Stott, John, 195, 221n30, 225, 225n55, 226
Stravinsky, Igor, 308, 308n4
Stuckey, Sterling, 85n16, 85n17
Sullivan, John W. N., 312, 312n16
Suppes, Patrick, 323n9
Swain, Scott R., 123n19, 124n22, 126n25
Sweet, William Warren, 165n1
Swete, Henry Barclay, 67n4, 68n8

Taylor, Charles, 227, 227n63
Taylor, Gardner C., 6, 299
Theodoret of Cyrus, 134n22–135n22, 146n93
Thévenaz, Louis J., 176n39–177n39, 179n45
Thielicke, Helmut, 292, 293, 293n6, 296, 296n11, 297, 297n13, 298n15, 299, 299n19, 299n21, 300, 300n23, 301, 301n26, 301n27, 302–3, 303n32, 305, 306n36
Thielman, Frank, 64, 77n26
Thompson, Philip E., 86n21, 92n2, 100n25, 103, 103n36
Thurian, Max, 254n20
Thurman, Howard, 310–313, 311n12, 315
Thurman, Sue Bailey, 311, 313
Tienou, Tite, 355, 356
Timothy, 29, 40, 109, 130, 146, 284
Titus, 29, 30, 32, 33
Tonstad, Linn Marie, 243, 244n47
Trinitarian God. *See* God
Tronchin, Theodore, 287
Trueblood, Elton, 229n75
Tryphaena, 77
Tryphosa, 77
Turner, Daniel, 206-7, 207n23, 207n24, 209n34, 209–10, 210n37, 212, 212n48
Turner, Laura, 227n64
Tylenda, Joseph N., 156n23, 156n25
Tyndale, William, 336

Ufford, Edward S., 302n31
Urbanus, 77

Ursinus, Zacharias, 153, 154, 160

Valens the Arian emperor, 138
Van Dyk, Leanne, 217, 217n1, 223n39, 224n49
Van Vlastuin, Willem, 162–63, 163n47
Vanhoozer, Kevin J., 109, 112n8
Vaughan, David J., 314n20
Virgin Mary, 20, 109, 252, 258, 272, 273
Voight, Jon, 196
Volf, Miroslav, 212, 212n47

Waldron, Jeremy, 327, 327n12, 329
Wallace, Bill, 339
Walton, John, 52n2, 54n4, 60n7
Ware, Timothy (Kallistos), 211, 211n43, 211n45
Warfield, Benjamin, 333
Washer, Paul, 35
Wedgewood, Ralph, 95n10
Wehner, Peter, 229, 229n73
Weigel, George, 262, 263n2, 265
Wells, David, 283, 283n7, 289
Wesley, John, 338, 339, 341
White, B. R., 203n6, 204n13
White, James F., 92n1, 102n30
Whitefield, George, 165, 166, 341
Whitman, Walt, 109
Wilberforce, William, 229, 267
Wilken, Robert Louis, 313–14, 314n19, 315, 315n23
Willebrands, Johannes, 256, 257–58
Williams, George Hunston, 4, 7
Williams, Roger, 81
Williams, William Carlos, 96n19
Willimon, William H., 9, 235, 235n13, 333, 334, 334n2
Winter, Bruce W., 75n23
Wittgenstein, Ludwig, 110
Wolff, Christoph, 314n21
Wolsterdorf, Nicholas, 340n20
Wood, Ralph C., 18
Woodbridge, John D., 9, 262, 263
Wren, Christopher, 337, 337n12
Wright, Shawn D., 88n30

Yahweh, 50, 51. *See also* God
Yoder, John Howard, 349, 349n2

Zagzebski, Linda Trinkhaus, 117n14

Zizioulas, John D., 98n22, 212n46
Zwingli, Ulrich (Huldrych), 5, 174, 210, 210n39, 240, 240n37, 240n38, 241, 242, 336

Index of Scripture

OLD TESTAMENT

Genesis

1:1—2:4	54
1:2	87
2:2–3	56
2–3	54, 55
3:17	37
4:26	52
9:2–5	58
12:1–3	51
12:7–8	58
12:8	52
15:19–21	51
17:1–14	51
24:2	122

Exodus

3:5	50
3:8	118
3:14	70
12–14	57
12:25–27	57
13:5	49
15:1–19	62
15:20–21	62
17:15	58
19:5–6	51
19:12	55
19:15	49
20:1–19	51
20:8–11	56
20:24–25	50
21:2	49
23:14–17	56
23:19	52
24:1–2	9, 13–14, 18, 55
24:1–11	51, 54
25:8	53
25:30	49
25–31	54
28:29–30	54
28:35	43, 51
28:41	50
29:38–42	58
29:44	50
30:10	55
30:37	50
31:12–17	56
32	61
32:1–10	68
34:23–24	56
34:27–28	51
35–40	54
40:10	50

Leviticus

1–7	58
3:11	58
4:2	58
4:20	59
5:5–6	59
5:7	57
5:15	18, 58
8:10–11	50
9:1–4	59
10:1–5	51
10:10	49

Leviticus *(continued)*

13–14	50
15:18	49
16	54, 57
16:8	10, 21–22, 57
16:21	60
17:11	58
17:12–14	58
18:24–30	50
19:2	37
19:18	37
20:26	51
22:25	58
23:5–14	57
23:15–21	57
23:23–25	57
23:26–32	57
23:33–43	57
24:5–9	49
26:3–13	57
27:8	57

Numbers

3:10	55
5:2–3	50
6:16–17	59
6:24–26	61
8:15	49
15:24–29	58
15:30–31	58
23:9	51
28:1–8	58
28:2	58
29:1–6	57

Deuteronomy

	62
1:8	51
4:2	118
4:6	51
4:7–8	50
4:13	51, 118
5:1–21	51
5:12–17	56
5:22	118
5:22–30	51
6:4–5	62
6:5	37
6:13	68
7:6	51
8:7–10	54
9:10	119
9:26–29	61
10:4	119
12:5	13–14, 52
12:23–24	58
16:13–17	57
16:16	58
16:16–17	56
16:17	57
26:1–11	57
26:5	10, 56
26:15	54
26:18–19	51
28:64	39
31:9	19, 119
31:10–13	119
31:30–44	62

Judges

5	62
12:1–7	57

Ruth

2:10	49

1 Samuel

	37
1:10	60
10:5–13	62
15	38
15:22–24	36
18:6	61
20:3	81
21:4[Hb. 5]	49
21:6[Hb. 7]	49

2 Samuel

1:17–27	60
23:1	62
24:24	58

Index of Scripture

1 Kings

5:17–18	53
6–8	55
7:13–14	53
7:15–22	54
8:27	52
9:3	52

2 Kings

3:15–19	62
19:15–34	60

1 Chronicles

6:33–46	62
7:14	53
14:1	53
15:1—16:6	62
15:4–6	61
15:16–22	61
16:37–42	61
16:38–42	62
23:30	61
25:1–6	62
28:9	53

2 Chronicles

2:7	13–14, 53
5:12	62
7	61
20:19	62
29:14	62
29:25–30	61
35:15	61, 62

Ezra

3:10–11	61
9:7	60

Nehemiah

11:17	62
11:23	61
13:27–47	61

Job

3:3, 7	60

Psalms

	62
3:13	51, 60
6	60
9	39
16:9	52
18	61
19:7	120
22:1–21	60
22:3 [Hb. 4]	61
22:22–31	60
24:3–4	59
26:6	59
30:1	61
32	60, 61
33	61
33:1–3	61
33:10–12	51
34	61
38	60
39:1	62
42:1	52
44	60
45–49	62
50:12–13	58
51	60
62:1	62
68:1	5, 26, 61
72–83	62
73:25	52
74	60
77:1	62
78:12–16	62
78:23	25, 244
78:54	54
84–85	62
86	39
87–88	62
88	62
99:9	49
100	61
102	60
106:6–12	62
107	61

Psalms (continued)

107:23–32	69
114	62
118	61
118:25	60
120	61
120–134	61
121	61
122:1	52
122:6	60
127	338
130	60
135	61
136	61
138	61
143	60
150:4	61

Isaiah

1:11	58
30:29	61
38	60
41:8	51
46:10	304
49:6	39
51:2	51
55:11	112

Jeremiah

7:1–15	53
7:2	52
26:6–9	53
51:45	296n12

Lamentations

	60

Ezekiel

3:15	296
3:17–21	298n16
3:22	300
3:22—11:24	300
10:3–19	53
11:22–23	53
11:25	300n25
33:25	58
36:20–21	39
37	299, 300
44:7	58

Hosea

	4:1–13, 38

Amos

5:1–2	60
6:5	62

Jonah

	1:6–16, 60

Habakkuk

	3, 62

Zechariah

2:12	54
8:9	52

APOCRYPHA

2 Macc

12:46	155

NEW TESTAMENT

Matthew

1:14	69
1:14	32, 70
1:23	69
1:32	69
1:51	69
2:2	11, 69
2:11	69
3:6	85
3:13–17	85
4:9	68
4:10	68

Index of Scripture

4:23–24	70
5:14	233
6:24	114
9:31	70
9:38	70
11:51	70
14:33	69
16	41
16:19	177
17:5	69
18	41
18:6	70
18:18	241
18:19	177
18:26	69
19:9	30
20:20	69
20:28	70
22:30	133
25	305
26:28	99
26:29	305
28	41
28:9	17, 69
28:18	121
28:19	79
28:20	40

Mark

3:14	122
16:2	73

Luke

1:46–55	73
2:29–32	73
4:6 7	68
4:8	68
9:2	122
9:31	294
11:2–4	73
24:25	102

John

3:8	87
6:57	98

13:35	299n22
17:4	42
17:11	63
17:17–19	63
17:21	89–90, 269
17:23	166
20:21–23	241

Acts

1:8	122
1:14	73
1:21–22	73
2:41	73, 294
2:42	294
2:42	46, 74
2:44–45	73
2:46	73
2:46–47	73
2:47	294
4:2	18, 73
4:32	34, 73
5:42	73
6:4	73
8:30–31	125
10:47	81
16	130
16:2	130
20:7	73
20:8–9	75
20:28	35
27	141
28	141

Romans

1:1	71
1:9	71, 72
1–11	293
1:16—15:13	64
1:18	65, 70
1:18–32	65, 70
1:21	65, 71
1:21–22	28, 32, 65
1:23	71
1:24	26, 28, 65
1:25	71, 113
1:26	65

Index of Scripture

Romans (continued)

Reference	Page
1:26–27	65
1:28	65
1:29–31	65
2:29	72
3:25–26	63
5:1–2	65
5:1–11	65
5:10–11	65
6	241
6:4	83
7:6	63
8:5	71
8:9–11	63
8:18–15	224
8:29	71
8:31	293
9:6–7	292n1
9–11	293
10:14	293n3, 299n20
12	293
12:1	71
12:1–2	3–10, 14, 20–21, 74
12:2	71, 73, 74, 76, 336
12:3–8	71
12:9–10	71
12:14	20–21, 71
12–16	293
13:1	118
13:1–7	71
13:1–10	74
13:8–10	71
13:11–13	71
14:1	71, 74
14:2–3	5, 13–23, 76
14:3	207n24
15:1	76
15:6	76
15:7	71, 74, 207n24
15:14	42
15:19	71, 72
16:3	6, 7, 12, 13, 77
16:3–16	76
16:5	75
16:10b	11b, 14–15, 76

1 Corinthians

Reference	Page
	42
1:13	40, 200
5	41, 46
5:7	63
5:18	75
5:19	75, 98
5:21	75
5:21–31	75
6	43
6:1–2	75
6:5–9	76
8:5–6	66
8–10	66
10:11	224
10:14	66
10:16	74
10:17	99
10:20	66, 99
11:1—14:40	74
11:2–16	75
11:4–5	13, 72
11:17–34	73, 74
11:18	20, 72
11:21–22	75
11:22	75
11:23–26	75
11:24	99
11:26	243
11:30	63
12	244
12:4–11	28–30, 72
12:28–29	74
13	43
13:1–13	75
13:2	43
13:13	75
14:3–5	12, 17, 26, 75
14:4–5	12, 19, 23, 72
14:8	118
14:12–16	32, 37, 74
14:23	26, 72
14:26	74
14:29	74
15:3–4	115
15:28	134
15:42	90
16:1–2	73

Index of Scripture

16:2	74

2 Corinthians

4:7	25
4:8–10	25
5:17	71
6:17	296n12

Galatians

1	40
1:6–10	296
3:6–9	292n1
4:4–6	48

Ephesians

1:3–14	65
1:6	65
1:12	66
1:14	66
2:1	66
2:2	66
2:3	66
2:7	66
2:8	271
3:10	40
4:1	63
4:1–16	40
4:18–19	66
4:19	66
4:22–24	71
4:23	75
5:1	71
5:8	233
5:14	74
5:15	75
5:17	75
5:18–20	74
5:18–21	75
5:19	74

Philippians

1:21	275
1:29	237
2:5	237
2:6	122
2:22	130
3:3	72

Colossians

1:10	63
2:12	88
3:3	241
3:9–10	71
3:12–15	76
3:15–17	74
3:16	74
4:2	73
4:15	75, 76

1 Thessalonians

2:13	111

2 Thessalonians

2:15	149
2.15	150

1 Timothy

1:2	130
1:19	109
2:5	156
2:6	48
2:14	40
3:15	40, 244
3:15–16	40
4:3	66
4:4	67
5	140

2 Timothy

1:2	130
1:5	130
2:15	111
3:16–17	295
4:19	76

Titus

1:3	48
1:6–9	29

Titus (continued)

2:11–15	32
3:5–7	25–26

Hebrews

1:3	121
2:17	63
5:8	294
5–10	63
7:27	103
8:5	53
9:1—10:1	53
9:11–14	63
10:1–18	63
12:1	338
13:17	298n17

1 Peter

	217n5
2:9	63, 351

2 Peter

	218n5
2:13	75

1 John

4:7–21	63
4:20–21	44

Jude

18	75

Revelation

1:10	73
4	67
4:3	67
4:4	67
4:6b-8a	67
4:11	67
5:9–10	351
7:9–10	350
13:2	4, 67
13:3	11–15, 67
13:4	67
14:6–7	67
15:3–4	74
18:4	296n12
18:9	68
18:10	68
18:13	68
21	244
21:2	35
21:5	120
22:18–29	118

GRECO-ROMAN WRITINGS

Aristotle

Nicomachean Ethics

8.11	77

Pliny

Epistles

10.96	74

EARLY CHRISTIAN WRITINGS

Augustine

City of God

	143
19.13	144n80

Confessions

	144
1.11	140n58
1.20	142n68
2.3	139n56
3.11	140n60
3.12	140n61
3.4	140n59
4.12	144n79
4.13	143n76
4.15	144n82
5.7	139n57

5.8	140n62
5.8, 5.9	139n55
6.1	140n64
6.1, 6.2,	142n71
6.2	142n72
8	239n35
9	142
9.10	145n89, 145n91
9.11	141n66
9.12	145n87
9.13	142n67
9.4	143n74
9.8	142n69
9.9	142n70, 143n73, 143n75, 145n85, 145n86

De Musica

143

Cyprian of Carthage

Epistle

72.21	233n3

Irenaeus

Against Heresies

5.2	241n41

Justin Martyr

1 Apology

67	73
67.8	73

www.ingramcontent.com/pod-product-compliance
Lightning Source LLC
Chambersburg PA
CBHW071757300426
44116CB00009B/1108